ESSE [illegible] FINANCE

Also in the HarperCollins Essential Series

Essential Psychology
G. C. Davenport

Essential Government and Politics
Jim Cordell

Essential Business Studies
Stephen Barnes

Essential Marketing
Tony Proctor

Series Editor Roger Gomm

ESSENTIAL ACCOUNTANCY & FINANCE

Bijon Kar

CollinsEducational

An imprint of HarperCollins*Publishers*

Published by
CollinsEducational
77–85 Fulham Palace Road
Hammersmith
London
W6 8JB

First published in 1993

British Library Cataloguing in Publication Data
is available on request from the British Library

ISBN 0–00–322263–2

Typeset by Ellis Associates
Cover design by Ridgeway Associates.
Printed in Great Britain by Butler and Tanner, Frome, Somerset.

In memory of my parents

Foreword

Every book in the Essential Series is designed carefully to put you in control of your own learning.

When you use this book, you will not only cover the core elements of your course but you will also benefit from the author's use of modern teaching and learning techniques, with the result that you will make the best possible use of your time.

This book has:

- an introductory section at the beginning of each chapter, which focuses your attention on its contents and which tells you exactly what you will have learned by the end of the chapter. These are your 'learning objectives'
- periodic summaries and reviews which regularly remind you of the content you are covering and so reinforce your learning
- notes in the margin of the text, where the author takes the role of a tutor: picking out key facts, highlighting and explaining difficult concepts and guiding you to a better understanding of the main text
- essay questions and other assignments which will give you exam practice and help you to develop your skills in presenting written work
- advice on study skills which gives valuable suggestions for making the best use of your study time and improving your learning. When you have developed these basic skills you will be much better equipped to direct and control your own learning.

Learning is not easy: nobody learns without effort. However, if you use this book effectively you will not only succeed in your course and in your exam but you will also enjoy the experience of learning.

Author's preface

This book is written in a user-friendly style and provides a sound introduction to Accounting and Finance. It is primarily intended for the AAT (Association of Accounting Technicians) – Preliminary and Intermediate – BTEC National Certificate Diploma and GCSE students. It will also be useful to any beginner in Accountancy and Finance. The main feature of the book is the use of a step-by-step approach to the theory and practice of Accounting and Finance. Each chapter begins with a list of learning objectives followed by a step-by-step explanation of the various concepts and ideas introduced in it. The main ideas are then summarized and re-emphasized in the form of marginal notes to help readers through the chapters. Though the major stress of the book is on Financial Accounting, it includes one chapter each on Personal Finance, Break-even Analysis, Investment Appraisal and Accounting and Information Technology which makes it a comprehensive book on Accounting and Finance. It is most up-to-date and includes a summary of FRS 1 (Finance Reporting Standard 1) and Cashflow statements which replaced SSAP 10 in March 1992. Other features of the book include: a large number of completely worked-out examples, a large number of self-assessed activities with answers and a graded selection of end-of-chapter activities and assignments (some of which are drawn from past examination papers of AAT and GCSE) with complete answers to more than half of these.

The author of any book receives help from a large number of people – the list is too long to give in full. However, special mention must be made of my ex-colleague David Palfreman, who mooted the idea of my writing the book. I must also thank Mr Sengupta, Philip Datta and my colleagues at Manchester College of Arts and Technology, particularly Mrs S. Chiam, for their valuable comments on the first draft of this book.

I must thank my publishers, particularly Roger Gomm, for their healthy cooperation.

My thanks also go to my elder son Arindam who did most of the wordprocessing of the manuscript and to Anita and Ronjon for accepting quietly the apparent indifference of their father during the writing of the book.

Finally, I wish to thank my wife Bharati for her patience, support and encouragement.

Contents

1 First principles

Chapter objectives

After completing this chapter you should be able to:

- understand the importance of finance to individuals and business organizations
- describe the different types of business organization that are found in the private sector
- state the major objectives of business organizations
- explain the functions of management
- discuss the role of accounting in the context of a business organization
- distinguish between financial and cost and management accounting
- state the main functions of an accountant
- identify the principal users of accounting information.

Introduction

This chapter examines the role of accounting in the world of business and finance, the main types of business organization and their main objectives. The principal functions of management are considered together with an explanation of how accounting can help managers to do their job. You will then begin to understand how accountants help both individuals and organizations in financial planning and control.

THE WORLD OF BUSINESS AND FINANCE

We live in a complex society. The world of business and finance as a key part of this society is equally complex. Business and finance comprise many different types of organization engaged in different activities. Depending on the type of activity they are engaged in, such organizations can be divided into **manufacturing**, **wholesaling**, **retailing**, **service** (such as transport companies, accounting firms, banks and insurance companies) and **non-profit making organizations** (such as charities, clubs and professional bodies). All these organizations have one thing in common: all of them either sell a product or provide a service that will satisfy human want. Also, with the exception of non-profit making organizations, all of them , as we shall see presently, aim at making a gain – a **profit**. This profit is expressed in terms of money.

Getting organized: information

Find out, at the start of your course:

- How long the course is, in hours per week and in total, and when the final examinations are. If you are directing your own studies without attending a course then at least find out when the examinations are.
- What home work and course work you will have to do.
- Which examination board sets your examinations. What is the content of the syllabus? How will you be assessed? A college library will have a copy of the syllabus and assessment. Obtain your own photocopy.

Getting organized: place

Identify a location in your home which is your study place and nothing else. Just a table and chair will do. With practice you will reach a point where the act of sitting in that chair, at that table triggers the work response in you. This will not happen if you choose your bed or the armchair in front of the TV as your study place.

Getting organized: time

- How will you fit study into your other commitments? You cannot simply add a course onto an already overfull life.You will have to reorganize your life to make time for study.
- At what time do you work most effectively? Not 'like to work' but work most effectively: there is a difference.
- For how long can you study **effectively** at a stretch? Practise and test your own learning until you know the answer to this question. For most people the answer is about one hour: then they need a short break.
- Studying for two hours every day is usually much more effective that a ten-hour stretch on Sunday.
- For each period of study, set yourself realistic objectives. In this book each chapter starts

with a set of targets or objectives. Use the chapter objectives to phase your study, and at the end of each chapter go back to the beginning to check how much you have achieved.

- Plan you study sessions and their objectives a week in advance. Things may not go exactly to plan but at least you will know what you have to do to make up for lost time.
- Keep lists of things to do. These should be specific e.g. 'work through examples of posting to the Ledger'.

Getting organized: equipment

The minimum you will need is:

- A4 narrow-lined paper
- A4 accounts paper
- a ring binder and file dividers
- card index cards – you can find or make your own box to keep them in
- pencils and a sharpener – it is always better to work accountancy exercises in pencil until they are correct
- a rubber
- a pen you find it easy to write with
- your textbook(s)
- a calculator; if you have a personal computer then any spreadsheet program will be useful. More advice on IT and accountancy is given in Chapter 23.

► Now go through all the getting organized sections and make a list of the things you should be doing and when you are going to do them.

Note making

In learning accountancy there are two kinds of things to make notes about.

Firstly there are terms and concepts. In this chapter for example the terms sole trader, partnerships and limited companies are explained. You need to know what these terms mean. The best way of storing this kind of information is on index cards which you can file alphabetically, or in any other way you find convenient. Avoid the temptation to write long notes on index cards. Instead write brief memory joggers and references to more complete information. For example a card on partnerships might read:

Partnerships

Owned/controlled between 2 & 20 partners – partnership agreement on capital supplied, responsibilities, salaries, commission, profits/losses

Usually unlimited liability but Limited Partnerships Act allows 'sleeping partners' with limited liabilities.

ref Kar pages XX-XX

see also **liability**

The other kinds of materials you will want to store are examples of accountancy procedures. In this book there are worked examples and activities for you to complete. These will make up your notes on accountancy procedures. Always head them so that you will know what they are when you look at them again. If the calculations illustrate the calculation of VAT; head them 'The calculation of VAT'. If they illustrate the measurement of profit, then head them 'The measurement of profit'. An understandable set of notes is your most important resource when it comes to revising for examinations.

Like individuals, business organizations need money: to set up their business, to buy various assets such as fixtures and fittings, plant and machinery and stocks of goods, to pay wages and salaries to their employees and to pay off many bills connected with the business. In other words, they need money to finance their operations. The availability of finance is therefore of utmost importance to business organizations. The provision of finance to both individuals and businesses is a specialized field of activity and in most countries large numbers of institutions and organizations have emerged with the primary function of providing finance, in the form of loans and advances, to individuals and organizations alike.

Types of business organization

There are many ways of classifying business organizations but the most commonly accepted mode is based on ownership. On this basis, businesses can be owned either publicly or privately. Examples of public ownership are the nationalized industries (British Rail, for example), local government and central government. The accounting for public enterprises is beyond the scope of this book. We shall therefore concentrate on the accounting needs of businesses in the private sector. Consequently, we begin with the classification of business organizations which are privately owned.

Basically, there are three types of business organization in the private sector:

1 **Sole traders**: These are usually small businesses that are owned by a single individual who also makes most managerial decisions. Capital is supplied by the owner her(him)self, supplemented by borrowings from friends, relations, banks or other financial institutions. The owner gets the profit or suffers the loss of the business. Her(his) liabilities are unlimited in the sense that (s)he is personally liable to the full extent of her(his) private assets for business debts.

You will find sole traders mainly in the retail trade (e.g. corner shops, newsagents), small scale service industries (e.g. electricians, plumbers) and small manufacturing and craft industries (e.g. furniture making, pottery).

2 **Partnerships**: These businesses are owned and controlled by two or more individuals who are known as partners. In general, the number of partners is restricted to 20. Usually, there will be a formal agreement between the partners for the smooth and efficient running of the business. The partnership agreement will cover such items as the amount of capital each partner is to contribute, the amount of salary or commission each partner is to receive and how profits or losses are to be shared among the partners.

Usually, partners will have unlimited liabilities for the debts of the business. However, the Limited Partnership Act allows a partnership between an active partner (whose liabilities are unlimited) and one or more **'sleeping' partners** (whose liabilities are limited to the amount of capital contributed). A sleeping partner does not participate in the actual running of the business but receives an agreed share of the profit.

Partnerships are a very common form of business organization for professional people such as doctors, solicitors and accountants. They are also found in small-scale businesses similar to those operated by sole traders.

3 **Limited companies**: These are formed by registration with the Registrar of Companies. When an application for registration is made, the promoters or founders of the company must sign a Memorandum of Association giving details such as the name, address, objects and share capital of the company, together with the Articles of Association which regulate the internal affairs of the company. On satisfactory completion of the requirements for registration, the Registrar will issue a Certificate of Incorporation which bestows upon the company a separate legal entity. This means that the company is a legal 'person' and can sue and be sued in a court of law.

The owners of such organizations are the **shareholders**. Their liabilities are limited to the value of their paid-up shares. There are two types of limited company: **private** (indicated by the letters 'ltd.' at the end of the name) and **public** (indicated by the letters 'plc.' at the end of the name). The main difference between these two types of company is simply that a public company can make an issue of shares to the general public whereas a private company may only sell its shares privately, that is, without advertising.

A business organization's objectives

Every organization must have a set of objectives, that is, a check-list of what it strives to achieve. A business organization makes a product or provides a service with a view to making a profit. Making a profit is a business objective - but how much profit?

There are at least three possible answers to this question.

► Maximizing profit

Firstly, the aim may be to **maximize profit**, i.e. to make as much profit as possible regardless of consequence. This 'quick grab' approach to profit may be all right as a short-term policy; it is unlikely to be sustained for a long period as it can damage the long-term prospects of a business.

► Satisficing profit

Secondly, the aim may be one of **satisficing profit**, i.e. making a satisfactory level of profit.

► Optimizing profit

Finally, the aim could be to **optimize profit**, i.e. to make the best attainable level of profit consistent with both short-term and long-term considerations. Which of these should be treated as a business objective is for the management to decide.

A non-profit making organization obviously cannot have a profit objective. Instead, it should aim at keeping its costs down and operating efficiently.

► Survival objective

Besides the profit objective, a business may have the objectives of survival and of growth. The **survival objective** implies that proper safeguards must be made against possible losses. It is based on what is called the 'mini-max approach', i.e. the aim should be to minimize the maximum expected loss whilst at the same time maximizing the minimum expected gain. The survival objective also implies liquidity, which refers to the availability of adequate funds (i.e. cash and near-cash assets such as bank deposits, debtors and short-term investment in securities) to meet contingencies.

► **Liquidity**: the availability of funds to meet short-term needs

► Growth objective

The **growth objective** is an extension of the survival objective. In an ever-changing business and economic environment, a firm must grow in order to survive. A firm cannot grow unless it can generate some funds for expansion from its operations. Growth also implies that a firm should be willing and able to adapt itself to change.

The business objectives outlined are all based on financial considerations. However, it is possible for a business to have non-financial objectives such as:

► Non-financial objectives

- customer or user satisfaction
- technical efficiency
- desire to attain or retain market leadership
- welfare of workers and good industrial relations
- social responsibility, e.g. safeguards against pollution.

THE MANAGEMENT FUNCTION

Different authorities on management have given different lists of management functions. However, the various functions of management can be summarized under three headings:

- planning
- control
- decision-making.

Functions of management

► Management planning

Planning: A scheme of activities that is considered to be attainable with the available resources in order to achieve some predetermined objectives or goals, the resources being money, machines, materials and staff.

The planning process begins with the formulation of business objectives or goals and extends into the ways and means by which these objectives can be fulfilled.

Control: The process by which managers ensure that resources are obtained and used effectively and efficiently to achieve the organization's objectives. Control means ensuring that the business plan is carried out as well as possible. This involves comparing actual performance with the plan and taking necessary action either to modify future performance or to revise the plan itself.

► Management control

Decision-making: The act of making a choice between alternatives. It involves making a formal judgement on a problem based on available information, the information usually being provided in quantitative form.

► Management decision-making

Most business problems relate to the outcomes of alternative courses of action. Information on them can never be perfect. Consequently, decision-making in business always involves an element of risk. For some problems quantitative information may not be available and decisions are normally based on the decision-maker's own experience and know-how. Such decisions, by their very nature, tend to be subjective. A good example of decision-making in business is selecting the most desirable investment from among a number of alternative projects.

The three elements of management in practice

The three elements of management function are inextricably interrelated. Planning is of little value without proper control and the control process itself may give rise to the modification or revision of the plan. Likewise, the formulation and implementation of a plan inevitably involves the decision-making process and decision-making itself is an integral part of planning and control.

Managers deal with people. Therefore they should maintain a good working relationship with the people under their authority and control and be able to motivate them to do their work. Managers plan, make decisions, motivate their staff and control the operations of the business. As we shall see later, they are assisted by accounting methods and techniques to perform their tasks.

It's time to recap on what you've learnt so far. Try the following assignment to test your understanding of the different terms and concepts introduced so far.

ACT **1.1**

Write either T or F against each of the following statements to indicate whether it is true or false.

- **a** A non-profit making organization has no objectives at all.
- **b** Decision-making in business can never be subjective.
- **c** Profit maximization is the only objective of a business.
- **d** Satisficing profit is another name for maximizing profit.
- **e** Business objectives may be guided by non-financial considerations such as customer satisfaction.

f Decision-making in business always involves an element of risk.

g A junior manager has no power of decision-making.

2 Write a short paragraph in answer to each of the following questions.

a What do you consider to be the most important objective(s) of a manufacturing firm?

b How does a private limited company differ from a public limited company?

c What in your opinion is the principal objective of any sporting club in your area?

d 'The nucleus of the management process is decision-making.' Explain.

► Answers in appendix

BUSINESS TRANSACTIONS AND THE ACCOUNTING PROCESS

Business transactions involve on the one hand giving or receiving goods and services and on the other hand receiving or paying cash now or at a later date. All business transactions thus fall into one of four possible types, namely, **cash sales, credit sales, cash purchases** and **credit purchases**. Since a business will be involved in hundreds and thousands of such transactions during a year, it is important that these should be systematically recorded, classified, analysed and presented in a form suitable for use by the management and other interested parties. The tasks of recording, classifying, analysing and presenting financial information are performed by accounting. Accounting is thus a **financial data processing system**. Today this is usually integrated into a comprehensive **Management Information System** which deals with other data in addition to financial data.

The accounting process begins with a business transaction. The primary documents of sales, purchases and other expenses are the **sales invoices, purchases invoices** and **vouchers** respectively. The information they contain will be recorded in the first instance in the books of original entry: the **Sales Day Book**, the **Purchases Day Book**, the **Cash Book** and the **Journal**. Today many businesses use computer packages to keep their accounting records. Their various 'books' will consequently be computer files. All this information will then be classified and entered in the main book of account, called the **Ledger**. From time to time and certainly at the year end the accounts in the Ledger will be balanced. A list of balances, called the **Trial Balance**, will be prepared. Finally, the accounting process will come to an end with the preparation and presentation of a set of **final accounts**, e.g. the **Trading and Profit and Loss** account and the **Balance Sheet**. These concepts and ideas will be developed further in later chapters.

SUBDIVISIONS OF ACCOUNTING

Financial accounting

► Book-keeping

Accounting begins with the recording of financial information. This recording function of accounting is commonly known as **book-keeping**. Besides book-keeping, accounting is also concerned with the construction of final accounts, i.e. the Trading and Profit and Loss account and the Balance Sheet, of different types of businesses such as sole traders and limited companies. This part of accounting is what is commonly known as **financial accounting**.

► Financial accounting

The main purpose of financial accounting is to prepare a set of accounts in accordance with legal requirements such as the Companies Acts, and of the Statements of Standard Accounting Practice, in order to ensure that the financial activities of a business are conducted fairly and squarely and that the interests of its owners, creditors and the general public are duly protected. In this sense, financial accounting may be aptly described as **stewardship accounting**.

Financial accounting is 'historical'. It records operations that have already occurred. Therefore it is of little use for management planning and control. Moreover, as financial accounting is usually concerned with the whole of the business unit, it does not provide adequate information on different aspects of the firm's operations. More detailed information is, however, of vital importance to managers for control and decision-making purposes. These deficiencies of financial accounting in relation to the needs of modern industrial society have been made good by the emergence of a branch of accounting called **cost and management accounting**.

Cost and management accounting

Cost accounting

► Cost accounting

Cost accounting has been defined by the Chartered Institute of Management Accountants as: 'the application of accounting and costing principles, methods and techniques in the ascertainment of cost and the analysis of savings and/or excesses compared with previous experience or with standards.'

This definition indicates two important areas of cost accounting:

- **cost ascertainment**: the determination of the cost of production of a unit, job, operation, process, department or service
- **standard costing and variance analysis**: the introduction and revision of costing standards to measure how actual performance varies from predetermined standards and to indicate to management the extent and causes of adverse variances. Costing standards are estimates of 'target' costs which are compared with actual costs as they are incurred. The difference between the target or standard cost and the actual cost is called the **cost variance**. If actual cost is lower than the standard cost, the cost variance is **favourable**. If, on the other hand, actual cost exceeds standard cost, the variance is **adverse** or **unfavourable**. Let's assume that the standard cost of a product is £20, but its actual cost is £25. Then the cost variance of this product will be £5 adverse (£20 – £25). In this case, management needs to find out the reasons for this adverse variance and take appropriate measures to rectify it.

Management accounting

► Management accounting

Management accounting is an extension of cost accounting. It uses all the principles and techniques of cost accounting and, in addition, some other quantitative (numerical) techniques drawn mainly from Statistics and Operational Research (i.e. the application of scientific methods to management problems) to help management in planning, control and decision-making. A comprehensive analysis of cost and management accounting is outside the scope of this book, but we shall

► See Chapter 17

make occasional references to some areas of cost accounting such as cost-volume-profit analysis in due course.

THE ROLE OF THE ACCOUNTANT

Very few people outside the accountancy profession have a clear idea of what an accountant does. Many people think that an accountant's job is utterly boring, as it involves recording and checking figures all the time. It is true that part of the job is to record financial information and to check the work of others, but to a great extent the job is to help individuals and organizations in financial planning and control. Accountants are managers of finance. Many accountants work as financial consultants helping people from all walks of life to choose the right course of action relating to money management. Their job can be varied and interesting.

► Qualifications

Accounting qualifications

- The Institute of Chartered Accountants (ACA/FCA)
- The Chartered Association of Certified Accountants (ACCA/FCCA)
- The Chartered Institute of Management Accountants (ACMA/FCMA)
- The Chartered Institute of Public Finance and Accountancy (CIPFA).

Qualified members of an accounting body can use the letters shown above after their name. Thus a qualified member of the Institute of Chartered Accountants describes her(him)self as either an Associate (ACA) or a Fellow (FCA) of the Institute.

Many ACAs/FCAs and ACCAs/FCCAs work in private practice providing auditing and financial/accounting services to their clients. Auditing refers to the checking of accounts and ensuring that they are correct. Financial/accounting services include the preparation of final accounts – the Profit and Loss account and the Balance Sheet – of all types of business and giving advice on tax and other financial matters. Some of the clients of these accountants are individuals who get advice on a variety of financial matters such as personal taxation, private pensions, mortgages and investment.

Some chartered accountants and certified accountants work in industry and commerce. Management accountants (ACMAs/FCMAs) are not qualified to audit; consequently their work in private practice is rather limited. Most of them work in industry and commerce. Public sector accountants work, as expected, mainly for local authorities. There is also a technician level accounting qualification provided by the Association of Accounting Technicians and the qualified members can use the designatory letters MAAT after their names. A MAAT can work either in industry and commerce or in private practice.

The accountant's work

In private practice, the work of an accountant varies from client to client. Similarly, work in industry and commerce will vary from organization to organization. It is therefore difficult to give a complete list of what an accountant does. However, the following are usual:

- recording of financial data into the relevant books of accounts
- control of cash – the preparation of the cash-flow budget
- preparation of the Trading and Profit and Loss account and the Balance Sheet

- preparation of the statement of source and application of funds
- assessment of financial performance
- preparation of the budget
- preparation of costing estimates
- preparation of the variance report for control purposes
- evaluation of investment projects
- arrangement for raising capital or loans including overdrafts
- auditing of accounts, i.e. checking of accounts to ensure that they represent a true and fair view of the business
- being a financial consultant or advisor.

THE FINAL ACCOUNTS OF A BUSINESS – A PREVIEW

The main aim of this book is to teach, in a systematic manner, the basic principles of financial accounting. First, though, let's look at an example of the end product of financial accounting: final accounts, the year-end financial statements of a company. Basically, there are two such financial statements:

- the Profit and Loss account (also known as the Income Statement)
- the Balance Sheet (also known as the Financial Position Statement).

Figure 1.1 (on page 10) illustrates the Income Statement for the year ended 31 December, 1989 and the Balance Sheet as at that date of a big British company, BP (British Petroleum) PLC.

Consider the BP statements carefully in the light of the notes below.

a Notice that both the Income Statement and the Balance Sheet are preceded by the word 'Group'. This means that BP, in addition to its own operations, owns more than 50 per cent of the shares of other companies, which are known as its subsidiaries. The financial statements reflect the operations of the whole group of companies under the control of BP PLC.

b Both the statements are accompanied by a number of notes (which are not reproduced here) that explain how the relevant figures are arrived at.

c 'Minority shareholders' interest' refers to the claims of outside shareholders of some of the subsidiary companies of BP PLC. The 'outside shareholders' are shareholders who are not members of the 'Group' but own some shares of the subsidiary companies. Their 'claims' refer to the share of profits and assets of the subsidiaries they are entitled to receive.

d Distribution to shareholders refers to the dividends paid or proposed to the shareholders. Dividends are part of the profits which the shareholders, as owners, receive each year.

e Earnings per ordinary share is arrived at by dividing the profit of the year, minus dividend paid to preference shareholders, by the number of ordinary shares in issue during the year. Preference shareholders are those who receive a 'fixed' rate of dividends each year. They also have a prior claim on the profits and the assets of the company.

f The Balance Sheet lists the assets (anything owned by the company), liabilities (anything owed by the company) and capital (money contributed by the owners, i.e. the shareholders to the business). All these terms will be explained in greater detail in a later chapter.

Figure 1.1 BP accounts

BP Income Statement for the year ended 31 December 1989

Group Income Statement

For the year ended 31 December 1989	Note	1989	£million 1988
Turnover	2	**29,641**	25,922
Replacement cost of sales		**22,095**	19,330
Production taxes	3	**1,242**	566
Gross profit		**6,304**	6,026
Distribution and administration expenses	4	**3,690**	3,333
Exploration and expenditure written off		**480**	495
		2,134	2,198
Other income	6	**803**	693
Replacement cost operating profit		**2,937**	2,891
Stock holding gain (loss)		**390**	(232)
Historical cost operating profit		**3,327**	2,659
Interest expense	7	**794**	582
Profit before taxation		**2,533**	2,977
Taxation	9	**744**	823
Profit after taxation		**1,789**	1,254
Minority shareholders' interest		**45**	44
Profit before extraordinary items		**1,744**	1,210
Extraordinary items	10	**390**	–
Profit for the year		**2,134**	1,210
Distribution to shareholders	11	**795**	823
Retained profit for the year		**1,339**	387
Earnings per ordinary share	12	**31.8p**	20.0p

Group Reserves

Group reserves at 1 January		**8,295**	7,802
Exchange adjustments		**268**	117
Shares purchased from KIO	27	**(2,423)**	–
Retained profit for the year		**1,339**	387
Other movements		**9**	(9)
Group reserves at 31 December	28	**7,490**	8,297

BP Balance Sheet for the year ended 31 December 1989

Balance Sheets

At 31 December 1989	Note	Group 1989	Group 1988	**£million** Parent 1989	Parent 1988
Fixed assets:					
Intangible assets	16	**1,672**	1,874	–	–
Tangible assets	17	**19,285**	18,926	–	–
Investments	18	**1,497**	1,437	**1,755**	2,333
Current assets:					
Stocks	19	**3,381**	2,503	–	–
Debtors	20	**5,361**	4,243	**3,865**	4,357
Investments	21	**151**	157	–	20
Cash at bank and in hand		**268**	183	3	3
		9,161	7,086	**3,857**	4,380
Creditors – amount falling due within one year:					
Finance debt	22	**2,531**	2,319	–	–
Other creditors	23	**7,037**	5,659	**811**	883
Net current assets		**(407)**	(892)	**3,046**	3,497
Total assets less current liabilities		**22,047**	21,345	**4,801**	5,830
Creditors – amounts falling due after more than one year:					
Financial debt	22	**5,758**	4,864	–	–
Other creditors	23	**1,936**	1,719	**18**	8
Provisions for liabilities and charges:					
Deferred taxation	9	**451**	389	–	–
Other provisions	24	**2,461**	2,241	–	–
Net assets		**11,441**	12,132	**4,783**	5,822
Minority shareholders' interest		**656**	614	–	–
BP shareholders' interest		**10,785**	11,518	**5,783**	5,822
Represented by					
Capital and reserves:					
Called up share capital	25	**1,346**	1,536	**1,346**	1,536
Share premium account	26	**1,752**	1,685	**1,752**	1,685
Capital redemption reserve	27	**197**	–	**197**	–
Reserves	28	**7,490**	8,297	**1,488**	2,601
		10,785	11,518	**4,783**	5,822

THE USERS OF ACCOUNTING INFORMATION

Different groups of people require financial information, such as depicted in Figure 1.2 to satisfy their differing needs. Broadly speaking, there are two principal users of accounting information, called **internal users** and **external users**. The internal users are the management group in an organization. The management of an organization requires financial information for planning, control and decision-making purposes.

Figure 1.2 *Users of accounting information*

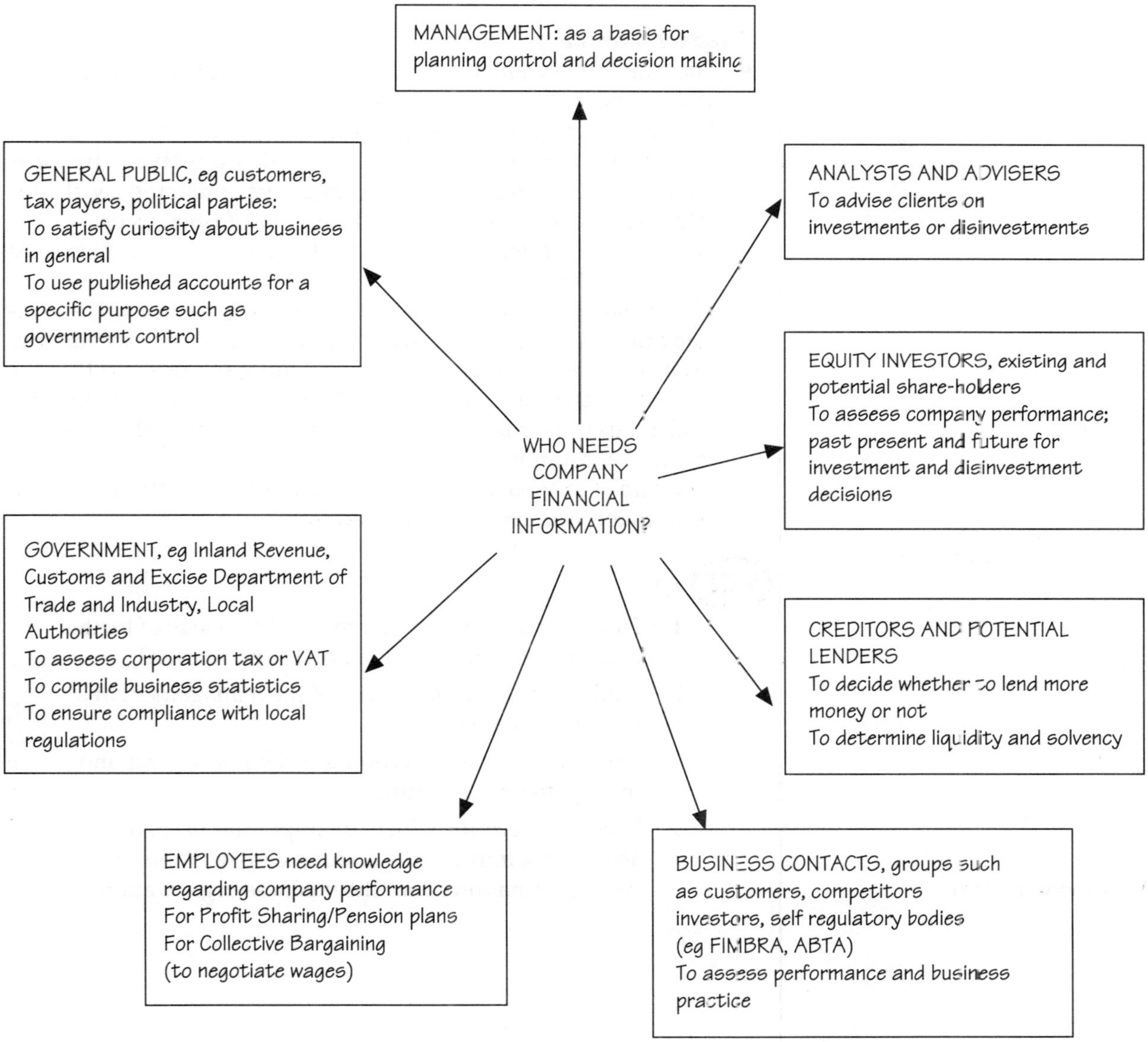

The external users of financial information

There are some users of financial information who are external to the organization. In 1975, the accounting profession in England published a document called the Corporate Report which identified seven different groups of external users of financial information. These seven groups of external users, together with one group of internal users, are shown in Figure 1.2 above.

ACT 1.2

Visit your public library and find the Business Directories (the librarian will direct you, if necessary). These directories list companies by the nature of their business. Either decide on a category which interests you (e.g. motor vehicles, pharmaceuticals) or a range of different kinds of business. Take down the addresses of some of the companies and write to each asking for their Annual Report and Accounts. These are free – and often very informative – documents. Use what you have learned in this chapter to understand their accounts.

Chapter summary

- There are three main types of business organization in the private sector: sole traders, partnerships and limited companies.
- The objectives of organizations differ and it is the task of top management to formulate the overall objectives. In most businesses earning the maximum profit consistent with stability and growth is the overriding set of objectives.
- The main functions of management are planning, control and decision-making.
- Management is aided by various accounting methods. These include financial accounting and cost and management accounting.
- Financial accounting is external accounting in the sense that the accounts prepared are intended for external parties such as shareholders and the Inland Revenue. This book is principally about financial accounting.
- Cost and management accounting is internal accounting in the sense that it is intended to aid managers.

ACT 1.3

1 How do the financial objectives of a college of further education differ from those of a supermarket?

2 Outline the major functions of the management of a business organization.

3 How does financial accounting differ from cost and management accounting?

4 Name five groups which are important users of accounting information and indicate why they require such information about the business organization.

► No answers given

2 Personal finance

Chapter objectives

By the end of this chapter you should be able to:

- identify the various sources of personal finance
- calculate different deductions that are made from personal income
- state the various uses of personal finance
- understand the difference between capital expenditure and revenue expenditure
- prepare a personal budget over a given period of time
- state the meaning of the following terms: earned income, investment income, gross income, net income, piece rate, time rate, incentive bonus scheme, index linkage, savings account, investment account, PAYE, SAYE, overdraft, personal loan, insurance premium(ia), sum assured, whole life policy, with profits insurance policy, unit trusts, unit-linked insurance policy, capital gains, dividends, capital expenditure, revenue expenditure, mortgage, hire purchase, superannuation, tax allowances/taxable pay, MIRAS, tax code, contracted out and contracted in National Insurance contributions, cash flow, personal cash flow budget.

PERSONAL FINANCE

Both individuals and business organizations need finance to satisfy their economic wants. Finance is a **resource** and financial problems relate to how we get finance and how we use it. The aim of this chapter is to give you an appreciation of financial principles as they apply to your personal life. Then in subsequent chapters these principles will be extended to the wider area of business.

Sources of personal finance

There are four major sources of personal finance:

- earned income
- State benefits
- investment income
- borrowing.

Earned income

Earned income or **earnings** or simply **income** is by far the most important source of personal finance. The vast majority of people receive **salaries** (if they are paid monthly) or **wages** (if paid on a weekly basis) from employment, either full-time or part-time. These people work for other people or organizations. There are also quite a large number of people who do not work for others: they work for themselves and are known as **self-employed persons**. For most salaried jobs, the annual earnings are more or less fixed, but in the industrial sector, because of the very nature of jobs, earnings of workers could vary a great deal from one week to another. In such cases, there are three basic methods of calculating wages. They are:

- time rate
- piece rate
- incentive bonus scheme.

► Time rate

The **time rate** is the most common method. Under this method total weekly wages or weekly gross wages are calculated as follows :

> ***Time rate***
> Total weekly wages = total hours worked per week × rate per hour

Example 2.1 Calculating gross wages on time rate

Data: hourly rate = £2.50
hours worked = 35
Calculate the total wages.

Solution

Wages = hours worked × rate per hour
= 35 × £2.50
= £87.50

► Piece rate

Under the **piece rate** method, the worker is paid on the basis of production. Wages are calculated as follows.

> ***Piece rate***
> Wages = units of production × rate per unit

Example 2.2 Calculating gross wages on piece rate

Data: units produced = 50
rate per unit = £1
Calculate the total wages.

Solution

Total wages = units produced × rate per unit
= 50 × £1
= £50

► Incentive bonus scheme

The **incentive bonus scheme** is usually a combination of the time rate and the piece rate. Under this scheme, a **basic time rate** is guaranteed and **bonus** is paid for production in excess of normal. There are many variations of calculating wages by this method, but below is a popular formula.

> ***Sample formula for incentive bonus scheme***
> Wages = time rate + $\frac{1}{2}$ (time saved × time rate)
> where time saved = time allowed – time taken

Example 2.3 Calculating gross wages with an incentive bonus scheme

Data: hourly rate = £2.50
hours worked = 40
units produced = 100
time allowed = 0.5 hour per unit
Calculate the total wages.

Solution

Time taken = 40 hours
Time allowed = 100 × 0.5 = 50 hours
Therefore, time saved = (50 – 40) hours
= 10 hours

$$\text{Total wages} = 40 \times £2.50 + \frac{1}{2}(10 \times £2.50)$$
$$= £100 + £12.50$$
$$= £112.50$$

► Overtime

In many organizations workers are paid overtime if they work more than the basic weekly hours. Overtime is usually paid at a premium, i.e. at a rate which is higher than the basic rate, e.g. at the rate of time and a half.

To record the time worked, most firms use a **clock card** or a **daily time sheet**. At the end of each week, total weekly hours will be calculated from these documents.

We've discussed a few methods of calculating wages. Now try the following to test your understanding of wage calculations.

ACT 2.1

The following information relates to a worker in a manufacturing firm for week 12:

Production in units = 120
Time worked = 40 hours
Time allowed = 0.5 hour per unit
Rate per hour = £3

The firm pays an incentive bonus equivalent to one half the time saved at the hourly rate.

Calculate the wages earned by the worker in week 12.

► Answer in appendix

State benefits

Many people do not have regular earnings from employment. Examples are full-time students, retired people with no occupational pensions and unemployed people. However, these people do receive financial benefits from the Government. Full-time students usually receive **grants** towards their fees and expenses from their local authorities. Old age pensioners receive **State pensions** and unemployed people get **unemployment benefits** from the Department of Social Security. There are also some other benefits, such as **sickness benefit**, which some people might receive from the Government from time to time. All these benefits constitute sources of income to the recipients.

Investment income

A decision to invest is preceded by a decision to save. When you decide to save, you decide in fact to abstain from present consumption so that the money saved is available for future use.

► Private and occupational pension contributions are 'investments' but pay-outs are counted as 'earned income'.

People save a part of their present earnings for a variety of reasons, but perhaps the most important incentive to save is to have regular income in the future, especially after retirement. Although the money saved can be invested in very many different ways, we consider the following are the most important channels of investment:

- the National Savings Movement
- building societies
- commercial banks
- insurance companies
- investments in stocks and shares.

The National Savings Movement

The National Savings Movement provides the following investment opportunities:

a ordinary savings accounts
b investment accounts
c National Savings Certificates/Bonds
d Index-linked Savings Certificates
e Premium Bonds.

► National Savings and investment accounts

The first two are normal savings accounts. With the **ordinary savings account**, the first £70 (which may be altered at any time by the Government) received as interest in any particular year is free of income tax but the rate of interest tends to be rather low. An **investment account** gives a much higher rate of interest and you receive the interest due as a 'gross' amount, i.e. before deduction of any income tax.

► National Savings Certificates

A **National Savings Certificate** gives a fixed rate of return over a fixed period. It is therefore a good investment during periods of high interest rates.

► Index-linked Savings Certificates

► Index-linkage; value up-rated to take account of inflation

Index-linked Certificates offer a fixed rate of return over and above the rate of inflation. Inflation is characterized by rising prices which means that the value of money (i.e. what money can buy) decreases. One way of arresting this reduction in the value of money in an inflationary situation is to invest money in index-linked certificates which makes your money grow at a faster rate than the rate of inflation.

► Premium Bonds

Premium Bonds represent an altogether different form of saving and investment. Buying a Premium Bond is similar to buying a ticket in a lottery where winning a prize depends entirely on luck. Although the holders of Premium Bonds do not get any interest on the money invested, their capital remains intact. Their bonds are included in weekly and other special draws which gives them the chance of winning a tax-free lump sum.

Building societies

► Paid-up share accounts
► High interest accounts

Building societies are very popular, particularly with small investors. Most societies provide a wide range of saving schemes such as **paid-up share accounts**, a number of **high interest accounts** and SAYE (Save As You Earn). There are two important factors which will determine the rate of interest you would expect from a building

society savings account. These are:
- the sum invested
- the period of investment.

If you invest a big sum of money for a long fixed period of time, you will be able to get a high rate of interest. Until 5 April 1991, income tax used to be deducted from the interest on the money invested in such accounts. Now the interest is paid 'gross'.

Under the **Save As You Earn** (**SAYE**) scheme, an investor agrees to save a fixed amount of money regularly for a fixed period of time, usually five years. The maximum amount a person can invest under such a scheme is governed by law and it varies from time to time. The amount of interest that is paid on such an investment is also fixed and free of income tax.

► Save As You Earn

We've just outlined the opportunities provided by building societies to the investors. It is extremely difficult to give a complete list of savings and/or investment accounts offered by the building societies as new accounts are continually being added to the wide range that already exists. However, you can easily obtain information about new investment opportunities from the societies themselves.

Commercial banks

The commercial banks such as the 'big four' – Barclays, National Westminster, Midland and Lloyds – provide a wide range of financial services both to individuals and to businesses. From the standpoint of personal savings, the most important is the **deposit account** which earns interest just like a building society account. Banks are now facing increasing competition from the building societies and as a consequence they too are offering new types of deposit or **saving accounts** with competitive rates of interest.

ACT 2.2

It's time you reviewed your savings. Go to the Post Office and collect their pamphlets on National Savings, go to a building society and to a bank and collect their information on savings. Look out especially for something called a **Tax Exempt Special Savings Account** (**TESSA**). For a given monthly sum saved, say £20, work out:

a which would give you the best overall return

b which would give you the best return while still giving you the opportunity to withdraw your money.

The answer will vary according to whether you are a tax-payer or not.

► TESSA: Tax Exempt Special Savings Account, a tax-exempt savings scheme

► No answer given

Insurance companies

Investment with an insurance company is usually undertaken for a long period of time and includes life cover. It takes the form of a **life assurance policy**. For such a policy, you make a regular monthly (or quarterly or half-yearly or annual) contribution, called the **premium**, to an insurance company over an agreed period of time. The premium depends on two main factors: the age of the person insured and the amount of the 'life' or insurance cover, called the **assured sum**.

► **Premium**: regular contribution to insurance scheme

There are two main types of life assurance policy: **whole life policies** and **endowment policies**. Under a whole life policy, your **beneficiary**

► Life assurance
- Whole life policies
- Endowment policies

(e.g. your spouse) gets the assured sum at your death. Under an endowment policy, you yourself will get the benefits on maturity of your policy. However, if you die before the maturity date, your beneficiary will be entitled to all the **benefits** stipulated in the policy. The benefits you or your beneficiary will get depend on the type of policy you have taken out. There are three main types of endowment policy:

- policies without profit
- policies with profit
- policies linked to unit trust.

On maturity of a 'without profit' policy, you will receive a lump-sum equal to the assured sum. For a 'with profit' policy, your entitlements on maturity will be equal to the sum assured plus the accumulated profit to date. The accumulated profit is the total profit actually made on your savings (i.e. the premia paid), which have been invested by the company. The amount you will receive from a unit-linked policy will of course depend on the market price of the unit on the date of maturity, or on selling the units. If you die before the maturity date, your beneficiary will receive either the sum assured or the sum assured plus accumulated profit depending on whether you have a without profit or with profit policy. In case of a **unit-linked policy**, your beneficiary will receive either a guaranteed sum or the value of the units at the date of your death if it is greater.

Investment in stocks and shares

People invest in stocks and shares of limited companies for two main reasons:

- to get a regular income in the form of **dividends**
- to get **capital gains** by selling their shares at a higher price than they had paid for them.

► **Dividends**: money paid out to investors in stocks and shares

Investing in shares does involve an element of risk as share prices may go down depending on the market forces of demand and supply. One way of lessening this risk and uncertainty and the probable loss from the downward movement of share prices is to invest in **unit trusts** rather than in the shares of one or two individual companies. Unit trust companies invest the investors' money in a number of companies with varying degrees of risk so that risks of loss are spread over a large number of companies.

► **Unit trusts** are companies which hold shares in a large number of other companies and issue their own 'units' (i.e. shares) to the investors. If you buy such units you are in effect buying a bit in each of the many companies whose shares are held by the unit trusts. You are therefore spreading the risk by investing in a unit trust.

Borrowing

Individuals need to borrow money when finance available from their current income and savings is not sufficient to obtain the goods and services they want. The borrowing needs of an individual are dependent on the type of **expenditure** (s)he has in mind. There are two main types of expenditure: **capital expenditure** and **revenue expenditure**. Capital expenditure refers to money spent on acquiring a capital good such as a motor car or a TV set, which is expected to last for several years. Revenue expenditure refers to money spent on items of recurrent nature such as food or petrol.The money needed for capital expenditure will normally be more than that for revenue expenditure. Also, borrowing for capital expenditure will usually be for a longer period than that for revenue expenditure.

Borrowing from commercial banks and building societies

Borrowing from banks and building societies may take several forms:

- overdrafts
- personal loans
- property mortgages.

Overdrafts

Overdraft facilities can be obtained by people who have **current accounts** with their banks. An overdraft is a facility whereby customers can take more money out of an account than they have put into it. The maximum amount that can be overdrawn and the maximum period for which this facility is granted are both to be negotiated with the bank manager. Interest is charged on a daily basis on the amount overdrawn at a rate which is normally a few percentage points above the **base rate**, which is regulated by the Bank of England.

► Bank overdrafts

► Not all building societies offer overdrafts.

► **Base rate**: rate of interest set by Bank of England; most loans are at a higher rate of interests than this.

Personal loans

A personal loan is a loan of fixed amount, for a fixed period at a fixed rate of interest. Repayment of the loan, together with the interest thereon, is spread over the agreed period and repaid in a number of equal instalments. Thus if you take a personal loan of £2,000 at 15 per cent p.a. for 2 years, your monthly repayment or instalment will be calculated as follows.

► Personal loans from banks

Sum borrowed = £2,000
Interest thereon = 15% of £2,000, for two years

$$= £\,\frac{2{,}000 \times 15 \times 2}{100}$$

= £600

Total to be repaid over two years = £2,000 + £600
= £2,600

$$\text{Monthly instalment} = £\,\frac{2600}{24}$$

= £108.33

Although the nominal rate, i.e. the rate at which interest is charged on the sum borrowed, seems to be fairly low, the **annual percentage rate**, i.e. the **APR** as it is called, will be rather high because interest is charged on the initial sum borrowed for the agreed period, even though part of the sum borrowed is being repaid every month. For this reason, personal loans from a bank tend to be more expensive than an overdraft for the same amount and for the same period; but banks are usually reluctant to grant overdraft facilities for a big sum for a period exceeding a year. For a significant capital expenditure, borrowers are forced to take up personal loans.

► **APR**: annual percentage rate of interest

Property mortgages

The purchase of a house is by far the most significant capital expenditure that an individual makes in a lifetime. Traditionally, building societies specialize in loans for house purchases. In recent years, however, many banks are providing **mortgage loans**. A mortgage loan requires that the property should be mortgaged with the lender. This means that the lender can take possession of the property if the borrower fails to make the necessary repayments.

► **Mortgages**: in house-purchase the security for the loan is usually the property being purchased. It can be repossessed if the borrower defaults on payments, and then it can be sold to repay the outstanding loan and interest.

► Hire purchase

Borrowing from finance companies

Many finance companies, such as Mercantile Credit Co, provide personal loans. They also provide **hire purchase** (HP) facilities. When you buy a durable or semi-durable product such as a washing machine, you can obtain HP facilities straight away from the supplier. The supplier will arrange the HP facilities with one of the finance companies and you don't need to visit or contact them. This is the great advantage of HP, but it has disadvantages too. Firstly you usually pay a great deal more interest for this facility than you would on a personal loan. Also you do not own the goods until you have paid the last instalment.

► Credit cards

Borrowing on credit cards

Credit cards are sometimes called 'plastic money'. A credit card, such a Barclaycard or an Access card, enables you to buy goods or services up to the value of your **credit limit**, from various retail outlets, garages, hotels and restaurants, cinemas etc. without paying at the time of purchase. You can also draw cash from the recommended banks and their **service tills**. At the end of each month you receive a statement showing the amount you owe them. If you pay the amount in full by the stipulated date, you do not pay any interest at all. However, if you decide to make a part payment (you can pay as little as five per cent of your total purchase for the month), you have to pay interest on the balance with your next payment. If you take out any cash through your credit card, you do not get any free extended credit facility, you have to pay interest on the cash drawn on a daily basis.

DEDUCTIONS FROM INCOME

► **Gross pay**: what you earn

► **Net pay**: what you get

A wage earner does not usually receive the full gross earnings in his/her pay packet. A number of **deductions**, some compulsory and some voluntary, are made from **weekly gross wages** or **monthly gross salary**. The amount after these deductions is called the **net pay** and this is the actual amount a person receives at the end of the week or month, as appropriate. A **pay slip** will accompany the net pay, which will show the details of all earnings and deductions.

An employer is obliged by law to make certain deductions from an employee's income. These deductions are called **compulsory deductions** and consist of the following:

- income tax
- National Insurance contributions
- superannuation contributions for certain approved pension schemes.

Voluntary deductions, on the other hand, are made at the request of the employee. Such deductions include trade union subscriptions and SAYE (Save as You Earn).

► Income tax

Income tax

Income tax is a major source of government revenue. The Government needs money to finance its operations. Most people in employment are liable to pay income tax, the actual amount depending on their personal circumstances. Income tax is deducted from an individual's income during a tax year which begins on 6 April of each year and continues until 5 April the following year.

You do not pay income tax on the whole of your earnings during a particular tax year. You are entitled to a number of allowances, depending on your personal circumstances, which will be deducted from your gross income to arrive at what is called your **taxable income**. You pay income tax on your taxable income only.

Personal allowances and income tax rates vary from year to year. The Chancellor of the Exchequer announces in his Budget Speech each year any changes in personal allowances and tax rates. For the 1991-92 tax year, the summary of the main allowances was as follows.

Income tax rates 1991/92

Bands of taxable income (£)	Rate (%)
0 – 23,700	25
over 23,700	40

Personal allowances and reliefs

a	Single person's allowances	£3,295
b	Married couple's allowance	£1,720

The tax rates and allowances for 1991/92 are given for illustration only and will not be used in our calculation of taxable pay and tax liability. Instead, we'll use imaginary figures for ease of calculation.

► Tax allowances
Taxable income: the amount you pay tax on, calculated by deducting tax allowances from pay.

For the 1992/93 tax year there is an additional tax band in which tax is paid at 20 per cent on taxable income between £1 and £2,000.

Personal allowances remain the same.

Superannuation contributions

Any superannuation contributions made by a person to an approved pension scheme are tax free.

► Superannuation contributions to an approved pension scheme

Example 2.4 Calculation of taxable income and tax liability

Susan Hardy is employed as a receptionist by a travel agent. Her present salary is £8,000 p.a. She is single and pays 5 per cent of her salary as superannuation contributions to her company's pension scheme. She has no other income.

Calculate her:

a taxable income

b income tax payable for the year.

Assume that a single person's allowance is £3,000 and the rate of income tax is 25 per cent.

Solution

	£
Gross income	8,000
Less superannuation contribution (5% of £8,000)	400
	7,600
Less personal allowance	
(Single person's allowance)	3,000
Taxable income	4,600
Income tax payable (25% of £4,600)	1,150

ACT 2.3

Since tax and personal allowances vary from year to year you should obtain the current rates. If you are a taxpayer these will have been sent to you, otherwise obtain them from the tax office (the address will be in *Yellow Pages*). Rework the examples in terms of the current rates.

► No answer given

Mortgage interest

► Tax relief on mortgages

► **MIRAS**: Mortgage Interest Relief At Source.

If you borrow to purchase your house, you are entitled to receive **tax relief** on the interest you pay to your lender. This relief was restricted to loans of £30,000 in 1992 but the figure may have changed by now. Tax relief is given through a scheme called **Mortgage Interest Relief At Source** (MIRAS). Under this scheme, the lending institution works out how much tax relief you would get on the interest payable, and deducts this amount from the gross interest payable. You therefore pay a smaller amount as interest to your lender.

The amount of tax relief is calculated by using the following formula.

Formula for mortgage interest tax relief

$$\text{Tax relief} = \frac{\text{amount of interest payable} \times \text{basic tax rate}}{100}$$

Example 2.5

Suppose that you have borrowed £20,000 from a building society at 14 per cent p.a. to buy your house, your tax relief under the MIRAS scheme will be calculated as follows.

			£
Gross interest payable	= 14% of £20,000	=	2,800
Less tax relief	$= £\ \frac{2800 \times 25}{100}$	=	700
Net interest payable per annum		=	2,100
Net interest payable per month	$= £\ \frac{2100}{12}$	=	£ 175

Note that we have assumed that the basic rate of income tax is 25 per cent. You therefore pay only £2,100 p.a. (or £175 per month), and not £2,800 p.a. to your building society.

PAYE

► **Employees** usually pay income tax on current earnings, week by week or month by month.

► The **self-employed** usually pay in two instalments a year on the preceding year's income.

You do not pay your income tax bill in one go. In Example 2.4, we worked out that Susan Hardy is liable to pay an income tax bill of £1,150. It would certainly be difficult to pay the whole amount in one go. Fortunately, she does not need to. The income tax due to the Inland Revenue from an individual who is working for someone else will be deducted by the employers from his/her gross income week by week or month by month, as the case may be, under the **Pay As You Earn (PAYE)** scheme. The employers will then pass the amount of tax deducted to the Inland Revenue. For self-employed persons, the situation is different. Their income tax liability will be calculated on the profits of their accounting year. They pay income tax in one go or by two instalments, on a **preceding year basis**. That is, they pay tax in 1990/91 on the profits they made in the accounting year ending in the tax year 1989/90.

Study the box titled 'How the PAYE scheme works' on the page opposite. Then check your understanding of personal income tax by doing Activity 2.4.

How the PAYE scheme works

1 Every person has to fill in a tax return form, usually on first employment and once a year around March or when the Inland Revenue requests a return.

In the **tax return form**, that person is required to give information about her/his earnings and expenses relating to the job. On the basis of this information, the Inland Revenue will provide the person with a **tax code** which will be used by his/her employer to work out the taxable pay. The tax code will take into account all the allowances the person is entitled to receive.
The tax code indicates the person's tax allowances.

2 The code number is equal to the sum of allowances and reliefs, without the last digit. This will be followed by a letter, usually signifying the type of allowances given.

The tax code for Susan Hardy in Example 2.4 for the year 1990/91 will be 300L. The letter L indicates that she has been given a single person's allowance. The letter H would indicate a married couple's allowance.

Notice that superannuation contributions are not taken into consideration in setting a tax code. The reason is that superannuation contributions are considered to be a charge and not an allowance and are automatically deducted from the gross income.

3 The Inland Revenue supplies the employers with the copies of Tax tables A, B, and C, and deduction sheets (known as P11s). Table A shows the tax free pay people are entitled to, week by week (for weekly paid workers) or month by month (for monthly paid workers) as appropriate. Table B shows the tax due at the basic rate and Table C at the higher rate.

4 The tax deducted by an employer is sent to the Collector of Taxes within 14 days of the end of each income month period.

ACT 2.4

1 Calculate the net annual and monthly pay receivable by each of the following.

a Eddie Banda, married, earning £8,500 a year

b Joanne Kemp, single, earning £10,000 a year, and making a contribution of 5 per cent of her gross salary to an approved superannuation fund

c Didar Singh, married, earning £25,000 a year and making a superannuation contribution of 5 per cent of his gross income to an approved pension scheme

Take the following tax rate and allowances.

Income tax rate	25%
Single person's allowance	£3,000
Married couple's allowance	£1,700

Note that the married couple's allowance is given to the husband in addition to the single person's allowance.

2 Calculate the net interest payable to the building society for each of the following.

a Julie Brown pays interest at 14% p.a. on a mortgage of £15,000

b Steve Taylor pays interest at 13.5% p.a. on a mortgage of £30,000

c Leslie Pitt pays interest at 14% p.a. on a mortgage of £60,000

► Answers in appendix

National Insurance contributions

National Insurance contributions are another compulsory deduction made by an employer from the income of employees. The employer also makes a contribution to the Department of Health and Social Security. By paying National Insurance contributions, an employee becomes entitled to certain benefits such as **unemployment, sickness** and **old-age pension benefits**.

There are four classes of National Insurance contributions:

Class I: all employees and their employers
Class II: self-employed persons
Class III: non employed persons
Class IV: self-employed persons, additional contributions based on profits.

To simplify matters, we shall concentrate on Class I contributions only.

The rates of Class I National Insurance contributions for 1991/92 were as follows.

Employer contributions	
Earnings (£p.w.)	*% of all earnings*
0 – 51.99	0
52 – 84.99	4.2% on £52.00 0.8% on excess
85 – 129.99	6.6% on £52.00 2.8% on excess
130 – 184.99	8.6% on £52.00 4.8% on excess
185 – 390.00	10.4% on £52.00 6.6% on excess
over 390.00	10.4% on £52.00 6.6% on £338.00 10.4% on excess

Employee contributions		
Earnings (£p.w.)	*% of all earnings*	
	*NCO**	*CO***
Earnings below £52 p.w.	0	0
Earnings above £52 p.w.		
0 – £52	2	2
£52.01 – £390	9	7
Above £390 p.w		
No further liability		

* *NCO* = not contracted out
** *CO* = contracted out

The **contracted out** rates are applicable to employees who have joined approved occupational pension schemes where their employers have elected to be excluded from the state earnings related scheme. In all other cases the **not-contracted-out** rates apply.

All the ideas presented so far relating to compulsory deductions are now illustrated in Example 2.6.

Example 2.6 Calculating compulsory deductions

John Hicks is a married man and his wife does not go out to work. His gross earnings for the tax year 1991-92 are expected to be £15,000. He makes a contribution of five per cent of his gross salary to his company's pension fund. He has a mortgage of £30,000 on his house and the current rate of interest is 14 per cent.

You are required to calculate:

- **a** his taxable pay
- **b** his income tax payable
- **c** his net pay for the year
- **d** the interest payable on his mortgage.

Solution

In working out this assignment, we've taken actual rate of income tax, personal allowances and NI contributions rate to illustrate how taxable pay, national insurance contributions etc. are calculated in practice.

		£	£
a	Gross pay		15,000.00
	Less superannuation contribution		
	5% of £15,000	750	
	Married person's allowance		
	(£3,295 + £1,720)	5,015	5,765.00
	Taxable pay		9,235.00
b	Income tax payable		
	25% of £9,235		2,381.25
c	Gross pay		15,000.00
	Less deductions:		
	Superannuation contribution	750.00	
	Income tax	2,308.75	
	NI contribution*	914.80	3,973.55
	Net pay		11,026.45
d	Interest on the loan		
	14% of £30,000	4,200	
	Less tax relief (under MIRAS)		
	25% of £4,200	1,050	
			3,150

*Calculation of NI contributions:

	£		£
Gross	15,000		
£52 × 52	2,704	@ 2%	54.08
	12,296	@ 7%	860.72
			914.80

Personal expenditure

We need money to get the goods and services we want. Food, clothing and shelter are no doubt the most important needs for most of us. Besides these basic needs, we need money for transport, entertainments, holidays and a host of other things. How much we can spend on each of these items will depend primarily on two factors:

- how strongly we feel the need for each item
- how much we can afford to spend.

How strong our need is for a particular thing will depend on a complex set of socio-psychological factors and in the end we have to decide it for ourselves. Once this decision is made, we are confronted with a second, purely financial decision. Our ability to afford a particular thing or a mix of things will depend mainly on three factors:

- present income
- past savings
- ability to borrow and to repay the loan together with the appropriate interest.

We've already discussed the sources of personal finance and dwelt, at some length, on the different options available to us for borrowing. Read the section on borrowing again to refresh your memory. Also, remember that expenses which we need to make on a regular basis are revenue expenditure. Expenses on durable or semi-durable goods which are expected to last for a reasonable length of time are capital expenditure.

Budgeting and the personal budget

A prudent individual always tries to balance income and expenditure, although for most of us it is not always an easy task. To control your **cash flows** – your cash inflows or incomings and your cash outflows or outgoings – you need a little forethought, that is, a bit of planning, regarding your cash receipts and payments. This is exactly what we do in a **personal budget**. A personal budget is simply an action plan, drawn up by an individual, which gives an account of expected income and expected expenditure over a given period of time. Since a personal budget implies planning for the future, it is important to estimate incomings and outgoings of cash for each plan period (which may be a week or a month) as accurately as possible. For most of us who work for other people, our expected income for the next few weeks or months is more or less certain and can be estimated with a high degree of accuracy. In the area of personal expenditure, some items such as mortgage payment or rent, community charges, insurance and transport costs are more or less fixed. Expenses on other items such as food, clothing, entertainments, etc. are generally variable, but are controllable within limits. The extent to which we need to control expenses on these variable items will be revealed by the personal budget.

If you notice that in a particular month, your expenditure is going far to exceed your income, you have basically two options:

- cut down your expenses and/or
- negotiate with your bank in good time for an overdraft or a personal loan.

To make additional funds available through an overdraft or a personal loan will save a lot of embarrassment and worry.

Figure 2.1 gives a typical layout for a personal cash (or cash flow) budget.

Sammy Patel
Cash Budget for the six months ending 31 December, 19x2

	July	Aug	Sept	Oct	Nov	Dec
Opening balance	X	X	X	X	X	X
Receipts (Schedule A)	X	X	X	X	X	X
Total cash available (X)	X	X	X	X	X	X
Total payments (Schedule B) (Y)	X	X	X	X	X	X
Closing cash balance/(deficit) (X – Y)	X	X	X	X	X	X

Figure 2.1
Layout of a personal cash budget

Preparing a personal cash flow budget involves the following steps:

1 Start with the estimated opening cash balance.

2 List all the sources of cash receipts e.g. pay, interest receivable, together with the expected amount from each source in the form of a schedule (Schedule A in our layout). Add the amounts for each month. This total, added to the opening balance listed in a above will provide the total amount of cash available during the month: the 'X' in our layout.

3 List all the payments that are to be made during each month in the form of a schedule (Schedule B in our layout). The sum of the individual items for a month will give you the total payments for that month: the 'Y' in our layout.

4 Total payments, i.e. the figure obtained in **3** above should now be subtracted from the sum of opening balance and total receipts, i.e., the 'X' obtained in **2** above, to obtain the closing cash balance. The closing balance may be either positive (showing a surplus) or negative (showing a deficit) depending on whether payments are less or more than the total cash available. It is customary to show a deficit within a pair of brackets, rather than putting a minus sign before the amount of deficit. Thus a deficit of £30 will be shown as (£30).

5 The closing balance of the current month or period will be the opening balance for the next month or period.

6 The budget will come to an end when the closing balance of the last month or period is determined.

Example 2.7 shows how a cash budget is prepared.

Example 2.7 Preparing a cash budget

Sandra Edwards is working as a clerical assistant in an office and is single. Her net income is £500 per month which is expected to remain unchanged for the next 12 months. She has a deposit account for a fixed sum of £1,000 with a bank which earns a net interest of 10 per cent per annum.

Her salary is paid into her bank current account. Also, the interest on her 'fixed' deposit account is credited to her current account twice a year, i.e. on 30 June and 31 December each year.

Sandra's 'fixed' expenditure is expected to be as follows.

Rent and community charge	£150 per month
Instalment on her car	£70 per month
Monthly car insurance premium	£20
Road tax due in December	£100
Gas bill due in October estimated at	£70
Electricity bill, paid through a budget account	£15 per month

Her 'variable' expenditure is expected to be:

Food and drink	£90 per month
Entertainment is usually	£100 per month,
but in December, it is to go up to	£150 per month
Petrol	£30 per month

Sandra expects a balance of £100 in her current account on 1 October.

Now draw up a cash flow budget for Sandra for the three months ended 31 December.

Solution

Schedule A

	October	*November*	*December*
	£	£	£
Receipts			
Salary	500	500	500
Interest on Deposit a/c	—	—	50
	500	500	550

Schedule B

	October	*November*	*December*
	£	£	£
Payments			
Rent	150	150	150
Instalment on car	70	70	70
Car insurance premium	20	20	20
Road tax	—	—	100
Gas	70	—	—
Electricity	15	15	15
Food	90	90	90
Entertainment	100	100	150
Petrol	30	30	30
	545	475	625

Sandra Edwards
Cash Budget for the three months ending 31 December

	October	*November*	*December*
	£	£	£
Opening balance	100	55	80
Receipts	500	500	550
Total cash available (*X*)	600	555	630
Total payments (*Y*)	545	475	625
Closing balance (*X* – *Y*)	55	80	5

Chapter summary

- There are four major sources of personal finance: earned income, state benefits, investment income and borrowing.
- For earned income three methods of calculating wages are especially common: time rates, piece rates and incentive bonus schemes.
- Investment income may come from investments in savings accounts, in insurance policies or in stocks and shares. The investments vary in their yields and in their security.
- Personal borrowings may be made from individuals or from organizations such as banks, building societies, finance companies or credit card companies. Borrowing normally requires the payment of interest. Different types of borrowing are associated with different levels of interest.
- Deductions are made from an individual's income. Some are compulsory. These include NI contributions and income tax.
- Personal expenditure can be divided into capital expenditure and revenue expenditure.
- Personal cash flow budgets can be prepared which enable individuals to plan their income and expenditure sensibly.

ACT 2.5

1 Calculate the weekly gross pay of the following workers, who worked the number of hours shown.

Caroline	46	Ian	42
Trevor	40	Elizabeth	44

The basic working week of the firm is 40 hours and overtime is paid over 40 hours at time and a half. The rate of pay is £2.95 per hour.

► No answer given

2 Susan Drummond is a stockroom assistant in a supermarket. The following details relate to her work during a certain week, with an hour for lunch each day, unpaid:

Monday	8.30 a.m. to 5.30 p.m.
Tuesday	8.30 a.m. to 6.30 p.m.
Wednesday	8.30 a.m. to 6.00 p.m.
Thursday	8.30 a.m. to 8.00 p.m.
Friday	8.30 a.m. to 5.30 p.m.
Saturday	8.30 a.m. to 5.30 p.m.

The rate of pay is £2.10 per hour plus time and a half for working after 5.30 p.m. and on Saturday.

Calculate Susan's gross wages for the week.

► Answer in appendix

3 The standard rate of production of an article is 10 units per hour. Workers are paid a bonus of 50 per cent of the time they have saved at their time rate. During a particular week the relevant figures for three workers were:

	Worker A	*Worker B*	*Worker C*
Hours worked	38	40	42
Units produced	360	440	480
Rate per hour	£2.50	£2.75	£2.60

Calculate the gross wage earned by each of the three workers.

► No answer given

4 John Rees works for a company in which the basic working week is 40 hours. He is paid a basic rate of £2 per hour for attendance and a piece rate dependent on how much he produces. The relevant piece rate can be obtained from the following table:

Production	*Piece rate*
Below 500 units	nil
From 500 to 1,000 units	5p per unit
From 1,001 to 1,500 units	10p per unit
Over 1,500 units	12p per unit

Calculate John's weekly gross wage if he produces:

a 499 units per week
b 1,250 units per week
c 1,700 units per week.

► Answer in appendix

For questions 5 and 6, take the following income tax rate, allowances etc.

Rate of income tax	25%
Personal allowances:	
Single person	£3,000
Married person's extra allowance given to husband	£1,720
NI contribution, flat rate on all earnings	6%

5 Sushila Patel works as a sales assistant in a supermarket and is single. She gets a salary of £8,000 per annum and has no other income.

She contributes 6 per cent of her gross salary to the company's pension scheme. Also, she pays an allowable (for tax purposes) subscription of £50 per annum to a trade union.

You are required to calculate Sushila's taxable income and tax liability for the current tax year.

► No answer given

6 Alan Dixon is a married man and his wife has no paid work. The following details relate to their financial position for the current tax year.

(i) Alan's annual salary: £14,750.

(ii) Alan pays 5 per cent of his salary into his company's pension fund.

(iii) Alan pays interest at 14 per cent on a mortgage loan of £20,000.

You are required to calculate:

a Alan's taxable income for the year
b His income tax liability for the year
c His net pay for the year
d The interest for the year Alan has to pay on his mortgage loan.

► Answer in appendix

7 Elaine Smith will start employment on 1 July. Her income and estimated expenses are as follows.

Income
Net monthly pay of £480.

Expenditure
(i) Rent of the flat which she intends to share with two others: £75 per month.
(ii) Share of gas and electricity bills, £75 per quarter payable in March, June, September and December.
(iii) Housekeeping: £200 per month.
(iv) Travel expenses: £20 per month.
(v) She intends to take up a life assurance policy in September, the premium is expected to be £8 per month.
(vi) Entertainments and clothing: £90 per month.
(vii) She will open a current account with the local branch of Barclays Bank plc with a cheque for £100 which she received on 25 June from her mother as a birthday present.

You are required to:

a Draw up a personal cash budget for Elaine for the first six months of her employment.
b Advise Elaine as to what she can do with any resulting surplus or deficit.

► No answer given

8 Eric and Paula are to be married on 1 April. They have already bought a house and all their savings have been used for house deposits, legal expenses and house furnishings. Their earnings and estimated expenses are as follows:

Net income
Eric: £600 per month.
Paula: £400 per month.

Expenditure
(i) Mortgage payment of £300 per month
(ii) Poll tax of £600 per annum, payable in ten equal instalments commencing on 1 May
(iii) Household insurance of £100 payable on 5 April
(iv) Car tax of £100 due in July
(v) Car insurance of £120 due in August
(vi) Gas and electricity: £120 per quarter, payable in June, September, December and March
(vii) Petrol: £60 per month

(viii) Car servicing due in September: £60

(ix) Telephone: £45 per quarter, payable in June, September, December and March

(x) Life assurance premium on their joint life: £20 per month commencing in May.

(xi) Entertainment and general expenses: £420 per month

► Answer in appendix

You are required to prepare a cash budget for Eric and Paula for the first six months of their married life.

3 The recording function of accounting 1 – the Ledger

Chapter objectives

By the end of this chapter, you should be able to:

- understand the meaning and significance of the accounting equation
- construct a simple balance sheet of a business
- state the different books of accounts that a business needs to maintain
- understand the principle of double-entry book-keeping and apply it to record financial transactions in the main book of accounts, the Ledger
- state the meaning of the following terms: accounting equation, balance sheet, trial balance, ledger, cash book, assets (fixed and current), liabilities (long-term, short-term), capital, horizontal and vertical formats, debit, credit, liquidity, books of orginal entry (or prime entry/subsidiary books), expenses, revenue.

DOUBLE-ENTRY BOOK-KEEPING

One of the main functions of accounting is to maintain proper records of financial transactions. This chapter deals with a system of record keeping which has been in use all over the world for centuries.The system is known as **double-entry book-keeping**. Every transaction is recorded twice, in two accounts. In this chapter this will be introduced through a well-known principle called the **accounting equation**.

The accounting equation and the Balance Sheet

Every business transaction will affect the financial position of a business, which at any point in time is given by the resources the business owns, called its **assets**, the money or money's worth the owner/s put into the business, called its **capital**, and the amount it owes to other people called its **liabilities**. The relationship between these three items is given by the **accounting equation**.

The accounting equation

$A = C + L$ where A = assets
C = capital
and L = liabilities

By the very meanings of the terms used, the two sides of the equation are necessarily equal. The total assets of the business (the A in our equation) must have been financed by capital (the C in our equation) or provided or borrowed by the owner/s (the L in our equation), or by a combination of the two.

► The accounting equation: assets equals capital plus liabilities

Assets: the resources owned by the business, including debts owed to it

Capital: the money or money's worth put into or kept in the business by the owners

Liabilities: the amount the business owes to others

The accounting equation is a useful means of working out any one of the three variables, provided the other two are known. Thus, for example, if the assets and the liabilities of the business at the end of a certain day are given to be £50,000 and £20,000 respectively, we can easily calculate that its capital is:

► Capital equals assets minus liabilities

$$C = A - L$$
$$= £50{,}000 - £20{,}000$$
$$= £30{,}000$$

The equation $C = A - L$ can be rewritten as $A - L = C$.

To conform to modern practice, we shall use this version of the accounting equation which can be easily translated into a very important statement of the financial position of a business, called the **Balance Sheet**.

► The Balance Sheet of a business is expressed $A - L = C$

Balance Sheets

Balance Sheets can be prepared in either **horizontal** (or **double-sided**) format, or **vertical** format. In the former, assets less liabilities ($A - L$ in our revised accounting equation) are now listed on the left-hand side (beware of the older text books where assets are shown on the right-hand side!) and capital on the right-hand side. The totals on both sides should of course be equal! In the vertical format, assets are listed first. Then liabilities are shown as a deduction from total assets. Just below the figure representing total assets minus total liabilities capital is listed. The two figures should, as expected, always agree.

The Balance Sheet in horizontal format

We shall start with the horizontal format and introduce the vertical format later on.

The Balance Sheet of a business will change after each and every transaction. Each transaction will have two effects on one or more of the three variables (that is A, C and L) in our accounting equation. This follows from the dual nature of a business transaction and is illustrated in Example 3.1.

Example 3.1 A Balance Sheet in horizontal format

The following transactions relate to the first three days' transactions of Joe Brown.

Day 1 Joe Brown started business with £20,000 in cash which he deposited in a business bank account.

Day 2 He bought premises on a building society mortgage of £25,000.

Day 3 He bought fixtures and fittings by cheque for £5,000.
He purchased stock by cheque for £10,000.
He bought further stock on credit from Jim Taylor, at £2,000.

You are required to prepare a Balance Sheet for Joe Brown at the end of each of the three days.

Solution

Day 1:

Joe Brown
Balance Sheet as at Day 1

	£	£		£	£
Bank		£20,000	Capital		£20,000

Day 2:

Joe Brown
Balance Sheet as at Day 2

	£	£		£	£
Assets:			Capital		20,000
Premises		25,000			
Bank		20,000			
		45,000			
Less Liabilities:					
Mortgage		25,000			
		20,000			20,000

Day 3:

Joe Brown
Balance Sheet as at Day 3

	£	£		£	£
Assets:			Capital		20,000
Premises		25,000			
Fixtures and fittings		5,000			
Stock		2,000			
Bank		5,000			
		47,000			
Less Liabilities:					
Mortgage	25,000				
Creditor: John Taylor	2,000				
		27,000			
		20,000			20,000

Let's now look at the effects of each of Joe Brown's transactions on the variables *A*, *C* and *L*, of the accounting equation, starting with Day 2.

	Transaction	*Effects*
Day 2:	Bought premises on a building society mortgage of £25,000.	Asset increased by £25,000. Liability increased by £25,000.
Day 3:	Bought fixtures and fittings by cheque for £5,000.	One asset, viz, fixtures and fittings increased by £5,000. Another asset i.e. cash reduced by £5,000.
	Bought stock by cheque for £10,000	Stock, an asset, increased by £10,000. Bank, another asset, decreased by an equivalent amount.
	Bought stock on credit from J. Taylor £2,000.	The asset stock increased by £2,000. Liabilities in the form of creditors increased by £2,000.

► You must remember that you are preparing the Balance Sheet for Joe Brown's business and not for him as an individual. The business is a separate entity from the owner, i.e. Joe Brown. From the standpoint of the business, its assets as at Day 1 consist of £20,000 in the business bank account; hence the left-hand side of the Balance Sheet shows only this. This money has been provided by the owner himself and constitutes the capital of the business which is shown as such on the right-hand side of the Balance Sheet. The accounting equation holds good.

A – *L* = *C*
£20,000 – 0 = £20,000

The business hasn't got any other liabilities.

► At the end of Day 2, assets consist of two items, viz, cash in the bank, £20,000 and premises worth £25,000, giving a total assets value of £45,000. Capital has remained the same, but since premises were bought on mortgage, the business owes £25,000 to the lender. Again, the accounting equation holds good.

A – *L* = *C*
£45,000 – £25,000 = £20,000

► At the end of Day 3, total assets minus total liabilities amount to £20,000 as listed on the left-hand side of the Balance Sheet. Stocks acquired amount to £12,000 – £10,000's worth being bought by cheque and the remainder on credit from J.Taylor. Capital remains the same as before but liabilities have increased by £2,000, as compared to Day 2, because of the purchase of some stocks on credit. Once again, the accounting equation appears to hold good.

A – *L* = *C*
£47,000 – £27,000 = £20,000

You should have noticed that the **dual nature** of business transactions is of paramount importance in preparing the Balance Sheet. The Balance Sheet always balances, because the effect of a transaction is either to alter the two sides of the accounting equation by an equal amount, or to increase one component of assets and to decrease another at the same time by an equal amount. This concept of duality of business transactions will be further developed in the context of writing up the main book of accounts, called the **Ledger** (see page 40).

The Balance Sheet in vertical format

Now that you are familiar with the horizontal format of the Balance Sheet, you can look at the alternative presentation in **vertical** format. Example 3.2 presents Joe Brown's Balance Sheet as at Day 3 (see Example 3.1) in vertical format.

► The Balance Sheet of a business is expressed $A - L = C$

Example 3.2 Balance Sheet in vertical format

Joe Brown
Balance Sheet as at Day 3

	£	£
Assets:		
Premises		25,000
Fixtures and fittings		5,000
Stock		12,000
Cash		5,000
		47,000
Less Liabilities:		
Mortgage	25,000	
J. Taylor (creditor)	2,000	
		27,000
		20,000
Financed by:		
Capital		20,000

The top part of the Balance Sheet simply lists the assets owned and the liabilities owed by the business on the given date and corresponds to the left-hand side of the accounting equation.

The bottom part lists the capital and corresponds to the right-hand side of the accounting equation.

► The Balance Sheet always balances because of the accounting equation.

The bottom part of the Balance Sheet begins with the expression 'Financed by'. This expression is used for clarity only and may be omitted if desired. Later on, when we shall be dealing with more complex Balance Sheets, we'll introduce slight modifications in the presentation of Balance Sheets in vertical format for greater clarity.

Now for an opportunity to test your understanding of the accounting equation *vis-à-vis* the Balance Sheet. Here is an assignment for you to do.

ACT 3.1

1 Complete the gaps in the following table.

	Assets £	*Liabilities* £	*Capital* £
a	17,800	?	13,500
b	?	8,300	19,200
c	15,300	2,800	?
d	?	12,650	40,750
e	?	6,900	30,250
f	40,500	?	30,250

2 Classify the following into assets and liabilities.

a Office equipment
b Bank overdraft
c Cash in hand
d Motor vehicles
e Stock of goods
f Loan from A. Lender
g Trade creditors
h Trade debtors
i Plant and machinery
j Land and buildings

3 Albert King had the following assets and liabilities on 31 December.

	£
Creditors	10,000
Debtors	15,000
Bank overdraft	5,000
Cash in hand	1,500
Stock of unsold goods	8,500
Furniture	4,200
Premises	25,000
Capital	39,200

Prepare Albert King's Balance Sheet as at 31 December in both horizontal and vertical formats.

► Answers in appendix

Classification of assets and liabilities

Assets are normally classified into two groups:

- fixed assets
- current assets.

Fixed assets are those which usually have a long life and are not held primarily for resale. Examples include buildings, machinery, motor vehicles, furniture, and long-term investment in stocks and shares of other companies.

► **Fixed assets** have a long life.

Current assets are those assets which are held for a relatively short time with the ultimate object of converting them into cash. Examples include stocks of goods, debtors (people who owe you money), cash at bank and cash in hand. For purposes of standardization, assets are usually listed in the Balance Sheet in a definite order. One such order

► **Current assets** are held for a short time.

► The order for listing assets

which is generally used is given below.

Fixed assets

Premises
Fixture and fittings
Plant and machinery
Motor vehicles

Current assets

Stock
Debtors
Bank
Cash

Fixed assets are listed in the descending order of their **permanency**, i.e. how long they are going to last. Current assets are listed in the ascending order of their **liquidity**, i.e. the ease with which they can be changed into cash.

There are two main types of liability:

- long-term liabilities
- short-term or current liabilities.

► **Long-term** liabilities are long-term debts.

► **Short-term** liabilities are debts due to be repaid within about 12 months.

Long-term liabilities are the indebtedness of the business which does not require repayment within the business's accounting period, which is usually 12 months. **Current liabilities** are short-term loans, such as debts for goods, which need to be repaid within the next 12 months.

The Balance Sheet – further considerations

The earlier presentation of Balance Sheets did not divide assets into fixed assets and current assets. Nor did it classify liabilities into long-term liabilities and short-term liabilities. This was to keep the essentials of the Balance Sheet as simple as possible. Now that we know the distinction between fixed and current assets, and between long-term and current liabilities, we can look at a standard Balance Sheet incorporating these two types of assets and liabilities. This is done in Example 3.3. From now on we shall follow this standard form in preparing Balance Sheets.

Example 3.3 Fixed and current assets, long-term and short-term liabilities

From the following list of balances extracted from the books of Pat Williams as at 31 December 19x9, prepare her Balance Sheet as at that date.

	£
Capital	45,000
Stocks	8,000
Premises	25,000
Debtors	10,000
Cash at bank	5,000
Fixtures and fittings	10,000
Motor vehicles	7,000
Loan from J. Smith	15,000
Cash in hand	500
Creditors	5,500

Solution

Pat Williams

Balance Sheet as at 31 December 19x9

	£	£
Fixed assets		
Premises		25,000
Fixtures and fittings		10,000
Motor vehicles		7,000
		42,000
Current assets		
Stock	8,000	
Debtors	10,000	
Cash at bank	5,000	
Cash in hand	500	
	23,500	
Less current liabilities		
Creditors	5,500	
Working capital		18,000
		60,000
Less long-term liabilities		
Loan from J. Smith		15,000
		45,000
Financed by		
Capital		45,000

Note:

1 First, all the fixed assets are listed in descending order of permanency. The values of these assets are then added to give us a sub-total of fixed assets which is £42,000.

2 Next, the current assets are listed in ascending order of liquidity. The values of these are put in the near-side column. The reason for this is to show how we arrive at the **working capital** of a business which is defined as the difference between current assets and current liabilities. The current asset values are then added to give us the sub-total of current assets.

► **Working capital** = current costs – current liabilities

3 The next step is to list the current liabilities. In this example, as we've just one item under this heading, i.e. creditors, we put the value of creditors just below the current assets total. We now subtract the current liabilities from the sum of current assets and put the figure in the column giving the fixed assets total. Against this figure, we write the expression 'Working capital'. Alternatively, you can write 'Net current assets'.

4 We now add the fixed assets total and the working capital to give us the total of £60,000. From this we take away the total of long-term liabilities, i.e. £15,000, to give us the final figure of £45,000. This figure represents the total net assets of the business. However, we normally do not write any description against this figure, following current practice.

5 The 'Financed by' figure simply lists the amount of capital which agrees with the total net assets figure.

Alternatively long-term liabilities may be listed under the heading 'Financed by', in which case both the top and bottom totals will be £60,000 as shown on the next page:

	£	£
		60,000
Financed by		
Capital	45,000	
Long-term liabilities		
Loan from J. Smith	15,000	60,000

THE BOOKS OF ACCOUNTS

The importance of proper record-keeping of financial transactions can hardly be over emphasized. The provision of adequate and regular financial information is vital to the success of a business. Such a provision of financial information is made possible by maintaining a set of books of accounts for recording various transactions. The books or computer files which a typical business will need for recording all its transactions are usually classified under three headings:

► Account books these days are often computer files but the term 'book' is still used for them.

- The **Ledger** – is the main or principal book of accounts.
- The **Cash Book** – used to record cash transactions only.
- **Books of original entry** or books of prime entry or subsidiary books.

Although in theory every transaction can be recorded straight away in the Ledger, it is convenient to classify all transactions into a number of categories according to their nature and to record them initially in the subsidiary books, to be transferred later on to the Ledger. How many such books a business needs will depend upon the nature and size of the business, but the following are considered to be the popular ones:

- the Sales Day Book
- the Purchases Day Book
- the Returns Inwards Book
- the Returns Outwards Book
- the Journal.

The rest of the chapter is devoted to the Ledger. The Cash Book and the subsidiary books are dealt with in the next two chapters.

Double-entry book-keeping and the Ledger

In stating the accounting equation we talked about the dual nature of all business transactions. To restate the **duality concept**: every business transaction involves two aspects – the **giving aspect** and the **receiving aspect**. Corresponding to these two aspects, there will be two entries in the main book of accounts (the Ledger) in two different accounts. Hence the name, double-entry book-keeping – each transaction is entered in two separate accounts in the Ledger. The double-entry system divides each page of the Ledger vertically in two halves – the left-hand side, called the **debit side**, and the right-hand side, called the **credit side**.

There is a definite set of rules for deciding which aspect (the giving aspect or the receiving aspect) of a given transaction is to be debited, i.e. entered on the debit side, and which one is to be credited, i.e. entered on the credit side of the ledger account.

This set of rules for debit and credit is as follows:
- debit the receiver or the receiving account
- credit the giver or the giving account.

It also follows from this set of rules that:
- every debit entry has a corresponding credit entry
- every credit entry has a corresponding debit entry.

This simple principle may be illustrated by taking a simple example. Let's assume that Kevin Jones, a retailer, buys a hundred boxes of chocolates at £1.20 each from North West Wholesalers Ltd., paying cash. In Kevin Jones' Ledger, the receiving account is the Purchase account and is to be debited whereas his Cash account is giving out £120 (100 × £1.20) and should therefore be credited. Likewise in North West Wholesalers Ltd.'s books, the Sales account, being the giving account, should be credited and the Cash account, being the receiving account, should be debited.

This example brings out one important fact that the 'duality' of a transaction does not mean, as many beginners in accounting assume, giving by one party and receiving by another. The double aspect of a transaction means that each party (both Kevin Jones and North West Wholesalers Ltd. in our example) receives value and gives value at the same time in the process of exchange.

The double-entry rules may now be restated in terms of the three variables: assets, liabilities and capital of the accounting equation as follows.

Recording assets, liabilities and capital

Assets:
- To record an increase in an asset, debit the asset account.
- To record a decrease in an asset, credit the asset account.

Liabilities:
- To record an increase in a liability, credit the liability account.
- To record a decrease in a liability, debit the liability account.

Capital:
- To record an increase in capital, credit the capital account.
- To record a decrease in capital, debit the capital account.

Notice that the rules for capital and liabilities are the same, but are exactly opposite to those for assets. This is what is to be expected as capital and liabilities on the one hand, and assets on the other, stand on opposite sides of the accounting equation in its original form. Thus, so long as you remember the two rules for assets, the remaining four can be easily deduced.

Expense accounts and revenue accounts

Besides assets, liabilities and capital, there will be two other distinct types of accounts which will be included in the Ledger. They are Expense accounts and Revenue accounts. Expenses are the costs of running a business, such as rent and rates, wages, and insurance. Revenues are the income or gains, such as interest received or rent received from subletting, which a business might enjoy. The double-entry rules for expenses and revenues may now be stated.

► **Expenses**: costs such as rent and rates, wages and insurance

► **Revenue**: income and gains such as interest and rents received

Expense accounts follow the same rules as those for assets.

> ***Recording expenses and revenues***
> - To record an increase in an expense, debit the expense account.
> - To record a decrease in an expense, credit the expense account.
>
> Likewise, revenues being the opposite of expenses, follow the expenses rules in reverse. That is,
> - To record an increase in a revenue, credit the revenue account.
> - To record a decrease in a revenue, debit the revenue account.

Drawings

► **Drawing**: money taken out of the business by an owner

The owner of a business may from time to time take out some money from the business for personal use. Such a withdrawal of money is called a **drawing**. It is therefore appropriate to open a new account in the Ledger, called the **Drawings account**. The accounting entries for drawings are as follows.

► Drawings in kind

> ***Recording drawings***
> - Debit Drawings account with the money taken out
> - Credit Cash or Bank account, as appropriate.

Ruling of the Ledger

The ruling of a traditional Ledger page is given in Figure 3.1.

Figure 3.1 A traditional Ledger page

DR					Name of account						CR
1	2	3	4	5	6	1	2	3	4	5	6

► The Ledger is always drawn in horizontal format.

Note:

1 **DR** is an abbreviation for debit, and indicates, as stated earlier on, the left-hand side.

2 **CR** is an abbreviation for credit and indicates, as stated before, the right-hand side.

3 There are six columns on either side of the Ledger page.
- Columns 1 and 2 are used to record the **month and date** of the transaction.
- Column 3 records a brief **narration** or **description** of the transaction.
- Column 4 is called the **'folio'** column, used for inserting the page number of the subsidiary book from which the transaction is posted to the Ledger.
- Columns 5 and 6 are used to record the **money value**, i.e. £ and p, of the transaction.

Before you start an account, write down its name in the centre of the page. Remember that the Ledger is simply a collection of accounts. Sufficient space should be left in between any two accounts so that all the transactions during the given period, affecting the accounts, can be entered.

Posting to the Ledger

Let's now see how transactions are posted or recorded in the Ledger accounts. This can be demonstrated by writing up a set of transactions, given in Example 3.3, in the Ledger.

Example 3.4 Posting to Anil Singh's Ledger

Post the following transactions in the books of Anil Singh.

► **Posting**: transferring records from one book to another

June

1 Started business with £15,000 in the bank.
2 Bought a motor van, paid by cheque – £4,500.
3 Bought office furniture on credit from AB Limited for £1,000.
4 Bought goods, paid by cheque – £5,000.
5 Sold goods for cash – £500.
6 Sold goods on credit to A. Hunter – £100.
7 Paid rent by cheque – £200.
8 Paid wages in cash – £100.
9 Received commission in cash – £50.
10 Cash sales – £600.
11 Anil Singh took out £100 in cash for his personal use.
12 Received a cheque from A. Hunter for £100.

Solution

After all the transactions are recorded, Anil Singh's Ledger accounts will appear as follows.

DR						**Capital a/c – Anil Singh**					CR
				£	p					£	p
						June	1	Bank		15,000	

DR						**Bank a/c**					CR
				£	p					£	p
June	1	Capital		15,000		June	2	Motor van		4,500	
June	12	A. Hunter		100		June	4	Purchases		5,000	
						June	7	Rent		200	

DR						**Motor van a/c**					CR
				£	p					£	p
June	2	Bank		4,500							

DR						**Office furniture a/c**					CR
				£	p					£	p
June	3	AB Ltd.		1,000							

DR						**AB Ltd. a/c**					CR
				£	p					£	p
						June	3	Office furniture		1,000	

DR					**Purchases a/c**					CR	
				£	p					£	p
June	4	Bank		5,000							

DR					**Sales a/c**					CR	
				£	p					£	p
						June	5	Cash		500	
						June	6	A. Hunter		100	
						June	10	Cash		600	

DR					**Cash a/c**					CR	
				£	p					£	p
June	5	Sales		500		June	8	Wages		100	
June	9	Commission		50		June	11	Drawings		100	
June	10	Sales		600							

DR					**A. Hunter a/c**					CR	
				£	p					£	p
June	6	Sales		100		June	12	Bank		100	

DR					**Rent a/c**					CR	
				£	p					£	p
June	7	Bank		200							

DR					**Wages a/c**					CR	
				£	p					£	p
June	8	Cash		100							

DR					**Commission received a/c**					CR	
				£	p					£	p
						June	9	Cash		50	

DR					**Drawings a/c**					CR	
				£	p					£	p
June	11	Cash		100							

The following notes explain how and why the 12 transactions given in Example 3.3 were entered in the different accounts in the Ledger of Anil Singh.

1 Every transaction affects two accounts. When an owner introduces money as capital into a business bank account, the names of the accounts involved obviously are:
   - Capital account – Anil Singh (i.e. the Capital account of the owner)
   - Bank account.

   Now the capital account of the owner is giving money to the business, therefore the Capital account is credited (remember the first rule: credit the giving account). The Bank account is receiving the £15,000 given by the owner and is therefore debited with £15,000 (remember the second rule: debit the receiving account). Alternatively, since an introduction of capital has the same effect as an increase in capital, Anil Singh's Capital account is credited. Since the receipt of £15,000 by the Bank account amounts to an increase in an asset, we've debited the Bank account. Note that every credit entry has a corresponding debit entry. In column 3, i.e. the narration column of each account, we've simply written the name of the other account. Thus in column 3 of the Capital account, we have written the word 'Bank' which is the name of the other account involved in this transaction. Similarly, in the Bank account, we've written the word 'Capital' in column 3 to describe the transaction. You should follow this practice of writing the name of the other account in the description column for posting every transaction to the Ledger.

2 When you buy an asset, for example a motor van as in this case, it represents an increase in the asset. You therefore debit the Asset account. As you have paid for the asset by cheque, your asset 'cash at bank' is reduced and you credit the Bank account. Notice again that a debit entry has a corresponding credit entry.

3 An asset is bought on credit. The two accounts involved are the asset account, viz. Office furniture account, and the creditor's account, viz. AB Ltd. Debit the Office furniture account, and credit AB Ltd.'s account (i.e. credit the liability account representing an increase in liability). The narrations follow the usual pattern.

4 The purchase of goods is different from the purchase of assets. Assets are bought to stay in the business, whereas goods are bought for resale. Therefore purchases of goods are to be recorded separately from the purchases of assets. The two entries are similar to those in **2** above. That is, debit the Purchases account, and credit the Bank account.

5 Sales tend to reduce the asset of stock of goods. The decrease of an asset requires a credit entry, and the Sales account is therefore credited. Cash from sales increases the asset cash, and hence the Cash account is debited. Alternatively, sales represent an increase in revenue, therefore credit the Sales account.

6 Credit the Sales account, but debit A. Hunter's account as he is a debtor.

7 Payment of rent is an expense and expenses are represented by debits. The Rent account is therefore debited, the corresponding credit entry being in the Bank account, as the asset 'cash at bank' is decreased by the amount of rent paid.

8 The same explanation as for rent above.

9 Commission received represents a revenue and, as you'll recall, revenues are shown as credits. Therefore, credit the revenue account, that is, Commission received account, and debit the Cash account, representing an increase in the asset cash.

10 The same explanation as in **5** above.

11 Withdrawal of money by the owner reduces the asset cash. Therefore credit the Cash account. The corresponding debit entry will be in the Drawings account, as it represents a reduction in capital.

12 As A. Hunter pays a cheque for £100, credit his account. The Business Bank account receives the money, therefore debit it.

13 In this example, nothing has been entered in the folio columns, as we are not given information regarding the subsidiary books. No cross reference is therefore possible.

Make sure that you understand and remember the rules of double-entry book-keeping. One way of doing this is to do a good number of examples involving the writing up of Ledger accounts. Here is one such example for you to try.

ACT 3.2

Write up the following transactions in the books of Anne McDermot.

March	1	Started business with £12,000 in the bank.
	2	Bought fixtures and fittings, paid by cheque, £1,200.
	3	Bought goods, paid by cheque, £6,500.
	4	Sold goods for cash, £600.
	5	Paid wages by cash, £90.
	6	Sold goods on credit to R. Simons, for £100.
	7	Cash sales, £450.
	8	Bought goods on credit from Modern Wholesalers Ltd., £2,000.
	9	Received a cheque from R. Simons, £100.
	10	Bought a motor van by cheque, £4,000.

► Answer in appendix

Balancing Ledger accounts

The accounts in the Ledger need to be **balanced** from time to time to obtain some key information, such as the amount of cash in hand. Balancing off an account represents a summarization process; it tells us the final state of an account. Thus when we balance a cash account, for example, we know exactly how much cash there is in hand.

► The **balance** of an account is the difference between the total of debit and the total of credit entries.

The balance of an account is the difference between the total of the debits or debit entries and that of credits or credit entries. If the total of debit entries exceeds the total of credits, the account is said to have a **debit balance**. If the sum of credits exceeds the sum of debits, the account is said to have a **credit balance**. If the two sides show exactly the same total, the account is said to have **no balance** at all. Normally, asset accounts and expense accounts will show debit balances, and liability accounts and revenue accounts will show credit balances.

► The running balance system used in computerized accounts is dealt with in Chapter 23.

Here is Anil Singh's Cash account, balanced. The following notes show how the balance was arrived at.

Balancing Anil Singh's account

DR			Cash a/c						CR	
			£	p					£	p
June	5	Sales	500		June	8	Wages		100	
June	9	Commission	50		June	11	Drawings		100	
June	10	Sales	600		June	11	Balance c/d		950	
			1150						1150	
June	12	Balance b/d	950							

1 Find out the totals of both the debit and credit sides. Use a piece of rough paper – do not write anything on the account as yet! Work out the difference, if any, between them.
2 The difference, as calculated in **1** above, is the **balance** and it is inserted on the side where the total is smaller. The expression 'Balance carried down' or the abbreviated form 'Balance c/d' is written in column 3, i.e. the description column, on the line after the last entry. It must be preceded by the date on which you are balancing the account.
3 A single line is ruled, and each side is totalled, the total being written on the line immediately below the ruled line ensuring that the two totals are written on a level with each other.
4 A double line is ruled just beneath the totals (which incidentally should be exactly the same) to indicate that the account is now balanced.
5 To complete the double entry, the expression 'Balance brought down' or the abbreviated form 'Balance b/d' is written in column 3 with the amount as shown against Balance c/d in columns 5 and 6 on the next line of the opposite side. It is dated with the date following the date of balancing. Thus if Balance c/d is dated as July 31, Balance b/d will be dated as August 1. The effect of introducing Balance b/d on the opposite side, is to cancel the entry Balance c/d, so that the original values of the entries made on both sides of the account are maintained. Thus the purpose of introducing the Balance c/d figure is not to 'fiddle' the accounts, but to ascertain the final state of an account on a given date.

The Trial Balance

A Trial Balance is a list of balances extracted from the accounts in the Ledger at any given time. Although it may be prepared at any time, it is customary to do so at month and/or year end.

There are two main reasons for preparing the Trial Balance. The first reason is to check the arithmetical accuracy of the Ledger entries. However, even when the Trial Balance balances, i.e. the debits total is exactly equal to the credits total, it does not guarantee that all the entries in the Ledger accounts are correct. As we'll see in Chapter 5, there are a number of errors which are not detected by the Trial Balance.

The second reason for extracting a Trial Balance is to obtain the necessary financial information, in summarized form, to prepare the final accounts, i.e. the Trading and Profit and Loss account and the Balance Sheet, of an organization.

► A Trial Balance is a list of balances extracted from the accounts in the Ledger. It is made to check the accuracy of the accounts and to obtain information for the final accounts.

To draw up a Trial Balance, list the name of each ledger account having either a debit balance or a credit balance. If the listed account shows a debit balance, write down the amount in the first column of values, entitled 'DR' or 'debit'. If the account has a credit balance, put down the amount in the second column, entitled 'CR' or 'credit'. When the listing of all the ledger accounts in this manner is complete, add up the figures in each column. The two totals should agree, assuming that there are no errors in the ledger accounts.

ACT 3.3

Follow the procedures demonstrated for Anil Singh's cash account and balance each of the accounts in his Ledger shown on pages 43–44.

► Check your results with the Trial Balance for Anil Singh given below.

Anil Singh
Trial Balance as at 12 June

	DR £	CR £
Capital		15,000
Bank	5,400	
Motor van	4,500	
Office furniture	1,000	
AB Ltd.		1,000
Purchases	5,000	
Sales		1,200
Cash	950	
Rent	200	
Wages	100	
Commission received		50
Drawings	100	
	17,250	17,250

Note:

1 The word 'account' or 'a/c' is omitted in the listing for clarity.
2 Note that A. Hunter's name does not appear on the Trial Balance. It is omitted as his account does not show any balance at all.
3 Our workings so far appear to be correct and the Trial Balance balances itself!

Sometimes, you may be asked to draw up a Trial Balance from a given list of balances. This is quite a simple task so long as you remember that balances in the assets and expenses accounts are always **debit balances**, and those in capital, liabilities and revenue accounts are **credit balances**. Only one account might give you a bit of a headache and this is the Bank account. Cash at bank is an asset and is normally represented by a debit balance. However, a bank account may be overdrawn with the prior consent of the bank manager. An overdrawn bank account represents a liability – as you owe the amount overdrawn to your bank. In your business bank account, an overdrawn amount will be shown as a credit balance.

Example 3.5 shows you how to prepare a Trial Balance from a list of balances given.

Example 3.5 Preparing a Trial Balance from a list of balances

The following balances were extracted from the Ledger of Patricia Anderson on 31 March.

	£
Sales	33,750
Purchases	18,100
Premises	25,200
Fixtures and fittings	1,500
Stock	3,500
Cash	250
Debtors	2,990
Creditors	3,050
General expenses	3,820
Capital: P. Anderson	18,560

From the above list of balances, prepare a Trial Balance for Patricia Anderson as at 31 March.

Solution

Patricia Anderson
Trial Balance as at 31 March

	£	£
Sales		33,750
Purchases	18,100	
Premises	25,200	
Fixtures and fittings	1,500	
Stock	3,500	
Cash	250	
Debtors	2,990	
Creditors		3,050
General expenses	3,820	
Capital: P. Anderson		18,560
	55,360	55,360

Note:
1 Sales represent an increase in revenue and therefore the Sales account shows a credit balance.
2 Purchases represent an expense and consequently the Purchases account shows a debit balance.
3 Premises, fixtures and fittings, stock, cash and debtors are all assets and are therefore shown as having debit balances.
4 General expenses are represented by a debit balance.
5 As expected, capital and liabilities (creditors) are shown as having credit balances.

Subdivisions of the Ledger

The Ledger contains records of all the transactions of a business. As the business expands or grows in size, so does the number of accounts in the Ledger. To improve the organization of financial information, it thus becomes desirable to classify the different ledger accounts into a number of classes. The classification of these accounts can be done in more than one way, but the following division of the ledger accounts is the most popular one. The examples, in our chart on page 50, are drawn from Anil Singh's Ledger.

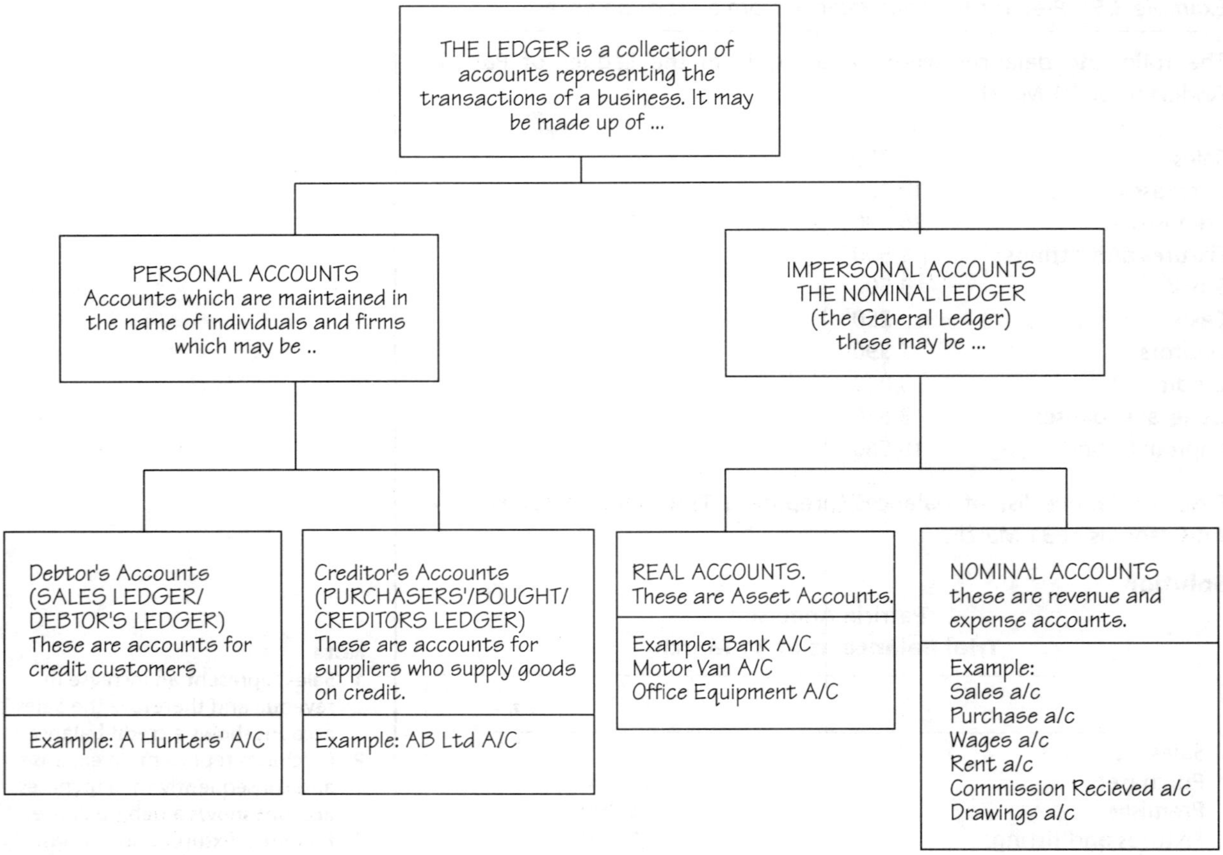

Figure 3.2 Subdivisions of the Ledger

Chapter summary

- The accounting equation states that the assets of a business are equal to the sum of its capital and liability: $A = C + L$. The total assets are financed by capital or borrowing or a combination of the two.
- An asset is anything that is owned by the business. Capital is the money or money's worth put into the business by the owners. A liability is anything that is owed by the business.
- The Balance Sheet is a financial statement for the business at a certain point in time. It can be prepared in horizontal or vertical format.
- A business has a number of books of accounts (although these need not be 'books' as such). These include:
  - o the Ledger – the principal book of accounts, which is itself subdivided into different ledgers representing different kinds of accounts
  - o the Cash Book – used to record cash receipts and payments (including cheques)
  - o books of original entry such as the Sales Day Book and the Purchases Day Book where credit sales and credit purchases are initially recorded.
- The two fundamental rules of double-entry book-keeping are:
  - o debit the receiver or the receiving account
  - o credit the giver or the giving account.

- Every debit entry has a corresponding credit entry and vice versa.
- A Trial Balance if correctly prepared should show that the debit total and the credit total are exactly the same.

ACT 3.4

For each of questions 1 to 5 put a tick against the letter representing the best choice from among the four possible answers given.

1 The cash account of J. Adams shows a debit balance of £80. It means that:
A There was £80 in hand
B The total money receivable was £80
C The total of money paid out was £80
D The total amount owing to other people was £80.

2 The accounting equation tells you that:
A Capital is equal to liabilities
B Assets are equal to the sum of capital and liabilities
C Assets are equal to capital minus liabilities
D None of the above.

3 In a Trial Balance, the purchases would be shown on the:
A Credit side
B Debit side
C Would not appear unless they were credit purchases only
D Would not appear unless they were cash purchases only.

4 B. Charles, a grocer, buys fixtures and fittings for cash. The entries in the Ledger would be:
A Credit Cash account, debit Fixtures and fittings account
B Debit Cash account, credit Fixtures and fittings account
C Credit Purchases account, debit Cash account
D Debit Fixtures and fittings account, credit Capital account.

5 The owner of a business takes out cash for his personal use. The entries in the Ledger should be:
A Debit Cash account, credit Drawings account
B Credit Bank account, debit Cash account
C Debit Bank account, credit Cash account
D Debit Drawings account, credit Cash account.

► Answers in appendix

6 Fiona Small commenced business on 1 May with £8,000 which she deposited in a business bank account. Her transactions during the first week of May were as follows.

	£
• Bought fixtures and fittings by cheque	2,000
• Bought stocks, paying by cheque	5,000
• Bought stocks on credit from AB Ltd	3,000
• Sold part of stocks on credit for cash	600
• Took a loan from Sandra Jackson	2,000

Show the dual effect of each of Fiona Small's transactions during the first week of May. The first one is done for you.

Fixtures and fittings account increases by	£2,000	(+ assets)
Bank account decreases by	£2,000	(– assets)

► Answer in appendix

7 Show the effects of the following transactions on assets, capital and liabilities, by putting a + or – sign before the appropriate accounts.

- Samina Ahmed started business with £10,000 in the business bank account.
- Bought stocks, paying by cheque, for £5,000.
- Bought furniture on credit from T. Jones for £1,000.
- Samina Ahmed put a further £2,000 cash into the business.
- Sold goods on credit to R.Traceman, £200.
- Received a cheque from R.Traceman for £200.
- Samina took out £200 cash for her personal use.

► No answer given

8 The following balances are extracted from the books of R. Jordan on 31 December.

	£
Premises	30,000
Stocks	10,500
Creditors	8,250
Bank overdraft	5,200
Fixtnres and fittings	2,150
Loan from A.Lender	5,000
Debtors	10,350
Motor van	5,550
Cash in hand	100
Capital	40,200

Prepare a Balance Sheet for the business of R. Jordan as at 31 December.

► Answer in appendix

9 Simon Singer has the following assets and liabilities as at 31 July.

Fixtures and fittings	£2,000
Motor vehicles	£4,500
Debtors	£6,250
Cash in hand	£500
Cash at bank	£2,100
Stocks	£5,150
Creditors	£5,500

During the first week of August, Simon Singer made the following transactions.

- Received £500 in cash from one of the debtors.
- Bought goods on credit £1,000.
- Took a loan of £5,000 from a bank, extended over 5 years.
- Paid a cheque for £1,000 to one of the creditors.

You are required to:

a Calculate Simon's capital as at 31 July.
b Prepare his Balance Sheet as at 7 August, after the above transactions have been taken into consideration.

► No answer given

10 Write up the ledger accounts of Jim Cox to record the following transactions.

March

1 Started business with £20,000 in the bank.
3 Bought fixtures and fittings paying by cheque £2,200.
4 Bought goods paying by cheque £8,000.
5 Bought additional goods on credit from Amanda Jackson, £2,500.
8 Cash sales, £750.
9 Sold goods on credit to R.Banda, £1,500.
10 Paid rent in cash, £250.
15 Paid Amanda Jackson; a cheque for £2,500.
18 Received a cheque from R.Banda for £1,000.
20 Cash sales, £500.
25 Paid wages in cash, £150.
27 Sold goods on credit to R.Banda, £500.
30 Took out £200 in cash for personal use.

► Answer in appendix

11 Enter the following transactions in the Ledger of Robert King.

September

1 Started business with a capital of £35,000: £30,000 in the bank and £5,000 cash.
2 Bought premises paying by cheque, £30,000.
3 Bought fixtures and fittings on credit from Office Supplies Ltd. £2,500.
6 Took out a loan of £5,000 from National Westminister Bank plc.
8 Bought goods paying by cheque, £6,500.
10 Paid wages in cash, £175.
12 Paid rates by cheque, £250.
15 Bought additional goods on credit from Gordon Gaddes, £2,500.
17 Sold goods on credit to:
(i) R. Johnson, £850
(ii) T. Kimpton, £700
(iii) P. Mistry, £990.
20 Cash sales, £750.
21 Paid wages, £175.
22 Paid cash to Gordon Gaddes, £2,500.
25 Received a cheque from P. Mistry, £990.
27 Paid insurance by cash, £150.
30 Received a cheque from R. Johnson, £750.

► No answer given

12 For each of the following accounts indicate by inserting a tick in the appropriate column whether the account would normally have a debit balance or a credit balance.

		Debit balance	*Credit balance*
a	Capital account		
b	Drawings account		
c	Cash account		
d	Wages account		
e	Premises account		
f	Sales account		
g	Purchases account		
h	Rent account		
i	Commission rec'd a/c		

► Answer in appendix

13 Enter the following transactions in the books of A. Simpson and balance off each account at the end of the month.

September
1 Started business with £10,000 in the bank.
2 Bought fixtures and fittings, paying by cheque, £1,800.
4 Bought goods paying by cheque, £6,500.
5 Cash sales, £490.
6 Sales on credit to J. Day, £250, I. Porter, £350, and L. Carter, £290.
7 Bought additional fixtures paying by cheque, £580.
10 Bought goods on credit from Northern Trading Company, £3,000.
12 Cash sales, £520.
14 Received a cheque from J. Day, £250.
17 Paid wages by cash, £200.
20 Sold goods on credit to I. Porter £250, L. Carter £300.
24 Paid rent by cheque, £350.
26 Paid a cheque for £2,000 to Northern Trading Company.
28 Received a cheque from I. Porter, £300.
30 Cash sales, £500.

► No answer given

14 Record the following transactions in the books of K. Harvey. Balance off all the accounts and then extract a Trial Balance as at 31 March.

March
1 Started business with £15,000 in the bank.
2 Bought fixtures and fittings paying by cheque, £2,150.
3 Bought goods by cheque, £8,750.
4 Cash sales, £375.
6 Bought goods on credit from D. Little, £2,100.
8 Paid wages by cash, £150.

10 Sold goods on credit to: R. Castle £250, W. Roberts £350, J. Bain £180.
12 Bought additional fixtures by cash, £120.
15 Cash sales, £350.
18 Paid rent by cheque, £250.
20 Received a cheque from R. Castle, £250.
22 Bought goods on credit from D. Green, £1,000.
25 Sold goods on credit to: W. Roberts £450 J. Bain £220.
28 Paid wages by cash, £180.
29 Received cheques from: W. Roberts £500; J. Bain £200.
30 Paid D. Green by cheque, £500.
31 Cash sales, £400.

► Answer in appendix

15 The following balances were taken from the Ledger of D. Pitt on 30 September.

	£
Creditors	10,100
Premises	25,000
Fixtures and fittings	2,500
Stock	10,000
Bank loan	5,000
Motor vehicles	6,500
Debtors	8,500
Bank	2,500
Cash	100
Capital	40,000

You are required to prepare a Trial Balance for D. Pitt as at 30 September.

► No answer given

16 The following balances were extracted from the books of Teresa London as at 1 March.

	£	£
Stocks		5,500
Debtors:		
Little	560	
Smith	500	
Johnson	100	1,160
Cash in hand		100
Cash at bank		2,140
Fixtures and fittings		2,000
Creditors:		
Day	150	
Choudhury	300	450
Capital: T. London		10,450

Transactions during March were as follows.

March

2 Cash sales, £200.
4 Sold goods on credit to: Little £250 , Smith £175 , Johnson £120.
6 Settled Day's account of 1 March by cheque.
10 Received a cheque from Smith for £500.
13 Paid wages in cash, £150.
16 Cash sales, £300.
20 Bought goods on credit from Day, £500.
24 Settled Choudhury's account of 1 March by cheque.

28 Received a cheque from Johnson, £220.
31 Paid wages in cash, £150.

You are required to:

a Show the opening balances as at 1 March in the appropriate accounts.
b Enter the above transactions in the appropriate accounts.
c Balance off each account.
d Draw up a Trial Balance as at 31 March.

Note: Stock account will show an opening debit balance of £5,500 as given. No other entries need to be made there.

► Answer in appendix

17 Distinguish between a real account and a nominal account. Give three examples of each.

► No answer given

18 For each of the transactions listed below, complete by inserting ticks in the appropriate columns the account to be debited, and the account to be credited.

Transaction	*Debit*			*Credit*		
	Personal	*Nominal*	*Real*	*Personal*	*Nominal*	*Real*
Goods bought on credit from I. Green, £500						
Sold goods on credit to A.Hutchinson, £250						
Paid wages to staff £100						
Drew cash for personal use, £150						
Bought office furniture for cash, £500						

► Answer in appendix

4 The recording function of accounting 2 – the Cash Book

Chapter objectives

By the end of this chapter, you should be able to:

- write up and balance a two-column cash book
- explain the meaning of cash discount and enter discount allowed and discount received in the accounting system
- write up and balance a three-column cash book
- prepare a bank reconciliation statement
- write up a petty cash book
- state the meaning of the following terms: cash book (two column and three column), cash discount, discount allowed, discount received, bank reconciliation, petty cash book, contra entries, trade discount, unpresented cheques, undeposited cash and cheques, dishonoured cheques, cheques r/d, imprest (or float), petty cash voucher.

THE CASH BOOK

In Chapter 3 we used the **Cash account** in the Ledger to record cash transactions, i.e. receipts and payments of cash. To record transactions involving cheques, we used another account called the **Bank account**. The title 'Bank account' is quite pertinent as cheques are realized into cash through the banking system. In most business organizations a large number of transactions involve cash and cheques, so it is convenient to put these transactions in a separate book. This is exactly what is done in the **Cash Book** which is in fact a combination of cash and bank accounts. We'll begin this chapter with a description of the Cash Book or, more appropriately, the **two-column Cash Book**, followed by a restatement of the rules for recording the receipts and payments of cash and cheques. Then we'll look at the idea of **cash discount**, and see how **discount allowed** and **discount received** are recorded in a more comprehensive Cash Book, called the **three-column Cash Book**.

► The Cash Book is a combination of cash and bank accounts.

Every business will receive a bank statement from its bank at regular intervals. The balance shown in a particular bank statement may not always agree with the balance obtained in the bank column of the Cash Book. For efficient control of cash flows, we therefore need to reconcile the two balances by preparing the **Bank Reconciliation Statement**.

Finally, we shall consider how to maintain a **Petty Cash Book** for recording expenses of frequent occurrence and of small value.

TWO-COLUMN CASH BOOK

► The Cash Book is both a book of original entry and part of the Ledger.

► The Cash Book uses the double-entry method.

► The two column Cash Book brings together the Cash account and the Bank account.

The Cash Book is both a book of original entry and a part of the Ledger. It is a book of original entry because all cash transactions are straight away recorded in the Cash Book. They do not go through any other book of accounts. It is also a part of the Ledger, because in writing up the Cash Book we follow the rules of double-entry, that is, we debit any money coming in (the receiving aspect), and we credit any money going out (the giving aspect). Just like the ledger page, the cash book page is divided vertically into two halves – the left-hand side is the debit side, and the right-hand side is the credit side.

The two-column Cash Book brings together the Cash account and the Bank account in one book. The ruling of the Cash Book closely conforms to that of the Ledger. The only difference is that in a two-column Cash Book, instead of two columns on each side for recording the value of the transaction, we have two pairs of such columns. The first pair is meant for recording cash transactions and is headed 'Cash', and the second pair is meant for transactions involving cheques and is headed 'Bank'. Figure 4.1 illustrates such ruling.

Figure 4.1 Ruling of a typical two-column Cash Book page

				Cash		Bank						Cash		Bank	
				£	p	£	p					£	p	£	p

Example 4.1 illustrates how the two-column Cash Book combines the Cash account and the Bank account into one account.

Example 4.1 Writing up the two-column Cash Book

The following are the Cash account and Bank account of S. Datta for the month of February.

DR						Cash a/c				CR	
				£	p					£	p
Feb	1	Balance b/d		200		Feb	2	Rent		150	
Feb	5	Sales		250		Feb	10	Wages		175	
Feb	15	A. Ward		175		Feb	28	H. Bromley		100	
Feb	26	Sales		300		Feb	28	Balance c/d		500	
				925						925	
Mar	1	Balance b/d		500							

DR			Bank a/c					CR
			£	p				£	p
Feb	1	Balance b/d	1,000		Feb	3	Rates	80	
Feb	7	AB Ltd	510		Feb	12	M. Hassan	535	
Feb	20	G. Cowley	275		Feb	19	K. Little	100	
Feb	25	R. Moore	105		Feb	26	Insurance	90	
					Feb	27	C. Baker	205	
					Feb	28	Balance c/d	880	
			1,890					1,890	
Mar	1	Balance b/d	880						

Combine the above two accounts together as they would appear in a two-column Cash Book.

Solution

Cash book

			Cash		Bank					Cash		Bank	
			£	p	£	p				£	p	£	p
Feb	1	Balance b/d	200		1,000		Feb	2	Rent	150			
Feb	5	Sales	250				Feb	3	Rates			80	
Feb	7	AB Ltd			510		Feb	10	Wages	175			
Feb	15	A. Ward	175				Feb	12	M. Hassan			535	
Feb	20	G. Cowley			275		Feb	19	K. Little			100	
Feb	25	R. Moore			105		Feb	26	Insurance			90	
Feb	26	Sales	300				Feb	27	C. Baker			205	
							Feb	28	H. Bromley	100			
							Feb	28	Balance c/d	500		880	
			925		1,890					925		1,890	
Mar	1	Balance b/d	500		880								

Entries in the Cash Book

Notice that all the entries in the Cash Book are made in strict chronological order. Notice also that for each transaction, there is only one entry in the Cash Book. Shouldn't there be two entries for every transaction? Yes, indeed. Then what has happened to the other entry for each of the transactions recorded above? Well, the other entry will be found on the opposite side of another account in the Ledger. Remember that the Cash Book is just one of two accounts of the Ledger necessary to record a single transaction. Thus for instance, the corresponding entry for Rent (on February 2) will be found on the debit side of the Rent account in the Ledger.

Remember the double-entry rules

- debit cash or cheques in (= receipts)
- credit cash or cheques out (= payments)

Two types of transaction affecting the Cash Book need special mention. The first one relates to the withdrawal of money from the business bank account for making cash payments, when the money in the till is insufficient for that. The second one relates to the deposit (or banking) of cash into the business bank account. For both these transactions we need to make two entries – one on each side of the Cash Book. These are the only exceptions to the general rule that in the Cash Book we record each transaction once only.

► Recording bank withdrawals in the Cash Book

Recording bank withdrawals in the Cash Book

To record the withdrawal of cash for business use from the bank account, we need to make the following entries.

1 Credit the 'Bank' column in the Cash Book as the withdrawal reduces the asset of cash at bank.
2 Debit the 'Cash' column in the Cash Book, as the receipt of cash from bank increases the asset of cash.

To record the banking of cash, the two entries above are reversed.

► Recording bank deposits in the Cash Book

Recording bank deposits in the Cash Book

1 Credit the 'Cash' column in the Cash Book, as the banking of cash reduces the asset of cash.
2 Debit the 'Bank' column in the Cash Book, as the deposit of cash increases the asset of bank balance.

► Contra entries cancel each other out: write C against each.

Both these transactions (cash paid into the bank, and withdrawal of cash from the bank) are merely internal transfers and they do not make the business any better or worse off. That is why they are known as **contra entries** – entries that cancel each other. The normal practice is to indicate this by writing the letter 'C' against each of the entries.

The three-column Cash Book

► The three-column Cash Book allows the recording of discounts.

The three-column Cash Book is an extension of the two-column Cash Book and contains three pairs of columns on each side of the Cash Book – the third pair is used to show the cash discount. But what is this cash discount?

The word 'discount' means 'allowance'. There are two types of discount used in business: trade discount and cash discount.

Trade discount represents an allowance or a reduction from the list price for bulk buying. This is automatically deducted from the list price in the invoice and constitutes the source of profits for traders. Since the invoice price is net of trade discount, there is no need to keep any record of such discounts.

► **Cash discount received**: reduction given to the business by suppliers for speedy payment

Cash discount is an inducement to credit buyers for prompt payment. The rate of discount and the period within which the payment is to be made to get this discount will usually be quoted on the sales document or the invoice. A business organization will experience two types of cash discounts: discount received and discount allowed.

Discount received refers to the allowance for speedy payment given to a business by its creditors, i.e. firms supplying the goods on credit.

► **Cash discount allowed:** reduction given to customer for speedy payment

Discount allowed refers to the allowance given by a business to its debtors, i.e. credit customers.

Don't confuse cash discounts with trade discounts. Trade discounts are not recorded.

Both these discounts are recorded in the Cash Book. This is done by adding another set of columns (one for £ and one for p) on each side of the Cash Book. Hence the name, **three-column Cash Book** – there are three pairs of columns on each side. The first one is for Discount; the second for Cash; and the third for Bank. The columns are always set in the order discount, cash and bank. Figure 4.2 illustrates the ruling of a typical three column Cash Book.

				Dis-count	Cash	Bank					Dis-count	Cash	Bank
				£	£	£					£	£	£

Figure 4.2 *A typical three column Cash Book page*

Entries in the three-column Cash Book

Discount allowed is entered on the left-hand side, and discount received is entered on the right-hand side of the Cash Book. Entries in the discount columns of the Cash Book do not constitute a part of the double-entry ledger system; they are for memorandum purposes only. Consequently, we do not need to balance the discount columns in the Cash Book – we simply show the total of each column. However this does not mean that these two transactions (discount allowed and discount received) are outside the double-entry system. They are very much part of the double-entry system, but the entries to record the dual aspect of each transaction are made in the ledger accounts.

► Enter discount allowed left, and discount received right.

Recording discounts in the Cash Book

- debit the Discount allowed account
- credit the personal account of the debtor with the amount of the discount

Similarly, the two entries for recording discount received are:

- debit the personal account of the creditor
- credit the Discount received account with the amount of the discount

It thus follows that we need two new accounts in the Ledger to complete the double entries affecting Discount allowed and Discount received.

Example 4.2 illustrates how to write up a three-column Cash Book, together with the necessary ledger accounts, to show the dual nature of transactions relating to discount allowed and discount received.

Example 4.2 Entering up the three-column Cash Book

Transactions of David Kemp

June

1 Opening balances: Cash £250, Bank £1,150
4 Cash sales £190
7 Bought goods paying by cheque, £1,000
8 Paid electricity bill by cheque, £90
12 Received a cheque for £200 from P. Fox in settlement of a £210 account (£10 discount allowed)
16 Paid B. Higgins, a creditor, a cheque for £110 in settlement for a £118 account (£8 discount received)
22 Cash sales £220
25 Received from M. Kumar (another debtor) a cheque for £105 in settlement of a £110 account (discount allowed £5)
28 Paid R. Jain (another creditor) a cheque for £210 in settlement of an account of £220 (£10 discount received)
30 Paid wages in cash £190

You are required to:

a Write up the three-column Cash Book of David Kemp and balance it off at the end of the month.

b Write up and balance off the personal accounts of the debtors and creditors.

c Write up the discount accounts.

Solution

Cash Book

			Discount	Cash	Bank				Discount	Cash	Bank
			£	£	£				£	£	£
June	1	Balance b/d		250	1150	June	7	Purchases			1000
June	4	Sales		190		June	8	Electricity			90
June	12	P. Fox	10		200	June	16	B. Higgins	8		110
June	22	Sales		220		June	28	R. Jain	10		210
June	25	M. Kumar	5		105	June	30	Wages		190	
						June	30	Balance c/d		470	45
			15	660	1455				18	660	1,455
July	1	Balance b/d		470	45						

Ledger accounts

DR		P. Fox a/c					CR		
			£	p				£	p
June	1	Balance b/d	210		June	12	Bank	200	
					June	12	Discount allowed	10	
			210					210	

DR				M. Kumar a/c					CR
			£	p				£	p
June	1	Balance b/d	110		June	25	Bank	105	
					June	25	Discount allowed	5	
			110					110	

DR				B. Higgins a/c					CR
			£	p				£	p
June	16	Bank	110		June	1	Balance b/d	118	
June	16	Discount recd.	8						
			118					118	

DR				R. Jain a/c					CR
			£	p				£	p
June	28	Bank	210		June	1	Balance b/d	220	
June	28	Discount recd.	10						
			220					220	

DR				Discounts allowed a/c					CR
			£	p				£	p
June	30	Total for the month	15						

DR				Discounts received a/c					CR
			£	p				£	p
					June	30	Total for the month	18	

Note:

1 The discount columns are not balanced. The total of each column is shown and later on transferred to the discounts accounts in the Ledger. Thus the total discount allowed of £15 is posted to the debit of the Discounts allowed account. However, the entry for each individual discount is shown as a credit entry in the appropriate personal account. On 6 June, P. Fox's personal account is credited with £10, being the amount of discount allowed. Discount allowed reduces the amount of debt owing by the debtor, that is, it reduces the asset debtor and is therefore credited. Discounts allowed in total, being similar to an expense, are shown as a debit entry in that account. The same reasoning – but in reverse order – applies to the entries in the personal accounts of the creditor and the Discount received account.

2 The double entries for every transaction made in the Cash Book are not all shown in this example. The corresponding credit entry for cash sales will be in the Sales account. The purpose of this example is to highlight the mechanics of writing up a three-column Cash Book, and not to demonstrate the complete system of ledger accounting.

The Bank Reconciliation Statement

Every business will receive a bank statement from its bank at regular intervals. The balance shown in a particular statement on a certain day may not always agree with the balance obtained in the Bank column of the Cash Book on that day. This apparent discrepancy between the two balances may be due to a variety of reasons. However, it is possible to categorize these reasons into two main groups:

► Often the bank statement does not tally with the bank column of the Cash Book. A reconciliation statement is required.

1 Items included in the Cash Book are not included in the bank statement because of time difference. Examples of this type of items are:
   - cheques paid out (which appear on the credit side of the Cash Book) but not yet presented for payment at the bank – **unpresented cheques**.
   - cheques received and cash ready to be banked (entered on the debit side in the Bank column) but not yet deposited at the bank – **undeposited cheques and cash**.

2 Some items in the bank statement may not appear in the Cash Book. Such items include:
   - interest and bank charges
   - standing orders for payments
   - direct debits (for payments)
   - dishonoured cheques e.g. cheques **referred to drawer (r/d)**
   - dividends received
   - cheques from customers paid through Bank Giro
   - interest received.

For efficient control of cash flows, an organization needs to reconcile these two balances. This is done by preparing a **Bank Reconciliation Statement**. There are two methods of doing this. The first is illustrated in Example 4.3.

► A Bank Reconciliation Statement is necessary for controlling cash flow.

Example 4.3 The Bank Reconciliation Statement – Method 1 with unadjusted Cash Book

The following is an extract from Jenny Clover's Cash Book for the month of September.

DR				Cash Book (Bank columns only)							CR
				£	p					£	p
Sept	1	Balance b/d		2,150		Sept	4	I. Crab		250	
Sept	5	J. Adams		120		Sept	15	AB Ltd		1,150	
Sept	20	R. Mciver		200		Sept	29	A. King		350	
Sept	28	S. Ray		150		Sept	30	Balance c/d		870	
				2,620						2,620	
Oct	1	Balance b/d		870							

Jenny Clover received a bank statement on 30 September from her bank, which is shown opposite.

Bank Statement					
			£	£	Balance £
Sept	1	Balance b/f			2,150 CR
	3	Cheque		120	2,270 CR
	11	Cheque	250		2,020 CR
	21	Cheque		220	2,220 CR
	21	AB Ltd	1,150		1,070 CR
	29	Bank charges		25	1,045 CR

Prepare a Bank Reconciliation Statement for Jenny Clover reconciling the two balances.

Solution

The first step in preparing the reconciliation statement is to tick those items which appear on both the Cash Book and the bank statement. After doing that, we find that the following entries in the Cash Book do not appear on the bank statement:

- S. Ray's cheque for £150 is not yet credited to the bank statement.
- a cheque given to A.King for £350, is not yet presented at the bank.

We also notice that one item, bank charges of £25, which appears as a debit item on the bank statement, does not appear in the Cash Book. Obviously, we need to make necessary adjustments for these three items in order to reconcile the two balances.

We start with the Cash Book balance. Then we add the unpresented cheques to this balance. The effect of the unpresented cheque on the Cash Book balance was to reduce it by £350. To bring this balance in line with the bank statement balance we need to add 350 to the Cash Book balance. Having done that, the next step is to deduct both bank charges and S. Roy's cheque for £150 which is not yet entered on the bank statement. Bank charges have the effect of reducing the bank statement balance. To bring the Cash Book balance in line with it we obviously need to subtract this amount, (i.e. £25) from the Cash Book balance. The completed reconciliation statement will appear as follows.

Bank Reconciliation Statement as at 30 September			
	£	£	£
Balance as per Cash Book			870
Add cheques issued but not yet presented:			
A. King			350
			1,220
Less bank charges		25	
Cheques received but not yet credited:			
S.Ray	150	175	
Balance as per bank statement			1,045

Have you noticed that the Cash Book balance is a debit balance, whereas the balance on the bank statement is shown to be a credit balance? This apparent contradiction can be resolved if we understand the meaning of debit and credit balances from the standpoint of each party to the transaction. Cash at bank, from the standpoint of the business, is an asset and is therefore a debit balance. From the standpoint of the bank, the balance outstanding in the name of the business is a liability and should be considered as a credit balance.

Bank reconciliation with unadjusted Cash Book: Method two

The second method of preparing the reconciliation statement is to start with the bank statement balance and, after adjustments for unpresented cheques etc, bring it to agree with the Cash Book balance. Basically, the procedure is the same as for the first method. The only difference is that all the adjustments are now reversed. You now **add** bank charges and bank cheques not yet entered on the bank statement, and **deduct** any unpresented cheques from the bank statement balance. Using this method, the reconciliation statement will appear as follows.

► There are three ways of constructing a reconciliation statement: two which leave the Cash Book unadjusted and one which adjusts it.

Bank Reconciliation Statement as at 30 September

	£	£
Balance as per bank statement		1,045
Add bank charges	25	
Banked cheques not yet entered on bank statement		
S. Ray	150	175
		1,220
Less unpresented cheques:		
A.King	350	
Balance as per Cash Book		870

Bank reconciliation with adjusted Cash Book

The task of preparing the reconciliation statement can be further simplified if we update the Cash Book with information such as bank charges, standing order etc, which appear on the bank statement, but not in the Cash Book. This will give us an adjusted Cash Book balance. We can then start with the bank statement balance and proceed with the adjustment for unpresented and undeposited cheques as before.

Bank reconciliation by adjusting Cash Book

Step 1 Tick those items which appear on the Bank Statement as well as the Cash Book.

Step 2 Update the Cash Book by entering any unticked items on the bank statement, such as bank charges, standing orders, interest received.

Step 3 Start preparing the Bank Reconciliation Statement itself:
- begin with the bank statement balance
- then add any undeposited cheques
- then deduct any unpresented cheques.

The figure thus obtained will give the balance as per the adjusted Cash Book.

Example 4.4 The construction of a bank reconciliation statement with the adjusted Cash Book.

The following are extracts from the Cash Book and the bank statement of Tony Archer.

DR			Cash Book (bank columns only)						CR	
			£	p					£	p
May	1	Balance b/d	1870		May	1	B.Gilbert		295	
May	5	Sales	200		May	7	MN Ltd		870	
May	8	R. Curtis	175		May	12	F. Gibson		210	
May	15	F. Knox	120		May	15	Office expenses		50	
May	20	Sales	215		May	20	Jackson and Sons		120	
May	28	K. Clarke	96		May	30	C. Young		20	
May	31	J. Stower	104		May	31	Balance c/d		1215	
			2,780						2,780	

Bank statement – Tony Archer					
			Debit £	Credit £	Balance £
May	1	Balance			1,870 CR
	5	Sundries		200	2,070
	6	551	295		1,775
	12	552	870		905
	13	Sundries		175	1,080
	15	Sundries		120	1,200
	20	Sundries		215	1,415
	20	554	50		1,365
	21	Credit transfer: K.Lamb		90	455
	30	Bank charges	30		1,425

You are required to:

(a) Write the Cash Book up to date, and state the new balance as on 31 May.

(b) Prepare a bank reconciliation statement as on 31 May.

Solution

DR			(Adjusted) Cash Book						CR	
			£	p					£	p
May	31	Balance b/d	1,215		May	31	Bank charges		30	
May	31	Credit transfer K. Lamb	90		May	31	Balance c/d		1,275	
			1,305						1,305	
June	1	Balance b/d	1,275							

Bank Reconciliation Statement as at 31 May	£	£	£
Bank statement balance			1,425
Add cheques received but not yet paid into bank:			
K. Clarke		96	
J. Stower		104	200
			1,625
Less cheques issued but not yet cleared:			
F. Gibson		210	
Jackson and Sons	120		
C. Young		20	350
Balance as per the (adjusted) Cash Book			1,275

The Petty Cash Book

As a business grows in size, it becomes necessary to divide the Ledger into a number of books, including the **Cash Book**, the **Personal Ledger** and the **Nominal Ledger**. It may also be necessary to subdivide further any book which has been separated from the Ledger. This is particularly relevant to the Cash Book. With the increasing size of the business, there will be many small expenses to be made over a given period of time. It will save a lot of time for the main cashier if (s)he is able to delegate this function of managing and recording numerous small payments which recur frequently. This is done in most organizations by maintaining a Petty Cash Book under the control of a junior but responsible member of staff.

The benefits of a Petty Cash Book

► **The Materiality Concept**: see Chapter 6

► The petty cash system saves entering large numbers of small transactions separately in the Cash Book

- It encourages a sensible division of labour. A junior accounts clerk can get on with recording petty or small expenses, and the main cashier can devote time and energy to more pressing needs of the accounts section.
- It avoids the need for making lots of entries of small and sometimes insignificant amounts in the main Cash Book. This will certainly reduce the likelihood of making errors in the Cash Book.
- It avoids the need for making too many entries in the Nominal Ledger under different expense accounts. Under a petty cash system, only the monthly totals of each account need to be posted to the Nominal Ledger. It thus saves time and reduces the chance of making mistakes in ledger posting.
- The Petty Cash Book will usually have a number of analysis columns so that the monthly or any periodic figures for each expense account are easily available.

► **Imprest** or **float**

The Petty Cash Book is usually maintained according to the **imprest system**. Using this system, the petty cashier always starts an accounting period (which may be a month or a week) with a sum of money called the **float** or **imprest**, which is received from the main cashier. At the end of the period (s)he gets back the amount which has actually been spent during the period. (S)he thus begins every period with the same float or imprest. This does not mean that the float cannot be altered at all. If circumstances demand, the float can be increased or decreased at any time but, normally, this sort of change is not made too frequently.

The petty cash system saves entering large numbers of small transactions separately in the Cash Book

Every payment made by the petty cashier must be supported by a voucher, and such vouchers are consecutively numbered from the beginning of the period for ease of reference. These vouchers may be needed to reclaim VAT (Value Added Tax) (of which you'll learn more in Chapter 7), and for internal audit, that is, an internal check by an independent officer of the organization.

► Petty cash vouchers

The ruling of a typical Petty Cash Book is shown in Figure 4.3.

Figure 4.3 *A typical Petty Cash Book page*

Rec. £ p	Date	Details	Folio F	Total £ p	1 £ p	2 £ p	3 £ p	4 £ p	5 £ p	6 £ p

Note:

Rec. = receipts
F = folio or voucher number
1 = VAT
2 = Postage
3 = Staff travelling expenses
4 = Office refreshments
5 = Motor expenses
6 = Sundries

Writing up the Petty Cash Book

1. The first two columns represent the debit side of the Petty Cash Book. On receipt of a float from the main cashier, the Petty Cash Book will be debited with the amount of the float. The corresponding credit entry will be made in the main Cash Book.
2. All payments will be recorded twice on the credit side of the Petty Cash Book – first in the 'total' column and second in the appropriate analysis column.
3. At the end of the given period, all the columns on the credit side will be totalled. The sum of the 'total' column should equal the sum of totals of all the analysis columns. This provides a check on the arithmetical accuracy of the entries made.
4. Now the debit column and the total column are balanced in the usual manner. The balance carried down in the total column is brought down on the debit side, and the petty cashier is given a reimbursement of the total expenses made during the period just ended, to raise the float to its normal level.
5. To complete the double entry, the total of each expense column is posted to the debit side of the appropriate expense account in the General Ledger.

Example 4.5 shows how a Petty Cash Book is written up.

Example 4.5 The Petty Cash Book

Andy Miller maintains a Petty Cash Book in his business. His main headings of small expenses are: VAT, office refreshments, motor and travel expenses, postage, cleaning, and sundry expenses.

The present monthly petty cash float is £130.
The balance brought forward from 1 March was £10.75.
The Petty Cash Book transactions during April were as follows.

Date	*Description*	*Voucher number*	*Amount* £	*VAT* £
April 1	Cash received from the main cashier*		119.25	
2	Taxi fares	1	6.00	
4	Office refreshments	2		1.80
5	Postage	3	10.20	
8	Petrol	4	5.00	0.60
10	Postage	5	8.75	
11	Office refreshments	6	2.20	
16	Petrol	7	5.00	0.60
20	Cleaning materials	8	8.90	
22	Replacement glass	9	20.50	3.08
24	Miscellaneous expenses	10	15.75	
25	Postage	11	12.70	
28	Taxi fares	12	6.75	
30	Postage	13	5.90	

*** Note**
The cash received on 1 April represents the reimbursement of expenditure incurred in March (£130.00 – £10.75 = £119.25).

a Write up the Petty Cash Book for Andy Miller for the month of April.

b Balance the Petty Cash Book and bring down the balance.

c Show the appropriate reimbursement on 1 May if Andy Miller decides to increase the petty cash float to £160 a month.

Solution

Petty Cash Book – Andy Miller

Recpts. £		Details	V. No.	Total paymts.	1 £ p	2 £ p	3 £ p	4 £ p	5 £ p	6 £ p
10.75	Apr 1	Balance b/d								
119.25	1	Cash received								
	2	Taxi fare	1	6.00		6.00				
	4	Office refres.	2	1.80						1.80
	5	Postage	3	10.20			10.20			
	8	Petrol	4	5.60	0.60	5.00				
	10	Postage	5	8.75			8.75			
	11	Office refres.	6	2.20						2.20
	16	Petrol	7	5.60	0.60	5.00				
	20	Cleaning mat.	8	8.90				8.90		
	22	Replacement glass	9	23.58	3.08				20.50	
	24	Misc. expenses	1	15.75					15.75	
	25	Postage	11	12.70			12.70			
	28	Taxi fares	12	6.75		6.75				
	30	Postage	13	5.90			5.90			
				113.73	4.28	22.75	37.55	8.90	36.25	4.00
	30	Balance c/d		16.27						
130.00				130.00						
16.27	May 1	Balance b/d								
143.73	1	Cash received								

V. = voucher

Column **1** = VAT

Column **2** = Motor and travel expenses

Column **3** = Postage

Column **4** = Cleaning

Column **5** = Sundry expenses

Column **6** = Office refreshments

Note:

1 Total for petrol and replacement glass equals the amount as shown in the transactions list plus VAT.

2 Reimbursement of £113.73 (i.e. the total expenditure for April) would have brought the float to £130, but now that Andy Miller wishes to raise the float to £160, a further £30 (£160 – £130) has been added to £113.73, bringing the total cash received to £143.73 (£113.73 + £30.00).

Chapter summary

- The Cash Book is a book of original entry, because all cash transactions can be entered into it immediately, and part of the Ledger, because the double-entry book-keeping method is used.
- The two-column Cash Book combines the Cash account and the Bank account. It follows the double-entry procedure. Each transaction is recorded only once, with the exception of withdrawals from and deposits to the bank. These are recorded twice.
- The three-column Cash Book is an extension of the two-column Cash Book which allows for the recording of cash discounts. Discounts allowed are allowances given by a business to its debtors (credit customers). They are debited in the Cash Book and credited in the personal account of the debtor. Discounts received are allowances for speedy payment given to a business by its creditors (firms supplying goods on credit). They are credited in the Cash Book and debited in the personal account of the creditor.
- A bank reconciliation statement deals with the routine discrepancies between statements received from the bank and the business accounts. There are two main ways of reconciling the Cash Book with the bank statement.

- A Petty Cash Book simplifies accounting by recording small expenditures of frequent occurrence. Petty cash accounting is sometimes called imprest accounting because an imprest or float gives the petty cash clerk a supply of money to make or reimburse purchases. At the end of a week or month the petty cash is reimbursed for what has been expended.

ACT 4.1

For questions 1 to 5, put a tick against the letter that represents the best answer from among the four alternatives given.

1 Cash discount is given:
  A Only when goods were paid for by credit cards
  B Only when goods are bought for cash
  C Only when goods are paid for by cheque
  D When accounts are settled according to the terms of payment.

2 The total of the Discount allowed column in the Cash Book is posted to:
  A The debit side of the Discount received account
  B The debit side of the Discount allowed account
  C The credit side of the Discount received account
  D The credit side of the Discount allowed account.

3 A credit balance of £500 on the Bank column of the Cash Book would mean that
  A There's cash in hand of £500
  B The book-keeper has made a mistake
  C The bank account is overdrawn by £500
  D Cash at bank is equal to £500.

4 When the Petty Cash Book is kept on the imprest system, then:
  A The petty cashier is reimbursed at the end of each period with the total expenses for the period
  B There is no need for analysis columns
  C A fixed amount is drawn from the cashier each period
  D None of the above is true.

5 A bank reconciliation statement tries to reconcile:
  A Cash receipts with cash payments
  B Bank balance with cash in hand
  C Bank statement balance with cash in hand
  D Bank statement balance with the balance on the Bank column of the Cash Book.

► Answers in appendix

3/11/94
Did this in class

6 Jason Davies had the following transactions during April.
April
  1 Started business with £10,000 in the bank
  2 Paid rent and rates by cheque – £500
  4 Bought goods by cheque – £5,000
  6 Cash sales – £450
  7 Paid a cheque to R. Thornton – £550
  8 Received a cheque from Brenda Wilson – £150
  10 Paid wages in cash – £150

15 Cash sales – £600
20 Paid T. Burton by cheque – £120
25 Cash sales paid direct into the bank – £150
30 Paid wages in cash – £150

You are required to write up the two-column Cash Book and balance it off at the end of the month.

► Answer in appendix

7 From the following particulars, write up the two-column Cash Book for Malinda Craven and balance it off at the end of the month.

July
1 Balances brought forward from last month: Cash £150; Bank £1,100 (DR)
3 Cash sales – £125
5 Paid electricity bill by cheque – £150
10 Received a cheque from Bob Kingsley – £200
12 Cash sales paid directly into the bank – £95
15 Paid wages by cheque – £215
18 Paid a cheque to Rebecca Smart – £350
20 Paid rent in cash – £250
21 Withdrew cash from bank – £500
25 Cash sales – £200
28 Cash purchases – £490
30 Received a cheque from AB Ltd – £520

► No answer given

8 Write up a two-column Cash Book for Shanti Sen from the following transactions and balance it off at the end of the month.

3/11/94

Did this in class.

December		£
1	Balances brought forward from last month	
	Cash	250
	Bank (credit balance)	500
2	Cash sales	400
5	Received a cheque from A. Rogers	210
10	Cash sales	420
11	Cash paid into bank	800
15	Paid a cheque to S. Kapoor	200
18	Cash sales paid directly into bank	400
20	Drawings by cheque	600
25	Paid insurance by cheque	225
26	Cash sales	375
28	Paid wages in cash	400
30	Paid a cheque to S. Hart	115
31	Received a cheque from R. Coping	90

► Answer in appendix

9 S. Zulu had the following transactions during November.

November
1 Started business with £16,000 in the bank
2 Withdrew £500 for business use
3 Bought goods by cheque £5,000
5 Cash sales – £200
6 Received a cheque for £475 from I. Hopkins in settlement of his account of £500, discount of £25 having been allowed
10 Paid L. Kimpton his account of £200 by cash £190, discount of £10 having been deducted

15 Cash sales directly put into the bank – £250
20 Jim Roberts, a debtor, paid his account of £500 by cheque £475, discount allowed being £25
25 Received £110 cheque from A. Stringer in settlement of £120
28 Paid a cheque to L. Bowen for £360 in settlement of £380 owing
30 Cash sales – £300
30 Paid wages by cheque – £400

You are required to:

a Write up a three-column Cash Book for S. Zulu and balance it off as on 30 November.
b Show the relevant discount accounts as they would appear in the General Ledger of S. Zulu.

► No answer given

3/11/94
Did this in class.

10 The following balances were extracted from the books of Anita Das on 1 April 19x8.

	£
Bank	300 (CR)
Cash	150 (DR)
R. Logan	300 (DR)
J. Coy	175 (DR)
B. Dillons	210 (DR)
E. Hague	80 (CR)
D. Crowther	195 (CR)
S. Singh	280 (CR)

Her cash/bank transactions during the month of April were as follows:

Cash received

April
6 Cash sales for the week £250, £200 banked straight away
13 Cash sales for the week, £300, £200 banked straight away
20 Cash sales for the week £325, £275 banked straight away
27 Cash sales for the week £250, £150 banked straight away

Cash paid

April
6 Shop assistant's wages for the week – £60
7 Electricity bill – £90
13 Shop assistant's wages – £60
15 Sundry expenses – £50
20 Shop assistant's wages – £60
25 Telephone bill – £90
27 Shop assistant's wages – £60

Cheques received

April
12 From R. Logan for £285 in settlement of account
20 From J. Coy for £165 in settlement of account
27 From B. Dillons for £199 in settlement of account

Cheques paid

April

10 To E. Hague for £76 in settlement of his account

15 For rent – £200

20 To D. Crowther for £185 in settlement of his account

25 To S. Singh for £260 in settlement of his account

You are required to:

a Write up a three-column Cash Book for Anita Das and balance it off as on 30 April.

b Show the personal accounts in Anita Das' Ledger as they would appear on 30 April.

c Show the Discount allowed and Discount received accounts in Anita's General Ledger.

► Answer in appendix

11 Jean Jones opened a greengrocer's shop on 1 April 19x4. She had £1,000 cash, of which she placed £900 into a bank account. The transactions of the shop during the month of April, were:

April		£
3	Purchased goods from T. Duke on credit	150.00
4	Paid half-year's rent by cheque	600.00
7	Cash sales for week	685.40
	Cash drawings by J. Jones	100.00
	Paid cash into bank	100.00
8	Purchased goods from B. Price on credit	75.50
	Purchased goods from R. Knight on credit	115.00
11	Paid T. Duke's account by cheque in full settlement	135.00
14	Cash sales for week	732.80
	Paid cash into bank	600.00
	Cash drawings by J. Jones	100.00
	Purchases from B. Prince on credit	125.00
18	Paid B. Prince by cheque	75.50
	Paid R. Knight by cheque, on account	50.00
19	Sales to J. Lord on credit	30.00
21	Cash sales for week	483.70
	Paid cash into bank	400.00
23	Purchases from R. Knight on credit	176.30
24	Bought cash register from ABC Ltd on credit	172.00
25	J. Lord settled his account by cheque (less 10% discount)	?
28	Cash sales for week	572.50
	Paid into bank	700.00
	Drawings by cheque – J. Jones	200.00

Note: You should calculate the amount of the cheque paid by J. Lord on 25 April.

From this information, you are required to:

a Record the appropriate transactions in a three-column Cash Book, and bring down the balances as at 30 April 19x4.

b Write up the ledger accounts of T. Duke, B. Prince, R. Knight and J. Lord, and bring down the balances as at 30 April 19x4.

(GCE JMB)

► No answer given

10/11/94
Did this in class.

12 J. Samuelson's Cash Book showed a balance at bank of £1,034 as at 31 December, 19x9. The bank statement showed a credit balance of £1,658 on the same day. The following discrepancies were discovered by comparing the Cash Book with the bank statement:

		£
(i)	Cheques paid into bank on 31 December 19x9 and not yet entered in the bank statement	392
(ii)	Cheques drawn and not yet presented for payment	690
(iii)	Items showed in the bank statement but not yet entered in the Cash Book:	
	Bank charges	34
	Payment of insurance premium by direct debit	260
	Dividends collected by bank	620

(a) Enter the items listed under (iii) above in the Cash Book and balance it off.

(b) Prepare a Bank Reconciliation Statement as at 31 December, 19x9.

► Answer in appendix

10/11/94
Did this in class.

13 Jane Banks, who is in business as a car dealer, prepares a Bank Reconciliation Statement weekly. The Bank Reconciliation Statement as at 5 November 19x8, in addition to bank charges of £25.60 not then recorded in the Cash Book, included only the following unpresented cheques:

Cheque number	£
162358	95.10
162361	147.64
162362	16.00
162364	38.90

The Cash Book, Bank columns only, of Jane Banks for the week ended 12 November 19x8 is as follows.

19x8		£	19x8		Cheque No.	£
7 Nov	Balance b/f	2,823.28	7 Nov	K. Supplies	162365	16.41
8	Sun Blinds	110.00	7	J. Bay	162366	273.69
8	John Bell	210.80	8	L. Simms	162367	116.20
9	T. Jones Ltd	169.00	8	M. Dint	162368	1,399.38
9	Jean Hill	1,921.00	8	D. Feint	162369	200.00
10	A. Wall – cheque	710.00	9	W. Young	162370	70.00
	Discount	6.00	9	S.M. Hotels	162371	47.00
11	D.D. Ltd.	29.00	10	Bank charges		25.60
12	Balance c/d	312.20	10	H. Meng	162372	139.10
			10	F. Grundy	162373	17.20
			11	P. Waters	162374	101.10
			11	V. Neall	162375	385.70
			12	H. Dent	162376	3,500.00
		6,291.28				6,291.28
			14 Nov	Balance b/d		312.20

The following bank statement has been received by Jane Banks.

Central Bank Plc Northtown Branch

Jane Banks **Statement of account** Account No. 547892

19x8		Payments £	Receipts £	Balance £
8 Nov	Opening balance			3,095.32
8	162366	273.69		2,821.63
8	162362	16.00		2,805.63
8	Bank Giro Credit		110.00	2,915.63
9	162368	1,399.38		1,516.25
9	162361	147.64		1,368.61
9	162365	16.41		1,352.20
10	Bank Giro Credit		379.80	1,732.00
10	162369	200.00		1,532.00
10	162367	116.20		1,415.80
11	162373	17.20		1,398.60
11	Car Dealers' Assos. Standing order	25.00		1,373.60
11	162372	139.10		1,234.50
11	Bank Giro Credit		2,631.00	3,865.00

The cheque prepared in favour of S. M. Hotels on 9 November was not dispatched and has now been cancelled; a proposed visit of Jane Banks to the Central Hotel owned by S. M. Hotels is not now to take place.

You are required to:

a Prepare a Bank Reconciliation Statement as at 12 November 19x8.

b Explain why it is necessary to prepare a Bank Reconciliation Statement.

(AAT)

► No answer given

17/11/94

Did this in class.

14 Write up a Petty Cash Book from the following particulars for the month of March and balance it off as at 31 March.

Make an analysis column for each of the following: postage, stationery, carriage and sundry expenses.

The amount of imprest is £80.

Transactions during the month of March

March		£
1	Cash in hand	25.00
1	Cash received from the Chief Cashier to make up the imprest	
1	Postage	5.90
2	Typing paper	10.60
4	Cleaning materials	3.75
9	Rail fares	6.30
12	Postage	5.95
19	Parcel post	4.90
21	Window cleaner	5.25
23	Bus fares	3.80
25	Postage	8.05
26	Envelopes	4.50
31	Taxi fare	5.30

Show the balance in hand on 31 March.

► Answer in appendix

5 The recording function of accounting 3 – the Day Books

Chapter objectives

By the end of this chapter, you should be able to:

- appreciate the role of subsidiary books in the accounting system of a business
- write up the various subsidiary books
- post transactions recorded in these books to the relevant accounts in the Ledger
- record in the Journal some transactions which cannot be recorded conveniently in the other day books
- explain how the various errors that are not revealed by the Trial Balance are corrected through the Journal
- explain the meaning of the following terms: day books, Sales Day Book, Purchases Day Book, Returns Outwards Book, Returns Inwards Book, the Journal, the Suspense Account, Credit Note, Invoice, T Accounts, narration, journalizing, errors of original entry, errors of omission, errors of commission, errors of principle, compensating errors, errors of reversal.

THE DAY BOOKS

The main book of accounts is the **Ledger** and it is maintained according to the principles of double-entry book-keeping, but a business deals with hundreds and thousands of financial transactions in a year, and this multiplicity of transactions makes it necessary to sort them out in some convenient groupings like credit sales, credit purchases, etc., before recording them in the Ledger. This initial sorting and classifying is done in a number of books of original entry. These books are also known as **books of prime entry**, or **subsidiary books**, **journals** or simply **Day Books**.

► Day Books are also called Journals, or books of prime entry, or books of original entry, or subsidiary books. They are often computer files rather than books.

This chapter explains how these books are written up and how the transactions recorded in them are eventually posted to the Ledger. The five main 'day' books are:

- the Sales Day Book
- the Purchases Day Book
- the Returns Inwards Book
- the Returns Outwards Book
- the Journal.

► The accounting system restated

Chapter 1 outlined the accounting process or system. It is worth explaining this system once again, so that we can understand the role of subsidiary books in it. A diagrammatic presentation of the accounting system of an organization is given in Figure 5.1.

Figure 5.1 *The accounting system*

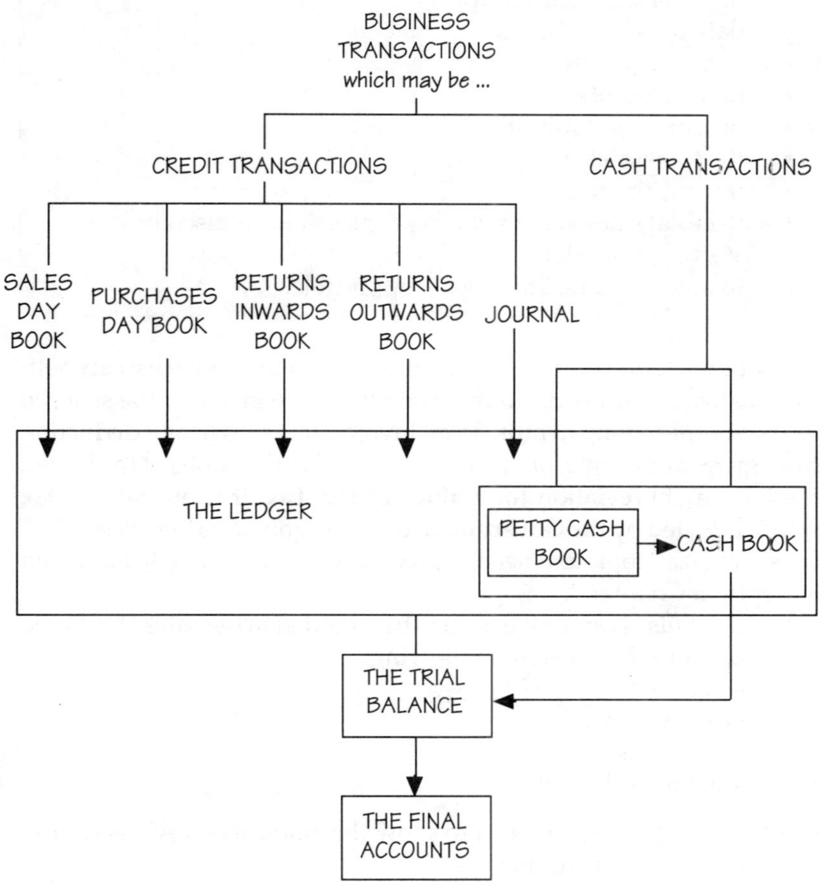

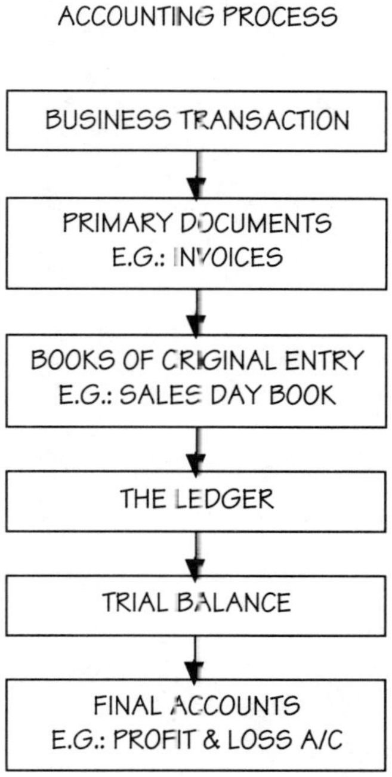

Credit transactions will be first recorded in one of the day books from the relevant source documents, for example **sales invoices** and **purchase invoices**. Likewise, cash transactions will be recorded in the **Cash Book**. The next step is to post these transactions to the relevant accounts in the Ledger. At the year end (or any time before that at the discretion of the management) a **Trial Balance** will be extracted from the balances of the Ledger and the Cash Book. The last step is to prepare a set of final accounts, i.e. the **Trading and Profit and Loss account** and the **Balance Sheet**. The accounting system in an organization thus begins with the financial transactions and ends in the preparation of year-end financial statements. The day books are written up from the source documents and extreme care needs to be taken so that no errors occur. An error at this stage will creep through all the subsequent stages in the accounting system.

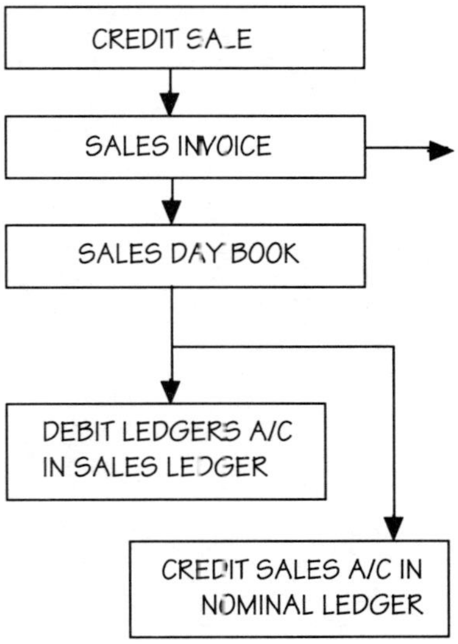

The Sales Day Book

The Sales Day Book is also known as the **Sales Journal**. It is used to record all credit sales, in strict chronological order, from the source documents, called **invoices**. An invoice is a document which is sent from the seller to the buyer, giving details of the transactions of the goods. Usually, an invoice will contain important pieces of information.

► **The Sales Day Book records all the credit sales from invoices.**

An invoice usually records:

- name of the selling firm
- date of sale
- name of customer
- invoice number
- quantity and unit price of goods
- the total sales value gross
- trade discount
- the total sales value net (gross sales value – discount)
- VAT if applicable
- total sales value and VAT if applicable.

All but two items (trade discount and VAT in the above list) are self-explanatory. A **trade discount** is an allowance given by the seller to the buyer for buying in bulk. In an invoice, it is shown as a deduction from gross sales value, but it is not recorded in the books of the buyer. **VAT** is an abbreviation for **Value Added Tax**. It is an indirect tax which is levied by the Government on some goods and services. VAT is a specialized topic and needs a great deal of explaining. It is covered in depth in Chapter 7.

Not all details given above need to be recorded in the Sales Day Book; it is enough to show just the following:

- date of sale
- name of customer
- invoice number
- the total net sales value.

If VAT is applicable, we need to show the amount of VAT as well as the sales total not including VAT.

The Sales Day Book will usually be totalled at the end of the day, but this can be done weekly or monthly if desired.

Posting from the Sales Day Book to the Ledger

When the Sales Day Book has been totalled, the transactions should be posted to the Ledger according to the following rules:

- debit each debtor's account in the Sales Ledger
- credit the total value of net sales during the period to the Sales account in the Nominal Ledger.

Figure 5.2 The ruling of a typical Sales Day Book page

Date	Customer's account	Invoice no.	Folio	Amount	
				£	p

A Sales Day Book page does not have two sides. The folio column is meant for inserting the appropriate ledger page number when posting the transactions to the Ledger. All other column headings are self-explanatory.

Example 5.1 Writing up a Sales Day Book

The following details relate to the business of H. Lord during the month of February.

February		Invoice number	Amount £
1	Credit sales to A. Lee	0971	200
3	Credit sales to B. Burns	0972	150
7	Credit sales to C. Coles	0973	180
12	Credit sales to D. King	0974	210
20	Credit sales to A. Lee	0975	250
28	Credit sales to C. Coles	0976	160

You are required to:

a Record the above transactions in the Sales Day Book of H. Lord.

b Post them, together with total February sales figure, to the relevant accounts in H. Lord's Ledger.

Note: you may ignore the folio column.

Solution

Sales Day Book

Date	Customer's account	Invoice no.	Folio	Amount £	p
Feb 1	A. Lee	0971		200	
Feb 3	B. Burns	0972		150	
Feb 7	D. Coles	0973		180	
Feb 12	D. King	0974		210	
Feb 20	A. Lee	0975		250	
Feb 28	C. Coles	0976		160	
	Total trans. to sales a/c			1,150	

Ledger accounts

A. Lee a/c (DR / CR)

DR				£	p	CR				£	p
Feb	1	Sales		200							
Feb	20	Sales		250							

B. Burns a/c (DR / CR)

DR				£	p	CR				£	p
Feb	3	Sales		150							

C. Coles a/c (DR / CR)

DR				£	p	CR				£	p
Feb	7	Sales		180							
Feb	8	Sales		160							

D. King a/c

DR											CR
				£	p					£	p
Feb	12	Sales		210							

Sales a/c

DR											CR
				£	p					£	p
						Feb	28	Sundry Debtors		1150	

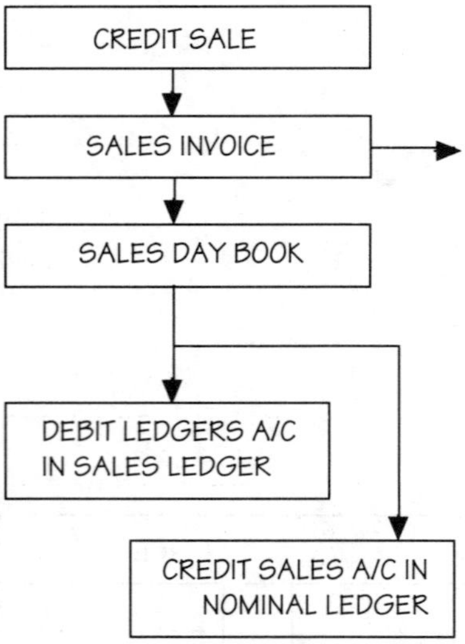

► The Purchases Day Book records all credit purchases.
Its source documents are invoices from suppliers.

Note the double entry rules:

- debit Debtor's account as it increases the asset debtors
- credit Sales account as it increases (sales) revenue.

The Purchases Day Book

This is also known as the **Purchases Journal**. It records all credit purchases, in order of date, from the source documents called the **purchase invoices**. The purchase invoice is simply the document which is sent to the buyer by the seller, giving the details of goods sent. You should note that the same document is a sales invoice to the seller and a purchases document to the purchaser.

Like the Sales Day Book, the Purchases Day Book is also totalled at the end of a day or at some convenient time.

Posting from the Purchases Day Book to the Ledger

After the Purchases Day Book has been totalled, the individual entries will be posted to the Ledger according to the following rules:

- debit the total value of purchases (net) during the period to the Purchases account in the Nominal Ledger.
- credit each creditor's account in the Purchases Ledger.

The ruling of the Purchases Day Book is identical to that of the Sales Day Book.

Example 5.2 Writing up a Purchases Day Book

From the following details, write up the Purchases Day Book of S. Hampson and then post the individual transactions and the total of the Purchases Day Book to his relevant ledger accounts.

March		Invoice No.	Amount £
1	J. Patel	01980	500
6	R. Drummond	01981	450
10	C. Nevin	01982	200
15	J. Patel	01983	420
25	R. Drummond	01984	175
31	C. Nevin	01985	275

Solution

Purchases Day Book

Date	Supplier's account	Invoice no.	Folio	Amount £	p
March 1	J. Patel	01980		500	
6	R. Drummond	01981		450	
10	C. Nevin	01982		200	
15	J. Patel	01983		420	
25	R. Drummond	01984		175	
31	C. Nevin	01985		275	
	Total transferred to Purchases account			2020	

Ledger accounts

J. Patel a/c

DR				£	p	CR				£	p
						Mar	1	Purchases		500	
						Mar	15	Purchases		420	

R. Drummond a/c

DR				£	p	CR				£	p
						Mar	6	Purchases		450	
						Mar	25	Purchases		175	

C. Nevin a/c

DR				£	p	CR				£	p
						Mar	10	Purchases		200	
						Mar	31	Purchases		275	

Purchases a/c

DR				£	p	CR				£	p
Mar	31	Sundry Creditors		2020							

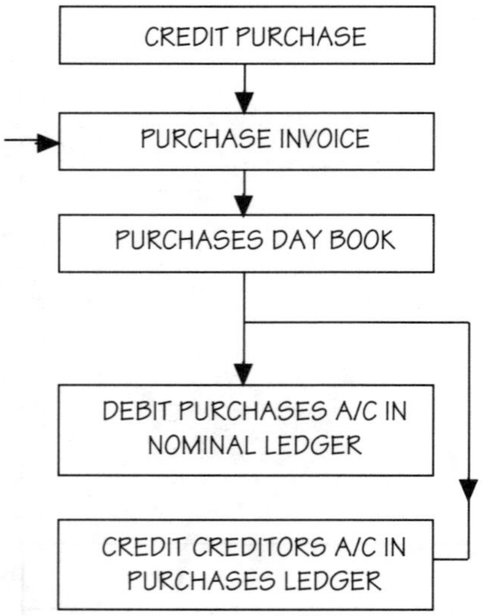

The Returns Inwards Book

This is also known as **Returns Inwards Journal** or **Sales Returns Journal**. In it is recorded any return of goods made by the customers, because the goods sent to them were faulty, or of the wrong specifications etc. On receipt of the returned goods, the seller should send a **credit note** to the customer, showing the amount of allowance or **credit** given to them for the goods returned.

The Returns Inwards Book is ruled in the same way as the Sales Day Book. As usual, the book will be totalled at the end of the day, or when convenient.

Posting from the Returns Inwards Book to the Ledger

The ledger entries for goods returned by customers are as follows:

- debit Returns Inwards account in the Nominal Ledger with the total value of returns during the period
- credit each debtor's account in the Sales Ledger.

Example 5.3 Writing up a Returns Inwards Book

► The Returns Inwards Book records goods returned by a customer.
Its source documents are credit notes sent to the customer, and debit notes sent by the customer.

Enter the following in the Returns Inwards Journal of C. Lloyd and post each individual entry and the total returns for the month in the appropriate ledger accounts.

May		Credit Note No.	Amount £
1	Goods returned by R. Adams	00050	50
10	Goods returned by A. Warner	00051	25
20	Goods returned by R. Adams	00052	15
31	Goods returned by A. Warner	00053	20

Solution

Returns Inwards Book

Date	Customer's name	Credit Note no.	Folio	Amount £	p
May 1	R. Adams	00050		50	
10	A. Warner	00051		25	
20	R. Adams	00052		15	
31	A. Warner	00053		20	
	Transferred to Returns Inwards account			110	

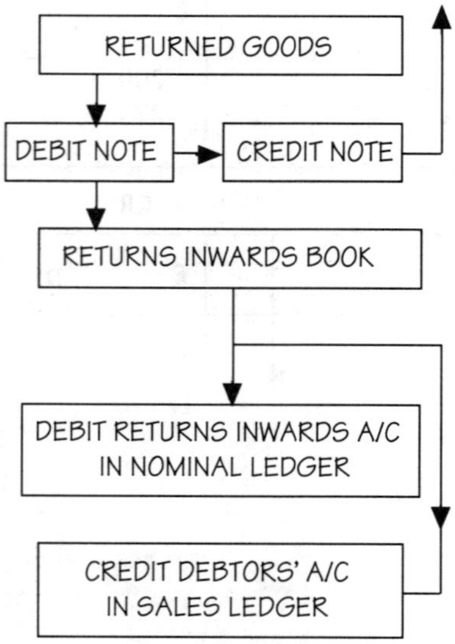

Ledger accounts

DR			R. Adams a/c					CR	
			£	p				£	p
					May	1	Returns Inwards	50	
					May	20	Returns Inwards	15	

DR			A. Warner a/c					CR	
			£	p				£	p
					May	10	Returns Inwards	25	
					May	31	Returns Inwards	20	

DR			Returns Inwards a/c					CR	
			£	p				£	p
May	31	Sundry debtors (returns for the month)	110						

Note:
In the description column of the Returns Inwards account, you can write 'debtors' **or** 'sundry debtors' **or** 'returns for the month'.

Remind yourself of the double-entry rules by noticing that each debtor's account is **credited** because return of good reduces the asset 'debtors' and it also increases the asset stock; this is shown by a debit entry in the Returns Inwards account. We could have obtained the same result by debiting the total returns in the Sales account but the accounting convention is to keep returns from customers in a separate account.

The Returns Outwards Book

This is also known as the **Returns Outwards Journal** or **Purchases Returns Book**. Returns outwards are the exact opposite of returns inwards. They refer to the return of goods made by the buyer to the seller, accompanied by a **debit note** stating the amount of allowance which the buyer should receive.

From these debit notes, the Returns Outwards Book is written in the usual manner.

► The Returns Outwards Book records goods returned to a supplier.
Its source documents are copies of debit notes sent with goods when returned and credit notes sent by the supplier.

Posting from the Returns Outwards Book to the Ledger

The double entries for returns outwards are as follows:

- debit each creditor's account in the Purchases Ledger with the relevant amount
- credit the Returns Outwards account in the Nominal Ledger with the total amount of returns for the period.

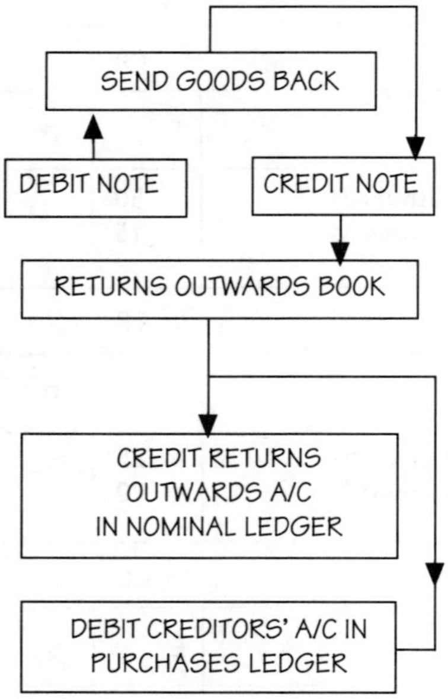

Example 5.4 Writing up the Returns Outwards Book

During the month of September, Jackie Redfern made the following returns of goods to the relevant suppliers.

September		Debit note no.	Amount £
1	To A. Kangwa	0018	100
10	To C. Houghton	0019	50
20	To A. Kangwa	0020	65
30	To C. Houghton	0021	75

You are required to write up the Returns Outwards Book for Jackie Redfern, post each individual transaction to the relevant account in the Purchases Ledger, and transfer the monthly total to the Nominal Ledger.

Solution

Returns Outwards Book

	Supplier's account	Debit Note no.	Folio	Amount £	p
Sept 1	A. Kangwa	0018		100	
Sept 10	C. Houghton	0019		50	
Sept 20	C. Kangwa	0020		65	
Sept 30	C. Houghton	0021		75	
	Transferred to Returns Outwards account			290	

Ledger accounts

DR **A. Kangwa a/c** CR

			£	p				£	p
Sept	1	Returns Outwards	100						
Sept	20	Returns Outwards	65						

DR **C. Houghton a/c** CR

			£	p				£	p
Sept	10	Returns Outwards	50						
Sept	30	Returns Outwards	75						

DR **Returns Outwards a/c** CR

			£	p				£	p
					Sept	30	Sundry creditors (returns for the month)	290	

The Journal

In the early stages of development of book-keeping, the Journal was the only book of prime entry in which the debit and credit aspects of all transactions were recorded before they were posted to the relevant ledger or **T accounts** (simplified ledger accounts without the usual columns for date, particulars, etc. They look like 'Ts'.). Nowadays, there are a number of other books of original entry, as described earlier in this chapter, in addition to the Journal. The Journal is used to record all those transactions which cannot conveniently be entered in any of the other books of prime or original entry. Its use nowadays includes:

- recording opening entries (i.e. assets, liabilities and capital) in a new accounting period
- recording of unusual transactions of infrequent occurrence like disposal of fixed assets, purchase of fixed assets on credit etc
- correcting errors.

► The Journal is a book of prime entry used when there are no special Day Books. It is used especially to:
- record opening entries
- record unusual transactions
- correct errors.

► **T accounts:** simplified format for ledger accounts

► If the Trial Balance does not balance a Suspense account is opened in the Journal.

Figure 5.3 Typical layout of a Journal

Date	Narration	Folio	DR Amount		CR Amount	
			£	p	£	p

The process of entering a transaction in the Journal is often called **journalizing**. To journalize a transaction, we need to record both its debit and credit aspects. As shown in Figure 5.3, the Journal has two pairs of money columns – one for debit, and the other for credit. We always make the debit entry first i.e. we write the name of the account to be debited in the 'narration' column, followed by the money value in the debit column. We then make the credit entry underneath and slightly indented, followed by the amount in the 'CR' column. Journalizing of the transaction is completed by writing a very brief account of the transaction, called the **narration**. In deciding which account is to be debited and which one to be credited, we follow the normal rules of double entry.

Example 5.5 Writing up the Journal

Enter the following in the Journal of Ian Cave:

October 1 **Assets**: Premises £20,000; Fixtures and fittings £1,000; Motor vehicles £8,500; Stock £5,000; Debtors – K. Singh £1,200; B. Riley £800; Cash at bank £5,250; Cash in hand £200.

Liabilities: Creditors – R. McDonald £2,500; K. Bush £1,750.

October 5 Sold a motor vehicle on credit to B. Johnson for £ 1,100.

Solution

The journal entries are as follows.

Date		Narration	Folio	DR Amount £	p	CR Amount £	p
Oct	1	Premises		20,000			
		Fixtures and fittings		1,000			
		Motor vehicles		8,500			
		Stock		5,000			
		Debtors					
		K. Singh		1,200			
		B. Riley		800			
		Bank		5,250			
		Cash		200			
		Creditors					
		R. McDonald				2,500	
		K. Bush				1,750	
		Capital*				37,700	
		Being the assets and liabilities at this date		41,950		41,950	
Oct	5	B. Johnson		1,100			
		Motor vehicles				1,100	
		Being the sale of motor vehicles (per invoice no. 00123) **					

* The figure for capital is obtained by deducting the total of liabilities (£4,250) from the total of assets (£41,950).

** You need to include this information if it is available.

It is important to understand that though we show separately the debit and credit entries in the Journal, it is not a part of the Ledger. The Journal is simply a diary of transactions – a book of original entry. Having journalized the transactions, we can open up new accounts in the Ledger (for opening entries) and/or post the journalized entries to the relevant accounts in the Ledger. Remember that the Journal is not a substitute for the Ledger but it is a complement to it.

Correcting errors using the Journal

► **Trial Balance**: see Chapter 3

A business will extract a **Trial Balance** at periodic intervals to check on the arithmetical accuracy of ledger and cash book entries. If the Trial Balance does not balance, i.e. the debit total is not equal to the credit total, some errors have been made in recording transactions. These errors usually arise because of overcasting and/or undercasting of amounts in the accounts. If the debit total is exactly equal to the credit total we should normally be tempted to conclude that our entries in the Ledger and Cash Book are correct, but this may not always be the case. There are several types of error which do not affect the Trial Balance and are not, therefore, revealed by it. These include:

► Different kinds of error

- errors of original entry
- errors of omission
- errors of commission
- errors of principle
- compensating errors
- errors of reversal.

These types of error are corrected by the use of the Journal. Let's now examine each of these errors in turn.

An error of original entry

► Errors of original entry

This refers to an incorrect figure that might have been used as the basis for the double-entry record. For example, a cash sale on 1 May for £97 is entered in the Ledger as follows:

DR	Cash account	£79	
CR	Sales account		£79

To correct this error, we need the following journal entries.

Correcting an error of original entry

The Journal

		DR £	DR p	CR £	CR p
May 2	Sales account	79			
	Cash account			79	
	Cash account	97			
	Sales account			97	
	Correction to original entry on May 1 which was transposed.				

Alternatively:

The Journal

		DR £	DR p	CR £	CR p
May 2	Cash account	18			
	Sales account			18	
	Correction of original entry on 1 May which was transposed. Originally entered as sale of £79 which should have been £97.				

We can correct this error in either of the two ways shown above. In the first method, the original entries are cancelled by making reverse entries in the Cash and Sales accounts. Then the two accounts involved are posted again with the correct figures.

The second method works out first the difference between the correct figure, i.e. £97, and the posted figure, £79. This difference indicates that both the accounts are understated by £18. The normal remedy is to bring the original figure to its correct level by debiting the Cash account and crediting the Sales account by £18.

An error of omission

► Errors of omission

This indicates that a transaction has been omitted altogether and it is not therefore reflected in the Trial Balance. To rectify this, we need to make the two relevant entries via the Journal in the usual manner.

► Errors of commission

An error of commission

This is where a transaction has been entered in the wrong account, but in the same group of accounts. For example, a credit sale of £ 100 to R. Simon is entered to R. Simpson, another debtor, by mistake. To correct this error, we need the following journal entries.

Correcting an error of commission

The Journal

		DR		CR	
		£	p	£	p
	R.Simon	100			
	R.Simpson			100	
	Correction of entry made in the wrong debtor's account				

► Error of principle

An error of principle

This occurs when a transaction has been posted to an account in the wrong group. A purchase of an asset incorrectly posted to the Purchases account, is an example of such an error. A motor van purchased from Nationwide Garages Ltd for £4,500, is originally posted as follows:

- debit the Purchases account with £4,500
- credit Nationwide Garages Ltd with £4,500.

This error of principle is rectified by making the following entry in the journal.

Correcting an error of principle

The Journal

		DR		CR	
		£	p	£	p
	Motor van account	4,500			
	Purchases account			4,500	
	Correction of overstated purchases and understated Motor van				

► Compensating errors

Compensating errors

These refer to two or more entries which tend to cancel each other out. The following example illustrates such errors. Consider the following two transactions recorded by a business on a certain day.

- Cash sales £600
- Paid rent in cash £600

The firm's book-keeper made the following entries only in the Ledger:

- credit the Sales account with £600
- debit the Rent account with £600.

We need four entries in all to record two transactions, but only two entries have been made in this case, which is incorrect. Yet the Trial Balance balances simply because the two remaining entries cancel each other. The debit entry for cash sales should have been made in the

Cash account, and the credit entry for rent paid, in the Cash account. The two errors have **cancelled** or **compensated** each other.

To correct the error the necessary journal entry is as follows.

Correcting compensating errors

The Journal

		DR		CR	
		£	p	£	p
	Cash account	600			
	Cash account			600	
	Correction of £ 600 each on the debit and credit sides of the cash account which cancel each other				

An error of reversal

► Errors of reversal

This refers to two entries which are the wrong way round. A cash sales of £ 200 should be made as follows:

- debit the Cash account with £200
- credit the Sales account with £200.

Instead the entries are made as follows:

- debit the Sales account with £200
- credit the Cash account with £200.

This is an example of an error of reversal. To rectify this error we need the following entry in the journal.

Correcting an error of reversal

The Journal

		DR		CR	
		£	p	£	p
	Cash account	400			
	Sales account			400	
	Receipt of £200 cash credited to Cash, debited to Sales in error. Correction of error is now effected.				

The amount is doubled in each case because we have first to cancel the original wrong entry of £200 and then we enter another £200 in its place thus giving a total of £400.

We've discussed the different types of error which do not affect the Trial Balance and how these errors can be corrected via the Journal. What remains now is to explain how errors which do affect the Trial Balance are corrected, but before we do so, try the following activity.

ACT 5.1

1 State two uses of the Journal.

2 Name six different types of errors that do not affect the Trial Balance.

3 Explain briefly the Journal entry needed to correct:
   a an error of principle
   b an error of reversal.

► Answers in appendix

The Suspense account

There are certain types of error which make the totals in the Trial Balance disagree i.e. the debit total is not equal to the credit total. The causes of such disagreement will include:

- undercasting and overcasting of some transactions
- one-sided entries
- incorrect additions giving rise to either overstated or understated balances in ledger accounts.

► When the Trial Balance does not balance a **Suspense account** is opened to make corrections.

To correct this apparent disagreement between debit total and the credit total, we need to open up a new account in the Nominal Ledger, called the **Suspense account**. The difference between the two totals is then put into the Suspense account. The Suspense account will show a debit if the debit total in the 'incorrect' Trial Balance is less than the credit total. It will be closed when the errors are detected and relevant postings are made in the accounts via the Journal.

Example 5.6 The use of the Suspense account

The Trial Balance of David Atkins extracted on 31 December 19x9 showed a shortage of £500 on the credit side. A Suspense account was consequently opened to balance the Trial Balance.
On 31 January 19x0, all the errors made during 19x9 were detected. They were as follows:

- the Sales account had been undercast by £300
- the Purchases account had been overcast by £250
- no entry had been made in the Bank account for £50 received as interest, although the Interest received account had been credited with £50.

You are required to:

a Show the journal entries with suitable narrations to correct the errors listed above.

b Write up the Suspense account showing the correction of the errors.

Solution

The Journal

		DR £ p	CR £ p
19x0			
Jan 31	Suspense account	300	
	Sales account		300
	Sales undercast by £300 in 19x9		
Jan 31	Suspense account	250	
	Purchases account		250
	Purchases overcast by £250 in 19x9		
Jan 31	Bank	50	
	Suspense account		50
	Interest received of £50 omitted from the bank account		

Ledger account

DR		Suspense a/c						CR	
			£	p				£	p
19x0									
Jan	31	Sales	300		Jan	1	Balance b/d	500	
	31	Purchases	250		Jan	31	Bank	50	
			550					550	

To correct an error, identify the account involved. Remembering the rules for double-entry book-keeping (debit an increase in asset/expense and credit a decrease in asset; debit a decrease in liability/capital/revenue and credit an increase in liability/capital/revenue) decide whether the account is to be debited or credited.

Finally, make the opposite entry in the Suspense account.

Chapter summary

- Books of original entry (Journals or Day Books) are used to record non-cash transactions including credit sales and credit purchases. Information is recorded in these books from source documents such as invoices, and later transferred or posted to the accounts in the Ledger.
- The Journal has special functions. It is used to record all those transactions which cannot be recorded in any other day books, and it is used to correct errors made in writing up ledger accounts.
- There are two main types of error. Errors of omission or commission do not affect the Trial Balance. Others tend to make the Trial Balance incorrect. The latter require a special account called the Suspense account.
- The opening entry of the Suspense account represents the difference between the two totals of the incorrect trial balance. When the errors are detected and corrected the Suspense account opening balance will disappear.

ACT 5.2

For questions 1 to 5 put a tick against the letter that represents the best answer from among the four alternatives given.

1 Credit sales are recorded in the first instance in:
- A The Ledger
- B The Cash Book
- C The Journal
- D The Sales Day Book.

2 When a customer returns goods to you, you:
- A Credit his account and debit Returns inwards account
- B Debit his account and credit Returns inwards account
- C Credit his account and debit Returns outwards account
- D Debit his account and credit Sales account.

3 When you return goods to your suppliers, the necessary ledger entries are:
- A Debit Returns outwards account and credit suppliers' accounts
- B Credit Returns outwards account and debit suppliers' accounts
- C Debit Returns inwards account and credit suppliers' accounts
- D Credit suppliers' accounts and debit Purchases account.

4 A suspense account is used:
- A To record returns outwards
- B To return returns inwards
- C To correct an error as shown in the unequal debit and credit totals in the Trial Balance
- D To record a prepayment or an accrual.

5 An error of commission means that:
- A Two or more errors cancel each other out
- B A total has been cast wrongly
- C An entry is made in the wrong account but in the same class of accounts
- D A transaction has been overlooked.

► Answers given in appendix

6 Record the following credit transactions in the Sales Day Book, post them to the relevant accounts in the Sales Ledger and post the total for the month to the Sales account in the General Ledger.

19x9			Invoice no.	£
June	1	Sold goods to R. Islam	00121	500
June	8	Sold goods to Brown and Brown Co	00122	1,000
June	20	Sold goods to R. Islam	00123	800
June	25	Sold goods to Brown and Brown Co.	00124	1,200
June	30	Sold goods to Joan Cummings	00125	600

► Answer in appendix

7 Write up the Purchases Day Book from the following details. Post the transactions and total purchases for the month to the relevant accounts in the Ledger.

19x2		Invoice	£
April 1	Bought goods on credit from Modern Wholesalers Ltd	MW891	2,000
April 10	Bought goods on credit from Ranjit Singh	RS521	800
April 15	Bought goods on credit from Modern Wholesalers Ltd	MW920	1,200
April 22	Bought goods on credit from Amanda Smith	AS830	600
April 30	Bought goods on credit from Ranjit Singh	RS600	700

► No answer given

8 Write the appropriate day books of John Crowther from the following details. Post the transactions and day book totals for the month to the relevant accounts in his Ledger.

19x3		£
Sept 1	Credit purchases from A. Chang	800
Sept 6	Credit purchases from Rani Patel	700
Sept 12	Credit purchases from A. Chang	900
Sept 15	Credit purchases from Rani Patel	500
Sept 20	John Crowther returned goods to A. Chang	200
Sept 25	Credit purchases from R. King	400
Sept 28	John Crowther returned goods to Rani Patel	150
Sept 30	Credit purchases from R. King	550

► Answer in appendix

9 The following balances were extracted on 1 May 19x2 from the books of H. Kimpton.

A. Moss	£250 (DR)
B. Curtis	£400 (DR)
C. Clarke	£315 (DR)
Sales account	£965 (CR)
Returns Inwards account	£210 (DR)

Credit sales during the month of May 19x2 were as follows.

		Invoice No	£
May 1	C. Clarke	00210	500
7	A. Moss	00211	750
15	C. Clarke	00212	650
May 22	B. Curtis	00213	590
29	A. Moss	00214	410
30	B. Clarke	00215	570

H. Kimpton sent credit notes to customers who had returned goods during May 19x2.

		Credit Note no	£
May 6	C. Clarke	015	50
12	A. Moss	016	80
20	C. Clarke	017	100
27	A. Moss	018	65
28	B. Curtis	019	25

You are required to:

a Write up the Sales Day Book for May 19x2.

b Write up the Returns Inwards Book for May 19x2.

c Show the opening balances in the relevant ledger accounts and post the transactions during May, including the Sales Day Book total and the Returns Inwards Book total for May to the appropriate accounts in H. Kimpton's Ledger.

► No answer given

10 The following balances were extracted from the books of G. Peck on 1 November 19x3.

Creditors:

A. Mahendra	£850 Cr.
B. Jacobs	£500 Cr.
C. Singh	£450 Cr.

Nominal Ledger accounts:

Purchases account	£2,000 Cr.
Returns Outwards account	£200 Cr.

Credit purchases during November, 19x3 were as follows.

		Name of suppliers	Invoice no	£
Nov	2	C. Singh	0701	500
	3	A. Mahendra	0810	800
	10	B. Jacobs	1122	920
	18	A. Mahendra	0999	750
	25	AB Ltd.	1987	990
	30	B. Jacobs	0678	620

G. Peck received credit notes from suppliers for purchases returns during November, 19x3.

		Name of suppliers	Credit note no	£
Nov	7	B. Jacobs	0089	150
	12	A. Mahendra	0190	200
	20	C. Singh	0825	175
	29	AB Ltd.	0930	100

You are required to write up:

a the Purchases Day Book for November, 19x3

b the Returns Outwards Book for November, 19x3

c the Purchases Ledger accounts of A. Mahendra, B. Jacobs, C. Singh and AB Ltd. for November,19x3

d the relevant Nominal Ledger accounts for November, 19x3.

► Answer in appendix

11 You are required to show the journal entries necessary to record the following transactions relating to the business of J. Wong:

a On 1 July 19x2, J. Wong bought a computer from North-West Computers Ltd for £1,100

b On 20 July 19x2, took goods out from his business for his personal use, valued at £100

c On 5 August 19x2, J Wong decided to write off a debt owing to him by J. Bloggs of £150 as bad debt

d On 20 August 19x2, J. Wong bought office furniture for £650 on credit from Office Furniture Ltd.

► No answer given

12 Show the journal entries needed to correct the following errors in Julie Taylor's books.

19x1		
Aug	1	£200 paid by B. Singh was credited to B. Singer's account
Aug	10	No entries were made for cash sales of £250
Aug	15	The purchase of a typewriter for £150 in cash was wrongly posted to the Purchases account
Aug	20	A credit sale of £265 to Rita Hughes had been entered in the correct accounts as £256
Aug	25	Discount received of £150 had been incorrectly entered on the credit side of the Discount allowed account
Aug	30	A sale of office desk for £50 had been entered in error in the Sales account

► Answer in appendix

13 The following balances relating to the assets and liabilities of Jane Davidson's business were extracted on 31 December 19x2:

	£
Premises	60,000
Fixtures	8,000
Stocks	10,000
Cash at bank	1,500
Cash in hand	500
Debtors	9,750
Creditors	10,250

Calculate Jane Davidson's capital and make appropriate journal entries to open her books.

► No answer given

14 The draft Trial Balance of Palimo Ltd as at 31 May 19x8 agreed. However, a subsequent audit revealed the following errors.

a Bank charges of £56 had been omitted from the Cash Book.
b The Purchases Journal had been overcast by £400.
c The Sales Journal had been undercast by £100.
d An invoice for £127 received from Beta plc had been entered into the Purchases Journal as £217. (This is quite independent of the error made in the Purchases Journal referred to above.)
e It is now considered prudent to write off the balance of £88 on Peter Shadey's account as bad.

Palimo Ltd maintains control accounts for debtors and creditors in its General Ledger. Individual accounts for debtors and creditors are maintained on a memorandum basis only.

Required:
Prepare journal entries to show how the above errors would be corrected.

Note: Dates and narratives not required.

Note: To answer this question, use a Debtors control account and a Creditors control account in place of individual debtors' and creditors' accounts respectively. You'll learn all about control accounts in a later chapter.

(AAT – Preliminary)

► No answer given

15 The draft Trial Balance of Tantin Traders as at 30 November 19x8 did not agree. An investigation of the books revealed the following errors.

- **a** Bank charges of £27.50 have been levied by the business's bank but have not been recorded in the business's Cash Book.
- **b** The discount received column of the Cash Book has been undercast by £88.52.
- **c** The Sales (Day) Book has been undercast by £999.
- **d** An invoice of £377.50 received from a supplier has been omitted from the Purchases (Day) Book.
- **e** Returns in of £220.75 from Dean Orton, a credit customer, have been posted in error to the credit of D. Norton's account. D. Norton is a credit supplier of Tantin Traders.
- **f** A credit note of £49.81 received from a supplier has been missed out completely from the records.
- **g** The balance on the Carriage Out account has been wrongly carried down as £761. It should be £716.

Tantin Traders maintain Control accounts for debtors and creditors. Individual customer accounts are maintained on a memorandum basis only.

Required:
Prepare journal entries (with narratives) to show how the above errors would be corrected.

(AAT – Preliminary)
► No answer given

16 The draft Trial Balance of Gordon Muir and Sons as at 31 May 19x9 did not agree and the difference was posted to a Suspense account.

The subsequent investigation revealed the following errors.

- (i) The Purchases Day Book has been overcast by £1,000.
- (ii) The Discount Allowed column in the Cash Book has been overcast by £100.
- (iii) Bank charges of £90 have been entered correctly in the Cash Book but have not been posted to the ledger.

Gordon Muir and Sons Ltd does not maintain control accounts as part of its double entry system.

Required:
Prepare journal entries to show how the above errors would be corrected.

Note: Dates and narratives are not required.

► No answer given

6 Accounting concepts and conventions

Chapter objectives

By the end of this chapter, you should be able to:

- understand the nature, meaning and significance of the accounting concepts or conventions
- state and explain a number of such concepts and conventions
- understand the meaning and importance of various statements of standard accounting practice.

CONCEPTS AND CONVENTIONS

Accounting seeks to achieve and maintain objectivity and commonly accepted standards, but it is not easy to do this because of the wide range of accounting treatments that are acceptable for specific business events or transactions. Thus, for example, the value of closing stock that a business might have at the end of the year, can be calculated in very many different ways. The absence of uniformity in the treatment of financial items or events makes it impossible to get a common basis for comparison and interpretation of the profit and loss accounts and/or balance sheets of two or more similar businesses at the end of a given period. For this reason there have been a number of attempts to standardize accountancy practice by proposing sets of concepts and conventions for common usage. It is impossible to give a complete set of such concepts, but the important ones are outlined in this chapter. You will also meet the Statements of Standard Accounting Practice (abbreviated as SSAP's) that have been developed by the accounting profession in recent years.

The concepts behind financial accounts

Following Bierman and Drebin, we can describe the various accounting practices or principles under three major headings:

- assumptions about the business environment
- operating conventions
- quality considerations.

► Bierman H. and Drebin A.R., *Financial Accounting, An Introduction*, Collier Macmillan 1972

Assumptions about the business environment

Accountants make, either explicitly or implicitly, certain important assumptions relating to business organizations and their environment, when they draw up their accounts. These include:

The Entity concept

► The Entity concept

This simply means that we should draw a distinction between the business and the owner. In other words, we should consider the business as a separate entity, distinct from the owner. This was emphasized in Chapter 2, when we saw that we should record the transactions of the business in its books, and not the personal transactions of the owner. For sole traders and partnerships, the law does not recognize this distinction but for companies it does, and it treats the company as a separate legal entity which means that a company can sue and be sued like an individual. Accountants, however, consider the business, whether it is a company or not, as a separate entity.

► The Going Concern concept

The Going Concern concept

This implies that we should assume that the business is going to be in existence for the foreseeable future, unless there is specific evidence to the contrary. This has an important effect on the valuation of assets. Under this assumption assets are normally valued at 'cost less accumulated depreciation'. If, however, we replace the continuity assumption with the assumption of immediate closure, for example, the valuation of assets should be made at a realistic market value which may be much lower than valuation at cost.

► The Stable Monetary Unit concept

The Stable Monetary Unit concept

Accounts are prepared on the assumption that the value of money remains unchanged over time. This assumption enables us to add up different values of stocks, for example, at cost, on different dates, at different prices. Without this assumption, we ought to have converted the different prices of the same goods on different dates to a common denominator with the consequent difficulties it would involve.

► The Periodicity concept

The Periodicity concept

This requires that financial statements are prepared regularly, at a given time interval, usually a year.

Operating conventions or concepts

Besides making a number of assumptions about business entities and the environment in which they operate, accountants also make use of a set of conventions in preparing the accounts of their clients which should reflect a true and fair view of the business. These conventions include:

► The Historic Cost convention

The Historic Cost convention

► **Current cost accounting** takes the effect of inflation into consideration.

► **Historic cost accounting** does not.

This convention implies that the basis of valuation of assets used by a business while preparing its final accounts is historic cost. In other words, all assets shown in the accounts are valued at the cost of acquiring them minus any depreciation thereon, if any. This convention has been subjected to criticisms in recent years. It is claimed that the historic cost concept does not reflect the true value of an asset in periods of inflation, i.e. rising prices. What we need, it is claimed, is a new basis of valuation like Current cost accounting which takes into account the effect of inflation on the assets of a business. Inflation accounting is a specialized area and is outside the scope of this book.

► The Money Measurement convention

The Money Measurement convention

This convention requires that all items included in the accounts must be measurable in monetary terms. There are some items which are of great importance to the operating efficiency and hence profitability of a business, yet they are not included in the financial statements simply because we cannot quantify them in financial terms. For example, what monetary value can be put on the quality and skill of staff in the organization? They together may constitute a valuable asset to the organization, yet we are unable to show them as such in the Balance Sheet as we cannot quantify this asset in terms of money. This convention brings out the impossibility of depicting a full picture of business through its periodic financial statements or accounts.

The Realization convention

This refers to the earning of profits. Revenue and hence profit is deemed to be **realized** i.e. earned, only when a definite sale has been made. A cash sale is realized at the point of sale i.e. when cash is received in exchange for goods or services. A credit sale is realized when the goods or services are passed on, together with an invoice, to the customer. Receipt of cash is therefore not a necessary condition for realization. Thus in the case of a manufacturer, revenue is not realized when goods are completed; it is realized only when the completed goods are actually sold to the customer.

► The Realization convention

The Accruals convention

This is also known as the Matching principle and states that revenue realized (whether actual cash is received or not) during a period, must be matched with the expenses incurred (whether paid or not) of the same period. The amount of an expense, such as wages due but not yet paid, is called an **accrued expense** and should be shown in the accounts. Likewise, any expense, such as an insurance premium, paid in advance for the next accounting period must be adjusted in the accounts.

► The Accruals convention or the Matching principle

The Duality convention

This convention constitutes the very basis of the double-entry book-keeping system. It states that every transaction has two aspects – the **giving** aspect and the **receiving** aspect. To record these two aspects, we should make one debit entry in one account and a corresponding credit entry in another account. Every debit entry must have a corresponding credit entry and every credit entry must have a corresponding debit entry. We have seen, in Chapter 2, that the accounts in the Ledger were entered according to this convention.

► The Duality convention is the basis of double-entry book-keeping.

Quality considerations

In applying the operating conventions to the accounts, an accountant needs to follow certain basic principles so that the accounts prepared give a true and fair view of the organization. Such principles include:

Objectivity

This implies that the accounts must be free from the personal bias of the accountant. One criterion of objectivity is that the accounts prepared by an accountant must be capable of being verified by an independent auditor. This ensures that subjective judgements on some transactions or events have been avoided, and the accounts are free of bias as far as they can be verified. It may not always be possible to be completely objective, but the element of subjectivity or personal liking and disliking in preparing the accounts should be kept to the minimum.

► The Objectivity consideration

Consistency

The consideration of consistency requires that similar items or transactions should be treated in exactly the same way from one accounting year to the next. Some items, such as depreciation, can be treated in the accounts in more than one way. Depreciation can be calculated by

► The Consistency consideration

either the **straight line method** or the **reducing balance method**. If one method is used in one year, and the other method is used in the next, profit figures and asset values will be distorted and will not provide an acceptable basis for comparisons of accounts between two or more years. To avoid this type of distortion we must be consistent in our treatment of accounts from year to year. However, this is not to say that we cannot, under any circumstances, change the treatment of some items in our accounts. We can and should do this if circumstances require it. In that event, we must show the effect of such changes on the profit of the year concerned.

Prudence

► The Prudence consideration, or the principal of conservation

This consideration, also known as the **principle of Conservatism**, means that in choosing a value for a certain item such as the closing stock, an accountant should select that value of the item which will understate rather than overstate the profit. In general terms, this concept requires that we must not anticipate revenue and profits; we should include them in our accounts only when they are actually realized, but we must provide for anticipated losses. As regards expenses, we should always use the maximum value rather than the minimum. The prudence concept implies that excessive optimism in profit calculations should be avoided as it might encourage the business person to undertake too risky a venture. The role of the accountant in this respect is to discount the risk factor.

Materiality

This consideration refers to the significance that is to be attached to a particular item in the accounts. For example, when a business buys a few staplers for office use they should, in theory, be treated as assets and should be shown as such in the Balance Sheet each year for as long as they last. Depreciation, as usual, should be charged on this. To do this in practice would be a sheer waste of time on the part of the accountant, and would increase administrative expenses by more than the value of the staplers. The fact is that the value of assets such as staplers is not sufficiently **material** i.e. significant, to justify giving them the same treatment as we would give assets such as premises. The best thing for us to do is to treat the staplers as a revenue item and show it as an expense in the Profit and Loss account in the year of purchase.

► The Materiality consideration

The Materiality concept thus tells us that items of insignificant value (i.e. not material items) should not be subjected to the application of rigorous accounting treatment. Instead, we use common sense to treat them in our accounts. What item is material, and what is not, will depend on the type, size and policy of businesses. For example, any capital expenditure of less than £500 may not be considered as material by big companies whose assets may run into millions of pounds. Such firms will treat this £500 as a revenue expense. But a small trader may consider this amount of assets as material and consequently depreciate it over a number of years.

Statements of Standard Accounting Practice (SSAPs)

The assumptions, concepts and conventions explained in the preceding pages are insufficient to bring about consistent and standardized approaches to an accounting report. In the 1960s the absence of uniformity and standardization in the preparation of the final accounts of firms, resulting in wide variations in reported profits, gave rise to demand, from accountants and non-accountants, for the remedy of such differences. The accounting profession responded to this demand by setting up the Accounting Standards Board (ASB), consisting of representatives from all the major accounting bodies in the United Kingdom. The main function of this body is to set standards in different areas of accounting in the form of a statement of standard accounting practice, better known as an SSAP. The first SSAP was published in 1970. Since then, a large number of SSAPs have been published. Twenty-five such statements had been listed at the date of writing this book.

► The SSAPs

The detailed examination of all these SSAPs is beyond the scope of this book. The purpose of introducing the SSAP is to make clear the presence of some standards today in financial reporting. Just to give an example, the SSAP number two identified four fundamental accounting concepts which should underlie the preparation of financial statements. These are:

- the Going Concern concept
- the Prudence concept
- the Accruals concept
- the Consistency concept.

We have already explained these earlier on in the chapter. In a later chapter, we'll refer to another SSAP (SSAP 10) when we discuss the sources and applications of funds of a business organization.

The SSAPs are only recommendations; they do not have the force of the law. Accountants are expected to follow them in preparing the accounts of firms.

Chapter summary

- Good financial reporting requires the application of some uniform principles and standards to narrow down the areas of difference and variety in accounting. This can be achieved by following a set of rules, variously known as assumptions, concepts, conventions, principles, postulates and practices.
- These rules are subdivided into three groups. The first group deals with those assumptions which affect the business entity and its environment. The second group is concerned with those conventions which will have a direct bearing on the preparation of operating statements. The last group deals with those principles which will directly affect the quality of financial reporting.
- Accountants are expected to follow some standards in preparing the financial statements of firms. These are provided by the statements of standard accounting practice which are issued from time to time by the Accounting Standards Board.

ACT 6

1 Explain briefly why we need accounting concepts and conventions.

2 State and explain two accounting concepts which will directly affect the quality of financial reporting.

3 What are the SSAPs and what useful purpose is served by them?

4 State and describe the four fundamental accounting principles identified in SSAP 2.

► No answers given

7 Value Added Tax

Chapter objectives

By the end of this chapter, you should be able to:

- understand the meaning and nature of VAT
- maintain the necessary accounts for VAT
- explain the effects of VAT on the financial statements of a business
- state the meaning of the following terms: VAT, input tax, output tax, analytical day book.

VALUE ADDED TAX

Value added tax, popularly known as **VAT**, was introduced in the United Kingdom in 1973 as a tax on the supply of goods and services. All businesses with an annual turnover in excess of an amount decided by the Chancellor of the Exchequer are subjected to this tax. This chapter begins with an examination of the nature of the tax, followed by an explanation of the book-keeping requirements relating to the tax. Finally, you will learn how to complete a VAT return that has to be forwarded to HM Customs and Excises Department quarterly.

The nature of VAT

Any business with turnover in excess of a certain minimum is regarded as a 'taxable person' and needs to be registered for VAT. The minimum turnover is decided by the Chancellor of the Exchequer and reviewed from time to time. On registration, a business is provided with a registration number which must be quoted on all business documents such as the invoice. It must charge VAT at the appropriate rate on all sales of taxable goods and services, i.e. goods and services that are subjected to VAT. At present, there are two rates of VAT: the **standard rate** which is fixed at 17.5% and the **zero rate** on some goods such as books and newspapers, food and children's clothes. On zero-rated goods, no tax is charged.

Input tax and output tax

To understand how VAT operates, you need to know the difference between an input tax and an output tax. The tax which a business charges on the goods supplied or services rendered by it is known as the **output tax**. The **input tax** is the tax which a business pays on the goods and services it buys. All registered sellers of taxable supplies can adjust the input tax they have paid on their purchases against the output tax they've collected on their sales. Only the **net** amount, i.e. output tax minus input tax, needs to be sent to the authorities every quarter. If, however, the input tax is more than the output tax, the business can claim a refund, equal to the difference, from the authorities. Payment of VAT is usually made with the VAT return.

► **Input tax:** charged on goods and services a business purchases

► **Output tax:** charged on goods and services a business supplies

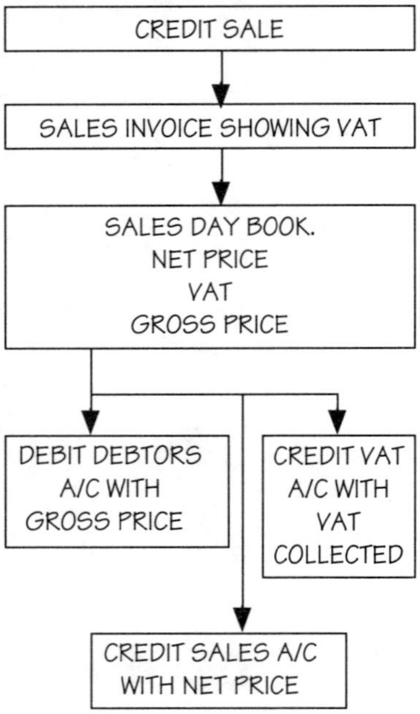

VAT is a tax levied on the value added by businesses at each stage of sales, from the first supplier to the ultimate consumer. This process of how VAT is paid at each stage of sales on value added is illustrated in Example 7.1.

Example 7.1 The payment of VAT

Allison sells goods to Brian for £200, Brian sells them to Clare for £250 and Clare sells them to Duncan, who is the ultimate consumer, for £300. All prices are excluding VAT.
Show how much VAT will be paid at each stage of sales assuming that Allison has no input tax to adjust against her output tax. The rate of VAT is 17.5%.

Solution

	Selling price (excluding VAT)	*VAT (output tax)*	*VAT (input tax)*	*VAT paid at each stage*
	£	£	£	£
Allison to Brian	200	35.00	NIL	35.00
Brian to Clare	250	43.75	35.00	8.75
Clare to Duncan	300	52.50	43.75	8.75
				52.50

Notice that Duncan, being the final consumer, cannot pass on the VAT to any body else and bears the entire burden of the tax. Allison does not pay any tax herself; she simply passes on the tax collected to the authorities. Brian and Clare, too, do not pay any tax; they simply act as collecting agents for VAT.

► Exempt goods and services

No VAT is charged on:
- postal services
- medical services
- finance, e.g. interest charge
- insurance premia
- betting and lotteries.

ACT 7.1

1 Give two examples of zero-rated supplies.
2 Who should register for VAT?
3 Give three examples of exempt supplies.

► Answers in appendix

ACCOUNTING FOR VAT

Output tax

A seller selling goods on which VAT is payable must keep a record of VAT charged or collected. Invoices should show:
- the selling price excluding VAT
- the amount of VAT
- the total price including VAT.

These three pieces of information should be recorded in the Sales Day Book, (see pages 79–82 for more about the Sales Day Book). A columnar Sales Day Book is obviously required for this purpose and it should contain three sets of columns, besides columns for date, particulars, invoice number and folio, to record the three sets of values: the **net price** (this is the price excluding VAT), VAT itself and the **gross price** (this is the price including VAT).

Once the transactions have been recorded in the Sales Day Book, they need to be posted to the appropriate ledger accounts. The debtors' accounts will be debited with the gross value because that is what they owe to the business. The Sales account in the General Ledger will be credited with the total net value of sales for the period, because that is what the business receives for its sales. If we stop at this stage, the double-entry principle will not work: the total of the debtors' accounts will exceed the sales value of the period by the amount of VAT charged. We therefore need a credit entry for the amount of VAT to maintain the balance between debit and credit. This is done by opening a new account, called the VAT account, in the General Ledger and crediting this account with the amount of VAT charged. The credit balance on the VAT account represents a liability – to HM Customs and Excise for the VAT collected. When this liability is discharged by the payment of the dues,

- debit the VAT account
- credit the Cash Book

with the amount paid.

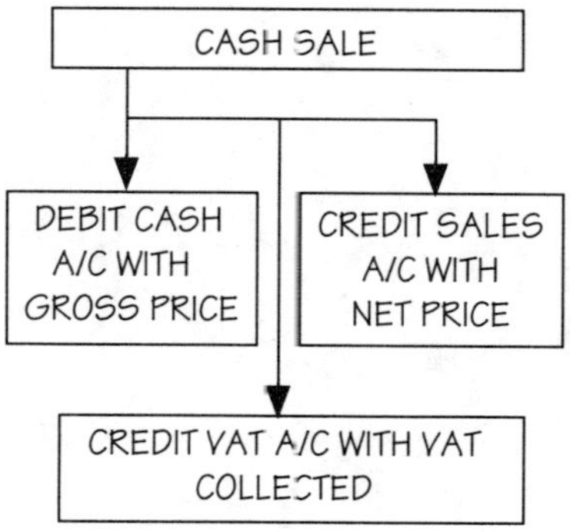

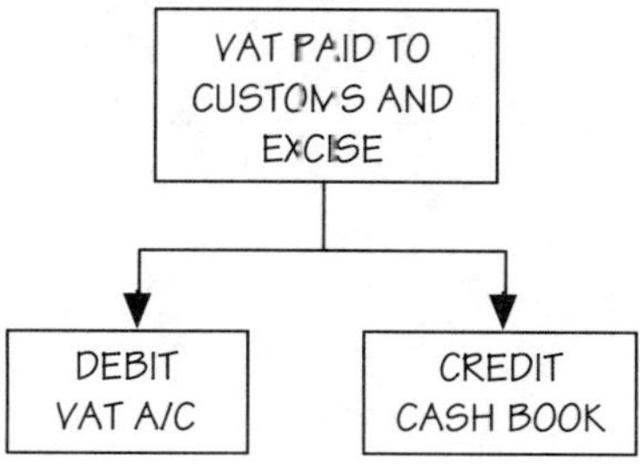

The book-keeping entries for cash sales involving VAT are as follows.

> ***Book-keeping entries for VAT: cash sales***
>
> - debit the Cash account with the total cash received
> - credit the Sales account with the net value of sales
> - credit the VAT account with the VAT collected.
>
> When VAT is paid to Customs and Excise:
>
> - debit the VAT account
> - credit the cash book
>
> with the amount of VAT.

Input tax

For more about the Purchases Day Book – see pages 82–83.

VAT paid on any credit purchases should also be recorded in an analysed Purchases Day Book which has separate columns to record the net value (the value excluding VAT), VAT and the gross value (the value including VAT) of purchases. These transactions will then be posted to the relevant ledger accounts as follows:

- debit the Purchases account with the total net value of purchases
- debit the VAT account with the amount of VAT
- credit creditors' accounts with the gross value of purchases.

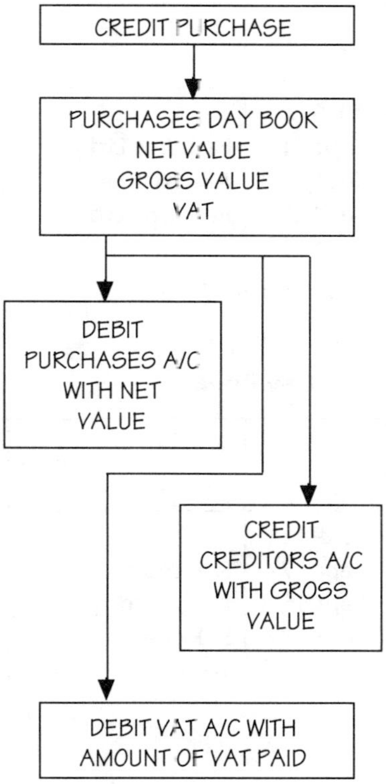

You will notice that VAT account will have entries on both sides: input tax on the debit side and output tax on the credit side. The balance on this account will be either a credit balance (i.e. a liability) or a debit balance (i.e. an asset). If it shows a credit balance, a cheque will be sent to the authorities to pay off the liability. If it shows a debit balance, a claim for the refund of the appropriate amount will be made to HM Customs and Excise. When the money is received from them, the asset **VAT receivable** will be realized.

Book-keeping entries for VAT: cash purchases

- debit the Purchases account with the net value
- debit the VAT account with the VAT paid
- credit the Cash or Bank account with the gross value.

Example 7.2 illustrates the recording of purchases and sales involving VAT.

Example 7.2 Recording purchases and sales involving VAT

Linda Stewart is a VAT registered trader and all her purchases and sales are subject to VAT at the standard rate of 17.5%. Her credit transactions for the month of September, 19x9 were as follows.

September

1	Bought goods from Fashions Ltd for £500
7	Sold goods to S. Jordan for £300
10	Bought goods from AB Ltd for £550
16	Sold goods to Alpha Ltd for £260
21	Bought goods from Fashions Ltd for £480
28	Sold goods to S. Jordan for £200
30	Bought goods from AB Ltd for £390

All the figures given above are excluding VAT.

You are required to:

a Write up Linda's Sales Day Book and Purchases Day Book.

b Post all the transactions to the appropriate accounts in Linda's Ledger.

c Balance off Linda's VAT account in her General Ledger.

Solution

Purchases Day Book **Page 1**

			Invoice no.	Folio	Net £ p	VAT £ p	Gross £ p
19x9							
Sept 1	Fashions Ltd			PL1	500	87 50	587 50
Sept 10	AB Ltd			PL2	550	96 25	646 25
Sept 21	Fashions Ltd			PL1	480	84 00	564 00
Sept 30	AB Ltd			PL2	390	68 25	458 25
	Total			GL2/3	1,920	336 00	2,256 00

Sales Day Book **Page 1**

			Invoice no.	Folio	Net £ p	VAT £ p	Gross £ p
19x9							
Sept 7	S. Jordan			SL1	300	52 50	352 50
Sept 16	Alpha Ltd			SL2	260	45 50	305 50
Sept 28	S. Jordan			SL1	200	35 00	235 00
	Total			G1	760	133 00	893 00

Purchases Ledger **Page 1**

DR						Fashions Ltd a/c					CR
				£	p					£	p
						19x7					
						Sept	1	Purchases	PDB1	587	50
						Sept	21	Purchases	PDB1	564	00

Page 2

DR						AB Ltd a/c					CR
				£	p					£	p
						19x7					
						Sept	10	Purchases	PDB1	646	25
						Sept	30	Purchases	PBD1	458	25

Sales Ledger **Page 1**

DR						S. Jordan a/c					CR
				£	p					£	p
19x9											
Sept	7	Sales	SDB1	352	50						
Sept	28	Sales	SDB1	235	00						

Page 2

DR						Alpha Ltd a/c					CR
				£	p					£	p
19x9											
Sept	16	Sales	SDB1	305	50						

General Ledger **Page 1**

DR						Sales a/c					CR
				£	p					£	p
						19x9					
						Sept	30	Total for month	SDB1	760	

Page 2

DR						Purchases a/c					CR
				£	p					£	p
19x9											
Sept	30	Total for month		1,920							

Page x

DR								**VAT a/c**			CR
				£	p					£	p
19x9 Sept	30	Total for month	PDB11	336		19x9 Sept	30	Total for month	SDB1	133	
						Sept	30	Balance c/d		203	
				336						336	
Oct	1	Balance b/d		203							

Note:

1. Note the rulings of the Purchases Day Book and the Sales Day Book contain two additional sets of columns to accommodate the recording of VAT. When additional sets of columns are added to a normal day book, it is known as an **analytical day book**. An analytical Sales Day Book may contain additional sets of columns for classifying sales, for example into products or geographical areas. The Purchases Day Book may similarly be used for purposes of classifying purchases.
2. The creditors' personal accounts show the gross value, i.e. purchase price plus VAT, whereas the Purchases account in the General Ledger shows the value of purchases net of VAT. The VAT account is therefore debited with the input tax.
3. The debtors' personal accounts record the gross value of sales, but the Sales account in the General Ledger records sales net of VAT. The output tax is entered on the credit side of the VAT account.
4. The VAT account is balanced off at the month-end, showing a debit balance of £203. This means that Linda can claim back this amount from HM Customs and Excise.

Calculations of VAT

When the selling price excluding VAT and the rate of VAT are given, calculations of VAT are straightforward:

VAT = net selling price × rate of tax

Thus VAT on a product, having a net selling price of £10 and being subjected to a 17.5% tax is simply £10 × 17.5% = £1.75. However, when the gross selling price together with the VAT rate is given, calculations of VAT and net selling price are as follows.

Calculation of VAT

$$\textbf{VAT} = \frac{\text{VAT percentage rate} \times \text{gross value of sales (or gross value of sales)}}{100 + \text{VAT percentage rate}}$$

$$\textbf{Net selling price (or net sales value)} = \frac{100 \times \text{gross selling price}}{100 + \text{VAT percentage rate}}$$

Alternatively,

Net sales value = gross sales value – VAT

Thus if the selling price of an article, including VAT is £46 and the rate of VAT is 17.5%, VAT on the article is $\frac{17.5}{117.5} \times £46 = £6.85$ and the net selling price is £46 – £6.85 = £39.15.

ACT 7.2

The following are the gross sales values of a number of transactions:

(i) £780
(ii) £1,000
(iii) £5.40

The rate of VAT is 17.5%. Calculate for each of the above:

a VAT
b net sales value.

► Answer in appendix

VAT on expenses and purchases of fixed assets

VAT on expenses and on fixed assets is treated in the same way as the input tax on purchases. Normally, expenses and fixed assets accounts should not include VAT. If, however, VAT on these items cannot be reclaimed, then it should be included in expenses or the cost of the fixed assets.

VAT and the final accounts

When a business is registered for VAT the final accounts should normally show all items, other than those on which VAT paid cannot be recovered, as net figures, i.e. exclusive of VAT. As a matter of fact, SSAP 5 requires that 'turnover shown in the Profit and Loss account should exclude VAT on taxable outputs'. In the Balance Sheet, amounts for debtors and creditors will appear as gross figures, because they represent the amounts owing to or owed by the business. In addition to these, there will be another figure in the Balance Sheet, provided the VAT account shows a balance on the date the Balance Sheet is prepared. A debit balance on the VAT account will be shown as a current asset (money reclaimable from HM Customs and Excise) and a credit balance (money owing to the tax authorities) will be shown as a current liability.

► A debit on the VAT account is an asset: tax reclaimable.

► A credit in the VAT account is a liability: tax owing.

Finally, according to SSAP 5, 'irrecoverable VAT allocatable to fixed assets ... should be included in their cost where practicable and material.'

VAT returns

Every VAT registered business has to complete a VAT return, obtainable from HM Customs and Excise, and forward it, together with any payment due, to the tax authorities every three months. The tax return includes the following details:

- VAT due
- VAT deductible
- net VAT payable or reclaimable
- value of outputs excluding any VAT
- value of inputs excluding any VAT
- declaration to the effect that information given on the form is true and complete.

Chapter summary

- VAT is a tax on the supply of goods and services. For suppliers it is an output tax. For purchasers it is an input tax.
- VAT should be recorded in the books of prime entry and the relevant accounts of the Ledger.
- The Purchases Day Book and the Sales Day Book should contain net and gross values of transactions and the amount of VAT. These are recorded in analytical day books for credit transactions and an analytical cash book for cash transactions.
- The double-entry rules for relevant ledger accounts are as follows:
  For sales:
  - o debit the customer's account with the gross value
  - o credit the VAT account with the amount of VAT
  - o credit the Sales account with net value of sales.

  For purchases and expenses:
  - o debit the VAT account with the amount of VAT
  - o debit the Purchases or Expense account with net value of purchases or expenses
  - o credit the supplier's account with the gross value of purchases or expenses.
- All items in the Profit and Loss account are shown net of VAT.
- In the Balance Sheet the amount of VAT due is shown as a current liability, and VAT reclaimable is shown as a current asset.
- VAT debtors and creditors are shown in terms of gross value of sales and purchases respectively.
- VAT-registered businesses are required to send a VAT return quarterly to HM Customs and Excise, together with any payments due.

ACT 7.3

1 What is VAT? What is meant by the terms 'zero rate' and 'standard rate'?

► No answer given

2 Distinguish between an input tax and an output tax in the context of VAT.

(extract from AAT)

► No answer given

3 Write brief notes on the requirements to register for Value Added Tax.

► No answer given

1/12/94 - Did this in class.

4 Rebecca Hanley is a sole trader. Her credit sales for the month of April are as follows.

19x4			£
April	1	To K. Roberts	160
	7	To M. Mohendra	200
	8	To Sen and Co.	250
	15	To K. Roberts	125
	20	To M. Mohendra	150
	25	To R. London	80
	30	To Sen and Co	150

All figures shown are net before adding VAT. The rate of VAT is 17.5%.

You are required to enter up the above transactions in Rebecca's Sales Day Book, Sales Ledger and the General Ledger.

► Answer in appendix

Homework – 1/12/94

5 The credit sales and purchases of AB Ltd for the month of June 19x3 were:

Net (after deduction of trade discount but before the addition of VAT)		£
June	1 Purchases from K. Fonda	500
	5 Sales to R. Dobbins	180
	10 Purchases from Northern Wholesalers Ltd	350
	12 Sales to AB Ltd	400
	15 Sales to Linda Web	50
	20 Purchases from K. Fonda	300
	25 Sales to R. Dobbins	250
	30 Purchases from Northern Wholesalers Ltd	500
	30 Sales to AB Ltd	350

You are required to write up the Sales and Purchases Day Books, Sales and Purchases Ledgers, and the General Ledger to record the above transactions.
Take the rate of VAT to be 17.5%.

► No answer given

6 B. Kent is a wholesaler cloth merchant. His books reveal the following VAT figures for his tax quarter beginning on 1 May and ending on 31 July 19x2.

	£
Output tax charged to customers	
May	20,508.74
June	21,304.06
July	18,600.15
Input tax on invoices from suppliers of goods	
May	6,380.62
June	5,791.56
July	5,621.35
Input tax on other items (eg. consumables)	
May	410.50
June	387.16
July	199.67

You are required to draw up the VAT account in B. Kent's General Ledger for the quarter and balance it off on 31 July 19x2.

► No answer given

7 During the quarter ended 31 May 19x6, the raw materials purchases by John Henry Limited, manufacturers of furniture, amounted to £181,590 before VAT at the standard rate of 15% and, in addition, the following items of expenditure occurred.

March		£	£
12	Highway Garage Limited		
	Motor van C478 TBR	9,500	
	VAT @ 15%	1,425	
		10,925	
	Vehicle excise duty	100	11,025
19	Smith Motors Limited		
	Motor van C379 KTA	8,000	
	VAT @ 15%	1,200	
		9,200	
	Vehicle excise duty	100	9,300

		£	£
	April		
23	Super Machines Limited		
	Used drilling machine		
	Number KXY54	8,200	
	VAT @ 15%	1,230	9,430
May			
7	Highway Garage Limited		
	Car repairs	210	
	VAT at 15%	31.50	241.50
20	Machine Repairs Limited		
	Renovation drilling machine		
	Number KXY54	500	
	VAT @ 15%	75	575

Note: This renovation was necessary before the drilling machine could be used in the factory.

The VAT due to the Customs and Excise Department on 28 February 19x6 amounting to £ 84,000, was paid on 20 March 19x6.

During the quarter ended 31 May 19x6, the company's turnover, before VAT, amounted to £800,000 and analysed for VAT purposes was as follows.

	Turnover £
Taxable – standard rate	620,000
zero rated	120,000
Non-taxable – exempt	60,000
	800,000

Required:

a Prepare the analytical Purchases Day Book for the three months ended 31 May 19x6 of John Henry Limited. **Note:** Raw material purchases for the three months ended 31 May 19x6 should be shown as one entry in the Purchases Day Book.

b Prepare the account for HM Customs and Excise – VAT for the three months ended 31 May 19x6 in the accounts of John Henry Limited.

(AAT)

► No answer given

8 Financial statements

Chapter objectives

By the end of this chapter, you should be able to:

- explain the difference between gross profit and net profit
- prepare a simple trading and profit and loss account for a sole trader
- prepare a balance sheet for a sole trader, after the trading and profit and loss account is completed
- understand the meaning of the following terms: profit and loss account, gross profit, net profit, opening/closing stocks, carriage inwards/outwards, drawings, trial balance.

Introduction

The work in this chapter demonstrates how profit or loss is calculated by preparing a **Trading and Profit and Loss account** from the information provided by the double-entry system, as explained in Chapter 3. After this, we shall see how the profit or loss of the year is dealt with in the Balance Sheet. We saw how the Balance Sheet is constructed in Chapter 3. The preparation of these accounts will be shown for the business of a **sole trader**. Partnership accounts and company accounts will be dealt with in chapters 18 and 19.

► The examples of financial statements in this chapter are for sole traders. Financial statements for partnerships and companies are dealt with in chapters 18 and 19.

► **Financial statements**: Income statement/Trading and Profit and Loss account/the Balance Sheet

THE MEASUREMENT OF PROFIT

Profit is simply the **income** of the business over a given period of time, usually a year. It represents the difference between **revenue** (sales) and **expenses**. There are two types of profit: gross profit and net profit.

Gross profit is the difference between the total value of sales, and cost of sales or cost of goods sold. **Net profit** is the difference between gross profit and all the expenses of running a business, such as rent and rates, electricity etc. Thus:

► **Profit** is the difference between revenue and expenses.

gross profit = sales – cost of sales

However, it may happen that during a certain period, a firm's cost of sales is more than the value of its sales. In such a situation, the firm will not be making any gross profit; instead, it will be operating at a **loss** and the amount of the loss will be given by a negative value of gross profit.

Net profit is the difference between gross profit and all incidental expenses of running the business such as rent and rates, electricity etc. Thus:

net profit = gross profit – expenses

When total expenses are greater than gross profit, net profit will be negative which again amounts to a loss. Remember that loss is the opposite of profit – a negative profit therefore represents a loss, whether it is a gross or a net figure. One word of caution: if we start with a gross loss then, to get the net loss, we need to add the total expenses to the gross loss.

► **Opening stock**: stock unsold at the beginning of the accounting year

► **Closing stock**: stock unsold at end of accounting year

If all the goods bought during a period are sold in that period, the cost of goods sold is simply the purchase cost of the goods in question. If, however, the business has some stock of goods at the beginning of the year, called the **Opening stock**, and has some unsold stock at the end of the year, called the **Closing stock**, the calculation is a bit more involved. In such a case, the cost of goods sold is calculated as follows:

cost of goods = opening stock + purchases – closing stock

Example 8.1 The calculation of gross profit and net profit

Calculate the gross profit and the net profit from the following details.

	£
Opening stock	6,000
Purchases	20,000
Closing stock	5,000
Sales	27,000
Sundry expenses	1,000

Solution

	£	£
Sales		27,000
Less cost of sales:		
Opening stock	6,000	
Add Purchases	20,000	
	26,000	
Less Closing stock	5,000	21,000
Gross profit		6,000
Less sundry expenses		1,000
Net profit		5,000

The calculation of gross profit and net profit has been shown in the form of an account deliberately, because it is important to get into the habit of doing accounts in their proper form, right from the beginning. The above presentation is called a Trading and Profit and Loss account, prepared in vertical format.

► **Returns outwards**

► **Returns inwards** – see Chapter 5

It is quite common in business to return part of the goods purchased to the suppliers because some are defective or because they do not conform to the required specifications. This type of returns (called **returns outwards**) needs to be deducted from the purchases figure to arrive at the true or **net purchases**. Likewise, when returns of goods are made to the business by customers (called **returns inwards**) it is necessary to adjust the sales figures by deducting the value of returns inwards from the value of sales.

► **Carriage inwards**: cost of transport of goods from supplier paid by purchaser

► **Carriage outwards**: cost of transport of goods paid by supplier

Sometimes the business has to pay transport cost (called **carriage inwards**) from the suppliers' premises to their own. This carriage inwards increases the cost of purchases and is therefore to be added onto the cost of purchases. **Carriage outwards**, i.e. the cost of delivering the goods to customers' premises, is a selling expense and is therefore to be deducted, together with other expenses, from the gross profit in order to calculate the net profit.

Quite a few new concepts have been introduced in the last few pages. Before you proceed any further, you should make sure that you understand them by doing the following assignments.

ACT 8.1

1 Calculate for each of the following, the cost of sales.
   - **a** Opening stock £3,000; Purchases £50,000; Closing stock £5,000
   - **b** Opening stock £4,900; Purchases £27,950; Closing stock £2,100
   - **c** Closing stock nil; Purchases £65,550; Returns outwards £2,750; Opening stock £9,275
   - **d** Purchases £45,780; Closing stock £4,780; Carriage inwards £1,250; Returns outwards £5,150; Opening stock £9,575

► Answer in appendix

2 Calculate, for each of the following, the gross profit or loss, and the net profit or loss.
   - **a** Sales £55,000; Cost of sales £32,000; Expenses £12,800
   - **b** Sales £75,000; Returns inwards £5,000; Cost of sales £60,250; Expenses £10,250
   - **c** Sales £64,750; Cost of sales £69,250; Expenses £12,800; Returns inwards £3,750

► Answer in appendix

3 Calculate, for each of the following, the cost of sales, the gross profit or loss and the net profit or loss.
   - **a** Sales £80,000; Purchases £50,000; Returns inwards £3,700; Returns outwards £5,000; Opening stock £5,000; Closing stock £6,000; Expenses £29,000; Carriage inwards £2,150
   - **b** Sales £75,500; Returns inwards £4,250; Purchases £55,555; Returns outwards £2,900; Carriage inwards £2,500; Opening stock £7,500; Closing stock £6,000; Expenses £17,865
   - **c** Sales £99,990; Purchases £94,880; Opening stock £9,999; Closing stock £1,880; Expenses £19,465; Returns inwards £5,450; Returns outwards £3,333; Carriage inwards £2,215

► Answer in appendix

THE TRADING AND PROFIT AND LOSS ACCOUNT

Like the Balance Sheet, the Trading and Profit and Loss account can be prepared either in horizontal format or vertical format. To begin with, we'll use both formats, but later on we shall be using the vertical format only, as it is the more popular one.

► **Trading and Profit and Loss account** or **Income Statement**

Although the Trading account and the Profit and Loss account may be considered as two distinct and separate accounts, the modern practice is to consider them as one account having two parts. In the first part, gross profit is calculated, and in the second, net profit.

► **Trading account** shows gross profit

► **Profit and Loss account** shows net profit. They are usually combined.

Example 8.2 illustrates the preparation of a Trading and Profit and Loss account from a given set of ledger accounts.

Example 8.2 Preparation of Trading and Profit and Loss account from given set of ledger accounts: sole trader

The following accounts have been taken out from the books of Clive Wallace on 31 December 19x9.

DR						Purchases a/c					CR
				£	p					£	p
19x9 Dec	31	Balance b/d		15,000							

DR						Sales a/c					CR
				£	p					£	p
						19x9 Dec	31	Balance b/d		28,000	

DR						Stock a/c					CR
				£	p					£	p
19x9 Jan	1	Trading a/c (stock on hand)		5,500							

DR						Sundry expenses a/c					CR
				£	p					£	p
19x9 Dec	31	Balance b/d		1,500							

Stock in hand at 31 December 19x9 was valued at £6,000.

You are required to:

a Prepare a Trading and Profit and Loss account for the year ended 31 December 19x9 in
  (i) horizontal format and
  (ii) vertical format.

b Show the appropriate entries in the ledger accounts of Clive Wallace, after the Trading and Profit and Loss account has been prepared.

Solution

a (i) Horizontal format

Clive Wallace
Trading and Profit and Loss account for the year ended 31 December, 19x9

	£		£
Opening stock	5,500	Sales	28,000
Add Purchases	15,000		
	20,500		
Less Closing stock	6,000		
Cost of Goods sold	14,500		
Gross Profit c/d	13,500		
	28,000		28,000
Sundry expenses	1,500	Gross Profit b/d	13,500
Net Profit (transferred to Capital a/c)	12,000		
	13,500		13,500

Note:

1 If the Trading and Profit and Loss account is prepared in horizontal format, it is considered to be a ledger account. The relevant figures are transferred to this account to the same side as they would appear in the ledger accounts as balances. Thus, the sales figure appears as a credit balance in the Sales account. It also appears on the credit side of the Trading and Profit and Loss account.

2 Gross profit is the balancing figure in the Trading part of the account and we describe this by writing 'c/d' against it. This is then brought down on the opposite side to begin the Profit and Loss section of the account. Again, net profit appears as a balancing figure. It is then transferred to the credit side of the Capital account as any profit made by the business belongs to the owner and it will increase his/her capital.

a (ii) Vertical format

Clive Wallace
Trading and Profit and Loss account for the year ended 31 December 19x9

	£	£
Sales		28,000
Less cost of sales:		
Opening stock	5,500	
Add Purchases	15,000	
	20,500	
Less Closing stock	6,000	14,500
Gross profit		13,500
Less Sundry expenses		1,500
Net Profit		12,000

Note carefully the layout and presentation of the account. The cost of sales needs some calculations and these are shown in a separate column. The calculated figure for cost of sales is not put in the working column, but in the end column which contains the sales figure. This is logical as we need to subtract the cost of sales from sales in order to get the gross profit (subtraction is easy if the figures involved are put in the same column!).

b Ledger accounts

DR					**Purchases a/c**					CR
				£	p				£	p
19x9 Dec	31	Balance b/d		15,000		19x9 Dec	31	Transferred to Trading a/c	15,000	

DR				**Sales a/c**					CR	
			£	p					£	p
19x9 Dec	31	Transferred to Trading a/c		28,000		19x9 Dec	31	Balance b/d	28,000	

DR				**Stock a/c**					CR	
			£	p					£	p
19x9 Jan	1	Trading a/c (balance on hand)		5,500		19x9 Dec	31	Transferred to Trading a/c	5,500	
19x9 Jan	1	Trading a/c (stock on hand)		6,000						

DR				**Sundry expenses a/c**					CR	
			£	p					£	p
19x9 Dec	31	Balance b/d		1,500		19x9 Dec	31	Profit/loss a/c	1,500	

The effect of the Trading and Profit and Loss account has been to balance off the Sales, Purchases and Sundry expenses accounts in the General Ledger, with no balances to be brought down to the next year.

The Closing stock figure

You may be wondering where the Closing stock figure comes from. It is not derived from any ledger account; it is found by valuing the stocks in existence, which means physically counting stocks at the end of the accounting year. It is then entered on the debit side of the Stock account and the double entry will be found in the Trading account. Notice that instead of putting Closing stock on the credit side of the Profit and Loss account, it is shown as a deduction from the sum of Opening stock and Purchases. As you know from elementary mathematics, two minuses make a plus; a credit entry put on the debit side as a deduction virtually amounts to a credit entry in its own right. Finally, this year's Closing stock will, of course, become the Opening stock for the next year, as indeed, last year's Closing stock gave us the Opening stock of the current year.

THE BALANCE SHEET

It is customary to construct a Balance Sheet for a business after its Trading and Profit and Loss account has been prepared. The purpose of preparing a Balance Sheet at this stage is to show the overall effect of various transactions made during the year on the three items: assets, liabilities and capital, listed in the Balance Sheet. The year-end figures for assets and liabilities will be obtained from the balances of the relevant accounts. Only the new capital figure needs to be worked out after the net profit is calculated in the Profit and Loss account. In the Balance Sheet, we start with the capital as at the beginning of the year. Then we add to it the amount of net profit made during the year.

If, however, a loss is made, we deduct it from the opening capital. From this sum, we deduct the amount of money taken out by the owner for his/her personal use, called **drawings**. The resulting figure is the capital as at the end of the year.

Example 8.3 The construction of the Balance Sheet of a sole trader after preparation of the Trading and Profit and Loss account

The following balances have been extracted from the books of David Hollamby, a sole trader, as at 31 December 19x9.

	£
Premises	35,000
Fixture and fittings	5,000
Net profit for the year	18,000
Capital as at 1/1/19x9	30,000
Stocks at 31/12/19x9	6,700
Cash in hand	500
Bank overdraft	2,400
Debtors	7,200
Creditors	9,000
Drawings	5,000

You are required to:

a Prepare David Hollamby's Balance Sheet as at 31 December 19x9.

b Show the Capital and Drawings accounts of David Hollamby as they would appear on 31 December 19x9.

Solution

a

David Hollamby
Balance Sheet as at 31 December 19x9

	£	£	£
Fixed Assets:			
Premises		35,000	
Fixtures and fittings		5,000	
			40,000
Current Assets:			
Stock		6,700	
Debtors		7,200	
Cash in hand		500	
		14,400	
Less Current Liabilities:			
Creditors	9,000		
Bank overdraft	2,400	11,400	
Working Capital			3,000
			43,000
Financed by:			
Capital			30,000
Add Net profit			18,000
			48,000
Less Drawings			5,000
			43,000

Note:

1 Pay particular attention to the layout of the Balance Sheet. We have made use of three columns, first, second and third from the left, for inserting the values of the items listed. In the third column, we've put all the final figures. The first and middle columns are used to show the necessary workings to arrive at the final figures to be inserted in the last column. Thus the Fixed assets total is entered in the last column, the individual asset values in the middle column, and the Liabilities are listed in the first column. The sum of liabilities is not put in the first column, but transferred to the second so that this amount can be deducted from the Current assets total. Finally, Working capital (or net Current assets) is inserted in the third column which is added to the Fixed assets total in order to give us a final figure of £43,000 in the top part of the Balance Sheet.

b Ledger accounts

Capital a/c – David Hollamby

DR			£	p				£	CR p
19x9					19x9				
Dec	31	Drawings a/c	5,000		Jan	1	Balance b/d	30,000	
Dec	31	Balance c/d	43,000		Dec	31	Profit and Loss Account	18,000	
			48,000					48,000	
					19x0				
					Jan	1	Balance b/d	43,000	

Drawings a/c

DR			£	p				£	CR p
19x9					19x9				
Dec	31	Balance b/d	5,000		Dec	31	Capital a/c	5,000	

2 Notice that the Drawings account does not show any balance at all. All the drawings by the owner during the year have already been transferred to the Capital account and there is nothing left to bring forward to the next accounting year.

At the year end, all the accounts in the Ledger will be balanced and a Trial Balance will be extracted. Also, the business will undertake stock-taking to value the Closing stock. The Trial Balance, together with the value of the Closing stock, will form the basis for the preparation of the final accounts. We'll now see, in Example 8.4, how a sole trader's final accounts are prepared from a year-end Trial Balance and the value of Closing stock is arrived at after a proper stock-taking.

Example 8.4 Final accounts for a sole trader prepared from year-end Trial Balance and value of Closing stocks

The following Trial Balance was extracted from the books of Alan Hope, a sole trader, as at 31 December 19x9.

Alan Hope
Trial Balance as at 31 December 19x9

	DR £	CR £
Capital at 1 Jan 19x9		36,650
Premises	29,200	
Fixtures and fittings	2,000	
Motor Van	6,000	
Purchases and Sales	56,000	84,045
Returns	545	400
Carriage inwards	250	
Carriage outwards	500	
Rates	1,700	
Rent received from subletting		1,200
Insurances	525	
Wages	8,895	
Discounts	405	300
Interest on loan	500	

Note:

1 In the Trial Balance two items are occasionally combined into one item in the listing and two figures are given against it – one in the debit column and the other in the credit column. This is quite often done, especially in examination questions, to test the candidate's understanding of ledger balances. Make sure you can identify which figure represents which. Take for example the item 'purchases and sales' from the Trial Balance. Purchases always represent a debit balance because they increase the assets. Sales, on the

Motor van expenses	1,750	
Sundry expenses	3,020	
Drawings	8,650	
Stock at 1 Jan 19x9	9,000	
Loan from Jean Halpin		5,000
Debtors and creditors	6,850	6,345
Cash in hand	150	
Bank balance		2,000
	135,940	135,940

The stock in hand on 31 December 19x9 was valued at £10,950.

You are required to prepare:

a A Trading and Profit and Loss account for the year ended 31 December 19x9

b A Balance Sheet as at 31 December 19x9.

Solution

a

Alan Hope

Trading and Profit and Loss account for the year ended 31 December 19x9

	£	£	£
Sales			84,045
Less Returns inwards			545
			83,500
Less Cost of sales:			
Opening stock		9,000	
Add Purchases	56,000		
Less Returns outwards	400		
	55,600		
Add Carriage inwards	250	55,850	
		64,850	
Less Closing stock		10,950	53,900
Gross Profit			29,600
Add other incomes:			
Rent		1,200	
Discount received		300	1,500
			31,100
Less Expenses:			
Carriage outwards		500	
Rates		1,700	
Insurances		525	
Wages		8,895	
Discount allowed		405	
Interest on loan		500	
Motor van expenses		1,750	
Sundry expenses		3,020	17,295
Net Profit			13,805

other hand, represent revenue, and are therefore shown as a credit balance. Likewise, of the two 'returns' figures, Returns inwards will be given by a debit balance and Return outwards by a credit balance. Again, Discounts allowed (representing an expense) is given by the debit figure, and Discounts received (being a gain) is shown as a credit balance. Debtors and creditors should not give you any problem! Debtors represent assets and therefore should be shown as a debit balance; creditors represent liabilities and are consequently given as a credit balance.

2 In line with common practice, we've prepared the accounts in vertical format. Look carefully at the layout of the accounts and try to remember it, as you'll be expected to do your final accounts in this way. Make provision for three columns in both the accounts. The main figures are always put in the third i.e. the last column. Any workings necessary to arrive at a major figure should be shown in the two preceding columns.

3 Returns inwards mean goods returned by the customers and are therefore deducted from the sales figure to get the net sales figure, or turnover as it is normally called.

4 Two adjustments have been necessary in this example to the purchases figure. Firstly, we have deducted the returns outwards figure from purchases to get the value of net purchases. Secondly we have added carriage inwards, as they tend to increase the purchase price, to it. We transferred the adjusted figure to the second or middle column in line with the first figure in the second column. For other calculations, e.g. net current assets in the balance, we transferred the figure one line below. You might be wondering why we adopt two rules for the same sort of adjustments. Well, the general practice is this: if you do need to write any description against the transferred figure, put it on the line following the line which contains the last figure in the preceding column. Otherwise put it on the same line.

5 A business may have income other than the income from its normal trading, such as rent received from subletting, discounts received, interest received etc. These incomes or gains are always added to the gross profit before other expenses are deducted from it.

6 Notice that carriage outwards is put together with other expenses. This is how it should be treated because carriage outwards is a selling expense. By contrast, carriage inwards, being a cost related to purchases, is shown in the trading section of the account as part of the cost of sales.

7 Notice that the bank balance is shown as a credit balance. What does this mean? It means that the business bank account is overdrawn and is therefore a liability. In the Balance Sheet, we've shown it as such.

8 In the Balance Sheet, we've deducted the long-term liability i.e. the loan from Jean Halpin, from the total net assets. This is in accordance with modern practice. Companies are obliged by law to show long-term liabilities in this way. For other businesses such as the sole trader and partnership, there are no such legal requirements; many accountants would like the company format to be extended to other types of businesses.

b

Alan Hope

Balance Sheet as at 31 December 19x9

	£	£	£
Fixed Assets:			
Premises			29,200
Fixtures and fittings			2,000
Motor van			6,000
			37,200
Current Assets:			
Stock		10,950	
Debtors		6,850	
Cash in hand		150	
		17,950	
Less Current Liabilities:			
Creditors	6,345		
Bank overdraft	2,000	8,345	
Net Current Assets			9,605
			46,805
Less Long-term Liabilities:			
Loan from Jean Halpin			5,000
			41,805
Financed by:			
Capital – 1 Jan 19x9			36,650
Add Net Profit (of the year)			13,805
			50,455
Less Drawings			8,650
			41,805

You might have noticed one interesting and very useful fact in the course of preparing the final accounts. Any item in the Trial Balance is used once only in either the Trading and Profit and Loss account or the Balance Sheet, but never in both of them. All items representing assets, capital and any other increase or decrease (e.g. drawings) therein and liabilities, should of course be transferred to the Balance Sheet; all the remaining items representing revenue and other expenses should be included in the Trading and Profit and Loss account. Before you actually start preparing the accounts, you may pencil in, in the Trial Balance, some codes such as T (meaning Trading account), PL (meaning Profit and Loss account), and BS (meaning Balance Sheet) against each item included in the Balance Sheet. This 'sorting' will help you to prepare the accounts quickly and accurately.

However, any additional information given outside the Trial Balance will have to be included in both the accounts. Take, for example, the case of 'Closing stock'. The value of Closing stock is given outside the Trial Balance and we've used this figure, as you'll see, twice: firstly in the Trading account, and secondly in the Balance Sheet under Current assets. These two entries are necessary in the accounts because of the dual nature of a transaction.

The Closing stock figure has not yet been recorded in the Ledger with the usual double entries. We therefore need two entries in our accounts. Firstly in the Trading account, Closing stock is seen as a reduction in the cost of sales. Secondly, in the Balance Sheet, it is treated as an asset on the balance sheet date.

This principle applies to any other information that is obtained at the last minute after the ledger accounts have been balanced. If you get in an assignment any additional information that is appended to the Trial Balance, don't forget to make two entries – firstly in the Trading and Profit and Loss account, and secondly in the Balance Sheet. This will come up again in subsequent chapters.

Chapter summary

- Businesses usually make a distinction between gross profit and net profit.
- Gross profit is the difference between the value of sales and the cost of sales.
- Net profit is the difference between gross profit and expenses.
- The Trading and Profit and Loss account, prepared in either horizontal format or vertical format, indicates how gross profit and net profit are ascertained.
- The year-end Balance Sheet indicates how the financial position of the business in terms of its assets, liabilities and capital has changed over the year.

ACT 8.2

For each of questions 1 to 5, put a tick against the letter representing the best choice from among the four possible answers given.

1 The following figures have been extracted from the records of a sole trader:
Sales £49,600; Purchases £25,000
Opening Stock £5,600; Closing Stock £7,000.
The cost of sales is:

A £26,000
B £23,600
C £25,000
D £49,600.

2 The double entry for the net profit is found:

A On the debit side of the Capital account
B On the credit side of the Capital account
C On the Bank account
D Nowhere, as it does not exist.

3 If the Closing stocks were overvalued, the gross profit would be:

A Overstated
B Understated
C Unaffected
D Undeterminable.

4 A Balance Sheet is:

A Another name for the Trial Balance
B A complete list of balances extracted from the Ledger
C A statement of assets, liabilities and capital of a business at a given time
D A specially ruled paper to balance an account.

► Answers in appendix

5 Working capital is:

A The difference between current assets and current liabilities

B The difference between fixed assets and current assets

C The sum of cash in hand and cash at bank

D Fixed assets plus current assets minus current liabilities.

► Answer in appendix

6 The following information was collected from the records of D. Spencer, a retailer, on 31 December 19x0.

	£
Stock – 1 Jan 19x0	5,000
Stock – 31 December 19x0	6,000
Purchases	35,500
Sales	50,000
Administrative expenses	2,500
Advertising expenses	1,500
Transport expenses (i.e. delivery of goods	1,000
Occupancy expenses	1,500

You are required to prepare a Trading and Profit and Loss account for the year ended 31 December, 19x0 in **(i)** horizontal format and **(ii)** vertical format.

► Answer in appendix

7 The following information relates to the business of I. Smart, a sole trader, as at 30 September 19x9.

	£
Sales	72,220
Purchases	48,715
Returns inwards	3,780
Returns outwards	4,030
Carriage inwards	500
Opening stock	9,850
Closing stock	5,780
Wages	9,950
Rent and rates	5,750
Carriage outwards	250
Sundry expenses	9,990

You are required to prepare a Trading and Profit and Loss account for I. Smart for the year ended 31 September 19x9 in **(i)** horizontal format and **(ii)** vertical format.

► No answer given

From now onwards, you should prepare your accounts in vertical format.

8 The following Trial Balance has been extracted from the books of Julie Hampshire, a sole trader, as at 31 March 19x0.

Julie Hampshire

Trial Balance as at 31 March 19x0

	DR £	CR £
Stock – 1 April 19x9	5,000	
Purchases	21,500	
Sales		35,150
Returns inwards	210	
Returns outwards		325
Rates	905	
Heating and lighting	1,720	
Wages	11,000	
Insurance	500	
Premises	38,000	
Fixtures and fittings	1,500	
Motor van	6,000	
Drawings	5,600	
Capital		65,425
Debtors	4,160	
Sundry expenses	825	3,250
Creditor		
Cash at bank	4,000	
Cash in hand	120	
Motor expenses	3,110	
	104,150	104,150

Stock at 31 March 19x0 was valued at £5,780.

You are required to prepare a Trading and Profit and Loss account for the year ended 31 March 19x0 and a Balance Sheet as at that date.

► Answer in appendix

9 The following is the Trial Balance of D. Ramsay as at 30 June 19x1.

	DR £	CR £
Premises	20,000	
Fittings	2,000	
Motor vehicle	6,500	
Sales		75,000
Purchases	50,000	
Carriage inwards	560	
Carriage outwards	625	
Stock – 1 July 19x0	7,850	
Returns inwards	650	
Returns outwards		750
Salaries and wages	14,500	
Rates	1,200	
Insurance	750	
Interest received		150
Debtors	9,550	
Creditors		12,150
Motor expenses	2,200	
Discounts allowed	600	
Discounts received		750
Cash in hand	200	
Sundry expenses	950	
Drawings	10,100	
Bank		1,435
Capital		38,000
	128,235	128,235

Stock at 30 June 19x1 was valued at £10,125.

You are required to prepare the following for D. Ramsay.

a A Trading and Profit and Loss account for the year ended 30 June 19x1

b A Balance Sheet as at that date.

► No answer given

10 The following Trial Balance was extracted from the books of Billy Cooper as at 31 December 19x0.

	DR £	CR £
Capital – B.Cooper		50,344
Stocks – 1 Jan. 19x0	21,980	
Purchases	74,294	
Carriage on purchases	260	
Land and buildings	25,000	
Fixtures	4,500	
Cash in hand	175	
Cash at bank	2,380	
Carriage outwards	615	
Commission received		1,250
Wages and salaries	14,785	
Interest on loan	1,000	
Loan from R.McKay		10,000
Debtors	12,350	
Creditors		9,780
Rates	1,250	
Heating and lighting	1,640	
Advertising	620	
Sundry expenses	790	
Repairs to building	1,125	
Drawings	10,500	
Sales		101,890
	173,264	173,26

Stock at 31 December was valued at £25,750.

Billy Cooper asks you to prepare the following.

a A Trading and Profit and Loss account for the year ended 31 December 19x0

b A Balance Sheet as at that date.

► Answer in appendix

11 The following is the Trial Balance of B. Obote as at 31 March 19x8.

	DR £	CR £
Returns	450	755
Discounts	495	565
Debtors and creditors	10,812	12,679
Purchases and sales	64,000	101,500
Drawings and capital – B.Obote	12,200	46,278
Fixtures	4,200	
Office machines	900	
Rates	2,500	
Heating and lighting	1,950	
Telephone charges	630	
Selling and distributing expenses	2,795	
Carriage inwards	870	

Stocks – 1 April 19x7	15,785	
Wages	16,280	16,280
Sundry expenses	950	
Cash in hand	210	
Bank		3,250
Premises	30,000	
	165,027	165,027

wages are in wrong column.

Stock at 31 March 19x8 was valued at £20,225.

You are required to prepare:

a A Trading and Profit and Loss account for the year ended 31 March, 19x8

b A Balance Sheet as at that date.

► No answer given

12 The following Trial Balance was extracted from the books of C. Dickens as at 31 December 19x2.

	DR £	CR £
Opening stock	12,000	
Purchases and sales	75,900	110,250
Returns	750	875
Carriage inwards	705	
Premises	30,000	
Fixtures	3,500	
Motor vehicle	7,000	
Debtors and creditors	15,900	16,800
Discounts	320	910
Cash in hand	250	
Cash at bank	2,225	
Rates	1,480	
Interior decorations	1,200	
Interest	750	
Loan from J. Austin		7,500
Salaries and wages	18,750	
Heating and lighting	1,830	
Motor expenses	2,310	
Insurance	950	
General expenses	880	
Drawings	8,200	
Capital – C. Dickens		48,565
	184,900	184,900

20/10/94

Did this in class.

Stock at 31 December 19x2 was valued at £20,190.

You are required to prepare for C.Dickens:

a A Trading and Profit and Loss account for the year ended 31 December 19x2

b A Balance Sheet as at that date.

► Answer in appendix

9 Adjustments to the final accounts 1 – accruals and prepayments

Chapter objectives

By the end of this chapter, you should be able to:

- deal with year end adjustments to revenue and expenses accounts
- make adjustments for accruals and prepayments in the final accounts
- understand the meaning of the following terms: accruals, prepayments, non-trading income, accruals (or matching) concept.

Introduction

In Chapter 8, we discussed how the final accounts of a sole trader are prepared. We saw that these accounts were part of the double-entry system with many of the accounts being closed off at the end of the accounting year.

This and the next two chapters extend these ideas further by examining how we deal with some additional information which might emerge at the end of the financial year and which has not yet been recorded in the ledger accounts. This additional information may relate, for example, to some unpaid and/or prepaid expenses. Again we may need to make provision for certain items such as **bad debts** (debtors who fail to pay off their debts) and **depreciation** on some fixed assets which lose part of their value because of normal wear and tear, obsolescence etc. We need to make adjustments to our accounts for these. We'll then show how these adjustments will affect our profit calculations in the Trading and Profit and Loss accounts and how they will affect the assets and liabilities in the Balance Sheet.

In this chapter, making adjustments to the final accounts for **accruals** and **prepayments** is explained. In Chapter 10, we shall deal with bad debts and provision for bad and doubtful debts. We shall discuss in Chapter 11 the necessary adjustments required for depreciation of fixed assets and see how the various adjustments can be incorporated in the form of an extended Trial Balance in order to simplify the task of preparing the final accounts with the necessary adjustments.

ACCRUALS AND PREPAYMENTS

Accruals

► **Accruals:** expenses due but not yet paid – a debit in the Profit and Loss account, a current liability in the Balance Sheet.

Accrual of expenses refers to expenses due but not yet paid, i.e. not paid by the end of the accounting year. In other words, accruals refer to any expenses incurred during a given period for which no payments have been made during the same period. This is quite common in business and arises because of normal delays in making payments, particularly when such payments are to be made at the year end and there is delay in receiving invoices or statements from the creditors.

Any expenses could accrue, but common examples of accruals are telephone charges, electricity and gas charges, and wages.

The **accrual or Matching principle**, as discussed in Chapter 6, requires that any expenses accrued during a period, whether they are actually paid or not, should be brought into the accounts to match up with the revenue of the same period. This therefore calls for adjustments to the accounts.

► **Accrual or matching principle**: see Chapter 6

Adjustment for accruals can be made by altering the ledger accounts (Example 9.1) or directly in the Profit and Loss account and Balance Sheet (Example 9.2).

The necessary adjustments for such expenses are illustrated in Example 9.1.

Example 9.1 Adjusting for accruals altering the ledger accounts

John Ashworth's Trial Balance prepared on 31 December 19x9, included the following item.

	£
Wages	10,520

It was later discovered that wages due but not yet paid at 31 December 19x9 amounted to £250.

You are required to show the necessary adjustments to:

a The Wages account

b The Profit and Loss account

c The Balance Sheet.

Note:

1 The Wages account is debited with the amount accrued. In the description column you can write either 'accrual' or 'balance c/d'. Notice that the amount of wages that has to be transferred to the Profit and Loss account is increased from £10,520 to £10,770.

2 The Profit and Loss account is shown in horizontal format, but it could as well be shown in vertical format.

Solution

a

DR		**Wages a/c**							CR
			£	p				£	p
19x9					19x9				
Dec	31	Balance b/d	10,520		Dec	31	Profit and Loss account	10,770	
Dec	31	Balance c/d (accrual)	250						
			10,770					10,770	
					19x0				
					Jan	1	Balance b/d (accrual)	250	

b

DR		**Profit and Loss a/c for the year ended 19x9 (extract only)**							CR
			£	p				£	p
		Wages	10,770						

c

John Ashworth
Balance Sheet as at 31 December 19x9 (extract only)

	£	£	£
Current Liabilities			
Accruals		250	

3 The Balance Sheet extract shows wages due, i.e. an accrual, as a current liability because the amount due has to be paid very early in the next accounting year. Notice that the Wages account shows a credit balance representing a liability.

Adjusting for accruals directly

Sometimes rather than altering the ledger accounts as shown in Example 9.1 accruals are dealt with directly on the Profit and Loss account and the Balance Sheet. In this case the Profit and Loss account (in vertical format) will appear as in Example 9.2.

Example 9.2 Adjusting for accruals directly (without altering the ledger accounts)

John Ashworth

Profit and Loss account for the year ended 31 December 19x9 (extract only)

	£	£	£
Expenses:			
Wages	10,520		
Add amount due	250		
		10,770	

You start with the Trial Balance figure for wages inserting it in the first column. Then you add the amount due or accrued to the Trial Balance figure and transfer the sum to the second column. This figure is the adjusted figure for wages.

The Balance Sheet will be the same as shown in Example 9.1.

Prepayments

► **Prepayments**: expenses paid for a future accountancy period – a debit in the Profit and Loss account, an asset on the Balance Sheet.

Prepayments are just the opposite of accruals. They refer to expenses paid during a certain accounting period, part of which relates to the next period. Examples of expenses which might be paid in advance are rent and rates, and insurance premia.

The accrual concept requires, once again, that expenses paid in advance for the next period are to be deducted from the amount shown in the Trial Balance so that the actual expenses of the period are matched with the revenue of the same period. Example 9.3 illustrates the necessary adjustments to the relevant accounts for prepaid expenses.

Example 9.3 Adjusting for prepayments by altering the ledger accounts

The following is the Rates account of Susan Kapadia for the year ended 31 December 19x1.

DR		Rates a/c						CR	
			£	p				£	p
19x1									
May	2	Bank	750						
Oct	6	Bank	750						

The rates due for the year amounted to £1,125 only.

You are required to:

a Show the necessary entries in the rates account for the prepaid amount and balance off the account.

b Show extracts from the Profit and Loss account for the year, and

Balance Sheet as at 31 December 19x1 to show how the rates prepaid are treated therein.

Solution

a

DR			Rates a/c					CR		
			£	p					£	p
19x1					19x1					
May	2	Bank	750		Dec	31	Profit and Loss account		1,125	
Oct	6	Bank	750		Dec	31	Balance c/d (prepayment)		375	
19x2			1,500						1,500	
Jan	1	Balance b/d (prepayment)	375							

b

Susan Kapadia
Profit and Loss account for the year ended 31 December, 19x1 (extract only)

	£	£	£
Expenses:			
Rates		1,125	
or alternatively,			
Rates	1,500		
Less amount prepaid	375		
		1,125	

Susan Kapadia
Balance Sheet as at 31 December 19x1 (extract only)

	£	£	£
Current Assets:			
Prepayments		375	

Note:

1. In balancing off the Rates account, we enter at the year end the actual amount of rates that should be charged for the year, i.e. £1,125, on the credit side with the description, 'Profit and Loss account'. The balancing figure of £375 represents the amount prepaid and appears on the credit side. Finally, the balance b/d appears on the left hand side.
2. If prepayment is already adjusted through the Rates account, the adjusted figure, i.e. £1,125 in this case, appears as an expense in the Profit and Loss account. If however, the Rates account has not yet been adjusted with the prepaid amount, the adjustment for the prepayment can be shown in the Profit and Loss account, as in the alternative answer above.
3. The amount prepaid is an asset because the person or organization receiving the amount – the local authority in this case – is a debtor and owes it to you. You can in fact get back the prepaid amount or a fraction thereof if you decide to close down and sell (if you own it) or leave (if you simply rented it) the premises before 31 March 19x2 (which is the local authority's financial year). It is therefore shown as a current asset in the Balance Sheet.

Unpaid and prepaid revenue receivable

A business may receive some income such as rent received from subletting part of the premises, or franchizing (e.g. letting part of the floor area to other organizations) which is not strictly speaking trading income. We call this **non-trading income**. Now this non-trading income, like an expense, may be unpaid or prepaid. We therefore need to adjust this to the accounts to conform to the accruals or matching concept.

Unpaid income

If a part of the income, such as rent for the year from subletting, remains unpaid, we still need to include the amount not received in calculating the income of the year. The actual entries necessary in the income account at the end of the financial year, together with the required adjustments in the Profit and Loss account and the Balance Sheet, are shown in Example 9.4.

Example 9.4 Adjusting for unpaid income

On 1 January 19x9, Jason Jacobs sublets part of his business premises and receives rent of £600 per quarter in arrears on the first day of April, July October and January. For the year ended 31 December 19x9, he received rent for the first three quarters.

You are required to:

a Show the rent receivable account as at 31 December 19x9, after you have made the appropriate adjustments for the rent income due, but not received.

b Show extracts from the Profit and Loss account and the Balance Sheet as at 31 December 19x9 to show how the rent income due is treated therein.

Solution

a

DR			Rent receivable a/c							CR
				£	p				£	p
19x9						19x9				
Jan	1	Profit and Loss account		2,400						
						April	1	Bank	600	
						July	1	Bank	600	
						Oct	1	Bank	600	
						Dec	31	Balance c/d (unpaid rent)	600	
				2,400					2,400	
Jan	1	Balance b/d		600						

Note:

1 You credit the rent receivable account with £600 (shown as balance c/d) to work out the expected income for the year which is then transferred to the Profit and Loss account. You will recall that any non-trading income is added to the gross profit of the year. This is exactly what we have done here.

2 Notice that against gross profit we have written 'b/f' (abbreviation for 'brought forward'). When we transfer a balance from one account to another, we usually write 'b/f'. Note that 'b/d' is reserved for bringing down the balance from the same account.

3 All the rest follows the same pattern as in Examples 9.2 and 9.3.

b

Jason Jacobs
Profit and Loss account for the year ended 31 December 19x9 (extract only)

	£	£	
Gross profit b/f			
Add other incomes:			
Rent	2,400		
Alternatively,			
Rent	1,800		
Add amount due	600	2,400	

Jason Jacobs
Balance Sheet as at 31 December 19x9 (extract only)

	£	£	£
Current assets:			
Rent receivable		600	

Income prepaid

An income prepaid represents the complete reversal of income unpaid. The prepaid amount is therefore deducted from the total money received, as it does not represent an income for the current period, and the resulting figure is added to the gross profit in the Profit and Loss account. The amount received in advance is a liability, as that money is owed to the tenant and is therefore included in current liabilities in the Balance Sheet. Example 9.5 illustrates this.

► **Income prepaid**: payment received in one accountancy period for goods or services to be delivered later: a liability

Example 9.5 Income prepaid

Mike McDermott has rented out part of his business premises at an annual rent of £2,000. For the year ended 31 March 19x2, he received by cheque, the following from his tenant.

19x1	May 1	£500
	Aug 1	£500
	Nov 1	£500
19x2	Feb 1	£1,000

You are required to:

a Show Mike's Rent receivable account as at 31 March 19x2, after the necessary entries of prepaid rent were made.

b Show how the rent received in advance will be shown in his Profit and Loss account for the month ended 31 March 19x2 and in his Balance Sheet as at that date.

Solution

a

DR		Rent receivable a/c							CR
			£	p				£	p
19x2					19x1				
Mar	31	Profit and Loss account	2,000		May	1	Bank	500	
					Aug	1	Bank	500	
Mar	31	Balance c/d (prepayment)	500		Nov	1	Bank	500	
					19x2				
					Feb	1	Bank	1,000	
			2,500					2,500	
					April	1	Balance b/d	500	

b

Mike McDermott
Profit and Loss account for the year ended 31 March 19x2
(extract only)

	£	£	£
Gross Profit b/f			
Add other incomes:			
Rent			2,000
Alternatively,			
Rent		2,500	
Less amount prepaid		500	2,000

Mike McDermott
Balance Sheet as at 31 March 19x2

	£	£	£
Current Liability Rent received in advance		500	

You can see that the treatment of income received in advance is similar to that of income due but not yet received but the entries are reversed. The effect of a 'received in advance' income is to reduce the net profit of the year whereas an 'income due but not yet received' increases the net profit. In a Balance Sheet, a prepayment of an income is shown as a liability whereas income due is shown as a current asset.

Now try the following assignment.

ACT 9.1

1 At the end of a certain year, a trader's Trial Balance shows heating and lighting as £2,500 with a footnote that the amount owing for this item is £175.
Now answer the following.
   a What is the generally accepted name for this £175?
   b Do you need to show this amount in the Profit and Loss account? If so, how? If not, why not?
   c Will this amount appear on the Balance Sheet? If so, where? If not, why not?

► Answer in appendix

2 Sultan's accounting year ends on 31 December each year. At the end of a certain year, the Insurances account, as given below, shows that £1,600 has been paid but the premium due for the year amounts to £1,200.

DR			Insurances a/c					CR	
			£	p				£	p
May	5	Bank	800						
Oct	8	Bank	800						

Balance off the Insurances account showing the amount that will be transferred to the Profit and Loss account.

► Answer in appendix

3 Explain briefly how you deal with an unpaid non-trading income such as Commission receivable in the final accounts of a sole trader.

► Answer in appendix

4 Balance off the following Revenue account for the year ended 31 December showing the amount to be transferred to the Profit and Loss account and the balance carried down. Also indicate whether the balance would be shown as a current asset, or as a current liability.

DR					Rent receivable a/c				CR
			£	p				£	p
					Jan	2	Bank	900	
					Apr	3	Bank	900	
					July	2	Bank	900	

The rent due each year is £3,600.

► Answer in appendix

Chapter summary

- Accruals are expenses which have been incurred but have not been paid by the accounting year end. An accrual will increase liabilities or reduce assets.
- Show the full amount of the expense incurred (Trial Balance figure plus amount accrued or due) on the debit side of the Profit and Loss account. Since an accrual is a liability, show this in the Balance Sheet as a current liability.
- Prepayments are expenses paid in advance of the current accounting year.
- For dealing with prepayments of expenses, enter the actual amount incurred (Trial Balance figure minus the amount prepaid) on the debit side of the Profit and Loss account. Since a prepayment is an asset, show this in the Balance Sheet as an asset.
- For unpaid revenue and prepaid revenue, credit the Profit and Loss account with the actual revenue receivable. This means that revenue not received must be added to the Trial Balance figure and prepaid revenue must be deducted from the Trial Balance figure. To complete the double-entry, show revenue due but not yet received as a current asset and revenue received in advance as a liability.

ACT **9.2**

For questions 1 and 2 put a tick against the letter representing the best choice from among the four possible answers given.

1 The Trial Balance showed general expenses as a debit balance of £4,500 and a note stated that £500 general expenses were due but unpaid. In preparing final accounts, you should:

A Debit Profit and Loss account with £4,500 and show £500 as a current liability in the Balance Sheet

B Debit Profit and Loss account with £5,000 and show £500 as a current liability in the Balance Sheet

C Debit Profit and Loss account with £4,000 and show £500 as a current asset in the Balance Sheet

D Debit Profit and Loss account with £5,000 and show £500 as a current asset in the Balance Sheet.

► Answer in appendix

2 The Trial Balance showed rent £3,000 on the debit side and a note stated that rent paid in advance amounted to £750. When preparing final accounts, you should:

A Debit the Profit and Loss account with £2,250 and show rent prepaid of £750 as a current asset in the Balance Sheet

B Debit the Profit and Loss account with £2,250 and show rent prepaid of £750 as a current liability in the Balance Sheet

C Debit the Profit and Loss account with £3,000 and show rent prepaid of £750 as a current asset in the Balance Sheet

D Debit the Profit and Loss account with £3,750 and show rent prepaid of £750 as a current liability in the Balance Sheet.

► Answer in appendix

3 The following information relates to the business of W. Faulkner for the year to 31 December 19x3.

(i) Rent:
Prepaid as at 31 December 19x2 £500; paid during 19x3 £4,000; owing as at 31 December 19x3 £300.

(ii) Motor expenses:
Paid in 19x3 £790; owing at 31 December 19x3 £60.

(iii) Insurance:
Paid during 19x3 £1,650; prepaid at 31 December 19x3 £150.

You are required to write up the Rent, Motor expenses and Insurance accounts in W. Faulkner's Ledger showing the transfers to the final accounts and the balances carried down to the next year.

► No answer given

08/12/94

Did this in class.

4 The following is the Trial Balance of Arthur King as at 31 December, 19x2.

	DR £	CR £
Premises	45,500	
Fixtures	4,500	
Motor van	12,600	
Stocks – 1 Jan 19x2	22,400	
Purchases	99,900	
Sales		120,250
Business rates	3,500	
Wages	6,800	
Heating & lighting	2,600	
Motor van expenses	5,750	
Returns inwards	600	
Discount received		800
Returns outwards		650
Discount allowed	560	
Sundry expenses	2,880	
Trade debtors	10,300	
Trade creditors		20,950
Cash in hand	800	
Bank overdraft		7,000
Drawings	8,400	
Insurance	2,860	
Capital		80,300
	229,950	229,950

The following information is also available.

(i) Stocks at 31 December 19x2 were valued at £25,880.

(ii) Wages due but not yet paid amounted to £250.

(iii) Insurance paid in advance amounted to £715.

You are required to prepare:

a A Trading and Profit and Loss account for the year ended 31 December, 19x2

b A Balance Sheet as at 31 December, 19x2.

► Answer in appendix

10 Adjustments to the final accounts 2 – bad debts and provision for bad and doubtful debts

Chapter objectives

By the end of this chapter, you should be able to:

- write up the bad debts and provision for bad debts accounts in the ledger
- make adjustments for bad debts and provision for bad debts to the final accounts
- understand the meaning of the following terms: bad debts, irrecoverable debts, specific bad debts, provision for bad debts.

BAD DEBTS

► Irrecoverable debts are written off and treated as business expenses in the Profit and Loss account.

There is always a risk that some customers of a business who buy goods on credit may not pay the amount due. A **bad debt** arises when a credit customer, i.e. a debtor, fails to pay his/her accounts. When all attempts to collect the money from the defaulter fail, the debt will be considered as irrecoverable and consequently be **written off**. Such irrecoverable debts will be treated as unavoidable business expenses and will be shown as such in the Profit and Loss account. Obviously, this will tend to reduce the net profit of the organization. Many businesses make a general provision for bad and doubtful debts as they know from experience that some debtors fail to pay their dues each year. This chapter explains how to deal with bad and doubtful debts in the accounting system of an organization.

► The Bad Debts account

When bad debts arise for the first time, you should open a new account in the ledger called the **Bad debts account**. The accounting entries for bad debts are as follows.

Entries for bad debts

- debit the Bad debts account
- credit the 'bad' debtor's account with the amount of the bad debt.

Example 10.1 Writing off bad debts

During the year ended 31 December 19x2, Derek Palmer considered the following debts to be bad, and decided that they should be written off on the dates shown.

31 March	A. King	£250
31 May	J. Gee	£150
30 Sept	R. Kelly	£200

You are required to show how these debts would be dealt with in Derek Palmer's Ledger.

Solution

DR				**A. King a/c**				CR	
			£	p				£	p
19x2 Jan	1	Balance b/d	250		19x2 Mar	31	Bad debts	250	

DR				**J. Gee a/c**				CR	
			£	p				£	p
19x2 Jan	1	Balance b/d	150		19x2 May	31	Bad debts	150	

DR				**R. Kelly a/c**				CR	
			£	p				£	p
19x2 Jan	1	Balance b/d	200		19x2 Sept	30	Bad debts	200	

DR				**Bad debts a/c**				CR	
			£	p				£	p
19x2 Mar	31	A.King	250		19x2 Dec	31	Profit and Loss account	600	
May	31	J.Gee	150						
Sept	30	R.Kelly	200						
			600					600	

Provision for bad debts and doubtful debts

When we can clearly identify the bad debts, we call them **specific bad debts**, and they are dealt with as shown in Example 10.1. In addition to specific bad debts, every business person will anticipate some debts recorded in the Sales ledger to be doubtful and possibly irrecoverable. If no action is taken to deal with doubtful debtors, the net profit calculated at the end of the year may be overstated. As this goes against the principle of Prudence or Conservatism, it is a common practice in business to make a provision for bad and doubtful debts. The amount of this provision can be decided either by inspecting each individual debtor account with a view to estimating the extent to which each debt is doubtful or by taking a certain percentage of total debts based on past experience. Once the amount of the provision for bad and doubtful debts is decided on, adjustments to the accounts will be made at the year end. The double-entry rules for such adjustments are as follows.

Note:

1 Note that an individual debtor's account is closed off as soon as the decision is taken that his/her debts are bad, by crediting it with the amount of the bad debts. The corresponding debit entry is made in the Bad debts account.

2 The Bad debts account is closed off by transferring the total amount to the Profit and Loss account, where it will be treated as an expense, on the last day of the accounting year.

3 Since the accounts of the debtors are balanced by writing off the debts, the amount they owed initially will no longer appear in the total debtors figure. There is therefore no need to make any adjustment to the debtors figure in the Balance Sheet.

► **Specific bad debts**: easily identifiable bad debts

► A provision for bad debts reduces net profit in the Profit and Loss account and decreases the total of debts in the Balance Sheet

► **The Prudence concept**: see Chapter 6

Adjustments for bad debts

- debit the Profit and Loss account
- credit the provision for bad and doubtful debts with the amount of the provision

The effect of creating a provision for a doubtful debt is to reduce both the Net profit in the Profit and Loss account, and the Total debtors figure in the Balance Sheet. Thus, in accordance with the Prudence concept, a provision for doubtful debts tends to understate rather than overstate the net profit earned during the year; it also makes the Debtors figure more realistic by recognizing the fact some debtors fail to pay their debts.

The amount of provision for doubtful debts may not remain the same year after year. At the end of each year, the provision needs to be reviewed in the light of recent experience and new evidence. If the amount of provision needs to be increased, the amount of the increase will be shown as an expense in the Profit and Loss account in that year. Correspondingly, the Debtors figure in the Balance Sheet should be reduced by the new provision, which once again will give a more accurate value of debtors. If, on the other hand, provision for bad debts has to be reduced by a certain amount from the previous year's figure, this will be treated as an unexpected gain in the Profit and Loss account. We can show the adjustment in the Profit and Loss account in two different ways. Either the amount of the decrease (i.e. reduction) can be added to the gross profit as we normally do with any revenue or gain or, alternatively, we can deduct the amount of the decrease from the sum of all expenses in the Profit and Loss account. Either way, the net effect will be the same; it will increase the net profit of the year. In the Balance Sheet, we deduct the new provision from the total Debtors figure in the usual manner.

Example 10.2 illustrates the adjustments that are required in the accounts relating to the provision for bad and doubtful debts.

Example 10.2 Adjustments required for provision for bad debts

The following year-end debtors balances have been extracted from the books of a business, which commenced business on 1 January 19x5.

Year ended	£
31 December 19x5	70,000
31 December 19x6	90,000
31 December 19x7	100,000
31 December 19x8	85,000

The business has decided to make a provision for bad and doubtful debts at the rate of 5 per cent of total debtors at the end of each year.

You are required to show for the years 19x5, 19x6, 19x7 and 19x8, the:

a Provision for bad debts account
b Extract from the Profit and Loss account
c Extract from the Balance Sheets.

Solution

a

DR		**Provision for bad debts a/c**	£	p				CR £	p
19x5					19x5				
Dec	31	Balance c/d	3,500		Dec	31	Profit and Loss a/c	3,500	
19x6					19x6				
Dec	31	Balance c/d	4,500		Jan	1	Balance b/d	3,500	
					Dec	31	Profit and Loss a/c	1,000	
			4,500					4,500	
19x7					19x7				
Dec	31	Balance c/d	5,000		Jan	1	Balance b/d	4,500	
					Dec	31	Profit and Loss a/c	500	
			5,000					5,000	
19x8					19x8				
Dec	31	Profit and Loss a/c	750		Jan	1	Balance b/d	5,000	
Dec	31	Balance c/d	4,250						
			5,000					5,000	
					19x9				
					Jan	1	Balance b/d	4,250	

Workings: Calculation of provision for bad debts

Year		£
19x5	5% × £70,000 =	3,500
19x6	5% × £90,000 =	4,500
19x7	5% × £100,000 =	5,000
19x8	5% × £85,000 =	4,250

In 19x6, provision increased by (£4,500 – £3,500) = £1,000. This amount is therefore charged to the Profit and Loss account.

In 19x7, provision is further increased by (£5,000 – £4,500) = £500, which is charged to the Profit and Loss account.

In 19x8, provision is reduced by (£5,000 – £4,250) = £750, which is considered as a gain and is added to the gross profit in the Profit and Loss account.

b

Profit and Loss account for the year ended 31 December

	19x5 £	£	19x6 £	£	19x7 £	£	19x8 £	£
Gross Profit b/f	*X*		*X*		*X*		*X*	
Add decrease in provision for bad debts								750
Less Expenses								
Provision for bad debts/								
Increase in provision for bad debts	3,500		1,000		500			

c **Balance Sheet as at 31 December**

	19x5 £	19x6 £	19x7 £	19x8 £
Current assets				
Debtors	70,000	90,000	100,000	85,000
Less provision for bad debts	3,500	4,500	5,000	4,250
	66,500	85,500	95,000	80,750

Now try the following assignment to test your understanding of the accounting requirement for dealing with bad debts and provision for them.

ACT 10.1

1 Why is a provision for bad debts made in the accounts of a business?

2 State the ledger entries required for dealing with bad debts.

3 What is the effect of bad debts on the profit of a business?

4 If a business decides to increase its provision for bad and doubtful debts from £150 to £250, how much will be shown as an expense in the Profit and Loss account and how much will be deducted from the debtors figure in the Balance Sheet?

5 A business decides to reduce its provision for bad and doubtful debts from £500 to £400, at the end of the current financial year. How would you show the necessary adjustments for this in both the Profit and Loss account and the Balance Sheet?

► Answers in appendix

Chapter summary

- Bad debts are debts which are irrecoverable and therefore treated as an expense. To write off a bad debt:
  - o debit the Bad debts account,
  - o credit the debtor's account.
- At the end of the year, bad debts are written off as an expense in the Profit and Loss account.
- When a general provision for bad debts is created for the first time:
  - o debit the Profit and Loss account
  - o credit the Provision for bad debts account, with the amount of the provision.

  If, however, an increase in the already existing provision is to be made, put the increase in provision only as an expense in the Profit and Loss account. For a decrease in provision, it is better to add the amount of decrease to the gross profit as the decreased provision is equivalent to an increase in revenue. In all the three cases, show the amount of provision at the end of the year as a deduction from debtors in the Balance Sheet.

ACT **10.2**

For questions 1 and 2, put a tick against the letter representing the best choice from among the four possible answers given.

1 The ledger entries required to record a provision for bad debts are:
  - **A** Credit the personal accounts of debtors and debit the Profit and Loss account
  - **B** Debit the Bad debts account and credit the Provision for bad debts account
  - **C** Credit the Provision for bad debts account and debit the Profit and Loss account
  - **D** Debit the Provision for bad debts account and credit the Profit and Loss account.

2 The Trial Balance shows provision for bad debts of £200 on the credit side and a note states that the provision is to be increased to £250. When preparing final accounts, you should:
  - **A** Debit the Profit and Loss account with £250 and show a provision for bad debts of £250 as a deduction from debtors in the Balance Sheet
  - **B** Debit the Profit and Loss account with £200 and show a provision for bad debts of £250 as a deduction from debtors in the Balance Sheet
  - **C** Credit the Profit and Loss account with £50 and show a provision for bad debts of £200 as a deduction from debtors in the Balance Sheet
  - **D** Debit the Profit and Loss account with £50 and show a provision for bad debts of £250 as a deduction from debtors in the Balance Sheet.

► Answers in appendix

3 On 31 December 19x2, Jim Drake's debtors totalled £20,000. He decided to make a provision for bad and doubtful debts at 10 per cent of debtors.
The debtors figure rose to £22,000 on 31 December 19x3 and Jim Drake decided to maintain the provision at its existing level.
You are required to show for each of the years ended 31 December 19x2 and 19x3:
  - **a** Provision for bad and doubtful debts
  - **b** The appropriate entries in the Profit and Loss account
  - **c** The appropriate Balance Sheet entries on 31 December of each of the two years.

► No answer given

4 The Trial Balance as at 31 May 19x9 of Tip Top Dealers Limited included the following.

	Debit £	Credit £
Purchases ledger control account	654.00	7,348.00
Sales ledger control account	12,360.00	716.00
Provision for doubtful debts		410.00
Bad debts recovered (received from K. L. Blaney)		970.00

Additional information:

(i) K. L. Blaney's bad debt was written off in the accounts for the year ended 31 May 19x7.

(ii) It had now been decided to write off the following debts, due to the company, as irrecoverable.

	£
L. Pink	210.00
G. Slack	50.00

(iii) The Provision for doubtful debts account is not used for actual bad debts written off or for bad debts recovered.

(iv) The company's continuing policy is to maintain a provision for doubtful debts at 2 per cent of outstanding debtors at each accounting year end.

Required:

a Prepare the Provision for doubtful debts account for the year ended 31 May 19x9 in the books of Tip Top Dealers Limited.

b Prepare the entry for debtors and creditors which will be included in the Balance Sheet as at 31 May 19x9 of Tip Top Dealers Limited.

(AAT)

► Answer in appendix

5 The following Trial Balance as at 31 December 19x5, has been extracted from the books of Pat Vine, a sole trader.

	DR £	CR £
Capital		72,091
Premises	59,900	
Fixtures	2,230	
Sales		139,078
Purchases	80,000	
Carriage	5,044	
Stock as at 1 Jan 19x5	11,927	
Cash in hand	177	
Cash at bank	1,002	
Drawings	7,600	
Rates and insurance	4,322	
Postage and stationery	3,051	
Debtors	12,120	
Creditors		6,701
Bad debts	877	
Provision for bad debts		130
Salaries and wages	28,420	
Advertising	1,330	
	218,000	218,000

The following additional information as at 31 December 19x5 is available.

(i) Wages are accrued by £550.
(ii) Insurance has been prepaid by £250.
(iii) £2,212 of carriage represents carriage inwards on purchases.
(iv) The provision for bad debts is to be increased by £100.
(v) Stock at the year end has been valued at £12,990.

You are required to prepare a Trading and Profit and Loss account for the year ended 31 December 19x5 and a Balance Sheet as at that date.

► **No answer given**

11 Adjustments to the final accounts 3 – depreciation of fixed assets and the extended Trial Balance

Chapter objectives

By the end of this chapter, you should be able to:

- calculate the depreciation of fixed assets by using different methods
- adjust for the provision of depreciation in the final accounts
- prepare an adjusted Trial Balance incorporating all year-end adjustments.

Introduction

This chapter begins with a definition of depreciation relating to fixed assets. Most businesses will need to calculate this to carry out their normal activities. The different methods of calculating depreciation and the accounting records that ought to be maintained in the books of a business are explained. The next step will be to show how depreciation will affect profit calculations in the Trading and Profit and Loss account and how it will affect the fixed assets in the Balance Sheet.

Finally we shall see how depreciation and other adjustments discussed in chapters 9 and 10 (such as accruals, prepayments and bad debts) can be incorporated in the form of an extended Trial Balance in order to simplify the task of preparing the final accounts with necessary adjustments.

► **Extended Trial Balances** simplify the job of preparing the final accounts

DEPRECIATION OF FIXED ASSETS

Fixed assets such as plant and machinery have a long life but do not last for ever. As they age, they diminish in value. This reduction in the value of an asset as it grows older is called **depreciation**. SSAP 12 defines depreciation as follows.

► **Depreciation**: the loss in value of a fixed asset

► Depreciation is an expense.

SSAP 12

'Depreciation is a measure of the wearing out, consumption or other loss of value of a fixed asset whether arising from use, effluxion of time or obsolescence through technology and market changes.'

It then goes on to say that 'depreciation should be allocated to accounting periods so as to charge a fair proportion to each accounting period during the expected useful life of the asset.'

Depreciation is a measure of the loss in value of an asset which has to be charged as an expense to the Profit and Loss account over its useful life.

Methods of calculating depreciation

There are different methods of calculating the depreciation that is to be charged each year to the Profit and Loss account as an expense. These include:

- the Straight line method
- the Reducing or Diminishing balance method
- the Sum of years digits method
- the Revaluation method.

► Four main methods of calculating depreciation

The first two are most popular in Britain, the third is really an extension of the second, and the fourth is used for assets with small value, such as loose tools.

We'll now discuss each of these methods in some detail. The following symbols are used in the different formulae used for calculating depreciation.

D = annual charge for depreciation
A = accumulated depreciation
C = cost of the asset
R = residual (scrap) value of the asset
n = number of years of the expected life of the asset
t = number of years of expected life left
V_b = value of assets at the beginning of the year
V_e = value of assets at the end of the year

The formulae for calculating depreciation are shown below.

Method	**Formula**
Straight line	$D = \frac{C - R}{n}$
Reducing balance	$D = r(C - A)$
where	$r = 1 - \sqrt[n]{\frac{R}{C}}$
Sum of years digit	$D = \frac{1}{n(n+1)/2} \times (C - R)$
Revaluation	$D = V_b - V_e$

The Straight line method

The Straight line method allows the total depreciation of an asset to be spread over its working life in equal instalments. Hence another name for this method is the **Fixed instalment method**. It is called the Straight line method because, if you plot the accumulated depreciation of an asset against the number of years of its useful life, you get a straight line. This is what is to be expected since the annual rate of depreciation is constant. This fixed annual rate of depreciation is calculated by the use of the straight line formula given above.

► The **Straight line method** spreads depreciation in equal instalments over the working life of an asset.

The annual charge is obtained by dividing the total depreciation – the '$C - R$' in our formula – by the number of years of expected life of the asset – the 'n' in our formula. Thus, if the cost of an asset is £11,000 with a residual value of £1,000 and the expected life span is 5 years, the annual charge for depreciation will be:

$$\frac{£11,000 - £1,000}{5} = £2,000$$

If, however, we assume the residual value to be nil, the annual charge will be:

$$\frac{£11{,}000}{5} = £2{,}200$$

which is in fact equal to:

$$\frac{£2{,}200}{£11{,}000} \times 100 = 20\% \text{ of cost.}$$

Thus the rate of depreciation, under the Straight line method, can be expressed as a fixed percentage of cost.

► The **Reducing balance method** calculates depreciation on the book or 'written down value' (WDV).

The Reducing balance method

Under this method, the annual depreciation charge is calculated by applying a fixed rate not on the original cost, as with the Straight line method, but on the **net value** or **book value** or **written-down value** (WDV). The WDV of an asset decreases as it ages; depreciation based on it is therefore called the **Reducing balance** or **Diminishing balance** method. The rate that is used to calculate the annual depreciation is given in our list of formulae, above. If, for example, the original cost of an asset is £5,000 and its residual value after 5 years is £500, the percentage rate for depreciation will be:

$$\text{Percentage rate (\%)} = 1 - \sqrt[n]{\frac{\text{residual value}}{\text{original cost}}}$$

$$= 1 - \sqrt[5]{\frac{500}{5{,}000}}$$

$$= 1 - \sqrt[5]{0.1}$$

$$= 1 - 0.631$$

$$= 0.369$$

$$= 36.9\%$$

The annual depreciation charge will be calculated by using the other formula given in our list:

$$D = r(C - A)$$

We'll use the percentage rate we have just calculated to work out the annual depreciation for five successive years.

Year	C or WDV = 'C – A'		*D*	*A*
	£		£	£
1	5,000	36.9% × £5,000 =	1,845	1,845
2	3,155	36.9% × £3,400 =	1,164	3,009
3	1,991	36.9% × £2,312 =	735	3,744
4	1,256	36.9% × £1,572 =	463	4,207
5	793	36.9% × £1,069 =	293	4,500

We can see that under the Reducing balance method, the annual depreciation gradually decreases as years go by, whereas under the Straight line method, annual depreciation remains the same throughout the working life of an asset. This is usually cited as an advantage of the Reducing balance method over the Straight line method. It is argued that in the later years of the working life of an asset, more maintenance and repairs requiring greater cost are needed and a lower depreciation charge in these years is therefore an advantage.

The Sum of years digit method

► Sum of years digit depreciation method

This method is an alternative to the Reducing balance method and uses the formula given above for calculating the annual depreciation of an asset. The steps involved in the calculation are as follows.

1 Find the sum of the digits representing the years up to the time of the asset's being scrapped. Thus if an asset is estimated to last five years, the sum of years digit represented by $n(n + 1)/2$ in our formula, will be equal to $5(5 + 1)/2 = 15$.
2 Divide this into our total depreciation i.e. the $(C-R)$ in our formula.
3 Multiply the result obtained in step **2** by the number of years of the asset's remaining life.

Example 11.1 Calculating depreciation by the Sum of years digit method

---

An asset costs £5,000 and is expected to last for five years with a residual value of £500. Calculate the depreciation that is to be charged to the Profit and Loss account in each of the five years by the Sum of digits method.

Solution

Sum of digits

Year	No. of unexpired years of asset's life (*t*)	Cost – residual value (*C* – *R*) £		Depreciation	£
1	5	5,000 – 500	= 4,500	$\frac{5}{15}$ × £4,500 =	1,500
2	4		= 4,500	$\frac{4}{15}$ × £4,500 =	1,200
3	4 3		= 4,500	$\frac{3}{15}$ × £4,500 =	900
4	2		= 4,500	$\frac{2}{15}$ × £4,500 =	600
5	1		= 4,500	$\frac{1}{15}$ × £4,500 =	300
					4,500

Note: that the value of '*t*' i.e. the number of unexpired years in the asset's expected useful life, is calculated from the beginning of the year. In fact, we get this set of values by reversing the set representing the number of years, given in column 1.

► **The Revaluation method**: used for calculating depreciation of assets of low value

The Revaluation method

► **The Materiality concept**: see Chapter 6

For assets of small value such as nuts and bolts, knives and forks etc. it is expensive and unnecessary to calculate the depreciation of each individual item. Here we apply the Materiality concept discussed in Chapter 6. Although a single nut or bolt is insignificant, the collection of loose tools is **material**. As regards depreciation of such items, we calculate the annual depreciation by revaluing them in total, and deducting this value from their original cost or value at the beginning of the financial year. Thus if some loose tools were valued at £5,000 at the beginning of the year, and £4000 at the end of the same year, the depreciation charge for the year will be (£5000 – £4000) or £1000.

ACT 11.1

1 A business depreciates its plant by the Straight line method. The plant costs £35,000 and had an estimated working life of 10 years with a residual value of £5000. Calculate the annual depreciation charge for the plant.

2 An asset, costing £15,000, has an estimated working life of five years. It is expected that the plant can be sold at the end of the fifth year for £2000. Calculate the percentage rate that should be applied to this asset in determining the annual depreciation charge under the Reducing balance method.

3 For the asset in question **1**, calculate the depreciation charges for years 1 and 2, under the Sum of years digit method.

4 A hotel valued its cutlery at the beginning of the financial year at £16,000. The same set of articles was valued again at £15,500 at the end of the year. Calculate the amount of depreciation that will be charged for cutlery to the Profit and Loss account.

► Answers in appendix

Ledger entries for depreciation

We have seen how depreciation is calculated under different methods. Which of these methods will be used in practice by a firm will have to be decided by the organization itself, but it is a good accounting practice to state the method used and to continue using it, in accordance with the principle of Consistency (see Chapter 6), until there is an over-riding need for a change (such as a change in management or management policy). Once depreciation on a fixed asset for a year has been calculated, we need to record this event in the Ledger of the business, remembering that every debit entry has a corresponding credit entry, and vice versa. The method of calculating depreciation has no effect on the way entries are made in the Ledger.

► **The Consistency principle**: – see Chapter 6

We do not make any entries for depreciation in the asset account, the only entries which are made there are those which relate to the sale and further purchase of the asset. A new account, called the **Provision for depreciation account**, will be opened up for each asset and it will show the accumulated depreciation of the asset year after year. The double entry is as follows.

► Depreciation is not recorded in the asset account

► Provision for depreciation account

- debit the Profit and Loss account
- credit the provision for depreciation account

with the annual charge for depreciation.

The advantage of this system is that it always shows the asset value at cost and provides a readily available figure for the accumulated depreciation at any year end.

Example 11.2 Double-entry recording for depreciation

Alan Crane started business on 1 January 19x6, the financial year ending on 31 December. He bought a motor vehicle for £10,000 and decided to depreciate it by 20 per cent per annum, using the Straight line method.

► Straight line method

You are required to show:

a the Motor vehicle account
b the Depreciation account
c the Profit and Loss extracts
d the Balance Sheet extracts

for each of the years 19x6, 19x7 and 19x8.

Solution

a

DR			Motor vehicle a/c						CR
			£	p				£	p
19x6 Jan	1	Bank	10,000		19x6 Dec	31	Balance c/d	10,000	
19x7 Jan	1	Balance b/d	10,000		19x7 Dec	31	Balance c/d	10,000	
19x8 Jan	1	Balance b/d	10,000		19x8 Dec	31	Balance b/d	10,000	
19x9 Jan	1	Balance b/d	10,000						

b

DR			Provision for depreciation – motor vehicle a/c						CR
			£	p				£	p
19x6 Dec	31	Balance c/d	2,000		19x6 Dec	31	Profit and Loss a/c	2,000	
19x7 Dec	31	Balance c/d	4,000		19x7 Jan	1	Balance b/d	2,000	
					Dec	31	Profit and Loss a/c	2,000	
			4,000					4,000	
19x8 Dec	31	Balance c/d	6,000		19x8 Jan	1	Balance b/d	4,000	
					Dec	31	Profit and Loss a/c	2,000	
			6,000					6,000	
					19x9 Jan	1	Balance b/d	6,000	

c

Profit and Loss account for the Year ended 31 December			
	19x6 £	19x7 £	19x8 £
Less expenses: Depreciation on Motor vehicles	2,000	2,000	2,000

d

Balance Sheet as at 31 December

	19x6		19x7		19x8	
	£	£	£	£	£	£
Fixed Assets						
Motor vehicle at cost10,000	10,000		10,000		10,000	
Less Depreciation to date	2,000		4,000		6,000	
		8,000		6,000		4,000

The disposal of a fixed asset

Fixed assets will normally be sold or scrapped at the end of their useful life. Sometimes it may be necessary to dispose of them before the end of their expected life span. In either case, entries need to be made in the relevant accounts to record this event. It is very unlikely that the money received from the sale of an asset will be exactly the same as its net book value. Calculations for depreciation are rarely completely accurate. In most cases there will be either a profit or loss on the disposal. The amount of profit or loss made on disposal can easily be calculated by balancing the relevant accounts.

► Asset disposal account

To do this we need to open a new account, called the **Asset disposal account**, in the Ledger. In the case of a motor vehicle sale it would be called the **Motor vehicle disposal account**. Then we make the entries in four distinct stages, as described below.

Stages in recording the disposal of an asset

First stage:

- debit the asset disposal account
- credit the asset account

with the cost price of the asset.

Second stage:

- debit the provision for depreciation (for the relevant asset) account
- credit the asset disposal account

with the accumulated depreciation already charged to the asset.

Third stage:

On receipt of the proceeds of the sale

- debit the Cash or Bank account
- credit the asset disposal account

with the amount of money received.

Fourth stage:

Balance the asset disposal account: the balancing figure will be either the profit (if it appears on the debit side) or loss (if it appears on the credit side) on disposal. Transfer the profit or loss made to the credit or debit side of the Profit and Loss account. Alternatively, add the profit on disposal to gross profit or deduct the loss from the gross profit.

Example 11.3 illustrates how to record the disposal of an asset and how to calculate the profit or loss on disposal.

Example 11.3 Recording the disposal of an asset and calculating profit and loss

A business ends its accounting year on 31 March each year. On 31 March 19x0, it sold a desk top computer ,which originally cost £2,000, for £500 in cash. The provision for depreciation on the computer to date stood at £1,200. You are required to make the necessary entries in the books of the business to record this transaction.

Solution

Computer a/c

DR									CR
			£	p				£	p
19x9 April	1	Balance b/d	2,000		19x0 Mar	31	Computer disposal a/c	2,000	

Provision for disposal – computer a/c

DR									CR
			£	p				£	p
19x0 Mar	31	Computer disposal a/c	1,200		19x9 April	1	Balance b/d	1,200	

Computer disposal a/c

DR									CR
			£	p				£	p
19x0 Mar	31	Computer a/c	2,000		19x0 Mar	31	Provision for depreciation	1,200	
					Mar	31	Cash	500	
					Mar	31	Balance transferred to Profit and Loss a/c	300	
			2,000					2,000	

Profit and Loss account for the year ended 31 March 19x0

	£	£
Gross Profit b/d Less Loss on the sale of computer	X 300	

Note:

The cash account is not shown as it does not involve any new concept. Note also that the Computer account and the Provision for depreciation account are both closed and do not leave any balances.

ACT 11.2

1 An asset which originally cost £2,500 and in respect of which the provision for depreciation stood at £2,000, is sold for £600. Calculate the profit or loss on disposal of the asset.

2 The written down value of an asset at the start of a year was £1,500. It was sold during the year for £1,200. How much profit or loss was made on the disposal of the asset?

3 State the book-keeping entries that are required to record the provision for depreciation on an asset.

4 An asset disposal account is normally opened up in the Ledger when a fixed asset is sold. What entries are required, in this account only, to determine the profit or loss made on disposal?

► Answers in appendix

ADJUSTING FOR BAD DEBTS, ACCRUALS, PREPAYMENTS AND DEPRECIATION

So far we've discussed three distinct types of adjustments: **depreciation** in this chapter, **bad debts** in Chapter 10 and **accruals and prepayments** in Chapter 9. Example 11.3 is a worked example which will consolidate the ideas developed so far.

Example 11.3 Adjusting for bad debts, accruals, prepayments and depreciation

The following Trial Balance was extracted from the books of Clare Younger on 31 March 19x1.

Clare Younger
Trial Balance as at 31 March 19x1

	DR £	CR £
Stock – 1 April 19x0	12,250	
Wages and salaries	14,750	
Rates	1,800	
Carriage inwards	900	
Motor expenses	6,500	
Motor vehicles at cost	20,000	
Provision for depreciation on motor vehicles – 31 March 19x0		10,000
Heating and lighting	2,150	
Insurances	1,900	
Premises	26,000	
Fixtures and fittings	5,000	
Provision for depreciation on fixtures and fittings		1,500
Debtors	16,800	
Creditors		21,250
Purchases	55,250	
Sales		90,750
General expenses	2,900	

Drawings	5,200	
Capital		50,770
Bad debts	600	
Provision for bad debts		750
Cash	800	
Bank	2,200	
Discount allowed	500	
Discount received		480
	175,500	175,500

The following additional information is also available.

(i) The year end stock was valued at £15,750.

(ii) Wages owing amounted to £1,250.

(iii) Insurance prepaid amounted to £475.

(iv) Provision for bad debts to be adjusted to 5 per cent of debtors at 31 March 19x1.

(v) Fixtures and fittings to be depreciated by 20 per cent on the Reducing balance method.

(vi) During the year, one motor vehicle which cost £10,000 and in respect of which the provision for depreciation stood at £8,000, was sold for £2,500. No entries were made in the accounts for this transaction.

(vii) Motor vehicles are to be depreciated at 20 per cent on the Reducing balance method.

You are required to prepare:

a Clare Younger's Profit and Loss account for the year ended 31 March 19x1

b Her Balance Sheet as at 31 March 19x1.

Solution

a

Clare Younger

Trading and Profit and Loss account for the year ended 31 March 19x1

	£	£	£
Sales			90,750
Less Cost of sales:			
Opening stock		12,250	
Add purchases	55,250		
Add carriage inwards	900	56,150	
		68,400	
Less closing stock		15,750	52,650
Gross profit			38,100
Add other incomes:			
Discount received		480	
Profit on sale of vehicle (W1)	500	980	
			39,080
Less expenses:			
Wages and salaries	14,750		
Add amount owing	1,250	16,000	
Rates		1,800	
Motor expenses		6,500	
Heating and lighting		2,150	
Insurances	1,900		
Less amount prepaid	475	1,425	
General expenses		2,900	

Bad debts		600	
Increase in the provision for bad debts (W2)		90	
Discount allowed		500	
Depreciation on fixtures and fittings		500	
Depreciation on motor vehicle (W3)		1,600	34,065
Net profit			5,015

b

Clare Younger

Balance Sheet as at 31 March 19x1

	Cost £	Dep. £	Net £
Fixed Assets:			
Premises	26,000		26,000
Fixtures and fittings (N4)	5,000	2,000	3,000
Motor vehicles (W5)	10,000	3,600	6,400
	41,000	5,600	35,400
Current Assets:			
Stock		15,750	
Debtors	16,800		
Less provision bad debts (W2)	840	15,960	
Prepayments		475	
Bank (W6)		4,700	
Cash		800	
		37,685	
Less Current Liabilities:			
Creditors	21,250		
Accruals	1,250	22,500	15,185
			50,585
Net Current Assets			50,770
Add Capital Net profit			5,015
			55,785
Less Drawings			5,200
			50,585

Workings:

W1 Profit on the sale of a motor vehicle:

	£	£
Sales		2,500
Less WDV :		
Cost	10,000	
Less depreciation to date	8,000	2,000
Profit		500

W2 Increase in the provision for bad debts :

	£
New Provision :	
5% × 16,800 =	840
Less old provision as per Trial Balance	750
Increase in provision	90

W3 Depreciation on motor vehicles :

	£	£
At cost		20,000
Less cost of MV sold		10,000
Cost at 31.3.x1		
		10,000
Less Provision for depreciation as per TB	10,000	
Less Provision for depreciation on MV sold	8,000	2,000
WDV		8,000
Depreciation for the year 20% × 8,000		1,600

W4 Fixtures and fittings : Provision for depreciation

	£
As per Trial Balance	1,500
Add depreciation of the year	500
To Balance Sheet	2,000

W5 Motor vehicles:

	£
Cost at 1.1x0	20,000
Less cost of MV sold	10,000
	10,000
Provision for depreciation:	
As per Trial Balance	10,000
Less depreciation on MV sold	8,000
	2,000
Add depreciation for the year	1,600
To Balance Sheet	3,600

W6

Bank as per the Trial Balance	2,200
Add cheque received from the sale of motor vehicle	2,500
	4,700

Note:

1 Note that all the adjustments for items given as 'additional information' have two entries – one in the Profit and Loss account and one in the Balance Sheet. This is to be expected as these adjustments have not as yet been posted to the relevant accounts in the Ledger.

2 The adjustments for the disposal of the motor vehicle are tricky. There are three things to calculate. First we work out the profit on the sale of the motor vehicle as shown in W1. Secondly, we need to calculate the depreciation for the year on the remaining motor vehicles. This is shown in W3. Finally we need to increase the Bank balance by the amount of the sale proceeds, i.e. by £2,500, because the amount has not as yet been debited to the Cash Book (see W6).

3 Notice the new layout given for showing the fixed assets in the Balance Sheet. If we have to list more than one fixed asset, this layout is generally followed. There are three columns to record the cost, accumulated depreciation and the net value, or book value or WDV of the assets concerned. Follow this layout from now on.

Adjustments and the extended Trial Balance

Sometimes it may be useful to prepare a rough Trading and Profit and Loss account and a Balance Sheet by proper groupings of the figures given in the Trial Balance. If there are no adjustments to be made at the end of the year, we need two additional columns in the Trial Balance – one for the Trading and Profit and Loss account and the other for the Balance Sheet. If, however, we need to make some adjustments for say, prepayments and accruals, we need an additional column in the extended Trial Balance. The mechanics of this extended Trial Balance are shown in Example 11.4.

Example 11.4 Adjustments and the extended Trial Balance

The following Trial Balance was extracted from the books of G.Gower as at 31 December 19x1.

G.Gower

Trial Balance as at 31 December 19x1

	DR £	CR £
Opening Stock	10,000	
Sales		90,500
Purchases	51,000	
Wages	11,750	
Rates	1,500	
Electricity	1,900	
Insurances	2,200	
Motor expenses	4,750	
General expenses	5,150	
Premises	20,000	
Debtors	10,500	
Drawings	5,000	
Creditors		14,000
Motor vehicles	7,000	
Fixtures	4,500	
Capital		32,750
Bank	1,500	
Cash	500	
	137,250	137,250

The following additional information is also available.

(i) Stock at 31 December 19x1 was valued at £9,250

(ii) Insurances prepaid amounted to £500

(iii) Wages owing totalled £2,150

(iv) Bad debts amounted to £500

(v) Provide for depreciation on motor vehicles at 20 per cent on cost

You are required to prepare the draft final accounts of G. Gower at the end of the year by the extended Trial Balance method.

Solution

Trial Balance			Adjustments			Profit and Loss a/c				Balance Sheet	
	DR £	CR £	(i)	DR £	CR £	DR £	CR £	DR £	CR £	DR £	CR £
Opening stock	10,000		=	9,250	9,250	10,000	9,250			9,250	
Sales		90,500					90,500				
Purchases	51,000					51,000					
				Gross Profit		38,750			38,750		
Wages	11,750		(ii)	2,150				13,900			
Rates	1,500							1,500			
Electricity	1,900							1,900			
Motor expenses	4,750							4,750			
General expenses	5,150							5,150			
Bad debts			(iv)	500				500			
Premises	20,000		(iii)		2,150					20,000	
Insurance	2,200		(ii)		500			1,700			2,150
Prepayments			(ii)	500						500	
Debtors	10,500		(iv)		500					10,000	
Creditors		14,000	(v)					1,400			14,000
Motor vehicles	7,000		(v)	1,400	1,400					5,600	
Fixtures	4,500									4,500	
Capital		32,750									32,750
Bank	1,500									1,500	
Drawings	5,000		(vi)							5,000	
Cash	500									500	
				Net profit				7,950			7,950
	137,250	137,250		13,800	13,800	99,750	99,750	38,750	38,750	56,850	56,850

Note:

(i) Notes in the adjustments column refer to the serial number of adjustments given in the additional information.

(ii) You might have noticed that for each adjustment, there are two entries – one debit and one credit in the adjustments column. This is necessary to ensure that the Trial Balance balances after the adjustments are made. Notice that this is ensured by the fact that the debit total and the credit total in the adjustments column, are exactly the same.

(iii) The first pair of figures in the Trading and Profit and Loss account refer to the trading figures. The closing stock figure is both a debit and credit in the adjustments column and once again in the credit side of the Trading account and the debit side of the Balance Sheet.

(iv) The gross profit is obtained by subtracting the total of debit entries (i.e. £10,000 + £51,000) from the total of credit entries, which in this case is (£9,250 + £90,550). This gives a gross profit of £38,750 which is inserted (as a balancing figure) in the debit column of the Trading account which is then transferred to the credit side of the Profit and Loss account.

(v) The expenses due are added to the relevant figures in the Trial Balance and these adjusted figures are then transferred to the debit column of the Profit and Loss account. To complete the double entry, accruals are shown on the credit column of the Balance Sheet as they represent liabilities. Prepayments are dealt with in the same way, but the entries are reversed. That is, prepayments are subtracted from the relevant Trial Balance figures before these are transferred to the debit side of the Profit and Loss account. Since they represent assets, they are shown on the debit side of the Balance Sheet.

(vi) Drawings are shown on the debit side as they appear on the debit side in the Trial Balance. However when you prepare the proper Balance Sheet, you should show drawings as a deduction from the sum of capital and net profit.

Chapter summary

- Depreciation is the reduction in value of an asset resulting from normal wear and tear, obsolescence or simply the passage of time.
- The four methods of depreciation discussed in this chapter are:
  - o the Straight line method
  - o the Diminishing balance method
  - o the Sum of years digits method
  - o the Revaluation method.
- The book-keeping rules for recording depreciation are:
  - o debit the Profit and Loss account
  - o credit the Provision for depreciation account with the annual charge of depreciation.
- In the Balance Sheet, accumulated depreciation is deducted from cost in order to get the net value of the asset. You should remember and follow the three-column approach to the listing of fixed assets as shown in Example 11.3.
- Year-end adjustments can be shown on an extended Trial Balance (a normal Trial Balance with additional columns) leading to the rough version of both the Trading and Profit and Loss account and the Balance Sheet.

ACT 11.3

19/01/95
No 1, 2 + 3
Did in class

For questions 1 and 2, put a tick against the letter representing the best choice from among the four possible answers given.

1 A machine costs £20,000 and is expected to have a working life of five years with a residual value of £5,000. The annual amount that should be charged for depreciation, using the Straight line method, is:
  - **A** £4,000
  - **B** £1,000
  - **C** £3,000
  - **D** £5,000.

2 A motor van costing £12,000 was depreciated by 25 per cent per annum, using the Diminishing balance method. Two years later it was sold for £6,000. The profit or loss made on the disposal of the van was:
  - **A** A loss of £6,000
  - **B** A loss of £750
  - **C** A profit of £750
  - **D** Zero.

► Answers in appendix

3 A machine costing £25,000 has an estimated life of five years with a scrap value of £5,000. Show the depreciation calculations for each year using:
  - **a** the Straight line method
  - **b** the Reducing balance method using a depreciation rate of 25 per cent per annum.

► No answer given

4 Alan Hurd bought a piece of equipment for £10,000 on January 1 19x1. On 1 January 19x5 he sold the old equipment for £2,500 and bought a replacement on credit from Johnson and Johnson Ltd for £13,000.
You are required to show:
  - **a** the Equipment account as it would appear on 31 December 19x5

b the Provision for depreciation of equipment account for 19x1, 19x2, 19x3, 19x4 and 19x5

c the Disposal of asset account as it would appear as at 31 December 19x5

d extracts from the Profit and Loss account and Balance Sheet as they would appear on 31 December 19x5.

► Answer in appendix

19|01|95
Homework.

5 The financial year of Muldane plc ended on 31 May 19x9. At 1 June 19x8, the company owned motor vehicles costing £124,000 which had been depreciated by a total of £80,000.

On 1 August 19x8, Muldane plc sold motor vehicles, which had cost £54,000 and which had been depreciated by £49,000, for £3,900 and purchased new motor vehicles costing £71,000. It is the policy of Muldane plc to depreciate its motor vehicles at 35 per cent per annum using the Diminishing balance method. A full year's depreciation is charged on all motor vehicles in use at the end of each year. No depreciation is charged for the year on assets disposed of during that year.

Required:

Show the following accounts as they would appear in the ledger of Muldane plc for the year ended 31 May 19x9 only:

a the Motor vehicles account

b the Provision for depreciation – motor vehicles account

c the Assets disposal account.

(AAT)

► No answer given

6 Since 1 October 19x7, the Sharp Edge Engineering Company Limited has been building up its own customers' delivery service, and accordingly, has purchased the following vehicles:

19x7			
1 October	Van	E676TVX	costing £28,000
19x8			
1 January	Lorry	E438CBA	costing £36,000
19x9			
1 February	Van	E779GMS	costing £16,000
1 July	Van	F934KTA	costing £24,000

Additional information:

(i) Lorry E438CBA proved to be unsuitable for the company's trade and was therefore sold on 31 December 19x8 to John Kerry for £21,680.

(ii) Van E779GMS was bought second-hand. Before joining the company's transport fleet on 1 April 19x9, this van was converted to meet the company's requirements. The conversion work was carried out in the company's own workshops, the following costs being incurred:

Direct labour	£1,880
Direct materials	£3,200
Variable overheads	£1,370.

Fixed overheads apportionment added at 25% of prime cost.

(iii) It is the company's policy to provide depreciation on motor vehicles at the rate of 20 per cent per annum on cost.
(iv) The company has a contract with the Fairdeal Insurance Company Limited under which each vehicle in the transport fleet is insured at an annual premium of £5,000; the first premium for each vehicle is paid the day the vehicle is bought.
(v) The company's accounting year end is 30 September.

Required:
Prepare the following accounts where relevant for each of the years ended 30 September 19x8 and 19x9 in the books of the Sharp Edge Engineering Company Limited:
a Motor vehicles at cost
b Motor vehicles provision for depreciation
c Lorry E438CBA disposal
d Motor vehicles insurance.

(AAT)

► Answer in appendix

7 The following Trial Balance was extracted from the books of A. Hope, a trader, as at 31 March,19x9.

A. Hope
Trial Balance as at 31 March, 19x9

	DR £	CR £
Capital		37,550
Premises	25,000	
Fixtures and fittings	2,000	
Motor van	6,000	
Drawings	10,000	
Stock – 1 April,19x8	9,000	
Purchases	56,000	
Sales		84,045
Returns inwards	545	
Returns outwards		700
Rates	1,100	
Insurance	425	
Salaries and wages	8,895	
Discount allowed	405	
Discount received		300
Interest on loan	500	
Motor van expenses	1,750	
Sundry expenses	3,020	
Loan from a friend		5,000
Creditors		6,345
Debtors	7,050	
Cash at bank	2,000	
Cash in hand	250	
	133,940	133,940

The following information is also available.
(i) Stock as at 31 March,19x9 was valued at £10,950.
(ii) Rates paid in advance at 31 March, 19x9 amounted to £150.

(iii) It is the company's policy to provide depreciation
(iv) Depreciation on fixed assets is to be provided for at the following rates:
Motor van – 20 per cent on book value;
Fixtures and fittings – 10 per cent on book value.

You are required to prepare:

a A Trading and Profit and Loss account for the year ended 31 March, 19x9

b A Balance Sheet as at 31 March, 19x9.

► No answer given

8 The Trial Balance of J. Slater at 31 March, 19x9 was as follows.

	DR £	CR £
Freehold premises	59,000	
Motor vans, at cost	15,650	
Provision for depreciation of Motor vans 31 March, 19x8		6,750
Capital		82,430
Drawing	13,127	
Wages and salaries	15,846	
Stock – 1 April, 19x8	13,930	
Balance at bank	6,615	
Bad debts	1,075	
Provision for bad debts		275
Debtors and creditors	11,320	11,380
Motor and delivery expenses	3,258	
Rates	700	
Purchases and sales	98,440	142,770
General expenses	4,644	
	243,605	243,605

Note:

(i) Stock at 31 March 19x9, £14,600.
(ii) Rates paid in advance at 31 March 19x9, £200.
(iii) The provision for bad debts is to be increased to £350.
(iv) Provide for depreciation of motor vans at 20 per cent on cost.
(v) Wages and salaries accrued at 31 March 19x9, £1,500.

You are required to prepare a Trading and Profit and Loss account for the year ended 31 March, 19x9 and a Balance Sheet as at that date.

► No answer given

9 The Trial Balance shown below was extracted from the books of J. Hopkins as at 31 December, 19x8.

J. Hopkins

Trial Balance as at 31 December, 19x8

	DR £	CR £
Purchases	60,800	
Sales		91,400
Returns	1,200	1,350
Carriage inwards	450	
Carriage outwards	310	
Motor expenses	1,864	
Salaries	5,310	
Discounts	309	210
Rent and rates	810	
Insurance	204	
Bad debts written off	1,516	
Provision for bad and doubtful debts – 1 Jan 19x8		805
Stocks – 1 Jan 19x8	31,630	
Debtors and creditors	22,460	11,960
Drawings	7,155	
Cash in hand	150	
Cash at bank	5,850	
Fixtures, at cost	11,000	
Motor van, at cost	9,400	
Provision for depreciation on Fixtures – 1 Jan 19x8		4,400
Provision for depreciation on Motor Van – 1 Jan 19x8		2,360
Capital		47,933
	160,418	160,418

The following additional information is available.
Stock at 31 December, 19x8: £36,530.
Insurance prepaid: £44.
Salaries outstanding: £506.
Provision for bad debts is to be increased to £880.
Provide for depreciation for the year:
Fixtures, £2,200; Motor van, £1,620.

You are required to prepare a Trading and Profit and Loss account for the year ended 31 December, 19x8 and a Balance Sheet as at that date.

► No answer given

10 Mr Chai has been trading for some years as a wine merchant. The following list of balances has been extracted from his ledger as at 30 April 19x7, the end of his most recent financial year.

	£
Capital	83,887
Sales	259,870
Trade creditors	19,840
Returns out	13,407
Provision for bad debts	512
Discount allowed	2,306
Discount received	1,750
Purchases	135,680
Returns inwards	5,624
Carriage outwards	4,562
Drawings	18,440
Carriage inwards	11,830
Rent, rates and insurance	25,973
Heating and lighting	11,010
Postage, stationery and telephone	2,410
Advertising	5,980
Salaries and wages	38,521
Bad debts	2,008
Cash on hand	534
Cash at bank	4,440
Stock as at 1 May 19x6	15,654
Trade debtors	24,500
Fixtures and fittings – at cost	120,740
Provision for depreciation on fixtures and fittings – as at 30 April 1987	63,020
Depreciation	12,074

The following additional information as at 30 April 19x7 is available.

(i) Stock at the close of business was valued at £17,750.
(ii) Insurances have been prepaid by £1,120.
(iii) Heating and lighting is accrued by £1,360.
(iv) Rates have been prepaid by £5,435.
(v) The provision for bad debts is to be adjusted so that it is 3 per cent of trade debtors.

You are required to prepare Mr Chai's Trading and Profit and Loss account for the year ended 30 April 19x7 and a Balance Sheet as at that date.

(AAT)

► Answer in appendix

11 The following Trial Balance has been extracted from the Ledger of Andrew Pye, a sole trader, as at 31 October 19x8, the end of Mr Pye's financial year.

Trial Balance as at 31 October 19x8

	DR £	CR £
Stock as at 1 November 19x7	22,000	
Purchases	223,000	
Sales		340,700
Discounts allowed	4,600	
Discounts received		5,500
Returns in	6,700	
Returns out		5,600
Wages and salaries	34,500	
Bad debts	3,100	
Carriage in	1,400	
Carriage out	2,200	
Other operating expenses	24,500	
Trade debtors	34,000	
Trade creditors		21,600
Provision for bad debts		450
Cash on hand	800	
Bank overdraft		23,400
Drawings	23,500	
Capital as at 1 Nov. 19x7		62,050
Property	50,000	
Equipment	64,000	
Provisions for depreciation (as at 1 November 19x7)		
property		10,000
equipment		25,000
	494,300	494,300

The following additional information as at 31 October 19x8 is available:

a Stock as at the close of business was valued at £23,700.

b 'Other operating expenses' were prepaid by £170.

c The provision for bad debts is to be adjusted so that it is 1 per cent of trade debtors.

d Depreciation had still to be provided for the year ended 31 October 19x8 as follows:
Property – 2 per cent Straight line method
Equipment – 30 per cent Diminishing balance method.

You are required to prepare Andrew Pye's Trading and Profit and Loss account for the year ended 31 October 19x8 and his Balance Sheet as at 31 October 19x8.

(AAT)

► No answer given

12 Control of working capital

Chapter objectives

By the end of this chapter, you should be able to:

- explain the importance of control accounts in the Ledger
- prepare a sales ledger control account
- prepare a purchases ledger control account
- understand the significance of stock control
- calculate stock values using FIFO, LIFO and AVCO methods
- understand the difference between perpetual and periodic valuation methods
- draft financial accounts using the different methods of stock valuation.

WORKING CAPITAL

Working capital is the difference between current assets and current liabilities. The major constituents of current assets are **stocks, debtors** and **cash** (both at bank and in hand), and the main item in current liabilities is **creditors**. To control working capital, we need to control stocks, debtors, creditors and cash. The need for control of working capital can hardly be over emphasized. An efficient and effective control of working capital will be reflected in higher profitability, better solvency and greater stability of the business. Many managers try deliberately to minimize working capital, but this objective may come into conflict with other objectives, such as expansion of sales of the business. Too quick an expansion of sales through extended credit, without having sufficient working capital to ensure liquidity, results in what is known as **overtrading**. The danger of overtrading is that it might drag the business quite quickly into insolvency and consequently liquidation. On the other hand, too 'safe' a level of working capital might result in an unprofitable use of that working capital. A balance needs therefore to be maintained between excessive trading and too little trading. The proper control of working capital will provide the managers with a means of attaining this.

► **Working capital**: differences between current assets and current liabilities

► **Current Assets**:
- stocks
- debtors
- cash

► **Current Liabilities**: mainly creditors

► **Overtrading**: too great a reliance on credit

► **Undertrading**: under-use of working capital

In this chapter, we'll deal with the control of three of the four major components of working capital: debtors, creditors and stock. We'll take up the control of liquid funds, i.e. cash, in a later chapter.

The control of debtors requires a procedure by which a check can be made on the accuracy of a large number of debtors' accounts. These are usually maintained together in one or more books, called the **Sales Ledger** or **Debtors Ledger**. One way of minimizing – or at least localizing – the potential errors that might creep into the debtors' accounts is to use a special account, called the **Sales ledger control account** or **Total debtors control account**. In such an account, the total of all transactions debited to the personal accounts of the credit customers will be debited. This total debtors figure is obtained for the Sales ledger control account directly from the Sales Day Book. Similarly,

► **The control of debtors**: the **Sales ledger control account**

► Sales or Debtors ledgers and the Sales ledger control/Total debtor control account.

► Sales ledger control a/c totals all transactions debited to debtors.

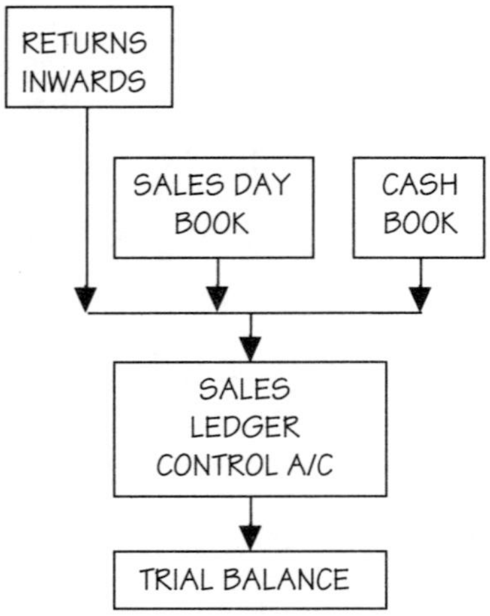

the total of all cash received from the debtors will be credited. This information can be directly obtained from the Cash Book. Now, if all the entries in the Ledger have been correctly posted, the Control account balance should agree with the total of the balances of all individual debtors' accounts kept in the Sales Ledger. Because we post the total of all debtors balances in the Sales ledger control account, it is also know as the **Total debtors control account**.

Besides checking on the accuracy of ledger postings in relation to debtors' accounts, the Sales ledger control account balance may be used in place of the individual debtor balances when the Trial Balance is prepared. Also, such a control account provides management with a means of detecting fraud as the control account is maintained in the General Ledger, under the direct supervision of a more senior officer in the organization. Finally, the control account can provide management with the total debtors figure as well as the total cash collected from the debtors, at short notice. This speedy provision of information to management will certainly improve the quality of control in relation to working capital, resulting in improved liquidity and profitability.

► The Sales ledger control account may be a double-entry or a memorandum account.

The Sales ledger control account may or may not be included within the double-entry system. If it is regarded as part of the double-entry system, the accounts of individual debtors will be treated as memorandum accounts. However, more usually the accounts of individual debtors are included within the double-entry system, as they are usually done, the Sales ledger control account must be treated as a memorandum account. Whether we treat the control account within or outside the double-entry book-keeping system, the entries in it will be exactly the same. In fact, the Sales ledger control account reproduces the information in the individual debtor's account. The only difference is that the amounts to be recorded in the control account – on either the debit or the credit side – should always be 'total' figures which should be obtained from the relevant books of original entry, such as the Sales Day Book, the Returns Inwards Book, the Cash Book and the Journal. If we remember this basic principle, writing up the control account will not cause any undue difficulty. The entries in the control account should always be made independently of the individual debtor's accounts and of the persons writing them up.

Remembering that the Sales ledger control account, kept in the General Ledger as a memorandum account, is a near replica of an individual debtor's account, let us list the main transactions and how they are to be entered in it.

Entries for the Sales ledger control account

1 Opening balances:
In a Sales ledger control account, there may be two opening balances, one being a debit balance, and the other being a credit balance. Normally, most debtors' accounts will show debit balances, but it is possible for a few customer accounts to show credit balances. This situation may arise if a customer has paid the same invoice twice – and temporarily becomes a creditor rather than a debtor, so the account will thus show a credit balance. The control account recognizes such possibilities.

2 Credit sales:
Debit the Sales control account with the periodic total of credit sales, as recorded in the Sales Day Book.

3 Cash received from customers:
Credit the control account with the periodic total of cash received from debtors recorded in the Cash Book.

4 Returns inwards:
Credit the control account with the periodic total of goods returned by customers, as recorded in the Returns inwards account.

5 Bad debts written off:
Credit the control account with the periodic total of bad debts, through the Journal.

6 Discount allowed:
Credit the control account with the periodic total of discounts allowed, as recorded in the cash book.

7 Dishonoured cheques:
Debit the control account with the periodic total of such cheques, to be derived from an examination of the journal.

8 Cash refund:
Debit the control account with the periodic total of cash refund to customers.

9 Contras:
If a credit customer of a business is also a supplier of goods to it, then the same person or firm is both a debtor and a creditor and will have two accounts – one in the Sales Ledger and the other in the Purchases Ledger. In such a case, it is normal practice to set off one against the other so that only the difference between the two amounts is actually received or paid. This would require contra entries in the two control accounts involved: the Sales ledger control account and the Purchases ledger control account, via the Journal. Any amount to be adjusted towards the payment of the debt will require a credit entry on the Sales control account, the corresponding debit entry being in the Purchases control account which we'll be discussing shortly.

After all these entries are made, the closing balance in the Sales ledger control account should be equal to the sum of the balances extracted from the individual debtor accounts in the Sales Ledger.

In Example 12.1, we can see how a Sales ledger control account is drawn up.

Example 12.1 Drawing up a Sales ledger control account

The following balances were extracted from the books of R. Daniels on 31 December 19x1.

	£
Opening balances:	
Debit balances in the Sales Ledger	12,250
Credit balances in the Sales Ledger	300
Totals for the year:	
Sales Day Book	100,290
Discount allowed	10,980
Payments received from customers	80,500
Returns Inwards journal	3,680
Bad debts written off	500
Dishonoured cheques	210
Cash returned to a customer who overpaid his accounts	50
Settlement by contra – suppliers' a/cs	2,990
Closing balances:	
Debit balances in the Sales Ledger	14,400
Credit balances in the Sales Ledger	550

You are required to prepare a Sales ledger control account for the year to 31 December 19x1.

Solution

Sales ledger control a/c

DR				£	p	CR				£	p
19x1						19x1					
Jan	1	Balance b/d		12,250		Jan	1	Balance b/d		300	
Dec	31	Sales		100,290		Dec	31	Discount allowed		10,980	
Dec	31	Dishonoured cheques		210		Dec	31	Cash		80,500	
						Dec	31	Returns		3,680	
Dec	31	Cash refund		50		Dec	31	Bad debts		500	
Dec	31	Balance c/d		550		Dec	31	Contras		2,990	
						Dec	31	Balance c/d		14,400	
				113,350						113,350	
19x2						19x2					
Jan	1	Balance b/d		14,400		Jan	1	Balance b/d		550	

The control of creditors: the Purchases ledger control account

► **Purchases ledger control account or Bought ledger control account**: totals all transactions credited to accounts of suppliers

As with debtors, the control of creditors can be achieved by maintaining a special account in the General Ledger, called the **Purchases ledger control account**, which is also known as the **Bought ledger control account** or the **Total creditors control account**. This account is similar to the Sales ledger control account, but shows the total of all transactions credited to the personal accounts of suppliers. This periodic total of creditors can be directly obtained from the Purchases Day Book.

The advantages of a Purchases ledger control account are similar to those of a Sales ledger control account. They include a check on the accuracy of the entries in the Purchases Ledger, a check on the possibility of fraud as the Control account is maintained independently of the individual creditors' accounts, and the provision of speedy and accurate information to management regarding creditors' balances and the amount of money paid to the creditors.

The Purchases ledger control account is almost a replica of an individual creditor's account in the Bought Ledger, the only difference being that the entries in the control account should always be periodic totals, which should be obtained from the books of prime entry such as the Purchases Day Book, the Returns Outwards Book, the Cash Book and the Journal. Items which increase the liabilities of the business, e.g. credit purchases, should be entered on the credit sides, and items which reduce the liabilities, such as cash paid to creditors, discount received and goods returned, should be entered on the debit side. Contras are dealt with by making an entry in each of the two control accounts, but on opposite sides, via the Journal.

► **Contras**: offsets of mutual indebtedness

One final point: just like the Sales ledger control account, the Purchases ledger control account may have two opening or closing balances i.e. a debit balance and a credit balance. A credit balance is what is normally expected, but there may be occasions when one or more creditors might, for example, have received more cash than they should, and this will be reflected in the creditors' accounts, and eventually in the control account as a debit entry, indicating that they owe this much to the company.

The preparation of a Purchases ledger control account is illustrated in Example 12.2.

Example 12.2 Preparing a Purchases ledger control account

The following information was extracted from the books of Joe Hunter on 31 March 19x1.

	£
Opening balances:	
Debit balance in the purchases ledger	2,500
Credit balances in the purchases ledger	55,750
Totals for the year:	
Purchases Day Book	150,000
Discount received	7,750
Payments made to creditors	100,000
Returns outwards Book	5,840
Debtor balances set off against creditor balances	6,330
Closing balances:	
Debit balances in the purchases ledger	3,150
Credit balances in the purchases ledger	86,480

You are required to write up Joe Hunter's Purchases ledger control account for the year to 31 March 19x1.

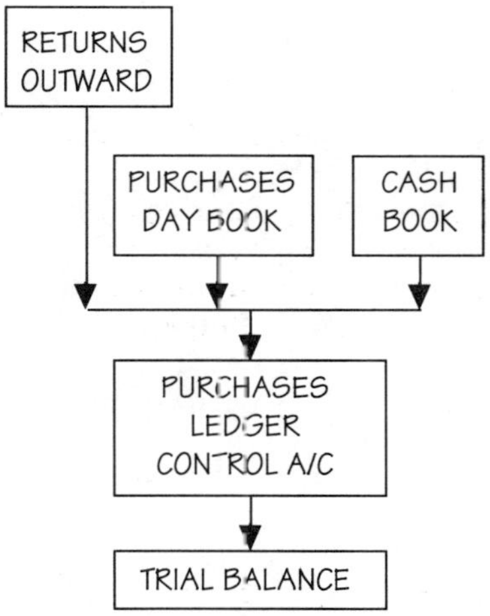

Solution

DR			Purchases ledger control a/c					CR	
			£	p				£	p
119x0					19x0				
April	1	Balance b/d	2,500		April	1	Balance b/d	55,750	
19x1					19x1				
Mar	31	Discount rec.	7,750		Mar	31	Purchases	150,000	
Mar	31	Cash	100,000		Mar	31	Balance c/d	3,150	
Mar	31	Returns Out.	5,840						
Mar	31	Debtors(contras)	6,330						
Mar	31	Balance c/d	86,480						
			208,900					208,900	
April	1	Balance b/d	3,150		April	1	Balance b/d	86,480	

► Control accounts are often called **adjustment accounts**

We have seen how control accounts included in the ledger system ensure that the entries in the Ledger based on the principle of double-entry, are correct. Because of this built-in measure of detecting errors, such ledgers are called **self-balancing ledgers** and the control accounts which testify to this self-balancing are called **adjustment accounts**. You should remember therefore that control accounts and adjustments accounts are one and the same thing.

Control of stock

The main objective of **stock control** is to control the flow of stocks of materials or goods into the store, and the flow of stocks into production or sales, to ensure that an optimum quantity of all materials or goods is stocked. The aim of this is to avoid overstocking and understocking.

Overstocking results in the uneconomic use of resources. This will eventually be reflected in the lowering of the overall profits of the organization. **Understocking** is equally bad as it leads to stocks of materials or goods running out. This inevitably disrupts or stops production and adversely affects the sales (and hence profit) of the organization.

Stock control is therefore linked with the control of stock levels. It is in fact based on four critical stock levels:

- maximum stock level
- minimum stock level
- re-order stock level
- re-order stock quantity.

Stock control involves presetting these four control levels (**critical levels**) for each item of stock and taking appropriate action if any stock item tends to deviate from these levels.

Maximum stock level

This is the level above which stock should not be allowed to rise. It is fixed for each item in the store after considering the following:

- rate of usage of materials or sales of goods
- cost of storage
- lead time, i.e. the time necessary to obtain deliveries of materials or goods *from the date of order*

- economic order quantity, i.e. the most desirable re-order quantity
- availability of storage space
- possible risk of deterioration or obsolescence.

Minimum stock level
This is the level below which stocks must not be allowed to fall. The main factors affecting it are:
- rate of usage of materials or sales of goods
- lead time between ordering and receiving replenishment of stocks
- possible cost of running out of stock.

Re-order stock level
This is the level at which a purchase requisition for replenishment of stock is made. It lies between the maximum stock level and the minimum stock level and is affected by:
- the rate of usage or sales
- the minimum stock level
- the lead time for delivery.

Re-order (stock) quantity
This is the quantity to be ordered at the re-order level. It is fixed after considering:
- the rate of usage or sales
- possible risks of obsolescence and deterioration
- quantity discount for bulk buying
- transport costs
- the cost of holding stock.

Stocktaking
Besides determining the critical stock levels, stock control systems maintain records of quantities and value of stock. These records are required for **stock valuation**, particularly at the end of the financial year. Stock is usually valued by determining the quantity and multiplying it by cost per unit or market price per unit. Quantities of stock as at a certain date will be usually determined after a physical stock count, known as **stocktaking**. There are two main methods of stocktaking:

► **Stock valuation**: usually calculated by counting quantity and multiplying by cost or selling price

Annual stocktaking
This involves counting and valuing all stock items on one or more particular day(s), usually towards the end of the accounting year.

Continuous stocktaking
This involves counting and valuing a few items each day throughout the year.

The annual stocktaking is administratively simple but, compared to continuous stocktaking, it has the following disadvantages:
- stock deficiencies and losses are not revealed in good time for preventive action to be taken
- it causes production or sales hold-ups during stocktaking
- there is too little time to count stock effectively.

Stocktaking is an area of administration in a business where computer technology has become important. We'll be considering the application of computers in Chapter 23, but remember that, in a computerized system, it is relatively easy continually to monitor the stock of every single item and annual stocktaking as such is no longer necessary.

Stores records

For recording different transactions of materials or goods, such as receipts, issues and transfers, two important documents are usually kept. They are **bin cards** and the **Stores Ledger**.

► Bin cards

Bin cards

There will be one bin card for each stock item. Bin cards are maintained by the store-keeper in the stores and contain a record of receipts, issues and balances in stock, in quantity only.

XYZ Limited

Bin card		Bin number	
Description of material		Normal quantity to order	
Code number		Maximum stock level	
Stores Ledger folio no.		Minimum stock level	
		Re-order stock level	

	RECEIPTS		ISSUES		BALANCE
Date	GRNo.•	Quantity	MRNo.••	Quantity	Quantity

- • Goods Received Note number
- •• Materials Requisition Note number

Figure 12.1
A bin card

► **Stores Ledger**: records movements of stocks into and out of the stores

► **Evaluated account**: shows quantity and value of stocks of goods available

Stores Ledger

A Stores Ledger contains an evaluated account of any movement of stocks to and from the stores. It is usually a loose-leaf file or a card index. Each item of stores will have a separate card or account. Diagram 12.2 shows a typical Stores ledger account.

XYZ Limited

Stores Ledger Account			
Material			
Code no.		Maximum stock level	
Bin no.		Minimum stock level	
Location		Re-order level	

	RECEIPTS				ISSUES				BALANCE		
Date	GRNo.•	Quantity	Rate	Value	MRNo.••	Quantity	Rate	Value	Quantity	Rate	Value

Figure 12.2
Stores ledger card

- • Goods Received Note number
- •• Materials Requisition Note number

Methods of valuing stock issues and closing stocks

If the items in stock were bought at a uniform price throughout, there would be no problem in valuing stores issues. Issues of materials to production, or cost of goods sold to customers, and the closing stocks of materials would be valued or costed at the uniform purchase price. However, the situation will be entirely different when materials are bought at different prices at different times. This will obviously create a problem in costing items. The problem is usually dealt with by selecting a method of valuing stores issued and closing stocks.

► Stock valuation

There are many different methods of stock valuation, but only three methods are common. These are:

- First In, First Out (FIFO)
- Last In, First Out (LIFO)
- Average Cost (AVCO).

These methods refer to the valuation of issues and not to the actual physical issue of materials or goods, which will normally be made in chronological order (i.e. old stocks will be issued first). We'll see what this means later.

What do we mean by each of these methods? Figures 12.3 to 12.5 based on Table 12.1 illustrate each of them. For simplicity, the Goods received note and Material requisition note numbers have been left out.

Table 12.1 *Receipts and issues of goods*

RECEIPTS			ISSUES (Sales)	
Date	Quantity	Price £	Date	Quantity
19x3			19x3	
Jan 2	500	2.00	Jan 12	300
Jan 10	250	2.20	Jan 20	250
Jan 15	300	2.50	Jan 28	200
Jan 26	250	2.60		

First In, First Out (FIFO) method

This method assumes that materials or goods received first will be issued first. Consequently, the price of the first batch will be used for all issues until the first batch is completely exhausted. The price of the second batch will then be used, and so on.

Using the data given in Table 12.1, a Store's ledger account is shown overleaf, in Figure 12.3, to illustrate the FIFO method of valuation. Look at this carefully now.

► FIFO

Figure 12.3 Stores ledger account: FIFO method

Date	RECEIPTS			ISSUES			BALANCE		
	Quantity	Rate £	Value £	Quantity	Rate £	Value £	Quantity	Rate £	Value £
19x2 Jan 2	500	2.00	1,000				500	2.00	1,000
Jan 10	250	2.20	550				500 + 250 750	2.00 2.20	1,000 550 1,550
Jan 12				300	2.00	600	200 + 250 450	2.00 2.20	400 550 950
Jan 15	300	2.50	750				200 250 + 300 750	2.00 2.20 2.50	400 550 750 1,700
Jan 20				200 + 50 250	2.00 2.20	400 110 510	200 + 300 500	2.20 2.50	440 750 1,190
Jan 26	250	2.60	650				200 300 + 250 750	2.20 2.50 2.60	440 750 + 650 1,840
Jan 28				200	2.20	440	300 + 250 550	2.50 2.60	750 + 650 1,400

The advantages and disadvantages of this method are as follows.

Advantages

- The method is simple to understand and easy to operate.
- Pricing under this method is in line with the ideal physical movement of stocks, i.e. oldest stocks are issued first.
- Issue prices are based on actual costs.
- Closing stock will reflect current prices.

► Advantages and disadvantages of the FIFO method

Disadvantages

- When prices change frequently, this method tends to be cumbersome and time-consuming.
- Issue price may not reflect current price.
- During a period of rising prices, this method will lead to costs being understated and profits overstated whereas during a period of falling prices the reverse occurs – costs are overstated and profits understated

Last In, First Out (LIFO) method

This method assumes that materials or goods received last are issued first. As a consequence the price of the last batch in stock will be used for all items until this batch (theoretically) is completely exhausted. The price of the previous batch received will then be used and so on.

► LIFO

Figure 12.4 illustrates this method of valuing issues and closing stock.

Figure 12.4 Stores ledger account: LIFO method

Date	RECEIPTS			ISSUES			BALANCE		
	Quantity	Rate £	Value £	Quantity	Rate £	Value £	Quantity	Rate £	Value £
19x2 Jan 2	500	2.0	1,000				500	2.00	1,000
Jan 10	250	2.20	550				500 + 250 750	2.00 2.20	1,000 + 550 1,550
Jan 12				50 + 250 300	2.00 2.20	100 + 550 650	450	2.00	900
Jan 15	300	2.50	750				450 + 300 750	2.00 2.50	900 + 750 1,650
Jan 20				250	2.50	625	450 + 50 500	2.00 2.50	900 + 125 1,025
Jan 26	250	2.60	650				450 50 + 250 750	2.00 2.50 2.60	900 125 + 650 1,675
Jan 28				200	2.60	520	450 50 + 50 550	2.00 2.50 2.60	900 125 + 130 1,155

The advantages and disadvantages of this method are as follows.

Advantages

- Cost of goods will generally reflect current prices.
- Valuation of closing stock tends to be conservative in an inflationary situation, as closing stock will be valued at earlier prices.

► Advantages and disadvantages of the LIFO method

Disadvantages

- When prices change frequently this method tends to be cumbersome and time-consuming.
- This method is unrealistic in the sense that it assumes the physical movement of stock to be the opposite of that actually followed.
- Closing stock will be understated in inflationary situations and overstated in deflationary situations.

AVCO

This method uses the average price for costing issues. The average price is calculated by dividing the total cost of goods in stock by the total units or quantity of goods in that stock. It is in fact a weighted average of stock prices. In other words:

► Average Cost (AVCO) method

$$\text{Average cost} = \frac{\text{value of goods in stock}}{\text{total quantity in stock}}$$

The average price or cost is calculated each time materials are received in store. Figure 12.5 shows how this method works.

Figure 12.5 Stores ledger account: AVCO method

Date	RECEIPTS			ISSUES			BALANCE		
	Quantity	Rate £	Value £	Quantity	Rate £	Value £	Quantity	Rate £	Value £
19x2 Jan 2	500	2.00	1,000				500	2.00	1,000
Jan 10	250	2.20	550				750	2.067	1,550
Jan 12				300	2.067	620	450	2.067	930
Jan 15	300	2.50	750				750	2.24	1,680
Jan 20				250	2.24	560	500	2.24	1,120
Jan 26	250	2.60	650				750	2.36	1,770
Jan 28				200	2.36	472	550	2.36	1,298

► Advantages and disadvantages of AVCO method

The advantages and disadvantages of the AVCO method are as follows.

Advantages

- It tends to smooth out fluctuations in purchase prices.
- As compared to LIFO or FIFO this method is less cumbersome and time-consuming since calculations of average price are limited to the number of receipts which are much less frequent than issues.
- The valuation of closing stocks is always made at a single price.

Disadvantages

- Material cost or cost of goods does not represent actual price.
- The average price may run to a number of decimal places.

Perpetual and periodic inventory valuation method

► **Perpetual inventory**: taking stock all the time

► **Periodic inventory**: taking stock at particular points in time

In the examples given so far we have seen FIFO, LIFO and AVCO used as **perpetual** methods of stock control, meaning that stock values are recorded perpetually throughout the year. There is an alternative which is known as **periodic stock valuation**. Using this method the exact date of issue of materials (or sales) during the year are ignored and, instead, calculations are made of the value of the closing stock in terms of the total quantity issued or sold during the period.

The LIFO method, on the basis of periodic valuation, assumes that the last batch of materials to come during the period are the first to be issued, instead of the last to be received before the issue was made. The FIFO method, will however, give the same value under both the methods.

The difference between the perpetual method and the periodic methods is illustrated in Example 12.3.

Example 12.3 Comparing perpetual and periodic inventory taking FIFO

From the following particulars, calculate the value of the closing stock using **(i)** FIFO **(ii)** LIFO **(iii)** AVCO methods on:

a a perpetual inventory basis
b a periodic inventory basis.

RECEIPTS	ISSUES	
19x2		
January 10 @ £ 20 each	April	8 units
August 20 @ £ 30 each	December	7 units

Solution

Perpetual inventory: FIFO

Date	RECEIPTS			ISSUES			BALANCE		
	Quantity	Rate £	Value £	Quantity	Rate £	Value £	Quantity	Rate £	Value £
19x2 Jan	10	20	200				10	20	200
April				8	20	160	2	20	40
Aug	20	30	600				2 + 20 22	20 30	40 + 600 640
Dec				2 + 5 7	20 30	40 + 150 190	15	30	450

Periodic inventory: FIFO
Value of closing stock = 15 units @ £ 30
= £ 450
The FIFO method gives us the same answer under both methods.

Example 12.4 Comparing perpetual and periodic inventory taking LIFO

Perpetual Inventory: LIFO

Date	RECEIPTS			ISSUES			BALANCE		
	Quantity	Rate £	Value £	Quantity	Rate £	Value £	Quantity	Rate £	Value £
19x2 Jan	10	20	200				10	20	200
April				8	20	160	2	20	40
Aug	20	30	600				2 + 20 22	20 30	40 + 600 640
Dec				7	30	210	2 + 13 15	20 30	40 + 390 430

Periodic inventory: LIFO

Under the periodic method, it will be assumed that the whole of the issues, that is, 15 units, have been made from the last lot received, that is, 20 units at £30 each. Consequently, the value of the closing stock will be: 5 units @ £30 + 10 units @ £20 = £150 + £200 = £350
The LIFO valuation will give two different answers under the two methods.

Example 12.5 Comparing perpetual and periodic inventory taking AVCO

Perpetual inventory: AVCO

Date	RECEIPTS			ISSUES			BALANCE		
	Quantity	Rate £	Value £	Quantity	Rate £	Value £	Quantity	Rate £	Value £
19x2 Jan	10	20	200				10	20	200
April				8	20	160	2	20	40
Aug	20	30	600				22	29.09	640
Dec				7	29.09	204	15	29.09	436

Periodic inventory: AVCO

Received 10 @ £20 = £200

$$\frac{20}{30} \text{ @ £30} = \frac{\text{£600}}{\text{£800}}$$

$$\text{Average cost (price)} = \frac{\text{£800}}{30} = \text{£26.67}$$

So the value of the closing stock = 15 units @ £26.67 = £400

The average cost under the periodic method is a single average for the whole period, whereas under the perpetual method a new average is calculated each time a new receipt is made. Results obtained under these two methods are therefore different.

It's time for you to have a go at a problem involving FIFO, LIFO and AVCO methods of stock valuation. Try the following assignment now.

ACT **12.1**

The following are particulars of the receipts and issues of Material X during the month of January 19X3.

Receipts	*Issues*
Jan 2 100 units @ £ 5	Jan 8 150 units
6 200 units @ £ 5.20	15 220 units
12 250 units @ £ 5.30	

Prepare and complete the Stores ledger account for Material X using:

a the FIFO method of valuation

b the LIFO method of valuation

c the AVCO method of valuation.

► Answer in appendix

FIFO, LIFO and AVCO methods compared

The effect of the different methods on cost of material used, closing stock and profit is illustrated in the following example.

Example 12.6

The following details were extracted from the records of a trader which sells only one product on 31 December 19x2:

Opening stock	400 units @ £12
Purchases	1,200 units @ £15
Closing stock	500 units
Wages	£1,500
Other expenses	£2,000
Sales	£25,000

You are required to prepare a Trading and Profit and Loss account for the year ended 31 December 19x2 using:

a the FIFO method of valuation

b the LIFO method of valuation

c the AVCO method of valuation.

► Carefully read through the solution paying particular attention to the working.

Solution

Valuation of closing stock of the product, based on periodic inventory valuation method:

a	FIFO method:	500 units @ £15	=	£7,500
b	LIFO method:	100 units @ £15	=	£1,500
		400 units @ £12	=	£4,800
		500		£6,300
c	AVCO method:	400 units @ £12	=	£4,800
		1,200 units @ £15	=	£18,000
		1,600		£22,800

So average price = $\frac{£22,000}{1600}$ = £14.25

Value of closing stock = 500 @ £14.25 = £7,125

Trading and Profit and Loss account for the year ended 31 December 19x2

	FIFO		LIFO		AVCO	
	£	£	£	£	£	£
Sales		25,000		25,000		25,000
Opening stock	4,800		4,800		4,800	
Add purchases	18,000		18,000		18,000	
	22,800		22,800		22,800	
Less Closing stock	7,500		6,300		7,125	
Cost of goods sold		15,300		16,500		15,675
Gross profit		9,700		8,500		9,325
Wages	1,500		1,500		1,500	
Other expenses	2,000		2,000		2,000	
		3,500		3,500		3,500
Net profit		6,200		5,000		5,825

You will see that the FIFO method tends to understate the cost of sales and overstate the closing stock and gross profit, whereas the LIFO method tends to do just the opposite, i.e. it overstates the cost of sales and understates both closing stock and gross profit. The AVCO method tends to present a compromise between the two: cost of sales, closing stock and gross profit – all of these lie between those obtained by the FIFO and LIFO methods.

Chapter summary

- Working capital is current assets minus current liabilities.
- The major components of working capital are: debtors, creditors, stocks and cash.
- The effective control of working capital is necessary in order to avoid overtrading and undertrading.
- The control of debtors and creditors in the accounting system requires the use of the Sales ledger control account and Purchases ledger control account respectively.
- Stock control aims at maintaining an optimum quantity of all materials or goods stocked, avoiding overstocking and under-stocking.
- The actual levels of stocks are regulated by:
  - maximum stock level
  - minimum stock level
  - re-order stock level
  - re-order stock quantity.
- The main methods of valuing stores issues and closing stocks are: FIFO, LIFO and AVCO.

ACT **12.2**

For questions 1 to 4 choose the letter corresponding with the best answer.

1 The balance on the Sales ledger control account is normally:
- **A** A debit balance
- **B** A credit balance
- **C** Either **A** or **B**
- **D** Greater than that in the Purchases ledger control account.

2 The balance on the Purchases ledger control account is normally:
- **A** A credit balance
- **B** A debit balance
- **C** Either **A** or **B**
- **D** Equal to the debtors figure in the Balance Sheet.

3 Discounts received are normally shown in the General Ledger:
- **A** On the debit side of the Purchases ledger control account
- **B** On the credit side of the Purchases ledger control account
- **C** On the debit side of the Sales ledger control account
- **D** On the credit side of the Sales ledger control account.

4 Re-order stock quantity is:
- **A** Exactly the same as maximum stock level
- **B** Another name for re-order level
- **C** Exactly the same as minimum stock level
- **D** The quantity to be ordered at re-order level.

► Answers in appendix

5 From the following information, prepare a Sales ledger control account for the month of November 19x0.

02/02/95
Homework.

	£
November 1:	
Sales ledger balances	10,980
Totals for November:	
Sales Day Book	55,890
Returns Inwards Book	2,125
Discounts allowed	1,735
Cash received from customers	54,943
November 31 sales ledger balances	8,067

► No answer given

6 From the following information, prepare a Purchases ledger control account for the month of April 19x2.

02/02/95
Homework.

	£
April 1 Purchases Ledger balances	25,690
Totals for April	
Purchases Day Book	83,938
Returns Outwards Book	3,540
Payments made to suppliers	75,350
Discounts received	2,129
April 30 Purchases Ledger balances	28,609

► Answer in appendix

7 The financial year of Holy Ltd ended on 30 November 19x8. The Trial Balance of the company as at that date reveals a difference in the books. You have been asked to draw up a Sales ledger control account and a Purchases ledger control account to help locate any errors.

The figures for debtors and creditors in the Trial Balance as at 30 November 19x8 were £9,075 and £63,443 respectively. These represent the totals of the balances of the individual debtors and creditors accounts in the Sales and Purchases Ledgers.

You are able to extract the following information for the year ended 30 November 19x8 from the books of original entry.

	£
Cash Book:	
Discounts allowed	5,680
Cash and cheques from customers	267,108
Discounts received	4,531
Cash and cheques paid to suppliers	238,730
Refunds given to customers	178
Customers' cheques dishonoured	512
Journal:	
Bad debts written off	1,433
Increase in the provision of bad debts	250
Set offs	1,002
Sales Journal	308,650
Purchases Journal	244,078
Returns in Journal	5,086
Returns out Journal	7,204

According to the audited accounts for the previous year debtors and creditors as at the close of business on 30 November 19x7 were £40,044 and £69,832 respectively.

You are required to:

a Draw up the relevant Control accounts.

b Suggest where an error might have been made. Give your reasons.

(AAT)

► No answer given

8 The following information has been taken from the records of ASA Film Supplies Ltd for the year ended 30 November 19x9.

	£
Total creditors as at 1 Dec 19x8 (per control account and reconciled list of balances)	96,504
Credit purchases for the year to 30 Nov 19x9 (per Purchases Day Book)	874,210
Returns from credit customers (per Returns Inwards Book)	17,533
Returns to credit suppliers (per Returns Outwards Book)	21,555
Bad debts (per Journal)	11,200
Suppliers' balances transferred to be set off against debit balances in Sales Ledger (per Journal)	5,454

Discount allowed to credit customers (per Cash Book)	22,226
Discount received from credit suppliers (per Cash Book)	16,350
Cash paid to suppliers (per Cash Book)	820,311

Required:

a Prepare a Creditors control account for the year ended 30 November 19x9.

A list of balances on the individual creditors' ledger accounts as at 30 November 19x9 totalled £106,984. During the subsequent checking of the books the following matters are discovered:

(i) An invoice from Lux Projectors, a supplier, for £531 has been erroneously entered into the Purchases Book as £351.

(ii) A debit note for £211 sent by ASA Film Supplies Ltd to Printox Ltd, a supplier, has been missed out completely from the records.

(iii) A page of the Purchases Book has been totalled and carried forward as £255,666. The correct total should have been £255,606.

b Prepare Journal entries to correct the above errors.

Assume that the control accounts are maintained as an integral part of the double-entry system and individual personal accounts are maintained on a memorandum basis only.

Note: Dates and narratives are not required.

c Compute the corrected balance on the Creditors Control account as at 30 November 19x9.

d Recalculate the total of the individual creditor balances as at 30 November 19x9.

e What conclusion can you draw if the figures in **c** and **d** above are the same?

(AAT)

► Answer in appendix

9 The following balances as at 1 November 19x8 were extracted from the books of Mary Saunders Ltd.

	Debit £	*Credit* £
Purchases ledger control a/c	1,436	16,892
Sales ledger control a/c	35,975	874
Provision for doubtful debts		1,100
Provision for discounts allowable		640

The following transactions took place during the year ended 31 October 19x9.

	£
Credit sales	417,920
Cash sales	91,210
Credit purchases	289,439
Cash purchases	12,960
Amounts received from credit customers	392,710

Paid to credit suppliers	264,360
Returns outwards to credit suppliers	9,400
Returns inwards from credit customers	11,556
Bad debts written off	1,927
Bad debt recovered	518
(relevant bad debts written off in 19x7)	

Additional information:

(i) The provision for doubtful debts at 31 October 19x9 is to be 5 per cent of amounts due to the company according to the Sales ledger control account.

(ii) The provision for discounts allowable at 31 October 19x9 is to be 2.5 per cent of the relevant amount derived from the Sales Ledger.

(iii) A dispatch of goods in October 19x9 to a credit customer has been charged out at the list price of £2,000 without adjusting for the trade discount due of 10 per cent.

(iv) It is the company's policy to record bad debts recovered in the Sales ledger control account.

(v) The trial balance as at 31 October 19x9 of Mary Saunders Ltd included the following.

	Debit £	*Credit* £
Purchases ledger control account	937	
Debtors ledger control account		572

Required:

a Prepare the following accounts for the year ended 31 October 19x9 in the books of Mary Saunders Ltd:
Purchases ledger control
Sales ledger control.

b Carry out a computation of the accounts to be included in the Balance Sheet as at 31 October 19x9 of Mary Saunders Ltd for the following items.
Trade debtors
Trade creditors.

(AAT)

► No answer given

10 Purchases and sales of a good by a retailer are as follows.

Purchases		*Sales*	
19x1			
Jan	100 units at £50 each	Mar	30 units at £75 each
Feb	50 units at £55 each	May	110 units at £77 each
Apr	80 units at £61 each	June	50 units at £80 each

There was no opening stock.
It is the policy of the business to use perpetual inventory method of stock valuation.

You are required to:

a Calculate the closing stock using **(i)** FIFO **(ii)** LIFO **(iii)** AVCO methods.

b Prepare the Trading account for the six months ended 30 June 19x1 using the different values of closing stocks obtained in **a** above.

► Answer in appendix

11 T. Hall provides you with the following information relating to one of the goods traded in by him.

		£
Opening stock:		
200 units valued as follows:		
LIFO basis	£10 per unit 200	2,000
FIFO	£15 per unit 200	3,000
Purchases during April 19x4:		
600 units at £16		9,600
Sales during April 19x4:		
600 units at £23		13,800

You are required to:

a Determine value of closing stock using (i) FIFO (ii) LIFO methods.

b Prepare Trading accounts for April using (i) FIFO (ii) LIFO methods.

► No answer given

12 You have been given the following information for the small retail business of A. Green for six months to 31 December 19x1.

Receipts		Sales	
July	260 @ £20 each	Aug	120 @ £26 each
Sept	140 @ £20 each	Oct	160 @ £26 each
Nov	180 @ £22 each	Dec	120 @ £26.50 each

Capital at 1 July 19x1 consisted of fixed assets £10,000 and bank £5,000.
Expenses for the six months were £600.

You are required to:

a Calculate the closing stock values at 31 December 19x1 using FIFO and LIFO methods on the basis of perpetual inventory method.

b Calculate the closing stock values at 31 December 19x1 using FIFO and LIFO methods on a periodic inventory basis.

c Draw up a Trading and Profit and Loss account for the six months ended 31 December 19x1 using FIFO and LIFO valuations on a periodic inventory basis.

d Prepare a Balance Sheet as at 31 December 19x1 using FIFO and LIFO methods on a periodic inventory basis.

► Answer in appendix

e On the basis of your results, state the relative merits of FIFO and LIFO methods of stock valuation.

► No answer given for part **e**

13 From the Day Books to the final accounts – a comprehensive example

Chapter objectives

By the end of this chapter, you should:

- have recapitulated what you have already learnt in chapters 2–6 and 8–12 (as listed below)
- appreciate the way in which all these procedures interconnect and together provide information for the solution of practical business problems.

Introduction

Preceding chapters introduced and explained different aspects of the accounting function of a business organisation, including:

- writing up the books of original entry – Chapter 3
- posting to the Ledger; balancing off the ledger accounts – Chapter 3
- writing up the two and three column Cash Books – Chapter 4
- extracting a Trial Balance from the Ledger and the Cash Book – Chapter 3
- correction of errors through the Journal and the Suspense account – Chapter 5
- preparation of the Trading and Profit and Loss account and the Balance Sheet – Chapter 8
- adjustments to the final accounts for accruals, prepayments, bad debts and provision for bad debts and provision for depreciation on fixed assets – chapters 9 and 10
- control of working capital by controlling debtors, creditors and stocks – Chapter 12.

It is to be hoped that you have understood the main concepts and ideas introduced in each chapter on its own. However it is important that you also understand the different procedures as part of a single process in which the accountant uses these bits and bytes of information to solve practical business problems, such as ascertaining the true profit of a business over a time period, or giving an accurate picture of a firm's financial standing at a given point in time.

To help you to appreciate the interconnectedness of accountancy procedures this chapter provides you with a simulated business problem which we shall work through together. This will involve accounting procedures running from the initial recording of transactions in the books of original entry through to the preparation of final accounts with year end adjustments. Checks and balances will be built into the example in the form of control accounts.

Example 13.1 From books of original entry to the final accounts

On 1 July 19x1, Robert Kirk's books disclosed the following balances.

	£	
Premises	30,000	
Fixtures and fittings at cost	3,000	
Motor vehicles at cost	10,000	
Debtors:		
R. King	2,500	
S. Patel	2,250	
C. Ibrahim	1,750	
R. Laker	3,900	
Stocks	11,600	
Cash	2,000	
Bank	5,500	(DR)
Provision for depreciation:		
Fixtures and fittings	900	
Motor vehicles	4,000	
Provision for bad debts	800	
Creditors:		
G. Banda	6,750	
A. Archibald	8,200	
J. Roy	4,600	
Capital – R. Kirk	47,250	

The balances on the Sales ledger control account and the Purchases ledger control account as at 1 July 19x1 were equal to the sum of debtors and creditors, as listed above, respectively.

During July, the following transactions were made.

July	1	Cash sales £500
	3	Goods sold on credit to: S. Patel £750; R. Laker £900
	4	Bought a word processor in cash for £1,000
	5	Paid office expenses in cash £110
	6	Bought goods on credit from: A. Archibald £1,000; J. Roy £1,500; G. Banda £500
	8	Cash sales banked straight away £450
	8	Paid wages in cash £200
	9	Received a cheque from R. Laker for £3,000
	9	Goods sold on credit to: R. King £2,000; C. Ibrahim £2,250; AB Ltd £3,000
	11	Paid insurance by cheque £600
	12	Cash sales £350
	14	Goods returned to Robert Kirk by: S. Patel £150; R. Laker £200
	15	Paid wages in cash £200
	16	Motor expenses paid in cash £80
	20	Received cheques from: R. King £4,325 (after deducting a cash discount for £175); S. Patel £2,250
	21	Robert Kirk returned goods to: A. Archibald £200; G. Banda £110
	22	Wages paid in cash £200
	23	Cash sales £450
	25	Paid G. Banda a cheque for £6,960 (after deducting a cash discount of £180)

26	Robert Kirk withdrew £800 from the bank for his personal use
27	Motor expenses paid in cash £100
28	Paid electricity bill by cheque £100
30	Cash sales £750
30	Paid a cheque for £8,550 to A. Archibald, in full settlement
31	Cash purchases £1,500
31	Received a cheque from C. Ibrahim for £3,800 in settlement of his account

On 31 July 19x1, Robert Kirk had gathered the following additional information.

(i) The stocks at 31 July 19x1, were valued at £8,000
(ii) Insurance was prepaid by £500
(iii) Wages owing amounted to £200
(iv) Depreciation to be provided on:
- Fixtures and fittings at 10 per cent on cost
- Motor vehicles at 25 per cent, using a reducing balance method
- Word processor at 24 per cent p.a. on cost

(v) No change to be made on the provision for bad debts

You are required to:

a Prepare the appropriate day books for Robert Kirk for the month of July 19x1.
b Write up his three-column Cash Book for the month.
c Journalize the opening entries.
d Enter all the entries from the books of original entry to the appropriate accounts in Kirk's Ledger. For this purpose, divide the Ledger into Sales, Purchases and General Ledgers.
e Write up the necessary control accounts in the General Ledger and balance it off on 31 July 19x1, preparing a schedule of debtors and creditors to check the accuracy of total debtors and creditors figures.
f Prepare a Trial Balance as at 31 July 19x1.
g Prepare a Trading and Profit and Loss account for the month ended 31 July 19x1 and a Balance Sheet as at that date.

Solution

The following abbreviations are used in the folio columns of the various accounts:

J = Journal
SDB = The Sales Day Book
PDB = The Purchases Day Book
RIB = The Returns Inwards Book
ROB = The Returns Outwards Book
CB = The Cash Book
GL = The General Ledger
SL = The Sales Ledger
PL = The Purchases Ledger

The number following the letter(s) represents the page number of the relevant book.

a The Day Books

The Sales Day Book

Page 5

19x1			£ p
July 3	S. Patel	SL2	750
3	R. Laker	SL4	900
9	R. King	SL1	2000
9	C. Ibrahim	SL3	2250
9	AB Ltd	SL5	3000
31	Transferred to Sales a/c in the General Ledger	GL8	8900

The Returns Inwards Book

Page 3

19x1			£ p
July 14	S. Patel	SL2	150
	R. Laker	SL4	200
	Transferred to Returns Inwards a/c in the General Ledger	GL10	350

The Purchases Day Book

Page 8

19x1			£ p
July 6	A. Archibald	PL2	1000
6	J. Roy	PL3	1500
6	G. Banda	PL1	500
31	Transferred to the Purchases a/c in the General Ledger	GL9	3000

The Returns Outwards Book

Page 2

19x1			£ p
July 21	A. Archibald	PL2	200
21	G. Banda	PL1	110
31	Transferred to Returns outwards Book in the General Ledger	GL11	310

b The Cash Book

The Cash Book

Page 20

19x1			D £	C £	B £				D £	C £	B £
July 1	Balances b/d			2,000	5,500	July 1	Word Proces.	GL14		1,000	
July 1	Sales	GL8		500		July 5	Office exp.	GL15		110	
July 8	Sales	GL8			450	July 8	Wages	GL16		200	
July 9	R. Laker	SL4			3,000						
July 12	Sales	GL8		350		July 11	Insurance	GL17			600
July 20	R. King	SL1	175		4,325	July 15	Wages	GL16		200	
July 20	S. Patel	SL2			2,250	July 16	Motor exp.	GL18		80	
July 23	Sales	GL8		450		July 22	Wages	GL16		200	
July 30	Sales	GL8		750		July 25	G. Banda	PL1	180		6,960
July 31	C. Ibrahim	SL3	200		3,800	July 26	Drawings	GL20			800
						July 27	Motor exp.	GL18		100	
						July 28	Electricity	GL19			100
						July 30	A. Archibald	PL2	450	1,500	8,550
						July 31	Balance purchases b/d	GL9		660	2,315
			375	4,050	19,325				630	4,050	19,325
Aug 1	Balance c/d			660	2,315						

c The Journal

The Journal

Page 10

19x1			DR £ p	CR £ p
July 1	1 Premises	GL2	30,000	
	Fixtures and fittings	GL3	3,000	
	Motor vehicles	GL4	10,000	
	R. King	SL1	2,500	
	S. Patel	SL2	2,250	
	C. Ibrahim	SL3	1,750	
	R. Laker	SL4	3,900	
	Stocks	GL4	11,600	
	Cash	CB20	2,000	
	Bank	CB20	5,500	
	Capital – R. Kirk	GL1		47,250
	G. Banda	PL1		6,750
	A. Archibald	PL2		8,200
	J. Roy	PL3		4,600
	Provision for bad debts	GL5		800
	Provision for depreciation:			
	Fixtures and fittings	GL6		900
	Motor vehicles	GL7		4,000
	Assets and liabilities at this date		72,500	72,500

d The Ledgers

The Sales Ledger

Page 1

DR				R. King a/c					CR
19x1				£	19x1				£
July	1	Balance b/d	J10	2,500					
July	9	Sales	SDB5	2,000	July	20	Bank	CB20	4,325
					July	20	Discount allowed	CB20	175
				4,500					4,500

Page 2

DR				S. Patel a/c					CR
19x1				£	19x1				£
July	1	Balance b/d	J10	2,250	July	14	Returns	RIB3	150
July	3	Sales	SDB5	750	July	20	Bank	CB20	2,250
					July	31	Balance c/d		600
				3,000					3,000
Aug	1	Balance b/d		600					

Page 3

DR				C. Ibrahim a/c					CR
19x1				£	19x1				£
July	1	Balance b/d	J10	1,750	July	31	Bank	CB20	3,800
July	9	Sales	SDB5	2,250	July	31	Discount allowed	CB20	200
				4,000					4,000

Page 4

DR				R. Laker a/c					CR
19x1				£	19x1				£
July	1	Balance b/d	J10	3,900	July	9	Bank	CB21	3,000
July	3	Sales	SDB5	900	July	14	Returns inwards	RIB3	200
					July	31	Balance c/d		1,600
				4,800					4,800
Aug	1	Balance b/d		1,600					

Page 5

DR				AB Ltd a/c					CR
19x1				£	19x1				£
July	9	Sales	SDB5	3,000	July	31	Balance c/d		3,000
Aug	1	Balance b/d		3,000					

The Purchases Ledger

Page 1

G. Banda a/c

DR 19x1				£	CR 19x1				£
July	21	Returns outwds.	ROB2	110	July	1	Balance b/d	J10	6,750
July	25	Bank	CB20	6,960	July	6	Purchases	PDB8	500
July	25	Discount recd.	CB20	180					
				7,250					7,250

Page 2

A. Archibald a/c

DR 19x1				£	CR 19x1				£
July	21	Returns Outwds	ROB2	200	July	1	Balance b/d	J10	8,200
July	30	Discount recd.	CB20	450	July	6	Purchases	PDB8	1,000
July	30	Bank		8,550					
				9,200					9,200

Page 3

J. Roy a/c

DR 19x1				£	CR 19x1				£
July	31	Balance c/d		6,100	July	1	Balance b/d	J10	4,600
					July	6	Purchases	PDB8	1,500
				6,100					6,100
					Aug	1	Balance b/d		6,100

The General Ledger

Page 1

Capital – Robert Kirk a/c

DR 19x1				£	CR 19x1				£
					July	1	Balance b/d	J10	47,250

Page 2

Premises a/c

DR 19x1				£	CR 19x1				£
July	1	Balance b/d	J10	30,000	July	31	Balance c/d		30,000
Aug	1	Balance b/d		30,000					

Page 3

DR			Fixtures and fittings a/c								CR
19x1				£		19x1				£	
July	1	Balance b/d	J10	3,000		July	31	Balance c/d		3,000	
Aug	1	Balance b/d		3,000							

Page 4

DR			Motor vehicles a/c								CR
19x1				£		19x1				£	
July	1	Balance b/d	J10	10,000		July	31	Balance c/d		10,000	
Aug	1	Balance b/d		10,000							

Page 5

DR			Provision for bad debts a/c								CR
19x1				£		19x1				£	
						July	1	Balance b/d	J10	800	

Page 6

DR			Provision for depreciation – fixtures and fittings a/c								CR
19x1				£		19x1				£	
						July	1	Balance b/d	J10	900	

Page 7

DR			Provision for depreciation – motor vehicles a/c								CR
19x1				£		19x1				£	
						July	1	Balance b/d	J10	4,000	

Page 8

DR			Sales a/c								CR
19x1				£		19x1				£	
						July	1	Cash	CB20	500	
						July	8	Bank	CB20	450	
						July	12	Cash	CB20	350	
						July	23	Cash	CB20	450	
						July	30	Cash	CB20	750	
						July	31	Credit sales total	SDB5	8,900	
										11,400	

Page 9

DR		Purchases a/c							CR
19x1				£	19x1				£
July	31	Cash	CB20	1,500					
July	31	Credit purchases for the month	PDB8	3,000					
				4,500					

Page 10

DR		Returns inwards a/c							CR
19x1				£	19x1				£
July	31	Returns for month	RIB3	350					

Page 11

DR		Returns outwards a/c							CR
19x1				£	19x1				£
					July	31	Returns for month	ROB2	310

Page 12

DR		Discount allowed a/c							CR
19x1				£	19x1				£
July	31	Total for month	CB20	375					

Page 13

DR		Discount received a/c							CR
19x1				£	19x1				£
					July	31	Total for month	CB20	630

Page 14

DR		Word processor a/c							CR
19x1				£	19x1				£
July	1	Cash	CB20	1,000	July	31	Balance c/d		1,000
Aug	1	Balance b/d		1,000					

Page 15

DR		Office expenses a/c							CR
19x1				£	19x1				£
July	5	Cash	CB20	110					

Page 16

DR			Wages a/c					CR
19x1				£	19x1			£
July	8	Cash	CB20	200				
July	15	Cash	CB20	200				
July	22	Cash	CB20	200				
				600				

Page 17

DR			Insurance a/c					CR
19x1				£	19x1			£
July	11	Bank	CB20	600				

Page 18

DR			Motor expenses a/c					CR
19x1				£	19x1			£
July	16	Cash	CB20	80				
	27	Cash	CB20	100				
				180				

Page 19

DR			Electricity a/c					CR
19x1				£	19x1			£
July	28	Bank	CB20	100				

Page 20

DR			Drawings a/c					CR
19x1				£	19x1			£
July	26	Bank	CB20	800				

Page 21

DR			Stocks a/c					CR
19x1				£	19x1			£
July	1	Trading a/c	J10	11,600				

e The control accounts

Page 22

DR					**Sales ledger control a/c**				CR
19x1				£	19x1				£
July	1	Balance b/d		10,400	July	31	Returns inwards	RIB3	350
July	31	Credit sales	SDB5	8,900	July	31	Discount allowed	CB20	375
					July	31	Cash	CB20	13,375
					July	31	Balance c/d		5,200
				19,300					19,300
Aug	1	Balance b/d		5,200					

Page 23

DR					**Purchases ledger control a/c**				CR
19x1				£	19x1				£
July	31	Returns outwards	ROB2	310	July	1	Balance b/d		19,550
July	31	Discount received	CB20	630	July	31	Credit purchases	PDB8	3,000
July	31	Bank	CB20	15,510					
July	31	Balance c/d		6,100					
				22,550					22,550
					Aug	1	Balance b/d		6,100

Note:

The sum of balances of the debtors' accounts is equal to the balance obtained from the Sales ledger control account. Similarly, the balance given by the schedule of creditors exactly equals the Purchases ledger control account balance.

Schedule of debtors

Name	DR Balance
	£
S. Patel	600
R. Laker	1,600
AB Ltd	3,000
	5,200

Schedule of creditors

Name	CR Balance
	£
J. Roy	6,100

f The Trial Balance

Robert Kirk

Trial Balance as at 31 July 19x1

	DR £	CR £
Cash in hand	660	
Cash at bank	2,315	
Debtors	5,200	
Creditors		6,100
Capital		47,250
Premises	30,000	
Fixtures and fittings	3,000	
Motor vehicle at cost	10,000	
Provision for bad debts		800
Provision for depreciation –		
Fixtures and fittings		900
Motor vehicle		4,000
Sales	11,400	
Purchases	4,500	
Returns inwards	350	
Returns outwards		310
Discount allowed	375	
Discount received		630
Word processor	1,000	
Office expenses	110	
Wages	600	
Insurance	600	
Motor expenses	180	
Electricity	100	
Drawings	800	
Stock	11,600	
	71,390	71,390

g The Trading and Profit and Loss account and Balance Sheet

Robert Kirk

Trading and Profit and Loss account for the month ended 31 July 19x1

	£	£	£
Sales		11,400	
Less Returns inwards			350
		11,050	
Less Cost of sales:			
Opening stock		11,600	
Add Purchases	4,500		
Less Returns outwards	310	4,190	
	15,790		
Less Closing stock		8,000	7,790
Gross profit			3,260
Add Discount received			630
		3,890	
Less Expenses:			
Discount allowed		375	
Office expenses		110	
Wages	600		
Add amount due	200	800	
Insurance	600		
Less amount prepaid	500	100	
Motor expenses		180	
Electricity		100	
Depreciation on:			
Fixtures and fittings (W1)	25		
Motor vehicles (W2)	125		
Word processor (W3)	20	170	1,835
Net profit			2,055

Workings

W1 Depreciation on Fixtures and fittings

Depreciation for the year = 10% × £3,000 = £300

the month = £300 × 12 = £25

W2 Depreciation on motor vehicle

	£
At cost	10,000
Less depreciation to 31 July 19x0	4,000
WDV at 1 July 19x1	6,000

Depreciation for the year $= 25\% \times \frac{£6,000}{12}$

Depreciation for the month $= \frac{£1500}{12} = £125$

W3 Depreciation on word processor

Depreciation for the month $= 24\% \times \frac{£1,000}{12}$

$= \frac{£240}{12} = £20$

Robert Kirk
Balance Sheet as at 31 July 19x1

	Cost £	Deprecn. £	Net £
Fixed Assets:			
Premises	30,000	–	30,000
Fixtures and fittings	3,000	925	2,075
Word processor	1,000	20	980
Motor vehicles	10,000	4,125	5,875
	44,000	5,070	38,930
Current Assets:			
Stocks		8,000	
Debtors	5,200		
Less provision for bad debts	800		
		4,400	
Prepayments		500	
Cash at bank		2,315	
Cash in hand		660	
		15,875	
Less Current Liabilities:			
Creditors	6,100		
Accruals	200	6,300	
Net Current Assets			9,575
			48,505
Financed by:			
Capital			47,250
Add Net profit of the month			2,055
			49,305
Less Drawings			800
			48,505

You will have noticed some accounts (mainly revenue and expense accounts) in the General Ledger have not been balanced. These accounts show their respective state at the time of preparing the Trial Balance. As you've already noticed in preparing the final accounts, we have made a number of adjustments relating to the additional information given, after the Trial Balance had been prepared. These adjustments would eventually go through the double-entry system. We'll now show these accounts as they would appear after the final accounts are made. This will give you an opportunity to compare and contrast a number of accounts prepared before and after the preparation of final accounts.

Page 1

DR				**Capital – Robert Kirk a/c**					CR
19x1				£	19x1				£
July	31	Drawings	GL20	800	July	1	Balance b/d	J10	47,250
July	31	Balance c/d		48,505	July	31	Profit and loss a/c		2,055
				49,305					49,305
					Aug	1	Balance b/d		48,505

Page 20

DR			**Drawings a/c**						CR
19x1				£	19x1				£
July	26	Bank	CB20	800	July	26	Capital a/c	GL1	800

Page 5

DR			**Provision for bad debts a/c**						CR
19x1				£	19x1				£
July	31	Balance c/d		800	July	1	Balance b/d	J10	800
					Aug	1	Balance b/d		800

Page 6

DR			**Provision for depreciation – fixtures and fittings a/c**						CR
19x1				£	19x1				£
July	31	Balance c/d		925	July	1	Balance b/d	J10	900
					July	31	Profit and Loss a/c		25
				925					925
					Aug	1	Balance b/d		925

Page 7

DR			**Provision for depreciation – motor vehicle a/c**						CR
19x1				£	19x1				£
July	31	Balance c/d		4,125	July	1	Balance b/d	J10	4,000
					July	31	Profit and Loss a/c		125
				4,125					4,125
					Aug	1	Balance b/d		4,125

Page 8

DR			**Sales a/c**						CR
19x1				£	19x1				£
July	31	Trading a/c		11,400	July	1	Cash	CB20	500
					July	8	Bank	CB20	450
					July	12	Cash	CB20	350
					July	23	Cash	CB20	450
					July	30	Cash	CB20	750
					July	31	Credit sales for the month	SDB5	8,900
				11,400					11,400

Page 9

DR			Purchases a/c						CR
19x1				£	19x1				£
July	31	Cash	CB20	1,500	July	31	Trading a/c		4,500
July	31	Credit purchases for the month	POB88	3,000					
				4,500					4,500

Page 10

DR			Returns inwards a/c						CR
19x1				£	19x1				£
July	31	Total returns for the month		350	July	31	Trading a/c		350

Page 11

DR			Returns outwards a/c						CR
19x1				£	19x1				£
July	31	Trading a/c		310	July	31	Returns outwards for the month	ROB2	310

Page 12

DR			Discount allowed a/c						CR
19x1				£	19x1				£
July	31	Total for month	CB20	375	July	31	Profit and Loss a/c		375

Page 13

DR			Discount received a/c						CR
19x1				£	19x1				£
July	31	Profit and Loss a/c		630	July	31	Total for month	CB20	630

Page 15

DR			Office expenses a/c						CR
19x1				£	19x1				£
July	5	Cash	CB20	110	July	31	Profit and Loss a/c		110

Page 16

DR					**Wages a/c**				CR
19x1				£	19x1				£
July	6	Cash	CB20	200	July	31	Profit and Loss a/c		800
July	15	Cash	CB20	200					
July	22	Cash	CB20	200					
July	31	Balance (accruals) c/d		200					
				800					800
					Aug	1	Balance (accruals) b/d		200

Page 17

DR					**Insurance a/c**				CR
19x1				£	19x1				£
July	11	Bank	CB20	600	July	31	Profit and Loss a/c		100
					July	31	Balance c/d (prepayments)		500
				600					600
Aug	1	Balance b/d (prepayments)		500					

Page 18

DR					**Motor expenses a/c**				CR
19x1				£	19x1				£
July	16	Cash	CB20	80	July	31	Profit and Loss a/c		180
July	27	Cash	CB20	100					
				180					180

Page 19

DR					**Electricity a/c**				CR
19x1				£	19x1				£
July	28	Bank	CB20	100	July	31	Profit and Loss a/c		100

Page 24

DR					**Provision for depreciation – word processor a/c**				CR
19x1				£	19x1				£
July	31	Balance c/d		20	July	31	Profit and Loss a/c		20
					Aug	1	Balance b/d		20

Page 21

DR			**Stocks a/c**						CR
19x1				£	19x1				£
Sept	1	Trading account	J10	11,600	Sept	30	Transfer to Trading		11,600
Oct	1	Trading account (stock on hand)		8,000					

Note:

1 A new account – Provision for depreciation – word processor, has been created when the asset is depreciated.

2 All but two accounts – Wages and Insurance – are in perfect balance; there is nothing to carry forward to the next period. Since the Wages account shows an accrual of £200, it is shown as a credit balance as it is a liability to the business. The Rent account shows a prepayment of £500 which represents an asset and is therefore a debit balance.

3 The opening stock is transferred to the Trading account and is closed at the end of the accounting period. A new entry (not balance b/d) is made on the debit side (Trading a/c – stock on hand) for the closing stock.

4 The revenue account e.g. Sales, is in balance. This is what normally happens, but a revenue account such as Rent receivable can show either an amount received in advance (a liability) or an amount due (an asset).

Chapter summary

- This chapter brought together the various parts of the accounting system developed earlier into a comprehensive whole. The accounting system begins with economic events – that is, business transactions – and culminates in the preparation of an income statement and a Balance Sheet. The whole process can be presented by the very simple flow chart as follows.

Transactions ➧ Day Books and Cash Book ➧ Ledger ➧ Trial Balance ➧ Final Accounts

- This process was illustrated by working out fully a comprehensive example.

ACT **13.1**

Refer to Example 13.1 given in the text and examine Robert Kirk's Balance Sheet as at 31 July 19x1. Robert Kirk made the following transactions during August 19x1.

August

1	Paid wages in cash £200
3	Bought goods on credit from MN Ltd 5000; J. Roy 1,000.
5	Sold goods on credit to: S. Patel 2,200; R.Laker 800; AB Ltd 3,500
6	Cash sales, £450
8	Paid wages in cash, £200
10	Motor expenses paid in cash £120
12	Received a cheque for £2,280 from R. Laker in settlement of his account.
15	Paid office expenses by cheque for £180
16	Cash sales paid direct into the bank, £660
20	Bought goods for cash, £400
21	Robert Kirk withdrew £500 from the business bank account for personal use
22	Received a cheque from AB Ltd for £2,800
23	Motor expenses paid by cheque for £100
25	Sold goods on credit to: S. Patel for £800; AB Ltd for £1,800
26	Cash sales £450
28	Settled J. Roy's account by cheque, £6,800
30	Received a cheque from S. Patel for £2,000
31	Sold goods on credit to AB Ltd £3,000

The following information should also be taken into consideration.

(i) Stocks at 31 August 19x1 were valued at £6,500
(ii) Wages due, but not yet paid £200
(iii) The insurance premium of £600 paid on 1 July 19x1 was for the period from 1 July to 31 December 19x1
(iv) Depreciation to be provided on:
- Fixtures and fittings at 10 per cent on cost
- Motor vehicles at 25 per cent, using the reducing balance method.
- Word processor at 24 per cent p.a. on cost.

(v) Provision for bad debts should be reduced to £500

You are required to:

a Write up the appropriate day books of Robert Kirk for the month of August 19x1.
b Write up the Cash Book for the month.
c Post the transactions during the month, to the appropriate accounts in the Sales Ledger, Purchases Ledger, and the Nominal Ledger repectively.
d Update Robert Kirk's control accounts to include the relevant transactions in August.
e Prepare a Trial Balance as at 31 August 19x1.
f Prepare Kirk's income statement for the month ended 31 August 19x1 and a Balance Sheet as at that date.

► No answer given

14 Accounting from incomplete records

Chapter objectives

By the end of this chapter, you should be able to:

- understand the meaning and significance of 'a statement of affairs' in the context of incomplete and single-entry records
- calculate the net profit of a sole trader by using the increased net worth method of finding profit
- reconstruct a number of relevant accounts such as the Cash Book, Total debtors control account and Total creditors control account
- prepare the final accounts from incomplete records through various adjustments and reconstructions.

INCOMPLETE ACCOUNTS

There are many small businesses such as corner shops and self-employed persons (e.g. plumbers, electricians, hairdressers etc) who do not maintain a proper set of books according to the principles of double-entry book-keeping. The main reasons for this are:

- these people have neither the time nor the expertise to write up the books themselves
- they cannot afford the services of a qualified book-keeper or accountant on a regular basis.

What they normally do is to keep a written record of their cash receipts and cash payments and possibly some form of records of their debtors and creditors. In many instances, such information would be incomplete. Yet they need to produce a Trading and Profit and Loss account and a Balance Sheet at the end of their accounting period, to find out how much profit or loss they have made over the year, and to forward a copy of each of these statements to the Inland Revenue for tax purposes. Most of them cannot prepare such statements themselves. They are therefore obliged to employ an accountant to prepare their final accounts. It is the job of the accountant to prepare a set of accounts, from the **incomplete** and **single-entry** records provided, which will give a true and fair view of the business.

This chapter explains how we can prepare a Trading and Profit and Loss account and a Balance Sheet from a set of single-entry records which often do not give a complete picture of the business at all. The term **single-entry** in this context simply means that transactions are recorded once only and not twice, as is the practice with double-entry book-keeping.

The basic approach

The basic approach to preparing final accounts of a business from incomplete records is to identify what information is missing, and then reconstruct some accounts as best as we can, by piecing together all the available items of information. This exercise is similar to putting together a jigsaw puzzle, or to solving a crossword puzzle. It requires a great deal of careful thinking and a lot of patience!

The minimum information we would need to prepare final accounts (not just determine the profit) from incomplete records includes:

- assets and liabilities at the start of the year and/or
- assets and liabilities at the end of the year, together with
- cash receipts and payments during the year.

If the opening and closing balances are known, total receipts or payments can easily be estimated by balancing the Cash or Bank account.

Once we've collected as much information as possible, we proceed as follows.

Steps in preparing accounts from incomplete records

1 Determine the owner's opening capital by preparing a statement of affairs at the beginning of the year. Sometimes it may be necessary to prepare such a statement at the end of the year to find the closing capital.
2 Write up a cash book from available information such as bank statements, till rolls etc. Expenses can usually be estimated.
3 Construct the Total debtors' and Total creditors' accounts to establish sales and purchases figures.
4 Now proceed to prepare the Trading and Profit and Loss account and the Balance Sheet.

There is no commonly accepted procedure for dealing with incomplete records problems. Nor is there any standard or model answer to single-entry problems. Everything depends on what information is and is not available. The four steps given above are for guidance only and should not be treated as a standard for all problems connected with single-entry and incomplete records.

Statement of affairs

► **Statement of affairs**: prepared instead of a Balance Sheet where figures are not derived from double-entry records

A statement of affairs is similar to a Balance Sheet and contains all the information that we would normally expect in a Balance Sheet. However, we do not call it a Balance Sheet, simply because the balances contained in it are not derived, as in the case of a Balance Sheet, from balances generated from the double-entry system.

The basis of the Balance Sheet is the accounting equation:

A(ssets) – L(iabilities) = C(apital)

This equation is of great value to us. It enables us, as we saw in Chapter 3, to determine the capital if we know the assets and liabilities of a business at a given time.

Let's now apply the accounting equation to determine the capital as at a certain date as shown in Example 14.1.

Example 14.1 Determining capital from incomplete records

The following information was provided by Harry Appleton as to his assets and liabilities on 31 December 19x9.

Assets: Stocks – £4,750; Fixtures and fittings – £1,200; Motor van – £7,900; Debtors – £3,400; Cash in hand – £900; Cash at bank – £1,500.

Liabilities: Creditors – £4,800

Ascertain Harry Appleton's capital as at 31 December 19x9.

Solution

Sum of assets = £4,750 + £1,200 + £7,900 + £3,400 + £900 + £1,500
= £19,650

Liabilities = £4,800

Therefore C = $A - L$
= £19,650 – £4,800
= £14,850

We can now prepare Harry's statement of affairs, as shown in Example 14.2.

Example 14.2 Harry Appleton's Statement of affairs

From the information supplied in Example 14.1 above, prepare Harry Appleton's Statement of affairs as at 31 December 19x9.

Solution

Harry Appleton
Statement of affairs as at 31 December 19x9

	£	£
Fixed Assets:		
Fixtures and fittings		1,200
Motor van		7,900
		9,100
Current Assets:		
Stocks	4,750	
Debtors	3,400	
Cash at bank	1,500	
Cash in hand	900	
	10,550	
Less Current Liabilities:		
Creditors	4,800	
Working Capital		5,750
		14,850
Financed by:		
Capital		14,850

► **Net worth**: equals capital

► Profit can be estimated by calculating any increase in the net worth of the business.

Profit estimation

Increased net worth method

The **net worth** of a business is the same thing as capital which is estimated, as we've seen several times before, by working out the difference between the sum of assets and the sum of external liabilities, i.e. liabilities to people outside the business. Now if the net worth of a business over a period of one year has increased, other things remaining the same, this increase in capital must have been due to **profit** made during the year. We can see, then, that the net profit for the year is equal to the increase in capital over the year. Thus:

> Net profit = capital at end of year – capital at start of year

The 'financed by' section of the Balance Sheet of a sole trader looks like this.

Capital	X_a
Add Net Profit	X
	X
Less Drawings	X
	X_b

The capital figure denoted by X_a above, represents capital at the beginning of the year, and the final capital figure, denoted by X_b represents capital at the end of the year. This means that difference in capital over the year plus drawings equals net profit of the year. We thus get another important formula for ascertaining net profit.

> Net profit = capital at end of year – capital at start of year + drawings for the year

Further refinements to the formula can be made if we are to estimate net profit by this method when additional capital is introduced by the owner in the course of the year. In such a situation:

> Net profit = capital at end of year – capital at start of year + drawings – capital introduced during the year

All the three formulae given above are useful to estimate net profit by the **Increased net worth method**. If, however, the net worth of a business, that is, its capital, decreases over a given period, then instead of a net profit, the business would have made a net loss. In terms of our formulae, the net profit figure will be a negative quantity representing a loss.

Example 14.3 illustrates the estimation of net profit by this method.

Example 14.3

Maggie Robertson provided the following information regarding her business.

	31 Dec 19x8	31 Dec 9x9
	£	£
Assets and Liabilities:		
Cash in hand	200	100
Cash at bank	1,500	

Bank overdraft		200
Motor vehicles	8,500	6,500
Fixtures	1,000	900
Trade debtors	500	1,950
Trade creditors	1,750	750
Stocks	4,500	6,200

You also ascertain the following.

(i) Maggie withdrew cash of £4,000 from the business for her personal use during the year ended 31 December 19x9.

(ii) On 1 January 19x9, she put £1,000 into the business as additional capital.

You are required to:

a Prepare statements of affairs at the end of 19x8 and 19x9.

b Estimate the net profit or loss earned by Maggie for the year ended 31 December 19x9.

c Show the capital section of Maggie's Balance Sheet as at 31 December 19x9.

Solution

a

Maggie Robertson
Statement of affairs as at 31 December 19x8

	£	£	£
Fixed Assets:			
Fixtures			1,000
Motor vehicles			8,500
			9,500
Current Assets:			
Stocks		4,500	
Debtors		500	
Cash at bank		1,500	
Cash in hand		200	
		6,700	
Less Current Liabilities:			
Creditors		1,750	
			4,950
			14,450
Financed by:			
Capital			14,450

Maggie Robertson
Statement of affairs as at 31 December 19x9

	£	£	£
Fixed Assets:			
Fixtures			900
Motor vehicles			6,500
			7,400
Current Assets:			
Stocks		6,200	
Debtors		1,950	
Cash in hand		100	
		8,250	

continues over

Less Current Liabilities:			
Creditors	750		
Bank overdraft	200	950	
			7,300
			14,700
Financed by:			
Capital			14,700

b Profit for the year to 31 December 19x9, is estimated as follows.

	£
Closing Capital	14,700
Less Opening Capital	14,450
Increase in Capital	250
Add Drawings	4,000
	4,250
Less Additional Capital introduced	1,000
Profit of the year	3,250

c

Maggie Robertson

Balance Sheet as at 31 December 19x9 (extract only)

	£	£
Financed by:		
Capital – 1 Jan 19x9		14,450
Add: Additional capital introduced	1,000	
Net Profit	3,250	4,250
		18,700
Less Drawings		4,000
		14,700

ACT **14.1**

1 John Green's assets and liabilities as at 31 March 19x1 were as follows.

Total assets £33,500

Total liabilities £20,150

Calculate his capital as at 31 March 19x1.

2 Sandra Moss' opening and closing capitals for an accounting year were £15,000 and £20,000 respectively. Estimate her profit or loss for the year on the assumption that:

a She did not withdraw any money out of the business.

b Her drawings during the year amounted to £2,000.

3 Simon Shaw's capital as at 1 January 19x1 was £18,500. During the year to 31 December 19x1, he introduced £2,000 as additional capital into his business. His drawings for the year amounted to £3,000. His capital on 31 December 19x1 was £21,000.

Estimate Simon Shaw's profit or loss during the year ended 31 December 19x1.

► Answers in appendix

Profit estimation

Gross margin and markup

Sometimes we may be provided with simple accounting ratios such as **gross margin percentage, markup percentage,** or **net profit percentage** which will help us to determine gross profit or net profit or some other missing figures such sales or cost of sales. But before we look at how to use these ratios, let's define the terms **margin** and **markup**.

Gross margin is another name for gross profit and is simply the difference between sales and cost of sales. When gross profit (GP) is expressed as a percentage of sales, it is called the **gross profit ratio** (or percentage). Thus:

► **Gross margin or gross profit**: difference between sales and cost of sales. Often expressed as a percentage.

$$\text{GP (\%)} = \frac{\text{GP}}{\text{sales}} \times 100$$

This ratio is useful for calculating either gross profit (when sales are given), or sales (when GP is given).

Markup is the amount that is added on to the cost of a product or service to arrive at the selling price. It is normally expressed as a percentage which is given by:

► **Markup**: amount added to cost of product to produce the selling price. Often expressed as a percentage.

$$\text{Markup (\%)} = \frac{\text{GP}}{\text{cost of sales}} \times 100$$

This ratio can be used to calculate either the gross profit or the cost of sales. Before we use the GP and the mark up ratios to determine some missing figures, we need to remember the following two independent relationships or equations:

- cost of sales + gross margin = sales
- cost of sales + mark up = sales

Let's now illustrate the use of these two ratios. Example 14.3 illustrates the use of the gross profit percentage and Example 14.4 uses the markup percentage.

Example 14.3 The use of gross profit percentage

Alec Dawson provided the following details for the year to 31 December 19x0.

	£
Stock at 1 Jan 19x0	5,650
Stock at 31 Dec 19x0	7,250
Sales	51,000

Alec's policy has been to apply a uniform gross margin of 33.3 per cent.

You are required:

a To calculate his gross profit.
b To calculate the value of the purchases for the year.
c To prepare Alec's Trading account for the year to 31 December 19x0.

Solution

a $\frac{\text{GP}}{\text{sales}} = 33.3\%$

So GP = 33.3% × sales

Therefore GP = 33.3% × £51,000

= £17,000

b We know that

cost of sales = opening stock + purchases – closing stock.

Again, cost of sales = sales – GP

= £51,000 – £17,000 = £34,000

Therefore opening stock + purchases – closing stock = £34,000

or £5,650 + purchases – £7,250 = £34,000

Purchases = £34,000 + £7,250 – £5,650

= £35,600

c

Alec Dawson

Trading account for the year ended 31 December 19x0

► The use of gross profit percentage to estimate gross profit

	£	£
Sales		51,000
Less cost of sales:		
Opening stock	5,650	
Add Purchases	35,600	
	41,250	
Less closing stock	7,250	34,000
Gross Profit		17,000

Example 14.4 The use of markup to estimate gross profit

The following details relate to Elaine Henderson's business.

	£
Stocks at 1.4.x0	8,252
Stocks at 31.3.x1	7,100
Purchases	25,000
Uniform markup in use – 25%	

You are required to:

a Calculate gross profit for the year.

b Calculate sales for the year.

c Prepare Elaine's Trading account for the year to 31 March 19x1.

Solution

a Mark up $= \dfrac{\text{GP}}{\text{cost of sales}}$

Cost of sales = opening stock + purchases – closing stock

= £8,252 + £25,000 – £7,100

= £26,152

Therefore $\dfrac{\text{GP}}{\pounds 26{,}152} = 25\%$

Therefore GP = 25% × £26,152 = £6,538

b Sales = cost of sales + gross profit

= £26,152 + £6,538

= £32,690

c

Elaine Henderson

Trading account for the year ended 31 March 19x1

	£	£
Sales		32,690
Less cost of sales:		
Opening stock	8,252	
Add purchases	25,000	
	33,252	
Less Closing stock	7,100	26,152
Gross Profit		6,538

► The use of markup to estimate profit

Now try to do the following assignment.

ACT 14.2

1 For Charlie Stuart's business, stocks at the start and at the end of the year are £6,500 and £7,500 respectively. Purchases are £15,000. You are required to calculate:

- **a** Sales, if the gross profit is constant at 40 per cent on sales
- **b** Sales, if the gross profit is constant at 33.3 per cent on cost
- **c** Gross profit, if sales for the year are £30,000
- **d** Gross profit percentage, if sales for the year are £50,000.

2 From the following details regarding Amanda's business, calculate:

- **a** Gross profit
- **b** Sales for the year.

	£
Stock 1.7.x0	8,000
Stock 30.6.x1	7,150
Purchases	20,000

Uniform mark up in use is 20 per cent

3 Bob Simple provides you with the following information regarding his business.

	£
Stock 1.1.x0	6,250
Stock 31.12.x0	5,900
Sales for the year	40,000

Uniform gross margin in use is 30 per cent.

Calculate Bob's:

- **a** Gross profit
- **b** Purchases, for the year.

► Answers in appendix

Reconstructing accounts to determine some key items

These might include sales and purchases.

Determining sales

We can find out the sales for a year from the records of cash receipts from customers and the opening and closing balances of debtors. This can be done in two ways: either by calculation or by reconstructing the Total debtors ledger control account. To determine sales by calculation we use the following rule:

> Sales = cash received from debtors – opening debtors + closing debtors

The same information can be obtained by constructing a Total debtors control account. The balancing figure in the Control account will give us the value of sales. In Example 14.5, we illustrate the calculation of sales as well as drawing up a Debtors control account.

Example 14.5 Determination of sales

The following details relate to the business of Arthur King.

	£
Cash received from customers	15,900
Debtors – 1.1.x1	6,750
Debtors – 31.12.x1	8,400

You are required to determine the sales for the year by:

a Calculation

b Using a Total debtors control account.

Solution

a

Sales = cash received from debtors – opening debtors + closing debtors
= £15,900 – £6,750 + £8,400
= £17,550

b

DR		Total debtors control a/c						CR	
			£	p				£	p
Jan	1	Balance b/d	6,750		Dec	31	Cash	15,900	
Dec	31	Sales (difference)	17,550		Dec	31	Balance c/d	8,400	
			24,300					24,300	

Note: The opening debtors balance is a debit balance as it represents an asset. Cash received from debtors reduces their indebtedness and therefore appears on the credit side. The closing balance b/d will be a debit balance, but the balancing operation will appear on the opposite side, i.e. the credit side. What remains now is to find the difference between the total on the credit side, i.e. £24,300, and the total on the debit side, i.e. £6,750, which is £17,550. This difference represents the sales of the year and is shown as such on the debit side.

Determining purchases

As for sales, we can determine purchases made during the year from the records of cash payments to the suppliers and the opening and closing balances of the creditors. We can do this either by calculation or by drawing up a Total creditors control account. The following rule is used to work out the purchases figure.

> Purchases = cash paid to creditors – opening creditors + closing creditors

The 'balancing' figure in a Total creditors control account will also give us the figure for purchases. These two ways of determining purchases are illustrated in Example 14.6.

Example 14.6 Calculating purchases

Felicity Snapper provides us with the following information relating to her business.

	£
Creditors – 1.4.x0	10,500
Creditors – 31.3.x1	12,250
Payments to creditors	40,750

You are required to ascertain purchases made during the year by:

a Calculation

b Using a Total creditors control account.

Solution

a

Purchases = cash paid to creditors – opening creditors + closing creditors

= £40,750 – £10,500 + £12,250

= £42,500

b

DR			Total creditors control a/c					CR	
			£	p				£	p
Mar.	31	Cash	40,750		April	1	Balance b/d	10,500	
Mar.	31	Balance c/d	12,250				Purchases (balancing figure)	42,500	
			53,000					53,000	

Determining expenses

Calculating expenses such as rent and rates, telephone bills etc, might require the usual adjustments for accruals and prepayments. If in doubt, go back to Chapter 9 and read it again.

► **Accruals and prepayments**: see Chapter 9.

Sometimes it may be necessary to construct an Expense control account similar to the Debtors control account, to determine the relevant expenses for the year. In determining the expenses, we must pay due attention to the different accounting concepts and conventions developed in Chapter 6. A proper understanding of the Matching principle, in particular, will be of great use in tackling many problems relating to incomplete records.

ACCOUNTING FROM INCOMPLETE RECORDS: A COMPREHENSIVE EXAMPLE

Let's now piece together all the ideas developed in this chapter by working out a comprehensive problem as in Example 14.7.

Example 14.7 A comprehensive example of accounting from incomplete records

Eric Hague is a trader who does not maintain a proper set of books. However, he has supplied you with the following information relating to his assets and liabilities at certain dates.

	As at 31 March 19x0	As at 31 March 19x1
	£	£
Stocks	5,750	6,150
Debtors	4,800	5,500
Creditors	6,250	6,900
Premises at cost	18,000	18,000
Fixtures and fittings at book value	1,600	1,200
Rates paid in advance	200	250
Wages accrued	300	200
Bank	500	–

Eric's receipts and payments for the year to 31 March 19x1, were as follows:

	£
Receipts:	
Cash sales	20,800
Receipts from debtors	30,650
Payments:	
Payments to suppliers	28,950
Rates	2,200
Wages to part time staff	3,600
General expenses	3,720
Drawings	4,200
Motor vehicle	8,300

The following additional information is also available:

(i) Eric pays all cash direct into the bank and makes all payments by cheque.

(ii) He charges depreciation on fixtures and fittings at 25 per cent p.a. on their book value as at the beginning of the year.

(iii) The vehicle was bought on 1 October 19x0, and is to be written off over five years assuming a resale value of £1,300 at the end of that period.

Eric asks you to:

a Prepare a Statement of affairs as at 31 March 19x0.

b Draw up a summarized bank account for the year to 31 March 19x1.

c Construct a Total debtors control account and a Total creditors control account.

d Prepare a Trading and Profit and Loss account for the year ended 31 March 19x1.

e Prepare a Balance Sheet as at that date.

Solution

a

Eric Hague
Statement of affairs as at 31 March 19x0

	£	£	£
Premises at cost			18,000
Fixtures and fittings			1,600
			19,600
Current Assets:			
Stocks		5,750	
Debtors		4,800	
Prepayments		200	
Bank		500	
		11,250	
Less Current Liabilities:			
Creditors	6,250		
Accruals	300	6,550	
Working Capital			4,700
			24,300
Financed by:			
Capital			24,300

b

DR **Summarized bank a/c** CR

			£	p				£	p
19x0					19x1				
Apr	1	Balance b/d	500		Mar	31	Creditors	28,950	
19x1					Mar	31	Rates	2,200	
Mar	31	Cash sales*	20,800		Mar	31	Wages	3,600	
Mar	31	Debtors	30,650		Mar	31	General expenses	3,720	
					Mar	31	Drawings	4,200	
					Mar	31	Motor vehicle	8,300	
					Mar	31	Balance c/d	980	
			51,950					51,950	
Apr	1	Balance b/d	980						

c

DR **Total debtors control a/c** CR

			£	p			£	p
19x0					19x1			
Apr	1	Balance b/d	4,800			Cash sales*	20,800	
19x1						Cash	30,650	
Mar	31	Sales	52,150			Balance c/d	5,500	
			56,950				56,950	

* **Note**: Cash sales figure is included in the Total debtors control a/c to determine total sales (not just credit sales) for the year.

Total creditors control a/c

DR			£	p				£	p CR
19x0					19x1				
Mar	31	Cash	28,950		Apr	1	Balance b/d	6,250	
Mar	31	Balance c/d	6,900				Purchases	29,600	
			35,850					35,850	

Workings

W1

Wages control a/c

DR			£	p				£	p CR
19x0					19x1				
Mar	31	Cash	3,600		Apr	1	Balance b/d	300	
Mar	31	Balance c/d	200		19x1				
					Mar	31	Profit and Loss a/c	3,500	
			3,800					3,800	

W2

Rates control a/c

DR			£	p				£	p CR
19x0					19x1				
Apr	1	Balance b/d	200		Mar	31	Profit and Loss a/c	2,150	
19x1					Mar	31	Balance c/d	250	
Mar	31	Cash	2,200						
			2,400					2,400	

W3

	£
Motor vehicle:	
Cost	8,300
Less Resale value	1,300
	7,000

Therefore annual depreciation $= \frac{£7{,}000}{5} = £1{,}400$ (for a full year)

Therefore depreciation for 6 months $= \frac{£1{,}400}{2} = £700$

d

Eric Hague

Trading and Profit and Loss account for the year ended 31 March 19x1

	£	£
Sales		52,150
Less cost of sales:		
Opening stock	5,750	
Add purchases	29,600	
	35,350	
Less closing stock	6,150	29,200
Gross Profit		22,950
Less expenses:		
Wages	3,500	
Rates	2,150	
General expenses	3,720	
Depreciation on fixtures and fittings	400	
Depreciation on motor vehicle (W3)	700	
		10,470
Net Profit		12,480

e

Eric Hague

Balance Sheet as at 31 March 19x1

	£	£	£
Fixed Assets			
Premises			18,000
Fixtures and fittings		1,600	
Less Depreciation		400	
			1,200
Motor vehicle		8,300	
Less Depreciation		700	7,600
			26,800
Current Assets			
Stocks		6,150	
Debtors		5,500	
Prepayment		250	
Bank		980	
		12,880	
Less Current Liabilities			
Creditors	6,900		
Accruals	200		
		7,100	
Working capital			5,780
			32,580
Financed by:			
Capital			24,300
Add Net profit			12,480
			36,780
Less Drawings			4,200
			32,580

Chapter summary

- There is no universally accepted procedure for preparing final accounts from incomplete records. The best method is to identify the key figures that are missing and try to evaluate them by reconstructing the appropriate accounts.
- The opening and closing capitals of a business can be determined by preparing two statements of affairs (similar to Balance Sheets) - one at the beginning and the other at the end of the year.
- Net profit of a business over a given period can be estimated by the Increased net worth method:

  Net profit = increase in capital (net worth) over the year
  plus drawings
  minus additional capital introduced during the year

- Gross or net profit can be calculated by using one or more accounting ratios such as gross profit percentage or markup percentage.
- Some other key values such as sales and purchases figures can be ascertained by constructing the Debtors control account and the Creditors control account respectively. The closing cash/bank figure can be determined by reconstructing the Cash Book.

ACT **14.3**

For questions 1 to 5 put a tick against the letter that represents the best answer from among the four given alternatives.

1 The percentage gross margin is 25 per cent and the sales are £50,000. The gross profit is:
A £12,500
B £37,750
C £25,000
D £72,500.

2 The opening and closing capitals of a sole trader with regard to a financial year are £50,000 and £55,000 respectively. If the owner withdrew £7,500 for his/her personal use, the net profit of the year was:
A £5,000
B £7,500
C £12,500
D £2,500.

3 A business sells goods at cost + 50 per cent. If sales are £100,000, the gross profit is:
A £150,000
B £50,000
C £66,667
D £33,333.

4 A business has the following details with regard to its credit sales: opening debtors £10,000; closing debtors £12,000; cash received from debtors during the year £35,000. Credit sales for the year are:
A £35,000
B £45,000
C £47,000
D £37,000.

► Answers in appendix

5 A sole trader always buys goods on credit. His creditors at the start of the year and at the close of the year were £23,000 and £20,000 respectively. The payments to his creditors during the year amounted to £50,000. His purchases for the year were:

A £70,000
B £73,000
C £47,000
D £53,000.

► Answer in appendix

6 Jim Hodges is a trader who does not keep a proper set of books of accounts.

The assets and liabilities of Jim at the start and close of a financial year were as follow.

	As at 1 Jan 19x1	As at 31 Dec 19x1
	£	£
Premises at cost	20,000	20,000
Fixtures at WDV	1,600	1,400
Stocks	6,350	5,980
Cash at bank	1,000	250
Cash in hand	200	300
Debtors	4,800	5,500
Creditors	7,000	6,200
Prepayments	500	350
Accruals	200	400

Additional information: during the year to 31 December 19x1, Jim's drawings amounted to £4,800.

You are required to:

a Prepare a Statement of affairs as at 1 January 19x1.
b Prepare a Statement of affairs as at 31 December 19x1.
c Determine from the statements prepared in **a** and **b** above, the net profit or loss made by Jim Hodges during the year to 31 December 19x1.

► Answer in appendix

7 Tom Green is a greengrocer who does not keep proper books of accounts. All his takings are in cash, from which he pays:

(i) £100 each week to himself for his personal use
(ii) £400 per month to his assistant
(iii) General expenses of £50 per week.

He pays the balance of the cash received into the bank. The following is a summary of his bank account for the year to 31 December 19x9:

	£		£
Balance b/f	1,700	Rent and rates	4,100
Cash banked	36,850		
		Purchases	25,600
		Sundries	500
		Motor vehicles	7,500
		Balance c/f	850
	38,550		38,550

Tom Green provides you with the following additional information.

	At 1 Jan 19x9	At 31 Dec 19x9
	£	£
Stocks	1,700	950
Trade debtors	800	550
Trade creditors	1,950	2,080
Rates paid in advance	100	120
Fittings at cost	4,000	?
Accumulated depreciation on fittings	1,440	?
Cash in hand	150	200

The motor vehicle was bought on 1 July 19x9 and depreciation on it should be charged at 25 per cent p.a. on cost. Fittings to be depreciated at 20 per cent on the Diminishing balance method.

You are required to prepare:

a A statement of Tom Green's affairs as at 1 January 19x9.

b A Trading and Profit and Loss account of Tom Green's business for the year ended 31 December 19x9.

c His Balance Sheet as at 31 December 19x9.

► No answer given

8 Mary Grimes, a retail fruit and vegetable merchant, does not keep a full set of accounting records. However, the following has been produced from the business records.

Summary of the Bank account for the year ended 31 August 19x8

	£		£
1 September 19x7 balance b/f	1,970	Payments to suppliers	72,000
Receipts from trade debtors	96,000	Purchase of motor van (E471 KBR)	13,000
Sale of private yacht	20,000	Rent and rates	2,600
Sale of motor van (A123 BWA)	2,100	Wages 15,100	
		Motor expenses	3,350
		Postage and stationery	1,360
		Drawings	9,200
		Repairs and renewals	650
		Insurances	800
		31 August 19x8 balance c/f	2,010
	120,070		120,070
1 September 19x8 Balance brought forward	2,010		

Assets and Liabilities other than balance at bank

	1 Sept 19x7	31 Aug 19x8
	£	£
Trade creditors	4,700	2,590
Trade debtors	7,320	9,500
Rent and rates accruals	200	260
Motor vans:		
A123 BWA – at cost	10,000	–
Provision for depreciation	8,000	–
E471 KBR — at cost	–	13,000
Provision for depreciation	–	to be determined
Stock in trade	4,900	5,900
Insurances prepaid	160	200

(i) All receipts are banked and all payments are made from the business bank account.

(ii) A trade debt of £300 owing by John Blunt and included in the trade debtors at 31 August 19x8, is to be written off as a bad debt.

(iii) It is Mary Grime's policy to provide depreciation at the rate of 20 per cent on the cost of motor vans held at the end of each financial year; no depreciation is provided in the year of sale or disposal of a motor van.

(iv) Discounts received during the year ended 31 August 19x8 from trade creditors amounted to £1,100.

You are required to:

a Prepare Mary Grime's Trading and Profit and Loss account for the year ended 31 August 19x8.

b Prepare Mary Grime's Balance Sheet as at 31 August 19x8.

(AAT)

► Answer in appendix

9 Jane Simpson, a retail trader, has been trying to keep her own accounting records and has extracted the following list of balances as at 30 April 19x9 from her accounts prior to the preparation of the annual accounts and Balance Sheet by James Lang, an accounting technician.

	£
Fixtures and fittings:	
at cost	8,000
provision for depreciation at 1 May 19x8	3,000
Motor vehicles:	
at cost	9,600
provision for depreciation at 1 May 19x8	5,600
Stock in trade	12,000
Trade debtors	7,000
Balance at bank	1,700
Trade creditors	6,900
Sales	132,000
Cost of sales	79,200
Establishment and administrative expenses	11,800
Sales and distribution expenses	33,500
Drawings	9,700
Capital	30,000

In preparing the annual accounts, James Lang made the following discoveries.

(i) The Trial Balance as at 30 April 19x9 prepared from the above list of balances did not balance.

(ii) The stock in trade at 30 April 19x8 should have been valued at £16,000 not £13,000 as included in the accounts for the year ended 30 April 19x8.

(iii) Provision is to be made for a commission for sales staff of 2 per cent of gross profit in the accounts for the year ended 30 April 19x9.

(iv) An entry in the Cash Book for the purchases of fixtures and fittings on 1 February 19x9 costing £4,500 has not been posted to the Ledger.

(v) Depreciation is to be provided for the year ended 30 April 19x9 as follows:
Fixtures and fittings 10 per cent per annum on cost
Motor vehicles 25 per cent per annum on cost.

(vi) A credit sale of £4,700 in March 19x9 was included correctly in the posting to the Sales account but recorded as £4,200 in the Debtors account.

(vii) Goods costing £600 withdrawn by Jane Simpson for her own use have not been recorded in the accounts.

You are required to:

a Prepare Jane Simpson's uncorrected Trial Balance as at 30 April 19x9.

b Prepare Jane Simpson's Trading and Profit and Loss account for the year ended 30 April 19x9 and Balance Sheet as at that date.

► No answer given

15 Accounting for non-profit making organizations

Chapter objectives

By the end of this chapter, you should be able to:

- explain the special accounts that are needed for non-profit making organizations.
- prepare a Receipts and Payments account
- draw up an Income and Expenditure account from the information contained in the Receipts and Payments account together with other information such as unpaid bills and prepayments
- prepare a Balance Sheet for a club or society.

NON-PROFIT MAKING ORGANIZATIONS

So far we have talked about organizations for which the main motive is profit making. There are many organizations in the private sector for which the primary aim is not to make a profit but to provide a service to their members. These non-profit making organizations are formed for social, sporting, educational, religious, political and charitable reasons. Although money making is not their stated objective, they still need money or income to finance their operation. Their sources of income are regular **subscriptions** and **donations** from their members and wellwishers. Some may supplement their income by running a bar and organizing fundraising activities such as wine and cheese parties.

► The usual accounting system for clubs and societies is a **Receipts and Payments account**.

This may not be adequate if the club has a large turnover and substantial assets.

Clubs or societies are accountable to their members for the income and outgoings (expenditure). Usually one member, known as the **treasurer**, will be elected each year to look after the finances of the organization. The treasurer may not have the time or the expertise to maintain a proper set of books of accounts. Most clubs and societies will maintain a record of cash receipts and cash payments in a Cash Book. At the end of the year, the treasurer will summarize these transactions in the form of a **Receipts and Payments account**. This may be sufficient to record their financial transactions if their activities are limited and if they do not own any notable assets other than cash, but a Receipts and Payments account alone may not give a true and fair view of the affairs of the organization if it owns assets and has liabilities to external parties. In this case, the organization will also need two other financial statements – an Income and Expenditure account, (similar to a Trading and Profit and Loss account for a profit-making organization) and a Balance Sheet. This chapter explains how such accounts or statements are prepared for non-profit making organizations.

The Receipts and Payments account for a non-profit making organization is a summary of the Cash Book.

The Receipts and Payments account

A Receipts and Payments account simply represents a summary of the Cash Book over a period of time, normally a year. It starts with the opening cash and bank balances. Money received is debited and money paid out is credited, just like a normal Cash Book. At the end of the financial year, it is balanced in the usual way to find the closing cash in hand or balance (or overdraft) at bank.

Example 15.1 shows how to write up a Receipts and Payments account.

Example 15.1 Writing up a Receipts and Payments account

The following information was drawn from the cash records of the treasurer of the Uptown Golf Club for the year ended 31 March 19x1.

	£
Opening cash in hand	150
Earnings from bar	3,975
Subscriptions	2,250
Payments for clubs, balls etc.	880
Payment for bar supplies	2,100
Donations	500
Postage and stationery	250
Collection for annual dinner	800
Expenses for annual dinner	850
Sundry expenses	150
Ground maintenance	990

You are required to to write up a Receipts and Payments account for the year ended 31 March 19x1.

Solution

Uptown Golf Club
Receipts and Payments account for the year ended 31 March 19x1

DR								CR	
19x0			£	p				£	p
April	1	Balance b/d	150						
19x1					19x1				
Mar	31	Bar earnings	3,975		Mar	31	Purchase of clubs	880	
Mar	31	Subscriptions	2,250				Purchase of bar supplies	2,100	
Mar	31	Donations	500				Postage and stat.	250	
		Collection for annual dinner	800				Payment for annual dinner	850	
							Sundry expenses	150	
							Ground maintenance	990	
							Balance c/d	2,455	
			7,675					7,675	
April	1	Balance b/d	2,455						

Note:

1 The ruling of the Receipts and Payments account is similar to a ledger. However, you can use a normal two-column Cash Book especially when you wish to show the cash and bank transactions separately.

2 Since the Receipts and Payments account is prepared at the year end, the dates for all the entries except that for the opening balance, are shown to be the last day of the financial year. The actual dates for the receipts and payments must have been recorded in the treasurer's Cash Book.

The Income and Expenditure account

An Income and Expenditure account for a club or society corresponds to the Trading and Profit and Loss account for a business organization. It can be prepared either horizontally or vertically and the method of preparing it is almost the same as that of a Trading and Profit and Loss account. However, in this account we do not show 'net profit or loss'. Instead of the term 'net profit', we write 'surplus of income over expenditure' and we substitute the term 'loss' by 'excess of expenditure over income', or 'deficit of income over expenditure'. These two expressions mean the same thing as net profit and net loss respectively, but it is inappropriate to use the terms profit and loss for a non-profit making organization.

► The **Income and Expenditure account** for a non-profit making organization is equivalent to the **Trading and Profit and Loss** account.

► See Chapter 8

When preparing the Income and Expenditure account, accounting concepts and conventions such as the **going concern, accruals, matching and prudence concepts** still apply. This will inevitably require some adjustments to certain revenue and expense items for accruals and prepayments. A good example of a revenue item requiring adjustment is the **subscription** collected from members.

► For non-profit making organizations write **surplus of income over expenditure**, not 'profit'.

An Income and Expenditure account is constructed to find the amount of surplus or deficit of income over expenditure for a year, and also to provide as much information as possible to the members. Many clubs and societies run bars for their members. In this case it may be necessary to prepare a Bar Trading account to determine how much profit or loss has been made. (It *is* quite acceptable to use the term **profit** or **loss** in the context of a trading account for a bar or shop run by a non-profit making organization.)

► Accounting concepts and conventions also apply to non-profit making organizations.

► See Chapter 6

We shall now look at some of the adjustments and special accounts in detail.

Subscriptions

Subscriptions are the major source of income for most clubs and societies, but subscriptions collected during a certain year may not always represent the true income of that year. Part of the subscriptions collected this year might have been unpaid subscriptions from the previous year; another part might have been subscriptions paid in advance for the following year. To find the amount of the subscriptions received for the current year, we need to prepare a Subscriptions account which will normally show two opening and closing balances – one a debit balance and the other a credit balance. **Unpaid subscriptions** refer to the amount owing by the members to the club, and are therefore considered to be assets (debtors) of the club. Consequently, in the subscriptions account they are shown as a debit balance. Likewise, any **subscriptions prepaid** are considered to be liabilities of the club to the members as they have not as yet received any benefits for the money they have paid. Accordingly they are shown as a credit balance in the Subscriptions account. Any subscriptions collected will be credited to the Subscriptions account, the corresponding debit entry being in the Cash Book. At the year end, the closing balances relating to unpaid and prepaid subscriptions will be entered, and the Subscriptions account will be balanced. The balancing figure which will appear on the debit side of the subscriptions account, will give the income of the year. Example 15.2 gives an illustration of a Subscriptions account.

Example 15.2 The Subscriptions account for a non-profit making organization

The treasurer of the Fairfield Sporting Club gives you the following information:

On 31 December 19x0, subscriptions in arrears amounted to £375 and subscriptions received in advance amounted to £120. Subscriptions received for the year to 31 December 19x1 totalled £19,750. This amount included £375 due at the end of 19x0 and £200 in advance for 19x2. Subscriptions outstanding at 31 December 19x1 amounted to £325.

You are required to use the information given above to write up the Subscriptions account of Fairfield Sporting Club for the year ended 31 December 19x1, indicating the amount that is to be transferred to the Income and Expenditure account.

Solution

DR					**Subscriptions a/c**		CR
		£				£	
	Balance b/d (in arrears)	375			Balance b/d (in advance)	120	
	Income and Expenditure a/c (balance)	19,620			Cash	19,750	
	Balance c/d (in advance)	200			Balance c/d (in arrears)	325	
		20,195				20,195	
	Balance b/d	325			Balance b/d	200	

Note:

1 The two figures representing 'balance c/d' and balance 'b/d' at the year end cancel each other and therefore appear on the opposite sides. Subscriptions due at the end of year represent an asset and are thus a debit balance (after being brought down). Initially, they are shown as a credit entry. The same reasoning applies to subscriptions received in advance.

2 As the Subscriptions account will be prepared at the year end anyway, dates are ignored.

Note that the amount transferred to the Income and Expenditure account is £19,620, as income for the year, not £19,750 (the actual cash received during the year). £19,620 is the balancing figure and is obtained by deducting £575 (£375 + £200 – the total on the debit side before the insertion of the balancing figure) from £20,195 (the total on the credit side). There is another way of calculating the subscriptions income of the year:

	£	£
This year's subscriptions paid in the previous year		120
Add Cash received this year		19,750
		19,870
Less Subscriptions in arrears for last year	375	
Subscriptions in advance for next year	200	
		575
		19,295
Add Subscriptions in arrears for current year		325
Subscription income for this year		19,620

Note:

Working on an accrual basis as in Example 15.2 shows the true income and expenditure for the period.

Working on a cash basis shows cash received and spent during the accounting period.

Example 15.2 has been worked out on the accruals basis. However, it is possible to show subscriptions income on the cash basis, i.e. to treat the actual cash receipts for the year as the subscriptions income to be transferred to the Income and Expenditure account. Using the data of Example 15.2 on this basis, income from subscriptions will be shown as £19,750.

There is yet another method, based on the Prudence concept, of calculating subscriptions for purposes of the Income and Expenditure account. The outstanding subscriptions at the year end are ignored under this method, because it is widely believed that members who have enjoyed the benefits of a club for a year, and yet have not paid their dues, have no intention of paying anything at all. It is therefore better to ignore subscriptions outstanding, otherwise the surplus of income over expenditure may be overstated. If the principle of Prudence is applied to the data of Example 15.2, the calculation of subscriptions for the year 19x1 will be as follows.

► Applying the Prudence concept

	£
Cash received during 19x1	19,750
Add amount received in the previous year for 19x1	120
	19,870
Less amount received in the current year for next year	200
Amount transferred to Income and Expenditure account	19,670

Don't be put off by the variety of methods. Unless anything is said to the contrary, stick to the Accruals concept and write up the Subscriptions account accordingly. Remember that any subscriptions outstanding that have no possibility of being collected, can be written off as a bad debt in the Income and Expenditure account.

Too strict an adherence to the Accruals concept could lead to disturbing problems. How shall we treat a one-off payment – such as an entrance fee? How do we deal with life membership fees which are collected once only? Both of these receipts can be dealt with in one of three ways.

- Treat them as income during the year of receipt and transfer them in full to the Income and Expenditure account.
- Transfer them to an accumulated fund which is used in the same sense as capital in the case of a trading organization.
- Credit the amount in the first instance to an Entrance Fee account or Life Membership account and then transfer in instalments as income to the Income and Expediture account, spread over an agreed number of years.

Any of these methods may be used to deal with either the entrance fees or the life membership fees. However, once a method has been selected, it should be used from year to year in accordance with the Consistency principle.

► Apply the Consistency principle

Trading by clubs and societies

As we saw above, a non-profit making organization can carry out some trading activities to improve its financial position. Many clubs, for example, run a bar; members would probably like to know how much profit or loss is made. It is usual to prepare a Bar Trading and Profit and Loss account in the same way as a business would prepare such an account. Some figures such as Sales or Purchases may not be readily available, so we should need to prepare a Total debtors control account or a Total creditors control account. This is covered in Chapter 14, under single entry and incomplete records. The profit (or loss) figure will be transferred to the Income and Expenditure account.

A Trading and Profit and Loss account relating to a bar or similar activities may be prepared either horizontally or vertically, but the vertical format is recommended. Example 15.3 demonstrates the preparation of such an account.

Example 15.3 Trading Account for a non-profit making society

The following details are extracted from the records of The 50 Plus Club for the year ended 31 July 19x0.

	31 July 19x9	31 July 19x0
	£	£
Bar stock	9,800	7,950
Creditors for bar supplies	6,500	7,120
Transactions during the year:	£	
Bar sales	50,500	
Payments for bar supplies	26,200	
Bar staff wages	9,700	

You are required to prepare a Bar Trading and Profit and Loss account for the year ended 31 July 19x0.

Solution

50 Plus Club

Bar Trading and Profit and Loss account for year ended 31 July 19x0

	£	£
Sales		50,500
Less cost of sales:		
Opening stock	9,800	
Add purchases (W1)	26,820	
	36,620	
Less closing stock	7,950	28,670
Gross profit		21,830
Less Expenses:		
Bar staff wages		9,700
Net profit		12,130

Workings

W1 Calculation of purchases

Creditors control a/c

DR	£		CR £
Cash	26,200	Opening balance	6,500
Closing balance	7,120	Purchases (difference)	26,820
	33,320		33,320

ACT **15.1**

1 The following details relate to a social club.

	As at 31 Dec 19x0	As at 31 Dec 19x1
	£	£
Subscriptions in arrears	475	315
Subscriptions in advance	225	180

Additional information:
Subscriptions collected during the year to 31 December 19x1, amounted to £12,580. These include all subscriptions in arrears as at 31 December 19x0.

Calculate the total subscriptions for the year 19x1 to be included in the Income and Expenditure account.
Note: A Subscriptions account is not required, but if you wish you may prepare one to support your answer.

2 A sports club runs a bar for its members. During the year to 31 March 19x2, it paid £25,800 in total to the suppliers and its sales totalled £40,500. Its opening and closing balances of stocks and creditors were as follows.

	Opening Balance	Closing Balance
	£	£
Stocks	12,900	11,850
Creditors	10,100	9,950

Prepare a Bar Trading account for the year ended 31 March 19x2.

► Answers in appendix

The Balance Sheet for a non-trading organization

Just as for a business, the Balance Sheet of a non-trading organization shows the financial position at a certain point in time. Balance Sheets for clubs and societies are constructed in exactly the same way as for a business, except that we use **accumulated fund** in place of the term 'capital'. The Balance Sheet of such organizations is sometimes known as the Statement of affairs.

► For non-profit making organizations **accumulated fund** is used instead of 'capital'.

Non-trading organizations do not usually maintain complete sets of books according to the double-entry system. Therefore, when preparing their financial accounts, it may be necessary to apply some of the techniques of incomplete records, as discussed in Chapter 14. For example, if the opening accumulated fund is not given, we need to calculate it, in the form of a Statement of affairs by deducting the total liabilities from the total assets.

Now study Example 15.4 which shows the preparation of a complete set of accounts for a non-trading organization.

► Balance Sheet or Statement of affairs: see Chapter 14

Example 15.4 Balance Sheet or Statement of affairs for a non-profit making organization

The following information is supplied to you by the Springfield Sporting Club, relating to the year ended 31 March 19x2.

(i) Assets and Liabilities as at 31 March 19x1:

	£
Subscriptions in advance	150
Subscriptions in arrears	350
Equipment	4,100
Bank	2,050
Bar stocks	5,250
Premises	120,000
Creditors for bar supplies	10,260

(ii) Summary of receipts and payments:

	£
Receipts:	
Subscriptions including £300 from last year	13,330
Bar takings	20,850
Donations	150
Annual dinner and dance (net)	800
Gate collections	1,325
Payments:	
Additional equipment	2,000
Creditors for bar supplies	13,200
Ground maintenance	2,110
Bar staff wages	6,350
Electricity	600
Rates	2,500
Insurance	250
General expenses	390

(iii) Additional information:

- It is decided to write off the subscriptions not received for the year ended 31 March 19x1.
- At 31 March 19x1 creditors for bar supplies amounted to £8,750.
- Bar stocks were valued at £6,500 at the year end.
- Electricity bill owing at 31 March 19x1 amounted to £275.
- Insurance paid in advance at the year end equalled £45.
- At 31 March 19x1, subscriptions received in advance and in arrears amounted to £250 and £290 respectively.
- It is the policy of the club to depreciate equipment by 10 per cent of the book value. No depreciation is charged in the year of purchase

You are required to prepare for the club:

a A Statement of affairs as at 1 April 19x1

b A Bar Trading account for the year ended 31 March 19x2

c An Income and Expenditure account for the year ended 31 March 19x2

d A Balance Sheet as at 31 March 19x2.

Solution

a

Springfield Sporting Club
Statement of affairs as at 31 March 19x1

	£	£	£
Fixed assets:			
Premises			120,000
Equipment			4,100
			124,100
Current assets:			
Bar stocks		5,250	
Debtors for subscriptions		350	
Bank		2,050	
		7,650	
Less current Liabilities			
Creditors (bar supplies)	10,260		
Subscriptions paid in advance	150	10,410	
Net current Liabilities			(2,760)
			121,340
Accumulated Fund			121,340

b

Springfield Sporting Club
Bar Trading and Profit and Loss account
for the year ended 31 March 19x2

	£	£	£
Sales			20,850
Less cost of sales:			
Opening stock		5,250	
Add Purchases (W1)		11,690	
		16,940	
Less Closing stock		6,500	10,440
Gross profit			10,410
Less Bar staff wages			6,350
Net profit			4,060

c

Springfield Sporting Club
Income and Expenditure account for the year ended 31 March 19x2

	£	£	£
Income:			
Subscriptions (W2)			13,220
Donations			150
Profit from the bar			4,060
Gate collections			1,325
Dinner and dance			800
			19,555
Less expenditure:			
Ground maintenance		2,110	
Electricity	600		
Add amount due	275	875	
Rates		2,500	
Insurance	250		
Less amount prepaid	45	205	
General expenses		390	
Depreciation on equipment		410	
Bad debts		50	6,540
Surplus of income over expenditure			13,015

d

Springfield Sporting Club
Balance Sheet as at 31 March 19x2

	£	£	£
Fixed assets:			
Premises			120,000
Equipment (W4)			5,690
			125,690
Current assets			
Bar stock		6,500	
Debtors (subs due) (W2)		290	
Prepayments		45	
Bank (W3)		11,105	
		17,940	
Less current liabilities			
Creditors (bar supplies)	8,750		
Creditors (for subs) (W2)	250		
Accruals	275	9,275	
Net current assets			8,665
			134,355
Accumulated fund – 1 April 19x1			121,340
Add Surplus of income over expenditure			13,015
Accumulated balance – 31 March 19x2			134,355

Workings

W1

DR	Creditors control a/c		CR
	£		£
Cash	13,200	Balance b/d	10,260
Balance c/d	8,750	Purchases	11,690
	21,950		21,950

W2

DR	Subscriptions a/c		CR
	£		£
Balance b/d	350	Balance b/d	150
Income and Expenditure		Cash	13,330
account	13,220	Bad debts written off50	
Balance c/d	250	Balance c/d	290
	13,820		13,820
Balance b/d	290	Balance c/d	250

W3

DR	Receipts and Payments a/c		CR
	£		£
Balance b/d	2,050	Additional equipment	2,000
Subscriptions	13,330	Creditors (bar supplies)	13,200
Bar takings	20,850		
Donations	150	Ground maintenance	2,110
Dance and dinner	800	Bar staff wages	6,350
Gate collections	1,325	Electricity	600
		Rates	2,500
		Insurance	250
		General expenses	390
Balance b/d		Balance c/d	11,105
	38,505		38,505

W4

Equipment	£
At book value – 1 April 19x1	4,100
Less Depreciation for the year	410
	3,690
Add Purchases during year	2,000
	5,690

Note:

1 In the Statement of affairs, the total liabilities are more than the total of current assets, giving net liabilities of £2,760, which is shown within a pair of brackets to indicate that it is a negative figure. This figure is then subtracted from – not added to – the fixed assets total to give the value of total net assets which is equal to the accumulated fund.

2 In these workings, it has been necessary to construct a Receipts and Payments account in order to find the closing bank balance. If the closing bank balance had been known, this account would not have been necessary.

Chapter summary

- Organizations such as clubs, societies and charities are called non-profit making organizations because their main objective is not to make money or profit but to provide a service to their members. However, such organizations still need to prepare a set of final accounts to present to their members and other interested parties, eg. the bank. Such accounts are basically of two kinds:
  - An Income and Expenditure account where we ascertain the amount of surplus or deficit of income over expenditure generated in the financial year.
  - A Balance Sheet in which assets, liabilities and accumulated fund, (the same thing as capital in the context of a trading organization), of the organization at the end of the year are shown.

ACT **15.2**

For questions 1 to 5, put a tick against the letter that represents the best answer from among the four alternatives given.

1 An Income and Expenditure account is similar to:
- **A** A Statement of affairs
- **B** A Balance Sheet
- **C** A Trading and Profit and Loss account
- **D** A cash account.

2 The following details were obtained from the records of the Green Club.

	At 1.1.19x0	At 31.12.19x0
Subscriptions in arrears	–	£200
Subscriptions in advance	£150	£250

Subscriptions received during the year to 31 December 19x0 amounted to £10,000. According to the accruals concept, the amount of subscriptions that should be shown in the Income and Expenditure account is:
- **A** £10,000
- **B** £10,150
- **C** £10,350
- **D** £10,100.

3 The Greyhound Club runs a bar for its members. The following details relate to the bar.

	At 31.3.19x1	At 31.3.19x2
	£	£
Stocks	5,000	6,000
Amount owing to suppliers	2,500	3,250

For the year to 31 March 19x2, bar takings amounted to £50,000 and payments to suppliers totalled £35,000. The profits from the bar were:
- **A** £15,250
- **B** £18,500
- **C** £12,000
- **D** £12,750

4 The balance on the Income and Expenditure account is:
- **A** The amount of cash in hand and/or cash at bank
- **B** Either a surplus or a deficit of income over expenditure
- **C** The value of the accumulated fund
- **D** The total amount of subscriptions received.

5 The balance on the Receipts and Payments account is:
- **A** The profit or loss for the year
- **B** The total amount of subscriptions received
- **C** The total amount of subscriptions due
- **D** The amount of cash in hand, and/or at bank.

► Answers in appendix

6 The following information relates to Allage Sporting Club as at 1 January 19x2.

	£
Land and buildings	150,000
Equipment	10,000
Bar stocks	5,000
Bank	10,000

A summary of the receipts for the year to 31 December 19x2 is as follows:

	£
Donations	5,750
Subscriptions:	
For 19x2	2,500
For 19x3	500
	3,000
Bar sale	4,500
Sales of lottery	2,000

A summary of payments for the year is as follows:

	£
Bar stocks	2,800
Purchase of equipment	3,000
Lottery ticket prizes	560
Insurance, water and rates	1,050
Lighting and heating	800
General expenses	972

At the year end, the treasurer discloses the following additional information.

(i) Bar stocks were valued at £4,800.
(ii) Subscriptions owing by members were £175.
(iii) Equipment (including additions) was valued at £9,750.
(iv) An electricity bill not yet paid, £250.
(v) Insurance paid in advance, £250.

You are required to:

a Prepare a Receipts and Payments account for the year ended 31 December 19x2

b Prepare an Income and Expenditure account for the year ended 31 December 19x2 and a Balance Sheet as at that date.

► Answers in appendix

7 You are the treasurer of the Capriol Club which encourages and promotes folk dancing. You have prepared the following analysis of bank and cash transactions for the year ended 31 October 19x8.

Capriol Club
Receipts and Payments account for the year ended 31 October 19x8

	£		£
Cash and bank balances c/f	1,400	Secretarial expenses	578
Members' subscriptions	2,321	Rent	1,800
Donation	940	Visiting speakers' expenses	1,070
Sales of Annual Rally tickets	670	Donation to National Association	210
		Prizes for Annual Rally	365
		Other costs of Annual Rally	110
		Stationery and printing	421
		Cash and bank balances c/f	777
	5,331		5,331

The following information is also available.

(i) Members' subscriptions in arrears were £150 as at 1 November 19x7 and £184 as at 31 October 19x8. Subscriptions in advance were £36 at 1 November 19x7 and £168 at 31 October 19x8.

(ii) Amounts owing to suppliers of prizes for the Annual Rally were £12 at 1 November 19x7 and £54 at 31 October 19x8. Stocks of rally prizes in hand were £45 at 1 November 19x7 and £38 at 31 October 19x8.

(iii) The Capriol Club owns equipment which cost £3,680 and which was valued at £2,897 at 1 November 19x7 and £2,150 at 31 October 19x8.

Required:

a Calculate the Accumulated Fund of the Capriol Club as at 1 November 19x7.

b Prepare the Income and Expenditure account of the club for the year ended 31 October 19x8 bringing out the surplus or deficit on the Annual Rally.

c Prepare the Capriol Club's Balance Sheet as at 31 October 19x8.

(AAT)

► No answer given

8 The Monarchs MCC is a club for motorcycle enthusiasts. The club secretary has prepared the following summary of the club's cash and bank transactions for the year ended 31 May 19x9.

The Monarchs MCC
Receipts and Payments account for the year ended 31 May 19x9

	£		£
Cash and bank balances b/f	540	Secretarial expenses	440
Members' subscriptions	6,127	Rent and rates	2,750
Donations	350	Meeting expenses	2,200
		Sales of regalia	1,880
		Annual affiliation fee to National Body	500
		Purchases of regalia	1,145
		Purchases of garage tools	583
		Stationery and printing	345
		Cash and bank balance c/d	934
	8,897		8,897

On 1 June 19x8, the club owned garage tools which had cost £2,115 and which were valued at £1,550. Garage tools as at 31 May 19x9 (inclusive of purchases during the year) were valued at £1,450.

The following additional information is available:

	1 June 19x8	31 May 19x9
	£	£
Subscriptions in arrears	278	220
Subscriptions in advance	90	135
Owing to suppliers of regalia	228	371
Stocks of regalia, at cost	255	298

Required:

a Draw up a summary Subscriptions account for the year ended 31 May 19x9.

b Prepare a Trading account for sales of regalia for the year ended 31 May 19x9.

c Prepare an Income and Expenditure account for the club for the year ended 31 May 19x9.

(AAT)

► Answer in appendix

9 The following account has been prepared by the treasurer of the Phoenix Model Engineering Society.

Receipts and Payments Statement for the year ended 31 March 19x9

	£		£
1 Apr x8			
Opening balance b/fwd	894	Purchase of building land	8,000
Subscriptions received	12,000	Purchase of machinery and tools	17,500
Sales of machinery and tools	21,000	Rent of temporary office and meeting place	600
Sales of tickets for annual national exhibition	300	Printing, stationery and postage	860
		Deposit in building society investment account	7,500
		Secretary's honorarium	150
		Coach to annual exhibition	110
		Admission charges to annual national exhibition	220
		31 March 19x9	
		Closing balance c/fwd	354
	35,294		35,294

The following additional information has been obtained from the society's records.

(i) In addition to the balances at bank shown in the above receipts and payments statement, the society's assets and liabilities were:

	1 April 19x8 £	31 March 19x9 £
Stocks of machinery at cost	1,200	600
Subscriptions due to the society	150	250
Wooden hut at valuation	1,300	—
Subscriptions prepaid by members	300	*
Outing to annual national exhibition	—	**

* To be determined
** See (iv) below

(ii) The annual subscription for the year ended 31 March has been £50 per member since 1 April 19x7.
All subscriptions due at 1 April 19x8 have now been paid.
The society's membership was 238 during the year ended 31 March 19x9.

(iii) All sales of machinery and tools are to members on a strictly cash basis.

(iv) Annual National Exhibition, £40 for tickets was owing by a member to the society on 31 March 19x9 and at that date the society owed £45 for the purchase of exhibition programmes distributed to members without charge.

(v) Since preparing the above receipts and payments statement, the treasurer has received a bank statement showing bank charges of £14 debited in the society's bank account on 30 March 19x9: no adjustment was made for these charges in the above statement.

(vi) Since the sale of the wooden hut on 1 July 19x8, the society has rented a temporary office and meeting place at an annual rent of £600 payable in advance.

You are required to prepare an Income and Expenditure account for the year ended 31 March 19x9 and a Balance Sheet as at that date for the society.

(AAT)

► No answer given

10 The following is a summary of the receipts and payments of the Miniville Rotary Club during the year ended 31 July 19x6.

Miniville Rotary Club
Receipts and Payments account for the year ended 31 July 19x6

	£		£
Cash and bank balances b/f	210	Secretarial expenses	163
Sales of competition tickets	437	Rent	1,402
Members' subscriptions	1,987	Visiting speakers' expenses	1,275
Donation	177	Donations to charities	35
Refund of rent	500	Prizes for competitions	270
Balance c/f	13	Stationery and printing	179
	3,324		3,324

The following valuations are also available.

	19x5	19x6
	£	£
Equipment (original cost £1,420)	975	780
Subscriptions in arrears	65	85
Subscriptions in advance	10	37
Owing to suppliers of competition prizes	58	68
Stocks of competition prizes	38	46

Required:

a Calculate the value of the Accumulated Fund of the Miniville Rotary Club as at 1 August 19x5.

b Reconstruct the following accounts for the year ended 31 July 19x6:
  (i) the Subscriptions account
  (ii) The Competition prizes account.

c Prepare an Income and Expenditure account for the Miniville Rotary Club for the year ended 31 July 19x6 and a Balance Sheet as at that date.

(AAT)

► Answer in appendix

16 Manufacturing accounts

Chapter objectives

By the end of this chapter you should be able to:

- explain the meaning and purpose of a Manufacturing account
- show the division of total cost of a manufacturing concern into its main components
- state the meaning of work-in-progress and make adjustments for work-in-progress to the Manufacturing account
- prepare a Manufacturing, Trading and Profit and Loss account from a given set of information
- prepare a Balance Sheet for a manufacturing business.

MANUFACTURING ACCOUNTS

In chapters 8 to 11, we prepared the final accounts for firms involved in **merchandizing**, i.e. buying and selling of goods. In this chapter we shall look at the final accounts of **manufacturing** organizations – businesses whose primary activity lies in the manufacture of goods for sale. Such businesses will prepare a Manufacturing account in addition to the Trading and Profit and Loss account.

► A **Manufacturing account** is prepared in addition to the Trading and Profit and Loss account.

The main purpose of the Manufacturing account is to find the **production cost** of goods produced during an accounting period. It will also show the breakdown of the cost of production into the main elements of costs – the **cost of materials used**, **direct wages**, other **direct expenses** and **production overheads**. The Manufacturing account, together with the Trading and Profit and Loss account, will show how the total cost of running the business can be broken down into its component parts, based on a division of the organization according the the function of different departments, namely: production, administration and finance, and selling and distribution costs.

► The main purpose of the Manufacturing account is to find production costs.

Analysis of production costs

The Manufacturing account shows the production cost of goods manufactured during a given period of time, usually a year, subdivided into three main categories of cost:

- cost of raw materials used
- prime cost
- production (or manufacturing or factory) expenses (or **overheads**)

Let's now look at each of these in further detail.

► Main categories of production costs:

- materials
- prime
- production.

Statement of cost of raw materials used

A statement of **cost of raw materials** (or simply materials) used or consumed can be prepared as follows.
Steps in preparing statement of materials costs

Step 1: Start with the opening stock of materials.
Step 2: Add net purchases (i.e. purchases less returns) of materials, including any carriage charge.
Step 3: From the total obtained in Step 2, deduct the closing stock of materials.

The figure thus obtained is the cost of materials used in production.

► Materials costs

An example should make this clear.

Example 16.1 Preparing a statement of materials costs

From the following details, prepare a statement of cost of materials used.

	£
Opening stock of materials	5,000
Purchases	52,000
Returns outwards	3,000
Carriage on purchases	500
Closing stock	4,500

Solution

The statement of cost of materials used would appear as follows.

	£	£
Opening stock of materials		5,000
Add Purchases	52,000	
Less Returns	3,000	49,000
Add Carriage on purchases		500
		54,500
Less closing stock		4,500
Cost of materials used		50,000

Now try the following assignment to test your understanding of 'cost of materials used'.

ACT 16.1

The following particulars are extracted from the books of a manufacturer.

	£
Opening stock of materials	7,500
Purchases	49,500
Returns outwards	2,250
Closing stock	8,250
Carriage on purchases	750

Prepare a statement of cost of raw materials used from the information given above.

23/02/95
Did this in class.

► Answer in appendix

Statement of prime cost

Prime cost is defined to be the sum of all direct costs connected with the manufacturing process.

► **Prime cost**: direct cost of production

> Prime cost = direct materials cost + direct wages + direct expenses

To prepare the statement of prime cost, you proceed as follows.

Step 1: Work out the cost of materials used, as in Example 16.1.

Step 2: Add direct (or manufacturing or production) wages and any direct expenses (costs, other than materials or wages, which are incurred for a specific product or saleable service, such as royalties) to the cost of materials used. The resulting figure is the prime cost.

Now go through the following example carefully.

Example 16.2 Calculating prime cost

In addition to the particulars listed in Example 16.1, you are given the following additional information.

	£
Manufacturing wages	25,000
Royalties	5,000

Prepare a statement of prime cost.

Solution

Statement of prime cost

► **Returns outwards and carriage**: see Chapter 8

► **Opening and closing stock**: see Chapter 8

	£	£
Opening stock of materials		5,000
Add Purchases	52,000	
Less Returns	3,000	49,000
Add Carriage on purchases		500
		54,500
Less closing stock		4,500
Cost of materials used		50,000
Add:		
Direct (Manufacturing) wages		25,000
Direct expenses (Royalties)		5,000
Prime cost		80,000

ACT 16.2

From the following information, prepare a statement of prime cost.

23/02/95
Did this in class

	£
Carriage on purchases	1,500
Closing stock of materials	8,900
Direct wages	27,500
Returns outwards	2,500
Opening stock of materials	10,000
Purchases	60,500
Royalties	5,000

► Answer in appendix

Statement of production overheads

Overheads (or overhead expenses) are the sum of all indirect expenses, i.e. expenses which are not directly connected with production. **Production overheads** (or factory overhead expenses) are the part of an organization's total overheads that relate specifically to production. All indirect expenses relating to the running of the workshop are **production** or **factory** or **works overhead**. Some examples of such overhead expenses are:

- factory rent and rates
- workshop supervisors' wages and salaries
- depreciation of plant and machinery
- insurance of workshop premises, including plant and machinery
- factory heating and lighting
- factory power.

► **Production overheads**: all indirect expenses relating to production

Combining the different costs: the Manufacturing account

At this stage we have to bring together the three categories of production costs to construct the **Manufacturing account**. This is done by adding the factory overhead expenses to the prime cost of production. The construction of a complete Manufacturing account is illustrated in Example 16.3.

Example 16.3 Constructing a Manufacturing account

The following balances are extracted from the books of John Appleby, a manufacturer, as at 31 December 19x9.

	£
Stock of raw materials – 1 Jan 19X9	7,500
Purchases of raw materials	80,000
Carriage on purchases	1,000
Royalties paid	1,000
Direct wages	20,000
Indirect (factory) wages	10,000
Factory rent and rates	4,750
General factory expenses	5,750
Returns outwards	500

Note:

(i) Stock of raw materials – 31 Dec 19x9, £10,000.
(ii) Direct wages due, but not yet paid, £740.
(iii) Depreciate plant and machinery at 10 per cent on cost. The cost of plant and machinery is £25,000.

You are required to prepare a Manufacturing account of John Appleby's business for the year ended 31 December 19X9.

Solution

John Appleby
Manufacturing account for the year ended 31 December 19X9

	£	£
Opening stock of raw materials		7,500
Add Purchases of raw materials	80,000	
Less Returns outwards	500	
	79,500	
Add Carriage on purchases	1,000	80,500
		88,000
Less closing stock of raw materials		10,000
Cost of raw materials used		78,000
Direct wages (W1)		20,740
Direct expenses: Royalties		1,000
Prime cost		99,740
Production overheads		
Indirect wages	10,000	
Factory rent & rates	4,750	
Depreciation on plant and machinery (Working 2)	2,500	
General factory expenses	5,750	23,000
Production cost of goods completed		122,740

Workings:

W1 Direct wages:

	£
As per list of balances	20,000
Add wages due, but not yet paid	740
	20,740

W2 Depreciation is 10% × £25,000 = £2,500.

Now it's your turn to prepare a Manufacturing account. Carefully work through Example 16.3 again then, by comparison, work out each step in the following assignment.

23/02/95

Did this in class

ACT 16.3

The following details relate to the production cost of Anne Hart's business for the year ended 31 March 19x0.

	£
Manufacturing wages	29,750
Indirect factory wages	12,250
Factory rent and rates	5,800
Royalties paid	1,200
Factory power	5,500
Factory heating and lighting	3,750
Factory general expenses	4,750
Depreciation of plant and machinery for the year	2,750
Purchases of materials	65,000
Carriage on purchases	900
Returns outwards	1,500
Stock of materials – 1 April 19X9	8,000
Stock of materials – 31 March 19X0	11,500

You are required to prepare a Manufacturing account for Anne's firm for the year ended 31 March 19x0.

► Answer in appendix

Work in progress

A Manufacturing account is prepared for a given period, say a year, which ends on a particular date. It is highly probable that on this day there will be some items of production which are only partly finished. There might also be a stock of partly finished products at the beginning of the accounting period. Therefore, an adjustment is made to the cost of production for the year. These stocks of partly finished goods are called **work in progress** or **work in process**. This is done by adding the opening stock of work in progress (WIP) to the cost of goods completed and then deducting the closing stock of WIP from the total. The final figure will represent the cost of goods completed during the period under consideration. These adjustments are illustrated in Example 16.4.

► **Work in progress (WIP):** adjusting for partly finished goods

Example 16.4 Adjusting for work in progress

Using the same figures as in Example 16.3, you are now given the following additional information.

	£
Opening work in progress	2,500
Closing work in progress	3,750

You are required to show the necessary adjustments for these items to the Manufacturing account in Example 16.3.

Solution

Adjustments for WIP

	£
Cost of goods completed	
(As per Manufacturing account in Example 16.3)	122,740
Add opening WIP	2,500
	125,240
Less Closing WIP	3,750
(Adjusted) Cost of goods completed	121,490

Now see if you can make the necessary adjustments to the Manufacturing account you prepared in Activity 16.3 in the light of the additional information provided in Activity 16.4.

ACT 16.4

Return to Activity 16.3. Make the necessary adjustments to your Manufacturing account to incorporate the following additional information.

	£
Stock of WIP – 1 April 19x9	5,150
Stock of WIP – 31 March 19x0	7,200

23/02/95
Did this in class.

► Answer in appendix

The Trading account of a manufacturer

Like a business engaged in merchandizing, a manufacturing business needs to prepare a Trading account to find out the amount of gross profit it has made over a given period of time. Gross profit is the difference between the value of sales (or simply sales) and the cost of sales.

Note:

* Sometimes it may be necessary for a manufacturing business to buy some stock of finished goods if actual production during a period is insufficient to meet current demand for their product. In that case, purchases of finished goods should be included in the cost of sales.

The cost of sales for a manufacturing firm is calculated as follows.

Opening stock of finished goods	X
Add Cost of goods produced	X
Add Purchases of finished goods *	X
	X
Less closing stock of finished goods	X
Cost of sales	X

The cost of sales subtracted from the value of goods sold will give you the gross profit over the accounting period.

An illustration of a Trading account of a manufacturing firm is given in Example 16.5.

Example 16.5 Trading account for a manufacturing firm

The following information, supplied by a manufacturing firm, relates to the year ended 31 May 19x0.

	£
Cost of goods completed during the year	100,000
Purchases of finished goods	25,000
Opening stock of finished goods	20,000
Closing stock of finished goods	15,750
Sales for the year	140,000

You are required to prepare a Trading account of the firm for the year ended 31 May 19x0.

Solution

Trading account for the year ended 31 May 19x0

	£	£
Sales		140,000
Less Cost of goods sold:		
Opening stock of finished goods	20,000	
Add:		
Cost of goods produced	100,000	
Purchases of finished goods	25,000	
	145,000	
Less Closing stock of finished goods	15,750	129,250
Gross profit		10,750

Here's another short assignment for you to try. Activity 16.5 will test your understanding of the Trading account of a manufacturing concern.

ACT **16.5**

Didar Singh is the owner of a small engineering firm. The following information relates to his business for the year to 31 March 19x0.

	£
Sales	100,000
Opening stock of finished goods	8,800
Closing stock of finished goods	9,250
Cost of goods manufactured during the year	57,500
Purchases of finished goods	10,000

You are required to prepare a Trading account for Didar Singh's business for the year ended 31 March 19x0.

► Answer in appendix

Profit and Loss account of a manufacturer

For any type of profit-making organization, whether manufacturing or not, the purpose of constructing a Profit and Loss account is to ascertain the amount of net profit (or loss) made during the accounting year.

Net profit is the difference between gross profit and all expenses (all expenses other than manufacturing expenses for a manufacturing concern, for these are normally included in the cost of the goods produced) of running the business.

► In a manufacturing concern expenses of production are usually included in the costs of products.

The preparation of the Profit and Loss account of a firm which produces goods for sale is similar in content to that of any other type of business. The only difference lies in the listing of the expense items in the Profit and Loss account. A manufacturing concern will normally group these non-manufacturing expenses under three headings:

- **financial expenses** or **overheads**
- **administration expenses** or overheads
- **selling and distribution expenses** or overheads.

► Non-production expenses are usually grouped under three headings:
- financial expenses/overheads
- selling and distribution
- administration.

Many companies combine administration and financial expenses into one group to get two – rather than three – groups of overheads corresponding to the main non-manufacturing functional departments of a manufacturing organization.

Accruals and prepayments in the manufacturing firm

Adjustments for accruals and prepayments to the final accounts are made in the normal way. Thus, for example, direct wages due *but not yet paid* have to be added on to the direct wages figure given in the list of balances. Any amount **prepaid** on any account is to be deducted from the Trial Balance figure.

► **Accruals and prepayments**: see Chapter 9

Adjustments for accruals and prepayments are also made to the Balance Sheet so that a true and fair view of the financial position of the firm may be obtained at any given time.

Any accruals should be included in current liabilities and any prepayments in current assets.

► Accruals are current liabilities.
► Prepayments are current assets.

The Balance Sheet of a manufacturer

The Balance Sheet of a manufacturing firm will contain three different types of stocks, but otherwise it is similar in content to that of any other business. The stocks are recorded under current assets as shown here.

► The manufacturer's Balance Sheet only differs from other Balance Sheets in listing three types of stocks.

Balance Sheet as at 19x9 (extract only)

Current assets	
Stocks:	
Raw materials	X
Work-in-progress	X
Finished goods	X
	X

THE COMPLETE FINAL ACCOUNTS OF A MANUFACTURER

To bring together all the different ideas developed in this chapter, work through the following complete worked example. Make sure you understand each stage in the process before going on to the next. Refer back to the text whenever necessary.

Example 16.6 The final accounts of a manufacturer

The following Trial Balance has been extracted from the books of Amos Banda, a toy manufacturer, as at 31 December 19x0.

	DR £	CR £
Capital		53,595
Drawings	5,000	
Plant and machinery (cost £80,000)	40,000	
Accounting machines (cost £5,000)	4,000	
Debtors	20,320	
Bank	7,850	
Creditors		18,750
Sales		170,000
Returns inwards	1,250	
Returns outwards		2,150
Carriage outwards	710	
Carriage on purchases	625	
Discount allowed	590	
Bank charges	330	
Insurance	600	
Commission on sales	1,750	
Rent and rates	1,800	
Factory power	3,220	
Lighting and heating	2,400	
Administrative salaries	10,200	
Salespersons' salaries	15,000	
Factory consumables	2,500	
Direct wages	30,700	
Factory indirect wages	16,500	
Purchases of raw materials	57,000	
Stocks at 1 Jan 19x0:		
Raw materials	6,350	
Work in progress	3,750	
Finished goods	10,000	
General administration expenses	2,050	
	244,495	244,495

The following additional information is also available.

(i) Stocks at 31 December 19x0:

Raw materials	£4,000
Work in progress	£2,500
Finished goods	£8,000

(ii) Rent and rates, lighting and heating and insurance are to be apportioned:
factory five-sixths, administration one-sixth.

(iii) Depreciation on plant and machinery and accounting machines at 10 per cent per annum on cost.

(iv) Direct wages due, but not yet paid, £900.

You are required to prepare a Manufacturing, Trading and Profit and Loss account for Amos Banda's business for the year ended 31 December 19x0 and a Balance Sheet as at that date.

Solution

Amos Banda

Manufacturing, Trading and Profit and Loss account for the year ended 31 December 19x0

	£	£	£
Opening stock of raw materials			6,350
Add Purchases of raw materials		57,000	
Less Returns outwards		2,150	
		54,850	
Add Carriage on purchases		625	55,475
			61,825
Less Closing stock of raw materials			4,000
Cost of raw materials used			57,825
Direct wages (Note 1)			31,600
Prime cost			89,425
Production overheads:			
Indirect factory wages		16,500	
Factory power		3,220	
Factory consumables		2,500	
Rent and rates (five-sixths)		1,500	
Lighting and heating (five-sixths)		2,000	
Insurance (five-sixths)		500	
Depreciation on plant and machinery		8,000	34,220
			123,645
Add Opening work in progress			3,750
			127,395
Less Closing work in progress			2,500
Cost of production (carried to Trading account)			124,895
Sales			170,000
Less Returns inwards			1,250
			168,750
Less Cost of sales:			
Opening stock of finished goods		10,000	
Add Cost of goods produced		124,895	
		134,895	
Less Closing stock of finished goods		8,000	126,895
Gross profit			41,855

continues on the next page

	£	£	£
Gross profit			41,855
Less:			
Administration overheads			
Salaries	10,200		
Rent and rates (one-sixth)	300		
Lighting and heating (one-sixth)	400		
Insurance (one-sixth)	100		
General expenses	2,050		
Depreciation on accounting machines	500	13,550	
Selling and distribution overheads:			
Salespersons' salaries	15,000		
Commission on sales	1,750		
Carriage outwards	710	17,460	
Financial overheads:			
Discount allowed	590		
Bank charges	330	920	31,930
Net profit			9,925

Amos Banda
Balance Sheet as at 31 December 19x0

	Cost £	Depreciation £	Net £
Fixed assets:			
Plant and machinery (Note 2)	80,000	48,000	32,000
Accounting machines (Note 2)	5,000	1,500	3,500
	85,000	49,500	35,500
Current assets:			
Stocks:			
Raw materials	4,000		
Work in progress	2,500		
Finished goods	8,000	14,500	
Debtors		20,320	
Bank		7,850	
		42,670	
Less Current liabilities			
Creditors	18,750		
Accruals	900	19,650	
Net current assets			23,020
			58,520
Capital			53,595
Add Net profit for the year			9,925
			63,520
Less Drawings			5,000
			58,520

Note:

		£
1	Direct wages as per Trial Balance	30,700
	Add wages due	900
		31,600

2 Accumulated depreciation figures are calculated as follows.

	Plant and machinery	Accounts machines
	£	£
Cost	80,000	5,000
Less Book value (as per Trial Balance)	40,000	4,000
Accumulated depreciation to 31 December 19x9	40,000	1,000
Add Depreciation for the year (10% of cost)	8,000	500
Accumulated depreciation to date	48,000	1,500

Chapter summary

- The profit statement of a manufacturing business contains three distinct sections:
  - o Manufacturing: This section shows production cost which is calculated by adding up cost of raw materials used, direct wages, direct expenses (if any) and factory overheads, with appropriate adjustments for opening and closing stocks of partly finished goods, called work in progress.
  - o Trading: This section shows gross profit which is calculated by subtracting cost of sales (= opening stock of finished goods + cost of goods produced – closing stock of finished goods) from the value of sales.
  - o Profit and Loss: This section shows net profit, calculated by deducting all non-manufacturing expenses, classified under headings of administration overheads, selling and distribution overheads and financial overheads, from gross profit.
- The Balance Sheet of a manufacturer is constructed in the normal way with the inclusion of three types of stocks (raw materials, work in progress and finished goods) under current assets.

ACT **16.6**

For questions 1 to 5 put a tick against the letter that represents the best answer from among the four possible alternatives given.

1 Prime cost is:
- **A** Fixed costs of production
- **B** Cost of raw materials used
- **C** The sum of all factory overheads
- **D** The sum of all raw materials used, direct wages and direct expenses.

2 Work in progress is:
- **A** The value of partly finished goods
- **B** The value of finished goods produced during the year
- **C** The value of closing stock of finished goods
- **D** The value of raw materials consumed.

3 Which of the following is a selling and distribution expense?
- **A** Factory foreman's wages
- **B** Interest on loans
- **C** Advertising
- **D** Direct wages

► Answers in appendix

4 The following details are obtained from a manufacturer's records.

Cost of raw materials used	£30,000
Direct wages	£10,000
Indirect wages	£6,000
Factory overheads	£12,000
Direct expenses	£2,500

The prime cost of the manufacturer is

A £40,000
B £42,500
C £48,500
D £60,500.

5 The following information relates to a manufacturing firm for the year ended 31 December 19x3.

	£
Prime cost	60,000
Factory overheads	25,000
Opening WIP	10,000
Closing WIP	8,000
Administrative overheads	15,000
Selling and distribution overheads	10,000

The cost of goods manufactured during the year is:

A £118,000
B £108,000
C £87,000
D £85,000.

► Answers in appendix

6 The following balances were extracted from the books of Dot Ashworth, a toy manufacturer, for the year ended 31 March 19x3.

	£
Stock of raw materials – 1 Apr x2	20,250
Work in progress – 1 Apr x2	15,750
Purchases of raw materials	160,900
Carriage on purchases	1,100
Manufacturing wages	65,750
Manufacturing power	20,320
Manufacturing expenses	7,830

The following additional information is also available.

(i) Stocks at 31 March 19x3:

Raw materials	£25,950
Work in progress	£20,370

(ii) Manufacturing wages due but not yet paid £530.

You are required to prepare a Manufacturing account of Dot Ashworth's business for the year ended 31 March 19x2 indicating clearly in your accounts:

a the cost of raw materials used
b the prime cost
c the value of cost of goods manufactured.

► Answer in appendix

02/03/95
Did this in class

7 The following balances were extracted from the books of Eddie King, a manufacturer, as at 31 December 19x4.

	£
Stocks – 1 January 19x4	
Raw materials	10,250
Work in progress	12,150
Finished goods	20,750
Raw materials purchases	190,850
Carriage on purchases	950
Direct wages	60,990
Depreciation on plant and machinery	5,125
Factory power	18,930
Indirect wages (factory)	15,375
Factory rent and insurance	16,200
Factory heating and lighting	3,020
General manufacturing expenses	2,070
Sales	390,850
Purchases of finished goods	15,890
Office rent and insurance	8,200
Office heating and lighting	1,910
Depreciation of office fixtures	560
General office expenses	1,985
Office salaries and wages	30,200

The following information is also available.

		£
(i)	Stocks at 31 Dec 19x4	
	Work in progress	10,750
	Finished goods	25,150
	Raw materials	12,325
(ii)	Direct wages due	250

(iii) Insurances paid in advance:
Factory – £500
Office – £125

(iv) A provision of £350 for bad debts is to be made.

You are required to prepare a Manufacturing, Trading and Profit and Loss account of Eddie King's business for the year ended 31 December 19x4.

► No answer given

8 The following balances as at 31 December 19x5 have been extracted from the books of William Speed, a small manufacturer.

		£
Stocks at 1 January 19x5:	Raw materials	7,000
	Work in progress	5,000
	Finished goods	6,900
Purchases of raw materials		38,000
Direct labour		28,000
Factory overheads:	Variable	16,000
	Fixed	9,000
Administrative expenses:		
Rent and rates		19,000
Heat and light		6,000
Stationery and postage		2,000
Staff salaries		19,380
Sales		192,000
Plant and machinery: At cost		30,000
	Provision for depreciation	12,000

continues on next page

	£
Motor vehicles (for sales deliveries):	
At cost	16,000
Provision for depreciation	4,000
Creditors	5,500
Debtors	28,000
Drawings	11,500
Balance at bank	16,600
Capital at 1 January 19x5	48,000
Provision for unrealized profit at 1 Jan x5	1,380
Motor vehicle running costs	4,500

Additional information:

(i) Stocks at 31 December 19x5 were as follows.

	£
Raw materials	9,000
Work in progress	8,000
Finished goods	10,350

(ii) The factory output is transferred to the Trading account at factory cost plus 25 per cent for factory profit. The finished goods stock is valued on the basis of amounts transferred to the debit of the Trading account.

(iii) Depreciation is provided annually at the following percentages of the original cost of fixed assets held at the end of each financial year:

Plant and machinery	10%
Motor vehicles	25%

(iv) Amounts accrued due at 31 December 19x5 for direct labour amounted to £3,000 and rent and rates prepaid at 31 December 19x5 amounted to £2,000.

You are required to prepare a Manufacturing, Trading and Profit and Loss account for the year ended 31 December 19x5 and a Balance Sheet as at that date.

Note: The prime cost and total factory cost should be clearly shown.

(AAT)

► No answer given

9 The following list of balances as at 30 April 19x0 has been extracted from the books of Fairdeal Manufacturers Limited which commenced business on 1 May 19x9.

	£
Factory plant and machinery	
at cost 1 May 19x9	120,000
Motor delivery vehicles	
at cost 1 May 19x9	25,000
Purchases of raw materials	41,000
Factory labour:	
machine operatives	36,000
supervisory	7,000
Factory plant and machinery repairs	8,710
Heat, light and power	24,750
Rates and insurance	2,550
General administrative expenses	9,400
Administrative salaries	12,090
Trade debtors	12,000

Trade creditors	7,100
Bank overdraft	4,900
Sales	136,500
Ordinary shares of £1 each, fully paid	120,000
Share premium account	30,000

Additional information:

(i) Raw material stocks, at cost, at 30 April 19x0 were valued at £3,000.

(ii) Work in progress at 30 April 19x0 was valued at £24,000.

(iii) Depreciation is to be provided on fixed assets at the following rates on cost:
Factory plant and machinery 10 per cent per annum
Motor delivery vehicles 25 per cent per annum

(iv) Rates and insurances prepaid at 30 April 19x0 amounted to £600; heat, light and power accrued due at 30 April 19x0 was £2,300.

(v) Rates and insurances and heat, light and power charges are to be apportioned three quarters to manufacturing and a quarter to the profit and loss account.

(vi) Manufactured goods are to be transferred from the Manufacturing account to the Trading account at wholesale prices; the wholesale price of goods manufactured during the year ended 30 April 19x0 was £100,000.

(vi) Finished goods stock at 30 April 19x0, at wholesale prices, was valued at £10,000.

You are required to:

a Prepare the Manufacturing, Trading and Profit and Loss account for the year ended 30 April 19x0 of Fairdeal Manufacturers Limited.

b Prepare the Balance Sheet as at 30 April 19x0 of Fairdeal Manufacturers Limited.

(AAT)

► No answer given

17 Break-even analysis

Chapter objectives

By the end of this chapter, you should be able to:

- understand the meaning and purpose of break-even analysis
- understand and calculate the P/V ratio (contribution-margin ratio) and break-even point
- construct the conventional break-even charts and profit-volume charts
- understand and calculate the margin of safety
- demonstrate the effects of changes in costs and selling prices on the break-even point
- state and explain the assumptions underlying the break-even analysis.

BREAK-EVEN ANALYSIS

► **Break-even analysis**: technique for showing inter-relations between sales, costs and net profits. Also called **cost-volume-profit analysis**

► **Break-even point**: point of zero net profit or loss

In this chapter we shall study break-even analysis, which involves a study of the inter-relations between sales, costs and net profits. This study of **cost-volume-profits relationships** is important to a business as it helps predict cost and profit behaviour in response to changes in volume. The knowledge of the break-even point, that is the point of zero net profit, provides valuable information regarding the desirability of certain courses of action contemplated by a business.

Break-even sales can be determined either by calculation or by graphs. Both these methods are illustrated in the following pages.

Cost behaviour: fixed and variable costs

► Fixed and variable costs

As the study of cost behaviour is an integral part of break-even (or cost-volume-profit) analysis, we'll begin with an explanation of how costs fluctuate in response to changes in volume or activity.

Total costs tend to increase (decrease) as volume or activity increases (decreases); but, some of these costs are fixed, some are semi-variable (or semi-fixed) and some are variable. Let's now have a closer look at each of these three components of total costs.

Fixed costs

► Fixed costs remain unaffected by changes in volume of production or levels of activity
Period costs = fixed costs

Fixed costs remain unaffected by changes in volume or activity but are fixed only in relation to a given period of time. Hence an alternative name for fixed costs is **period costs**. More typically, fixed costs are fixed for a given range of output or activity. Both these possibilities are illustrated in Figures 17.1 and 17.2 below.

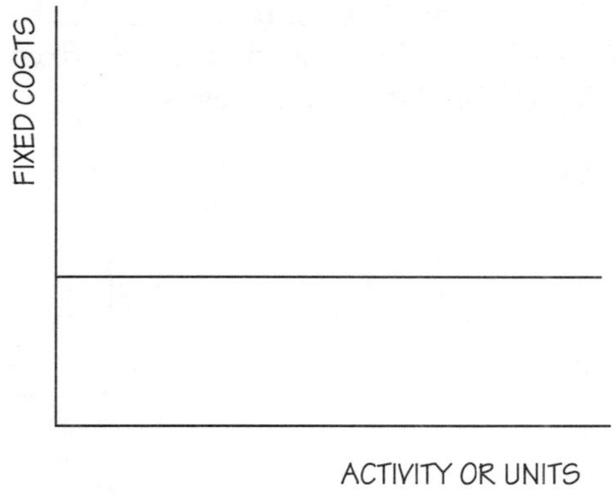

Figure 17.1
Fixed costs – assumed to be constant at all levels of activity

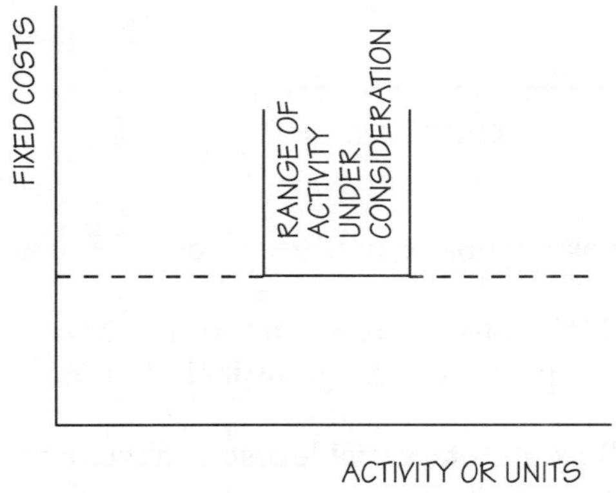

Figure 17.2
Fixed costs – assumed to be constant for a given range of activity

Algebraically, fixed costs can be represented by the following equation:

Equation 17.1

Fixed costs = K
where K is a constant.

Translated into a graph, this equation will always be represented by a horizontal straight line at a level of costs corresponding to the value of K.

Some costs which are normally regarded as fixed for a given range of activity, may increase by a significant amount for an increased range of activity. These costs are shown as **step costs,** as illustrated in Figure 17.3.

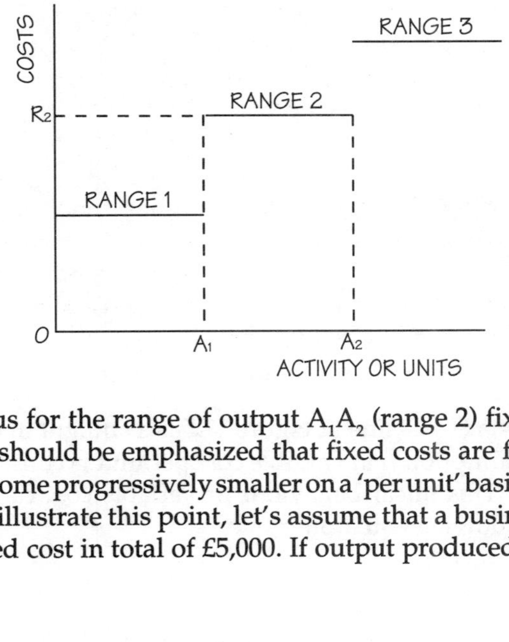

Figure 17.3
Step costs – different fixed costs levels for different ranges of activity or output

► As unit costs, fixed costs decrease as volume of production increases

Thus for the range of output A_1A_2 (range 2) fixed costs will be OR_2.

It should be emphasized that fixed costs are fixed only in total but become progressively smaller on a 'per unit' basis as volume increases. To illustrate this point, let's assume that a business incurs a monthly fixed cost in total of £5,000. If output produced during the month is

1000 units, the average fixed cost will be £5. If output is 2,000, fixed cost per unit will be £2.50, and so on. The behaviour of unit fixed costs (average fixed costs) is depicted in Figure 17.4 below.

Figure 17.4
Unit fixed costs-fixed costs per unit decreases as output increases

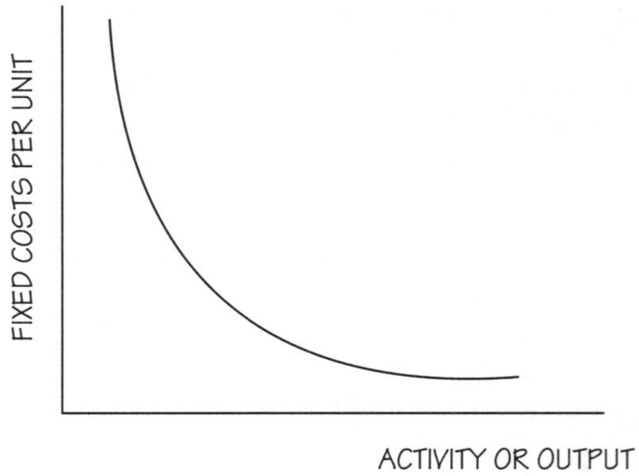

Variable costs

Variable costs increase as volume of production or level of activity increases.

Total variable costs (TVC) vary in direct proportion to output or activity, but variable costs per unit (average variable cost, AVC) may be uniform or constant.

Figures 17.5 and 17.6 illustrate total variable costs behaviour and unit variable cost behaviour respectively. Look at these carefully now.

Figure 17.5
Total variable cost (TVC) behaviour: TVC increases in direct proportion to output or activity.

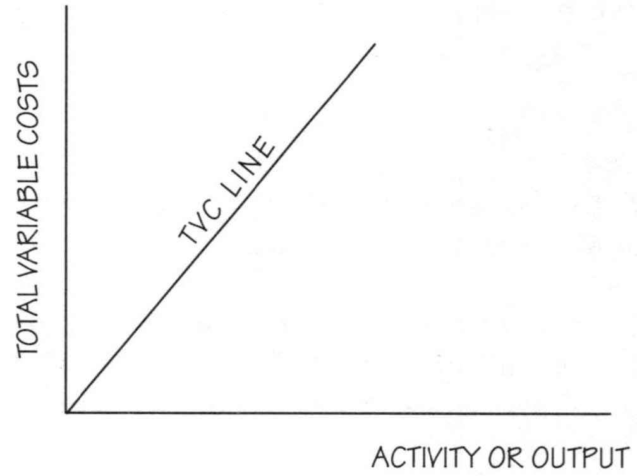

Notice that the variable costs of producing nothing is nil, hence the TVC line begins at the origin.

Figure 17.6
Average variable cost (AVC) behaviour.

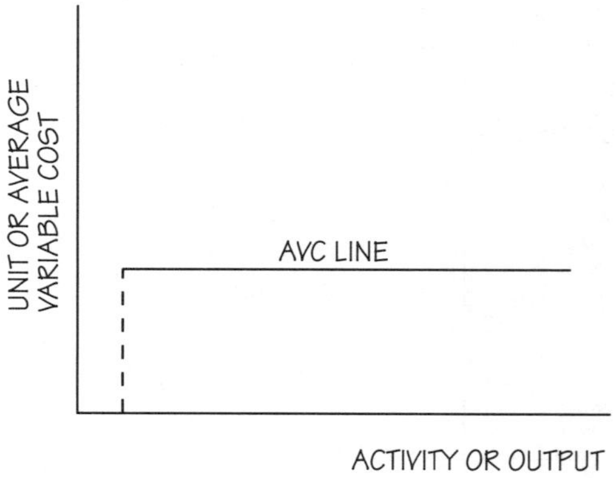

Notice that AVC line begins at a level corresponding to unit 1. (The AVC of zero output is 0/0 which is meaningless.)

The **total variable costs** (TVC) line in Figure 17.5 is a straight line as it is drawn on the assumption that variable cost per unit is constant. It is therefore linear. This linear behaviour of variable cost can be represented by the following equation:

Equation 17.2

$C = mx$
where C = variable cost in total
x = unit of output
m = a constant representing average variable cost.

It is, however, possible for variable costs to vary in a non-linear fashion, as illustrated in Figures 17.7 and 17.8, but, in the short term, it is realistic to assume that variable costs behave in a fairly linear fashion.

► Sometimes variable costs behave in a non-linear way. i.e. as unit costs they vary with levels of production.

Figure 17.7
Non-linear VC behaviour

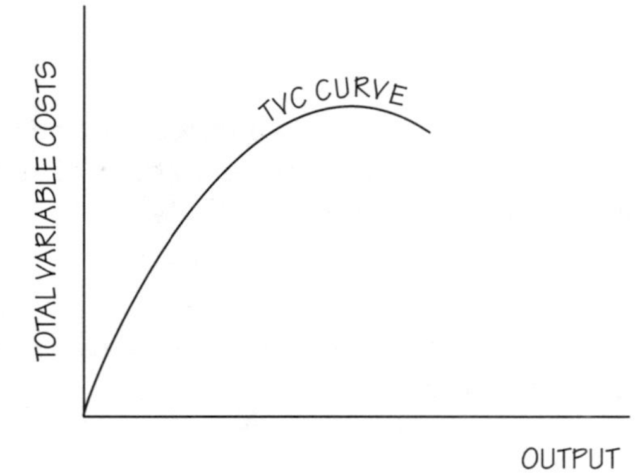

Notice that the TVC curve is convex (from above) indicating that an additional unit of output causes a less than proportional increase in cost.

Figure 17.8
Non-linear VC behaviour

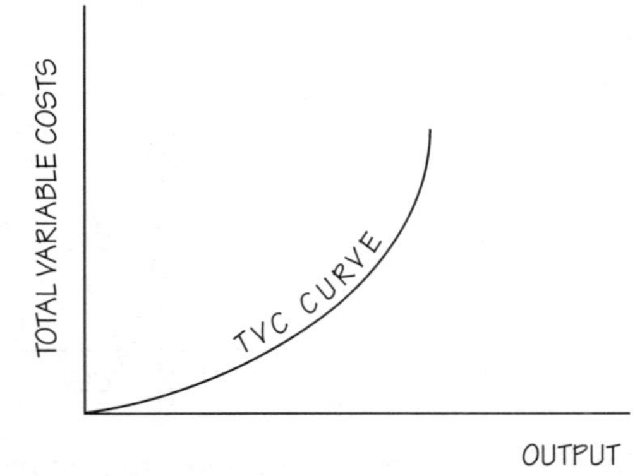

Here the TVC curve is concave (from above) indicating that an additional unit of output causes a more than proportionate increase in cost.

Semi-variable or semi-fixed costs

Semi-variable or semi-fixed costs contain elements of both fixed and variable costs. A typical example is telephone charges which contain a fixed standing charge and a variable element related to units of calls made.

Linear semi-variable (or semi-fixed) cost behaviour may be represented by the following equation.

Equation 17.3

$S = K + mx$
where S = semi-variable (or semi-fixed) costs
K = fixed element of S
m = variable cost per unit
x = number of units.

Notice that Equation 17.3 is obtained by combining Equations 17.1 and 17.2 representing fixed costs and variable costs respectively.

Figure 17.9 illustrates a linear semi-variable cost function.

Figure 17.9
Linear semi-variable cost behaviour

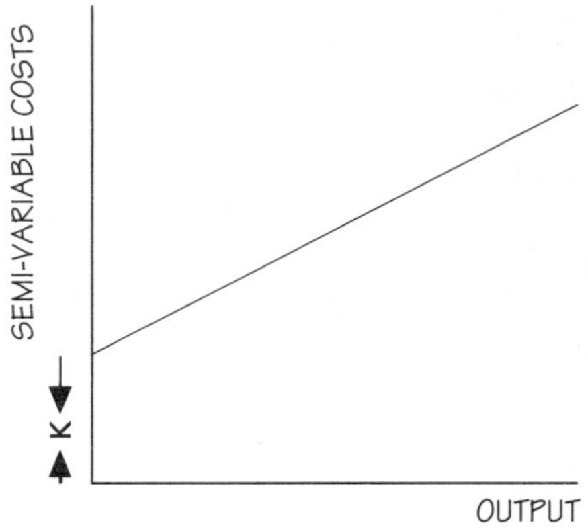

k represents the fixed element of the semi-variable cost.

It is possible for the semi-variable costs behaviour to be **non-linear** or **curvilinear**. You should find you produce two illustrations of semi-variable cost curves when you do the following activity.

ACT **17.1**

Complete Figures 17.10(a) and 17.10(b) by drawing two non-linear semi-variable cost curves.

Figure 17.10
Non-linear semi-variable cost curves

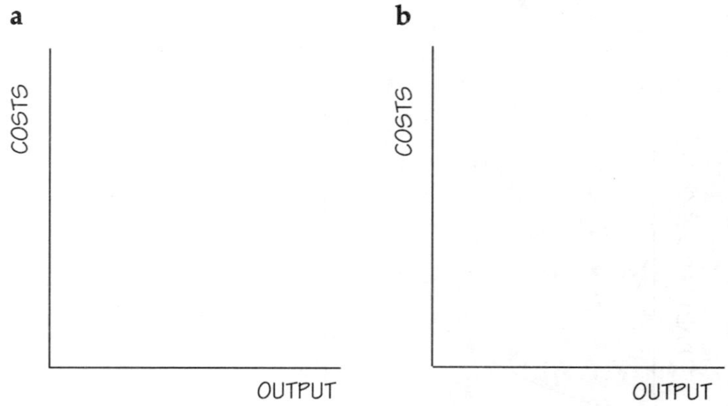

► Answer in appendix

The segregation of **semi-variable** (or semi-fixed costs) into their fixed and variable parts is important for break-even analysis. This is usually done by making intelligent **estimates** of individual expenses, by drawing a **scatter diagram** or by applying the statistical **method of least squares** and **regression analysis**. However, the detailed analysis of these various methods of segregating semi-variable costs into their fixed and variable parts is beyond the scope of this book.

BREAK-EVEN (OR COST-VOLUME-PROFIT) ANALYSIS

Break-even analysis, or more appropriately, cost-volume-profit analysis explains the interconnections between costs, volume and profits at various levels of activity.

As such it is an invaluable tool of profit analysis. Many short-term decisions relating to the profitability of certain courses of action are taken on the basis of break-even analysis.

The concept of the **break-even point** (BEP) is an important part of break-even analysis. The BEP is the **point of zero net profit**. The firm at the BEP makes neither a profit nor a loss – it just breaks even. Consequently, at the BEP,

Sales = total cost.

There are two basic methods for determining a break-even point:

- the contribution-margin method
- the graphical method.

Let's look at each of these methods in turn.

► Two methods of break-even analysis are:

- contribution-margin
- graphical method.

Contribution-margin method

This method uses a number of simple concepts and formulae to calculate the break-even point and other related values.

Concepts and formulae for contribution-margin method

1 Contribution = sales – marginal cost (or variable cost). Contribution can be calculated for any level of activity or output. Thus contribution per unit equals selling price (per unit) minus marginal cost per unit. Similarly, contribution from 100 units equals sales (revenue) from 100 units minus marginal cost of 100 units.

2 P/V ratio (profit/volume ratio) = $\frac{C}{S}$

where C = contribution
S = sales

The P/V ratio is more appropriately known as the contribution-margin ratio as it relates contribution to sales (volume).

3 BEP (in units) = $\frac{\text{FC}}{\text{CPU}}$

where FC = fixed cost
CPU = contribution per unit.

4 BEP (in £sales) = $\frac{\text{FC}}{\text{P/V ratio}}$

5 Sales volume needed for a target profit (in units) = $\frac{\text{FC} + \text{TP}}{\text{CPU}}$

where TP = target profit

6 Sales volume needed for a target profit (in £) = $\frac{\text{FC} + \text{TP}}{\text{P/V ratio}}$

All the above formulae are derived from the definition of the relevant terms such as variable or marginal cost, fixed cost and contribution, and the fundamental income equation:

Sales = fixed costs + variable costs + net profit

To illustrate the derivation and use of formula 4, let us consider Example 17.1.

Example 17.1 Using Formula 4

Selling price	20	100%
Variable cost	15	75%
Contribution	5	25%
Fixed cost	£35,000	

Now P/V ratio or contribution margin ratio = $\frac{C}{S} = \frac{5}{20} = \frac{1}{4} = 25\%$

The same figure is given in the second column of the example. To find the break even sales, we can use Formula 4 so that:

$$\text{BEP (in £sales)} = \frac{\text{FC}}{\text{P/V ratio}} = \frac{£35{,}000}{1/4}$$

$$= £140{,}000$$

Alternatively, we could get the same result by simple deduction, starting from the definition of contribution-margin ratio. A 25 per cent contribution-margin ratio indicates that for each pound of sales, 25 per cent is available for the recovery of fixed costs and net profit:

(£35,000 + 0) × 0.25 = £140,000 sales needed to break even.

The use of all the formulae will now be illustrated in the following example.

Example 17.2 Using all the formulae for the contribution margin method.

Data	£
Selling price (per unit)	30
Variable cost per unit	20
Fixed Cost for the year	40,000

You are required to calculate:

- **a** contribution per unit (CPU)
- **b** P/V ratio
- **c** BEP in units
- **d** BEP in £sales
- **e** net profit or loss from sales of £150,000
- **f** the value of sales needed to make a profit of £40,000
- **g** sales in units needed to make a profit of £40,000.

Solution

a CPU = selling price (per unit) – variable cost per unit

= £30 – £20

= £10

b $\text{P/V ratio} = \frac{C}{S} = \frac{£10}{£30} = \frac{1}{3} = 0.33 \text{ or } 33.3\%$

c $\text{BEP in units} = \frac{\text{FC}}{\text{CPU}}$

$= \frac{£40{,}000}{£10} = 4{,}000 \text{ units}$

d $\text{BEP in £sales} = \frac{\text{FC}}{\text{P/V ratio}} = \frac{£40{,}000}{1/3} = £120{,}000$

e Net profit/loss from sales of £150,000.

$\text{Sales volume (in £) needed for a target profit} = \frac{\text{FC + TP}}{\text{P/V ratio}}$

$\text{or } £150{,}000 = \frac{£40{,}000 + \text{TP}}{1/3}$

$£150{,}000 \times \frac{1}{3} = £40{,}000 + \text{TP}$

£50,000 – £40,000 = TP

TP = £10,000

f $\text{Sales value needed for a target profit} = \frac{\text{FC + TP}}{\text{P/V ratio}}$

$= \frac{£40{,}000 + £40{,}000}{1/3}$

$= \frac{£80{,}000}{1/3}$

= £240,000

g $\text{Sales volume (in units) needed for a TP} = \frac{\text{FC + TP}}{\text{P/V ratio}}$

$= \frac{£40{,}000 + £40{,}000}{£10} = \frac{£80{,}000}{£10}$

= 8,000 units

ACT **17.2**

Try this activity to test your understanding of the different formulae introduced so far.

1 The following data are obtained from the records of a company for a calendar year.

Present Production and Sales	10,000 units
Selling price per unit	£25
Variable cost per unit:	
Direct materials	£7.00
Direct labour	£4.00
Variable overheads	£4.00
Fixed cost (total)	£40,000

You are required to calculate:

a the contribution per unit
b the P/V ratio
c the break-even point in units
d the break-even point in £sales
e the profit or loss when sales amount to £130,000
f the sales (in units) required to earn a profit of £50,000
g the sales (in £) required to earn a profit of £60,000.

2 The following data are obtained from the records of a company for two successive years:

	First year	Second year
	£	£
Sales	100,000	120,000
Profit	20,000	25,000

You are required to calculate:

a the P/V ratio
b the break-even point in sales.

3 From the following information calculate:

a the P/V ratio
b the BEP (in £sales)
c the sales necessary to make a profit of £50,000.

	£	£
Sales		200,000
Cost:		
Variable	120,000	
Fixed	60,000	180,000
Net Profit		20,000

► Answers in appendix

Graphical method for break-even analysis

► Graphical method

The BEP can be determined graphically by constructing what is called a **break-even chart** (BEC). The BEC shows the following information at various levels of activity or output:

- fixed costs, variable costs and total costs
- sales value
- profit or loss
- break-even point, that is, the point at which neither a profit nor a loss is made
- margin of safety, that is, the difference between actual sales or activity and break-even sales or activity.

► Margin of safety: difference between actual sales and BEP

► **BEC**: break-even chart

The first step in the construction of a break-even chart is to segregate all costs into their fixed and variable components.

Construction of a break-even chart

A break-even chart is usually drawn on graph paper and involves the following steps.

1. Draw the axes and choose suitable units to represent the relevant variables on each axis.
   Activity or output is usually measured on the horizontal axis – the so called x-axis (the level of activity can be expressed as a percentage of capacity, in units or in £of sales); variable costs, fixed costs, total costs and sales on the vertical axis – the so called y-axis.
2. Draw the sales line. This is done as follows.
   a Select any sales volume, say 10,000 units.
   b Multiply the sales volume, i.e. 10,000 units, by the price per unit, say £10, to find the sales value, that is,
   10,000 × £10 = £100,000.
   c Plot sales value (£100,000) against sales volume (10,000 units). Call it S. Join S and O, the origin of the graph. The line OS is the sales line which gives you the sales values corresponding to different sales volumes. The sales line is a straight line simply because the selling price is assumed to remain constant.
3. Draw the fixed cost line. It should be a horizontal line joining the vertical axis at the level of the fixed cost, say £30,000. Call it C.
4. Draw the total cost line. The procedure is as follows.
   a Determine the total variable cost of a convenient level of activity or output. If you choose the output level 7,000 units, and the variable cost per unit is £5, then total variable cost is 7,000 × £5 = £35,000. Add this to the fixed cost, that is £35,000 + £30,000 = £65,000.
   This will be the total cost of producing 7,000 units.
   Plot £65,000 against 7,000 units on your graph. Call the point so plotted T.
   b Join the points C (the point on the vertical axis representing fixed cost) and T. The line CT is the total cost line. Again it is a straight line and we've implicitly assumed that variable cost per unit remains unchanged.

The BEC is given by the point of intersection of the sales line and total cost line. This point gives you the sales quantity and sales value where total sales value just equals total cost. It is a **point of zero profit**.

Figure 17.11 depicts the completed break-even chart. Our chart is constructed from the following information.

Selling price	£10
Variable cost per unit	£5
Fixed cost	£30,000

Work through steps 1-4 (above) again, this time studying Figure 17.11 carefully and relating the steps to it. The BEC is also known as a cost-

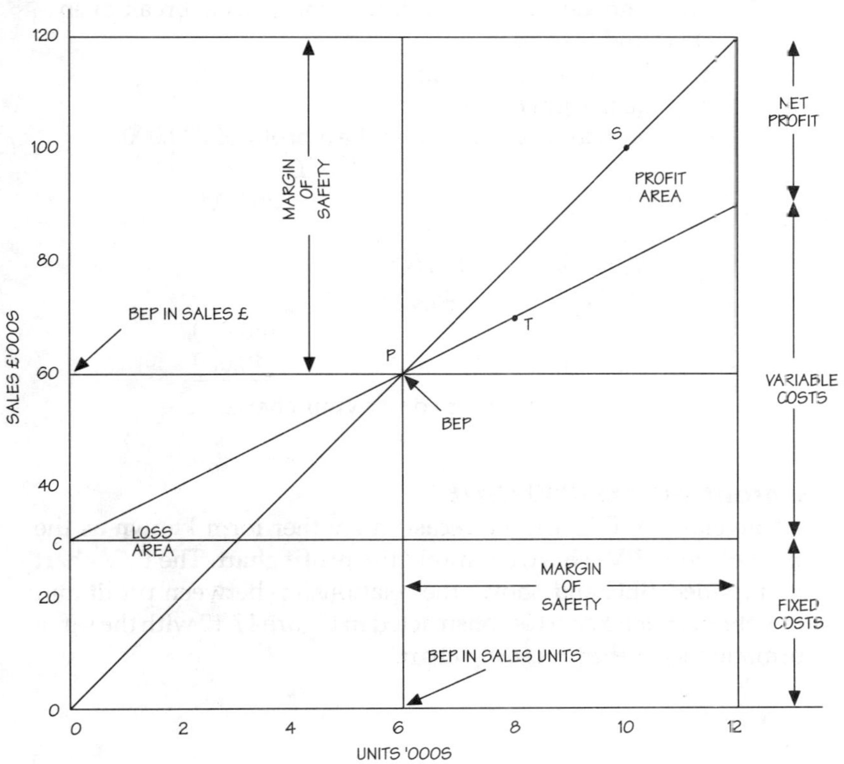

Figure 17.11
The completed break-even chart

volume-profit (C-V-P) chart. It shows the BEP (the point P in Figure 17.11 – 6,000 units or £60,000). It also shows the profit or loss at any level of output. To the left of the BEP, we have the loss zone, and to the right, the profit zone, as shown in the figure.

Finally, the BEC also shows the margin of safety.
If actual sales amount to 12,000 units or £120,000,
the margin of safety equals £120,000 – £60,000 = £60,000 or
12,000 units – 6,000 units = 6,000 units.

It's time for another activity. This one is designed to test your understanding of BEC and BEP.

ACT 17.3

1 A company makes a single product and its cost and revenue profile for the current year is as follows:

Selling price	£20
Variable cost per unit	£5
Fixed costs per annum	£30,000
Estimated sales (at 100% capacity)	10,000 units

You are required to draw a break-even chart. Determine from your graph:

a the BEP
b the expected profit or loss at the maximum production level (at 100 per cent capacity)
c the margin of safety at the production and sales level of 10,000 units.

► Answer in appendix

2 From the following information construct a break-even chart and find from it:

a the break-even point

b the margin of safety

c the sales necessary to make a profit of £20,000.

	£	£
Sales		200,000
Cost:		
Variable	120,000	
Fixed	40,000	
		160,000
Net Profit		40,000

Use graph paper to draw your charts.

► Answer in appendix

The profit volume (P/V) chart

► P/V chart or Profit chart

The conventional BEC can be recast in another form known as the **profit/volume (P/V) chart**, or simply the **profit chart**. The P/V chart is a simplified BEC and shows the relationship between profit and sales volume. Such a chart is constructed in Figure 17.12 with the same information as in the preceding chart.

Figure 17.12
The profit volume chart

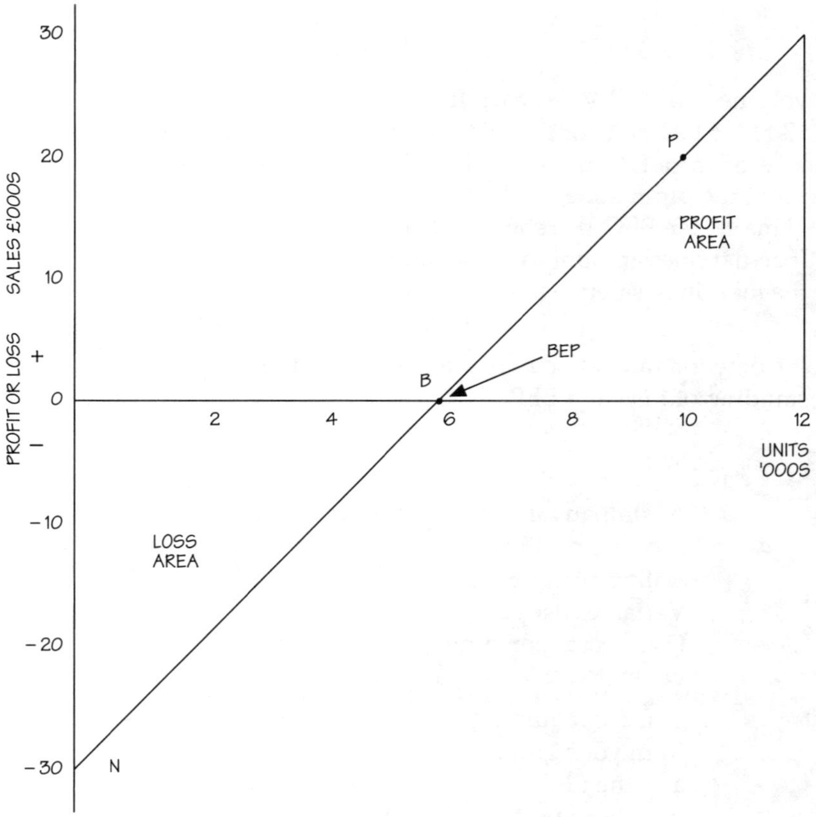

Steps in constructing the profit -volume chart

1 Choose your axes and decide on the units to be used. The horizontal axis will represent sales volume either in units or pounds-sterling. The vertical axis will measure profits above the origin, and losses below the origin.

2 At zero volume, the net loss will be equal to the amount of fixed costs: £30,000 in this example. This amount is plotted against the zero volume and is shown by the letter N.

3 Select any level of volume, say 10,000 units, and work out the net profit or loss resulting from this volume of production and sales.
Total revenue from 10,000 units at £10 per unit is 10,000 × £10 = £100,000. The total cost for producing these units will be £30,000 (fixed cost) plus £50,000 (variable cost) i.e. £80,000. (The variable cost is the product of units produced (10,000) and variable cost per unit (£10)). This will give a net profit of £20,000 from the production and sale of 10,000 units.

4 Plot the net profit of £20,000 against 10,000 units, represented by the letter P.

5 Join N and P. The line NP is the profit-volume line.

The BEP is given by the point of intersection of the profit-volume line and the horizontal axis: 6000 units.

The BEP is given by the point of intersection between the profit-volume line and the horizontal axis. It is shown by the letter B in Figure 17.12. The BEP is 6,000 units as before.

Try assignment 17.4 now.

ACT **17.4**

From the following particulars, draw a profit-volume chart.

Units produced and sold	25,000
Fixed cost	£40,000
Variable cost per unit	£10
Selling price	£15

From your graph find:

a the break-even point
b the margin of safety when 25,000 units are produced and sold
c the profit or loss from the sale of 20,000 units.

► Answer in appendix

Assumptions behind the break-even analysis

► Limiting assumptions

The break-even or the cost-volume-profit analysis is based on a number of limiting assumptions. They are:

- All costs can be segregated into their fixed and variable elements.
- Fixed costs will remain unchanged over the activity range being considered – the **relevant range.**
- Variable costs vary proportionately with activity so that variable costs per unit remain constant over the relevant range.
- Production methods and operating efficiency will remain unchanged.
- The difference in stock levels at the beginning and end of a period is insignificant and that they are valued at variable cost only.
- For a multi-product firm, the product mix will remain unchanged.

Uses and limitations of break-even analysis

Uses and advantages

1 The break-even analysis – in particular, the break-even chart – is easy to understand. Facts presented to management in graphical form are more easily understood than those contained in operating statements.
2 An understanding of cost behaviour patterns and cost-volume-profit relationships may be of invaluable help to management in the area of decision-making.
3 The strengths or weaknesses of a business and its profit earning capacity can be studied from both the P/V chart and the conventional BEC by studying the margin of safety (MOS). Many policy decisions, such as increasing the activity level, reducing fixed costs, or increasing the selling price, may be taken on the basis of MOS depicted on the BEC.
4 Alternative sales mixes can be evaluated easily by means of break-even analysis.

Limitations

1 The assumptions underlying the break-even analysis are essentially static. A change in any one of them will make the BEC out of date. Moreover, some assumptions are greatly unrealistic. Fixed costs may not remain unchanged for different activity levels. A more realistic presentation of fixed costs would have been a stepped fixed cost. Variable costs and sales are assumed to be linear. In reality, they are more often non-linear than linear.
2 The BEC shows relations between cost, volume and profits which are valid only in the short run. This makes them of little use in long-term planning.
3 The effect of various sales mixes on profits cannot be studied from a single conventional BEC but a P/V chart can overcome this.
4 The break-even analysis does not generally take into account capital employed which is one of the principal factors in many policy decisions. Exclusive reliance on BEC for policy decisions may not therefore be safe and reliable.

Chapter summary

- The break-even analysis shows the relationship between costs, volume and profit at different levels of activity. The break-even point, that is, the point of zero profit is just one of the many such points that depict the interconnections between these three variables.
- The break-even point can be determined either by calculation or by graphical methods.
- The most commonly used formula for calculating the BEP is:

$$\text{BEP (in £sales)} = \frac{\text{fixed cost}}{\text{P/V ratio}}$$

$$\text{where P/V ratio} = \frac{\text{contribution}}{\text{sales}}$$

- Graphically, the BEP can be determined by drawing a break-even chart in which the BEP is given by the intersection of the sales line and the total costs line.

ACT **17.5**

For questions 1 to 5 put a tick against the letter that represents the best answer from among the four possible alternatives given.

1 The break-even point of a business is where:
- **A** Fixed costs are equal to variable costs
- **B** Total costs are equal to sales revenue
- **C** Variable costs are equal to sales revenue
- **D** Fixed costs are equal to sales revenue.

2 If a selling price of a product is £20, the variable costs per unit is £12, then the total contribution from the sale of 5,000 units is:
- **A** £160,000
- **B** £100,000
- **C** £60,000
- **D** £40,000.

3 A business produces a single product of which the marginal cost is £10 per unit. Its fixed costs for the year are £20,000. If the selling price is £15, the break-even sales are equal to:
- **A** £20,000
- **B** £60,000
- **C** £200,000
- **D** £300,000.

4 The contribution per unit of a product is £10 and its fixed costs are £50,000 per annum. An annual profit of £20,000 can be made from the sale of:
- **A** 5,000 units of the product
- **B** 500,000 units of the product
- **C** 7,000 units of the product
- **D** 3,000 units of the product.

5 Margin of safety is:
- **A** Another name for marginal cost
- **B** The difference between fixed cost and marginal cost
- **C** The same thing as contribution margin
- **D** The difference between actual or expected sales and the break-even sales.

► Answers in appendix

6 ABC Ltd has the following structure of costs and revenues:

Selling price	£20
Variable cost per unit	£12
Fixed costs per annum	£50,000

You are required to:
- **a** Find the contribution per unit
- **b** Find the contribution in total from 50,000 units
- **c** Compute the P/V ratio
- **d** Determine the break-even point in units
- **e** Determine the break-even point in pounds-sterling
- **f** Compute the margin of safety when 50,000 units are produced and sold
- **g** Draw a conventional break-even chart

h Draw a P/V chart.
i Determine (either from one of your charts or by calculation) sales in units that are necessary to attain a net profit of £30,000.
j Demonstrate on your P/V chart the effect of a 10 per cent increase in fixed costs on the P/V ratio, the break-even point and the margin of safety
k Show on your P/V chart the effect of a 10 per cent decrease in selling price on the P/V ratio, the break-even point and the margin of safety.

► Answer in appendix

7 Outline briefly the limitations of the break-even analysis.

► No answer given

8 The selling price of a product is £30 and its variable cost per unit is £20. Fixed costs for the year are £30,000.

You are required to:
a Prepare a schedule showing the number of units in thousands up to 10,000 units, fixed costs, variable cost, total cost, sales revenue and profit/loss.
b Draw a break-even chart from the data in your schedule, indicating clearly the break-even point.
c Draw a profit-volume chart from the relevant data in your schedule, indicating as before the break-even point on your chart.

► No answer given

9 From the following information, calculate:
a The break-even sales in units
b The value of break-even sales.

	Per unit	Percentage of sales
	£	%
Selling price	25	100
Variable cost	15	60
Contribution	10	40

Fixed costs per month £35,000

► Answer in appendix

10 Alan Buxton invested £60,000 in a business which yields a gross profit of 35 per cent on sales value. His annual outgoings for wages, rent, and other expenses amount to £18,000. In addition to their wages, the assistants are paid a commission of 5 per cent on sales.

Required:
a Calculate the annual sales necessary to:
(i) break even, i.e. yield neither profit nor loss
(ii) yield a net profit of 20 per cent on Alan's investment.
(iii) yield a net profit of 30 per cent on the investment.
b Calculate the profit/loss if Alan's annual sales amounted to £42,000.
c Calculate the annual sales necessary for Alan to break even if he were able to move to equally acceptable premises with an annual rental of £3,000 less than that which he is currently paying.

(AAT)
► No answer given

11 A trader's gross profit rate is 25 per cent of the sales volume of his merchandise. His weekly expenses amount to £1,000.

Required:

a Draw a chart showing weekly sales up to £10,000 and the costs relating thereto.

b Read from your chart:

(i) the break-even point, i.e. the sales value at which total outgoings equal the sales value

(ii) the sales value which will earn a net profit of £1,000

(iii) the net profit/loss earned by sales of £3,200.

(AAT)

► Answer in appendix

18 Partnership accounts

Chapter objectives

By the end of this chapter, you should be able to:

- describe the meaning and significance of a partnership
- draw up partners' Capital and Current accounts
- prepare the Appropriation account and incorporate it into the final accounts of a partnership
- show the necessary accounting entries in the books of the partnership relating to the retirement of an existing partner
- define 'goodwill' and the necessary adjustments regarding the creation of goodwill
- show the closing entries connected with the dissolution of a partnership
- use the following terms: Current account, Appropriation account, Realization account and goodwill.

PARTNERSHIPS

The accounting system developed so far has been concerned with **sole traders**' businesses, that are owned and controlled by a single individual. **Partnerships** are owned and controlled by two or more individuals. In a partnership business each owner is a **partner**. The maximum number of partners is usually restricted to 20, although it is possible in some businesses such as firms of accountants to have an unlimited number of partners.

This chapter extends the basic principles of the double-entry system to partnerships, paying particular attention to recording the capital contributed by the different partners and of the partners' transactions with the business – the division of profits or losses among the partners, the retirement of a partner , the admission of new partners and the dissolution of the partnership business itself.

The formation of a partnership

A formal definition of partnership is given in the Partnership Act of 1890:

> *'The relationship which subsists between persons carrying on a business in common with a view to profit'.*

Partnership represents a business relationship set up with the explicit purpose of making a profit. There are no specific legal requirements for forming a partnership. It is possible to form a partnership by verbal agreement of how to run the business. However, it is desirable to form a partnership by written agreement called a **deed of partnership**. Such a deed will normally include the following details.

The Partnership Deed

- the name of the business
- the object of the business
- the capital to be introduced by each partner
- the ratio at which profits and losses are to be shared
- whether interest is to be paid on partners' capitals, and if so, at what rate
- whether interest is to be charged on partners' drawings, and if so, at what rate
- salaries to be paid to the partners
- arrangements relating to the death and the retirement of partners.

► The Partnership Deed

In the absence of such a deed, the **Partnership Act** of 1890 will apply to the partnership. The main provisions of the Act are as follows:

- Each partner is allowed to take part in the running of the business.
- Profits and losses are to be shared equally by all the partners.
- No interest is payable on partners' capitals.
- No remuneration for managing the partnership is payable to any partner.
- Interest at 5 per cent p.a. is allowed on any loans to the business.
- The admission of a new partner should be approved by all the existing partners.

Usually, each partner has **unlimited liability** which means that partners are 'severally and jointly responsible' for any debts of the business, to the extent of their personal possessions. However, there is one exception to this general rule. The **Limited Partnership Act** of 1907 allows a partnership to have limited partners whose liabilities are limited to the capital they have contributed, providing there is at least one general partner who agrees to take full liability for the debts of the business.

Capital and Current accounts

We have seen that a sole trader's accounting system requires only one Capital account. In case of a partnership there has to be one Capital account for each of the partners. For example , a partnership of two persons will need two Capital accounts in the Partnership ledger. However, if the number of partners is not too large, Capital accounts can be kept in columnar form – with as many pairs of money columns, on either side of the ledger, as there are partners. The Capital accounts of the partnership of two persons A and B, are shown in columnar form in Figure 18.1.

► Partnerships require more than one Capital account.

Figure 18.1 *Columnar Capital accounts*

Capital accounts

				A		B					A		B	
				£	p	£	p				£	p	£	p

► In Partnership accounts profits and losses are not recorded in the Capital account but in the Current accounts of the partners.

The Capital accounts of the partners are sometimes referred to as **Fixed** Capital accounts, since only the permanent capitals of the partners will be recorded there. The share of profits or losses of the partners will be recorded, unlike the sole trader's business, into a separate account, called the **Current account**. Each of the partners will have a Current account, the ruling of such an account being exactly the same as that of a Capital account. Besides the share of profits or losses, the Current account records the following transactions between the partners and the business:

► Entries of Current accounts

- drawings
- interest on capital
- interest on drawings
- salaries.

At the end of the year, when the Balance Sheet of the partnership is drawn up, the 'Financed by' section contains the balances of both sets of accounts – the Capital and Current accounts. This is shown in the relevant section of the Balance Sheet in Figure 18.2.

Figure 18.2 The 'Financed by' section of the Partnership Balance Sheet

Balance Sheet as at 19x9 (extract only)

	£	£	£
Financed by:			
Capital accounts:			
A		X	
B		X	X
Current accounts:			
A		X	X
B		X	X
			X

The Appropriation account

A sole trader's Trading and Profit and Loss account ends when the net profit or loss is determined. This is then transferred to the credit of the Capital account. With a partnership, this account extends beyond the net profit stage into another section, called the **appropriation section**. The appropriation section may be called the Appropriation account in its own right, but the modern practice is to consider it as another section of the Trading and Profit and Loss account.

► The Appropriation account shows the distribution of profits among partners

The purpose of the appropriation section is to show how the net profit of a business is distributed or divided or **appropriated** among the partners. Remember, though, that interest on partnership capital and salaries to partners are *not* expenses of a business, but appropriations of profits. That is why these items are not shown in the profit and loss section of the income statement, but are shown in the appropriation section as deductions from the net profit. The net profit, after the deduction of these items, will be divided among the partners, in their profit-sharing ratio. If, however, the appropriation section is laid out horizontally, all the appropriations will appear on the debit side and the net profit, as usual, on the credit side.

Sometimes the partnership business may charge interest on the drawings of the partners. The interest so collected is an income to the business, and therefore should be added to the net profit. In the horizontal format, however, interest on drawings will be shown on the credit side as it represents a revenue or income to the business.

You might have guessed by now that there is a definite connection between the Current accounts of the partners and the Appropriation account of the business. Every item that appears on the Appropriation account will have a corresponding 'opposite' entry on the Current accounts of the partners. Thus a debit entry (shown as a deduction in the vertical format) on the Appropriation account will have a corresponding credit entry on the Current accounts and vice versa. This list below shows the accounting entries required for recording the items which will appear in both the Appropriation account and the Current accounts.

Entries for Appropriation and Current accounts of partnerships

Item	*Debit*	*Credit*
Interest on capital	Appropriation a/c	Partner's Current a/cs
Interest on drawings	Relevant partners' Current a/cs	Appropriation a/c
Salaries	Appropriation a/c	Relevant partners' Current a/c
Share of profits	Appropriation a/c	Partners' Current a/c
Share of losses	Partners' Current a/c	Appropriation a/c

Example 18.1 demonstrates the construction of the Appropriation account in both horizontal and vertical formats, and the transfer of the different items shown in it to the partners' Current accounts.

Example 18.1 The Appropriation account

The following information relates to the partnership business of High and Tech.

(i) Capitals: High – £20,000; Tech – £30,000
(ii) Current account balances as at 1 Jan 19x2: High – £500 (DR); Tech – £1,000 (CR)
(iii) Net profit for the year ended 31 December,19x2: £40,000
(iv) Interest at 10 per cent p.a. to be paid on partners' fixed capitals
(v) Drawings during the year: High – £800; Tech – £2,000
(vi) Interest on drawings: High – £40; Tech – £100
(vii) Salaries: Tech – £8,000
(viii) High and Tech share profits in the ratio of 3 : 2

You are required to:

a Prepare the Appropriation account of the partnership for the year ended 31 December 19x2 in both horizontal and vertical formats.

b Show the Current accounts of the partners in columnar form as they would appear on 31 December 19x2, after all the necessary transactions were posted therein.

Solution

a In vertical format

High and Tech

Appropriation account for the year ended 31 December 19x2

	£	£	£
Net Profit b/f			40,000
Add Interest on Drawings:			
High		40	
Tech		100	140
			40,140
Less Appropriations:			
Interest on capital:			
High	2,000		
Tech	3,000	5,000	
Salary – Tech		8,000	13,000
			27,140
Share of profits:			
Tech – 3/5		16,284	
High – 2/5		10,856	27,140

In horizontal format

High and Tech

Appropriation account for the year ended 31 December 19x2

DR			£	p	CR			£	p
19x2					19x2				
Dec	31	Interest on Capital High: 2,000 Tech: 3,000	5,000		Dec	31	Net profit b/f	40,000	
							Interest on drawings: High: 40 Tech: 100	140	
		Salary: Tech	8,000						
		Share of profits: High: 16,284 Tech: 10,856	27,140						
			40,140					40,140	

Current account

19x2			High £ p	Tech £ p	19x2			High £ p	Tech £ p
Jan	1	Balance b/d	500		Jan	1	Balance b/d		1,000
		Drawings	800	2,000					
Dec	31	Interest on Drawings	40	100	Dec	31	Interest on Capital	2,000	3,000
Dec	31	Balance c/d	16,944	20,756	Dec	31	Salary		8,000
					Dec	31	Share of Profits	16,284	10,856
			18,284	22,856				18,284	22,856

Note that the Current account of High shows a debit balance which means that his account is overdrawn. In the Current account, the opening or the closing balance may be either a debit balance or a credit balance.

Example 18.2 gives a complete set of final accounts of a partnership.

Example 18.2 Final accounts for a partnership

East and West are in partnership, sharing profits and losses in the ratio of 3 : 2. The following is the list of balances extracted from their books at 31 December 19x1.

	DR	CR
	£	£
Sales		79,000
Purchases	40,000	
Discount allowed	600	
Returns inwards	400	
Wages	15,500	
Advertising	3,000	
Heating and lighting	2,500	
Insurance	1,500	
Sundry expenses	2,500	
Stock at 31 Dec 19x0	12,000	
Bad debts	400	
Premises, at cost	34,000	
Fixtures (Cost £5,000)	3,000	
Debtors	11,000	
Creditors		8,000
Bank	2,600	
Discount received		500
Capital a/cs:		
East		30,000
West		20,000
Current a/cs:		
East		2,500
West		1,000
Drawings a/cs:		
East	8,000	
West	4,000	
	141,000	141,000

The following additional information is available.

(i) Stock at 31 Dec. 19x1, £16,890.
(ii) Wages accrued, £500.
(iii) Insurance prepaid, £400.
(iv) A provision for bad debts is to be created at 5 per cent of debtors.
(v) Depreciation on fixtures is to be charged at 10 per cent p.a. on cost.
(vi) Interest is to be paid on partners' capitals at 10 per cent p.a.
(vii) A salary of £9,500 p.a. is to be paid to East.

You are required to prepare:

a A Trading and Profit and Loss account for the year ended 31 December 19x1.

b Partners' Current accounts, in columnar form, for the year ended 31 December 19x1.

c A Balance Sheet as at that date.

Solution

East and West

Trading and Profit and Loss account for the year ended 31 December 19x1

	£	£	£
Sales			79,000
Less returns			400
			78,600
Less Cost of sales:			
Opening stock		12,000	
Add purchases		40,000	
		52,000	
Less closing stock		16,890	35,110
Gross Profit			43,490
Add discount received			500
			43,990
Less expenses:			
Discount allowed		600	
Wages	15,500		
Add amount due	500	16,000	
Advertising		3,000	
Heating and Lighting		2,500	
Insurance	1,500		
Less amount prepaid	400	1,100	
Sundry expenses		2,500	
Bad debts		400	
Provision for bad debts (5% X 11,000)		550	
Depreciation on fixtures		500	27,150
Net Profit			16,840
Less appropriations:			
Interest on capital:			
East	3,000		
West	2,000	5,000	
Salary – East		9,500	14,500
			2,340
Share of profits:			
East 3/5		1,404	
West 2/5		936	2,340

East and West

Balance Sheet as at 31 December 19x1

	Cost £	Deprecn. £	Net £
Fixed assets:			
Premises	34,000	–	34,000
Fixtures	5,000	2,500	2,500
	39,000	2,500	36,500
Current assets:			
Stock		16,890	
Debtors	11,000		
Less provision for bad debts	550		
		10,450	
Prepayments		400	

Bank		2,600	
		30,340	
Less Current Liabilities			
Creditors	8,000		
Accruals	500	8,500	
Net Current Assets			21,840
			58,340
Financed by:			
Capital accounts:			
East		30,000	
West		20,000	
			50,000
Current accounts:			
East		8,404	
West		(64)	8,340
			58,340

Current accounts

			East	West				East	West
19x1			£ p	£ p	19x1			£ p	£ p
Dec	31	Drawings	8000	4000	Dec	31	Balance b/d	2500	1000
Dec	31	Balance c/d	8404		Dec	31	Int. on Cap.	3000	2000
					Dec	31	Salary	9500	
					Dec	31	Share of profit	1404	936
					Dec	31	Balance c/d		64
			16,404	4000				16,404	4000
19x2					19x2				
Jan	1	Balance b/d		64	Jan	1	Balance b/d		8404

Note:

1 When preparing the Trading and Profit and Loss account of a partnership you must give the appropriation section whether or not you've been specifically asked to do so.

2 Note that the depreciation figure for the Profit and Loss account has been calculated as 10% of cost i.e. 10% of £5000 = £500. But in the Balance Sheet you show the accumulated depreciation to date. The accumulated depreciation at 31 December 19x0 was £5,000 (cost) – £3,000 (book value) = £2,000.
Add the current year's depreciation to it to get the accumulated depreciation of
£2,000 + £500 = £2,500 to date.

3 The Current account of West as at 31 December 19x1 shows a debit balance and this is shown in the Balance Sheet, within a pair of brackets to indicate that the account is overdrawn. This figure is in fact subtracted from East's balance to arrive at the total of the two Current accounts.

An alternative method of showing the Current account balances is to show all the year end entries in the Balance Sheet itself as follows.

Current accounts:

	East £	West £	
Opening balance	2,500	1,000	
Add interest on capital	3,000	2,000	
Add Salary	9,500	–	
Add Share of profits	1,404	936	
	16,404	3,936	
Less drawings	(8,000)	(4,000)	
	8,404	(64)	8,340

You are strongly advised, however, to show the Current accounts of the partners as your workings and then to put the final balances of these accounts in the Balance Sheet in the way we've done it in this example.

Changes in partnership

A change in a partnership occurs and technically it ceases to exist, and a **new partnership** comes into being if any of the following happens:

- admission of a new partner
- retirement or death of an existing partner
- a change in the profit-sharing ratio.

In each of these circumstances, adjustments for goodwill and revaluation of assets have to be made so that the existing and/or retiring partners get a fair share of the goodwill and any increase in the value of assets. The books of the old business are then closed and new books are opened for the new business.

► **Goodwill**: the value of the reputation and connections of a business

Goodwill

Goodwill is an intangible asset and it is a value given for the long-standing reputation and connections of a business. It is extremely difficult to evaluate goodwill until and unless the business is sold as a going concern. There are different methods of calculating the value of goodwill theoretically but a study of these methods is outside the scope of this book. For our purposes it will be sufficient to accept the value of goodwill which is agreed between the partners in the event of any of the changes mentioned above. The need for revaluation arises when the values of some or all of the assets have significantly changed. The existing partners should benefit from an increase in the value of assets on revaluation. At the same time, they will suffer a loss if the asset value has gone down. It is therefore fair that the assets of a business should be revalued if any of the changes mentioned earlier occurs. Let's now consider each change in turn and see what type of accounting entries are required to record the change.

Admission of a new partner

The existing partners should agree on the terms of admission of a new partner. In most cases, the new partner will be required to bring in some cash as his/her capital on admission in exchange of an agreed share of the profits in the business. The accounting entries will be as follows.

- Debit the new partnership Cash Book
- Credit the new partner's Capital account

It is likely that the new partner will be required to pay an agreed sum of money for the goodwill of the business. This can be done in any of the following ways.

1 The premium for goodwill is directly paid to the old partners who share the amount in their old profit-sharing ratios. In such a case, no entries need to be made in the books.
2 The agreed amount is first paid to the business and is shared out immediately between the old partners in their old profit-sharing ratios. This method is similar to the first. The only difference is that in the first method there is no record of this transaction whereas in the second, the transaction is fully recorded.
3 The amount paid by the new partner for goodwill remains in the business but is credited to the old partners' Capital accounts in their old profit-sharing ratios.
This is recorded in the books of the new partnership as follows:

- Debit new partnership Cash Book with the amount of cash received
- Credit old partners' Capital accounts with the cash received divided in their old profit-sharing ratios

Sometimes the new partner may not have sufficient cash to pay for goodwill. In this case, goodwill will be treated as an asset of the new business and a goodwill account will be created. The accounting entries for recording this will be:

- Debit the (newly created) Goodwill account with the agreed value of goodwill
- Credit old partners' Capital accounts with the value of the goodwill divided in their old profit-sharing ratios

After goodwill has been created in this way, the new partners may not like to show it as an asset in their books. In other words, they would like to write off the goodwill. The accounting entries for this are as follows:

- Debit Capital accounts of all partners, including the new partner, in the new profit-sharing ratios
- Credit the Goodwill account

Example 18.3 gives an illustration of the accounting entries required in relation to the admission of a new partner.

Example 18.3 Accounting entries for admitting a new partner

A and B in are partnership, sharing profit and losses equally. On 31 December 19x1, their Capital accounts show the following balances: A – £25,000; B – £25,000. On the same day, they decide to admit C as a new partner. C puts £25,000 into the business as his capital. The new partners agree to share the profits and losses equally. It was agreed that the goodwill for the business was to be valued at £21,000.

You are required to show the goodwill accounts and the partners' Capital accounts in the new business if:

a goodwill stays in the business as an asset

b goodwill is written off immediately after the new partnership was formed.

Solution

a

DR		**Goodwill a/c**					CR	
			£	p			£	p
Dec	31	Capital a/cs A – 10,500 B – 10,500	21,000					

DR		**Capital a/c**							CR		
			A £	B £	C £				A £	B £	C £
19x1 Dec	31	Balance c/d	35,500	35,500	25,000	19x1 Jan	1	Balance b/d	25,000	25,000	
						Dec	31	Cash			25,000
						Dec	31	Goodwill	10,500	10,500	
			35,500	35,500	25,000				35,500	35,500	25,000
						19x2 Jan		Balance b/d	35,500	35,500	25,000

b

DR		**Goodwill a/c**					CR	
			£	p			£	p
19x1 Dec	31	Capital a/c A – £10,500 B – £10,500	21,000		19x1 Dec	31	Capital a/cs A – £7,000 B – £7,000 C – £7,000	21,000

DR		**Capital a/c**							CR		
			A £	B £	C £				A £	B £	C £
19x1 Dec	31	Goodwill	7,000	7,000	7,000	19x1 Jan	1	Balance b/d	25,000	25,000	
Dec	31	Balance c/d	28,500	28,500	18,000	Dec	31	Cash			25,000
						Dec	31	Goodwill	10,500	10,500	
			35,500	35,500	25,000				35,500	35,500	25,000
						19x2 Jan	1	Balance b/d	28,500	28,500	28,500

Retirement or death of a partner

If a partner retires or dies, the remaining partners have to pay him/her or his/her beneficiary the amount due to him/her. This might require a revaluation of assets and/or an estimate of goodwill. The retiring or deceased partner will receive an appropriate portion of goodwill and surplus of revaluation based on the old profit-sharing ratio. The treatment of goodwill will be more or less the same as with the admission of a new partner.

Revaluation

When assets are to be revalued, a **Revaluation account** is opened. The necessary accounting entries are as follows.

If there is an **increase** in asset value:

- Debit the Asset account
- Credit the Revaluation account with the increase in asset value

If there is a **decrease** in asset value, the entries are reversed.

- Debit the Revaluation account
- Credit the Asset account with the reduction in asset value

The Revaluation account is then balanced. The surplus or deficit (i.e. net increase or net decrease) on the Revaluation account will then be transferred to the Capital accounts of the old partners in the old profit-sharing ratios. A surplus will be credited and a deficit will be debited to the Capital accounts.

Example 18.4 illustrates the use of the Revaluation account.

Example 18.4 The Revaluation account

Abdul, Brian and Chang are in partnership, sharing profits and losses equally. Their Balance Sheet as at 31 March 19x2 was as follows.

	£	£
Fixed Assets:		
Freehold Premises		30,000
Fixtures and fittings		10,000
Delivery vans		25,000
		65,000
Current Assets:		
Stocks	30,000	
Debtors	20,000	
Bank	10,000	
	60,000	
Less Current Liabilities:		
Creditors	15,000	
		45,000
		110,000
Capital accounts:		
Abdul		40,000
Brian		40,000
Chang		30,000
		110,000

Chang decided to retire on 31 March 19x2 and the following valuations were agreed:

	£
Goodwill	21,000
Freehold premises	70,000
Fixtures and fittings	7,000
Delivery vans	20,000
Stocks	26,000
Debtors	19,000

The money due to Chang should be paid straight away. Abdul and Brian also agreed to admit Elaine as a new partner on 31 March 19x2, who would introduce cash equal to the value of Chang's capital after the assets had been revalued. They agreed to share profits and losses equally.

You are required to:

a Prepare a Revaluation account.

b Show the assets accounts and the partners' Capital accounts as they would appear after revaluation.

c Prepare a Balance Sheet of the new partnership as at 31 March 19x2.

Solution

DR		**Revaluation a/c**							CR
			£	p				£	p
19x2					19x2				
Mar	31	Fixtures and fittings	3,000		Mar	31	Goodwill	21,000	
Mar	31	Delivery vans	5,000		Mar	31	Freehold premises	40,000	
Mar	31	Stocks	4,000						
Mar	31	Debtors	1,000						
Mar	31	Capital a/cs							
		Abdul £16,000							
		Brian £16,000							
		Chang £16,000	48,000						
			61,000					61,000	

DR		**Bank a/c**							CR
			£	p				£	p
19x1					19x2				
Apr	1	Balance b/d	10,000		Mar	31	Capital – Chang	46,000	
19x2					Mar	31	Balance c/d	10,000	
Mar	31	Capital – Elaine	46,000						
			56,000					56,000	
Apr	1	Balance b/d	10,000						

Freehold premises a/c

DR								CR	
			£	p				£	p
19x1					19x2				
Apr	1	Balance b/d	30,000		Mar	31	Balance c/d	70,000	
19x2									
Mar	31	Revaluation	40,000						
			70,000					70,000	
Apr	1	Balance c/d	70,000						

Goodwill a/c

DR								CR	
			£	p				£	p
19x2					19x2				
Mar	31	Revaluation	21,000						

Fixtures and fittings a/c

DR								CR	
			£	p				£	p
19x1					19x2				
Apr	1	Balance b/d	10,000		Mar	31	Revaluation	3,000	
					Mar	31	Balance c/d	7,000	
			10,000					10,000	
19x2									
Apr	1	Balance b/d	7,000						

Delivery vans a/c

DR								CR	
			£	p				£	p
19x1					19x2				
Apr	1	Balance b/d	25,000		Mar	31	Revaluation	5,000	
					Mar	31	Balance c/d	20,000	
			25,000					25,000	
19x2									
Apr	1	Balance b/d	20,000						

Stocks a/c

DR								CR	
			£	p				£	p
19x1					19x2				
Apr	1	Balance b/d	30,000		Mar	31	Revaluation	4,000	
					Mar	31	Balance c/d	26,000	
			30,000					30,000	
19x2									
Apr	1	Balance b/d	26,000						

Debtors a/c

DR			£	p			CR	£	p
19x1 Apr	1	Balance b/d	20,000		19x2 Mar	31	Revaluation	1,000	
					Mar	31	Balance c/d	19,000	
			20,000					20,000	
19x2 Apr	1	Balance b/d	19,000						

Capital a/c – Abdul

DR			£	p			CR	£	p
19x2 Mar	31	Balance c/d	56,000		19x2 Apr	1	Balance b/d	40,000	
					19x2 Mar	31	Revaluation	16,000	
			56,000					56,000	
					Apr	1	Balance b/d	56,000	

Capital a/c – Brian

DR			£	p			CR	£	p
19x1 Mar	31	Balance c/d	56,000		19x2 Apr	1	Balance b/d	40,000	
					19x2 Mar	31	Revaluation	16,000	
			56,000					56,000	
					Apr	1	Balance b/d	56,000	

Capital a/c – Chang

DR			£	p			CR	£	p
19x2 Mar	31	Bank	46,000		19x2 Apr	1	Balance b/d	30,000	
					19x2 Mar	31	Revaluation	16,000	
			46,000					46,000	

Capital a/c – Elaine

DR			£	p			CR	£	p
19x2					19x2 Mar	31	Bank	46,000	

Abdul, Brian and Elaine

Balance Sheet as at 31 March 19x2

	£	£
Fixed Assets:		
Goodwill		21,000
Freehold Premises		70,000
Fixtures and Fittings		7,000
Delivery Vans		20,000
		118,000
Current Assets:		
Stocks	26,000	
Debtors	19,000	
Bank	10,000	
	55,000	
Less Current Liabilities:		
Creditors	15,000	
Net Current Assets		40,000
		158,000
Capital accounts:		
Abdul		56,000
Brian		56,000
Elaine		46,000
		158,000

Changes in profit-sharing ratios

A change in the profit-sharing ratio of a partnership causes the old partnership to cease and the new partnership to come into being. Revaluation of assets and the creation of goodwill are very common in cases of changing profit ratios. Since there are no other additional accounting entries involved we need not discuss changes in the profit-sharing ratios any further.

Dissolution of partnerships

A partnership may come to the end of its life for a number of reasons. These include the death or retirement of one or more partners, or disagreement between partners, bankruptcy, or take-over bids. Whatever the reason for dissolving the partnership, its assets are sold, liabilities are settled and the accounts are closed. We need a special account called the **Realization account**, to record the closing entries and to determine the profit or loss made on realization of the assets. These realization profits or losses are then transferred to the Capital accounts of the partners in their profit-sharing ratios.

Below is a brief account of the steps and the relevant accounting entries involved in closing the books of the partnership on dissolution.

Closing the Books of a partnership

Step 1: Transfer the balances on the provision accounts – e.g. Provision for depreciation accounts – to the relevant asset account, to determine the net value of the assets:

- Debit the Provision account
- Credit the appropriate asset account with the balance on the provision account

Step 2: Close off the assets account, other than the Cash Book, by transferring the balances to the Realization account:

- Debit the Realization account
- Credit the relevant asset accounts with the balance on the relevant asset accounts

Step 3: When assets are realised – i.e. sold – then:

- Debit the Cash Book
- Credit the Realization account with the proceeds of the sale

Step 4: If a partner takes over an asset at an agreed value:

- Debit the partner's Capital account
- Credit the Realization account with the agreed value of the take-over

Step 5: For any expenses incurred regarding realization:

- Debit the Realization account
- Credit the Cash Book with the amount of the expenses incurred

Step 6: For any discounts received:

- Debit the Creditors' accounts
- Credit the Realization account with the amount of discounts received

Step 7: When creditors are paid:

- Debit the Creditors' accounts
- Credit the Cash Book with the amount paid

Step 8: Now balance the Realization account to determine whether a profit or a loss has been made on realization. If a profit on realization is made:

- Debit the Realization account
- Credit the partners' Current accounts with the profit divided among them in their profit-sharing ratios

If however, a loss is made, the entries will be reversed.

Step 9: If a partner has loaned out some money to the business, it must be paid now:

- Debit the partner's Loan account
- Credit the Cash Book with the amount of the loan

Step 10: Close off the Current accounts by transferring their balances to the respective Capital accounts. If a Current account shows a credit balance:

- Debit the Current account
- Credit the Capital account with the balance on the Current account

If however, a Current account shows a debit balance, the entries are reversed:

- Debit the Capital account
- Credit the Current account with the balance on the Current account

Step 11: Use the remaining balances in the Cash Book to settle the partners' Capital accounts:

- Debit the partners' Capital accounts
- Credit the cCash Book

If one of the partners has a debit balance on his/her Capital account, he/she should introduce new cash equal to the debit balance to settle the account. If he/she is unable to pay, the rule in Garner *v.* Murray applies, but an explanation of this rule is outside of the scope of this book.

Example 18.5 demonstrates how the books of a partnership on dissolution are closed.

Example 18.5 Closing the books of a partnership

Peter and Jean are in partnership sharing profits and losses equally. Their Balance Sheet as at 31 March 19x2 was as follows.

	£	£	£
Fixed Assets:			
Premises			35,000
Motor Vehicles			15,000
			50,000
Current Assets:			
Stocks		20,000	
Debtors		10,000	
Bank		8,000	
		38,000	
Less Current Liabilities:			
Creditors		13,000	
			25,000
			75,000
Capital accounts:			
Peter			40,000
Jean			35,000
			75,000

On 31 March 19x2, they decided to dissolve the partnership and the assets realized were as follows.

(i) The premises were sold for £80,000.
(ii) Peter took over the motor vehicles at an agreed valuation of £12,000.
(iii) Stocks were sold for £16,000.
(iv) The debtors paid £9,500.
(v) The creditors were paid in full, after deducting the discount received of £500.
(vi) The expenses of realization which amounted to £1,000, were paid.

You are required to make the entries necessary to close the books of the partnership and show the ledger accounts in their final form.

Solution

Premises a/c

DR			£	p				£	p CR
19x1 April	1	Balance b/d	35,000		19x2 Mar	31	Realization	35,000	

Motor vehicles a/

DR			£	p				£	p CR
19x1 April	1	Balance b/d	15,000		19x2 Mar	31	Realization	15,000	

Stocks a/c

DR			£	p				£	p CR
19x1 April	1	Balance b/d	20,000		19x2 Mar	31	Realization	20,000	

Debtors a/c

DR			£	p				£	p CR
19x1 April	1	Balance b/d	10,000		19x2 Mar	31	Realization	10,000	

Creditors a/c

DR			£	p				£	p CR
19x2 Mar	31	Realization	500		19x1 April	1	Balance b/d	13,000	
Mar	31	Bank	12,500						
			13,000					13,000	

Bank a/c

DR			£	p				£	p CR
19x1 Apr	1	Balance b/d	8,000		19x2 Mar	31	Realization(Exp)	1,000	
19x2 Mar	31	Realization: Premises	80,000		Mar	31	Creditors	12,500	
Mar	31	Realization: Stocks	16,000		Mar	31	Capital a/cs		
Mar	31	Realization: Debtors	9,500				Peter	46,500	
							Jean	53,500	
			113,500					113,500	

DR		**Realization a/c**							CR
			£	p				£	p
19x1					19x2				
Mar	31	Premises	35,000		Mar	31	Bank: Premises	80,000	
Mar	31	Motor vehicles	15,000		Mar	31	Cap. a/c Peter: Motor vehicle	12,000	
Mar	31	Stocks	20,000		Mar	31	Bank: Stocks	16,000	
Mar	31	Debtors	10,000		Mar	31	Bank: Debtors	9,500	
Mar	31	Expenses	1,000		Mar	31	Discount received	500	
Mar	31	Capital a/cs Peter – £18,500 Jean – £18,500	37,000						
			118,000					118,000	

DR		**Capital a/cs**											CR
			Peter		Jean					Peter		Jean	
			£	p	£	p				£	p	£	p
19x2							19x1						
Mar	31	Realization Vehicles	12,000				Apr	1	Balance b/d	40,000		35,000	
Mar	31	Bank	46,500		53,500		19x2						
							Mar	31	Realization	18,500		18,500	
			58,500		53,500					58,500		53,500	

Note: The important accounts for purposes of realization are the Bank, Realization and Capital accounts.

Chapter summary

- A partnership is a business which is owned by two or more individuals. Accounting for partnership follows the general system of accounting developed in the earlier chapters of the book. However, there are a few points relating to the accounts of partnerships which require special considerations.
- You need one Capital account in the Ledger for each of the partners. Moreover, capital introduced by the partners is normally regarded as fixed and because of this, no other entries are made in the Capital accounts.
- Besides a Capital account, each partner will have another account in the Partnership Ledger, called the Current account, to record transactions like interest on capital, interest on drawings, salaries, and share of profits and losses.
- The Trading and Profit and Loss account does not come to an end with the determination of net profit or loss, but continues to show the division of profits amongst the partners. This extension of the Trading and Profit and Loss account is known as the appropriation section.
- In the 'Financed by' section of the partnership, you show the balances of both the Capital and Current accounts of the partners.
- Special accounting requirements are related to the admission of a

new partner, the retirement, resignation or death of an existing partner and changes in the profit -sharing ratios.

- All of the above require
  - an estimation of the value of the reputation of the firm or 'goodwill' and
  - a revaluation of assets.
- On dissolution of a partnership, the books of the business are closed off via a special account called the Realization account.

ACT 18.1

For each of questions 1 to 5 put a tick against the letter representing the best choice from among the four possible answers given.

1 Where fixed capitals are maintained in a partnership, then partners' drawings are transferred to:
- **A** The credit of the partners' Current accounts
- **B** The debit of the partners' Current accounts
- **C** The credit of the partners' Capital accounts
- **D** The debit of the partners' Capital accounts.

2 A partner's salary is:
- **A** Credited to the Appropriation account and debited to the Profit and Loss account
- **B** Credited to the partner's Capital account and debited to the Profit and Loss account
- **C** Credited to the partner's Current account and debited to the Appropriation account
- **D** Credited to the Appropriation account and debited to the partner's Current account.

3 When we balance off a partner's Current account, we get:
- **A** A debit balance always
- **B** A credit balance always
- **C** Either a debit balance or a credit balance
- **D** A debit balance and a credit balance at the same time.

4 T and V are in partnership sharing profits and losses at the ratio of 2 : 3. The net profit for the year is £25,000. T is to receive a salary of £5,000 p.a. The respective shares of profits of T and V will be:
- **A** T £8,000; V £12,000
- **B** T £10,000; V £15,000
- **C** T £10,000; V £10,000
- **D** T £12,500; V £12,500.

5 Key and Board are in partnership sharing profits and losses equally. The net profit of the year is £30,700. Interest on drawings are: Key – £200, Board – £100. Interest on partners' capitals are: Key – £2,000, Board – £3,000. The shares of profits for each partner will be:
- **A** £15,350
- **B** £15,500
- **C** £17,700
- **D** £13,000.

► Answers in appendix

6 Radha and Krishna are in partnership, sharing profits and losses equally. Their fixed capitals are: Radha £20,000, Krishna £25,000. Krishna is entitled to a salary of £6,000 per annum. Interest on capital is to be paid at 10 per cent p.a.

The following information is available relating to the year ended 30 June 19x2.

(i) The net profit of the year is £30,000.
(ii) Drawings during the year: Radha £2,500; Krishna £5,000.
(iii) Interest to be charged on drawings of the year: Radha – £150; Krishna – £350.

You are required to prepare:

a The appropriation section of the Trading and Profit and Loss account for the year ended 30 June, 19x2.
b The partners' Current accounts for the year.

► Answer in appendix

7 Right, Left and Middle are in partnership. Their deed of agreement includes the following.

(i) Profits and losses are to be shared in the ratios, Right 2/5, Left 2/5, and Middle 1/5.
(ii) Annual salaries of £8,000 and £6,500 are to be paid to Right and Left respectively.
(iii) Interest at 10 per cent is to be paid on partners' fixed capitals.
(iv) Interest at 10 per cent is to be charged on partners' drawings.

The following additional information is also given.

- The partnership made a profit of £60,000 in the year ended 31 December 19x5.
- The balances on partners' Capital and Current accounts as at 1 Jan, 19x5, were:

	Capital a/cs £	Current a/cs £
Right	40,000	2,000 DR
Left	40,000	1,000 CR
Middle	20,000	750 CR

- Drawings and interest on drawings in 19x5 were:

	Drawings £	Interest on Drawings £
Right	8,000	400
Left	6,000	300
Middle	2,000	100

You are required to prepare:

a The partnership appropriation section
b Partners' Current accounts for the year ended 31 December 19x5.

► No answer given

8 The following accounts remained in the Ledger of Alpha and Beta after they had prepared their Trading account for the year ended 31 September, 19x9.

	DR £	CR £
Capital accounts:		
Alpha		50,000
Beta		40,000
Current accounts:		
Alpha		100
Beta		400
Drawings:		
Alpha	7,680	
Beta	9,300	
Cash at bank	4,200	
Cash in hand	260	
Rent income		2,200
Office expenses	1,560	
Rates and insurance	1,660	
Heating and lighting	2,720	
Wages	26,580	
Stock – 31 September, 19x9	38,840	
Debtors and creditors	28,000	43,000
Motor van	6,400	
Furniture	2,800	
Premises	70,000	
General reserve		10,000
Gross profit		54,300
	200,000	200,000

The following additional information is available.

(i) Profits and losses are shared equally by the partners.

(ii) 10 per cent interest is to be allowed on partners' capitals.

(iii) Alpha is entitled to a monthly salary of £400.

(iv) Unused stationery as at 31 September 19x9 was valued at £100.

(v) Depreciation is to be provided at 20 per cent on book value of motor van and furniture.

(vi) A provision for bad and doubtful debts is to be created at 2 per cent of debtors.

(vii) Insurance prepaid at the close of the year amounted to £150.

(viii) Wages owing at 31 September 19x9 amounted to £200.

(ix) £1,000 should be transferred to general reserve.

You are required to prepare:

a A Profit and Loss (including appropriation) account of the partnership for the year ended 31 September 19x9

b Partners' Current accounts in columnar form

c The firm's Balance Sheet as at 31 September 19x9.

► No answer given

9 The following Trial Balance has been extracted from the ledger of K. Mount and N. Print who are trading in partnership.

Mount and Print
Trial Balance as at 30 November 19x9

	DR £	CR £
Property	300,000	
Equipment	260,000	
Provision for depreciation		
(as at 30 November x9)		
property		40,000
equipment		178,750
Stock as at 1 December 19x8	41,200	
Purchases	301,630	
Sales		603,160
Wages and salaries	78,600	
Bad debts	1,530	
Provision for bad debts as at		
30 November 19x9		943
Loan interest	4,200	
Carriage in	4,280	
Returns in	1,270	
Other operating expenses	25,600	
Depreciation	63,250	
Debtors	62,900	
Creditors		43,090
Cash on hand	820	
Cash at bank	1,370	
Drawings:		
K. Mount	58,930	
N. Print	40,800	
Long-term loan (14%)		30,000
Current accounts:		
K. Mount	980	
N. Print		1,417
Capital accounts:		
K. Mount		250,000
N. Print		100,000
	1,247,360	1,247,360

The following information is available.

(i) Stock at close of business on 30 November 19x9 was valued at £45,900.

(ii) The partners have agreed the following scheme for the appropriation of profits.

Interest on partners' capital: 12% per annum

Partnership salaries:

K. Mount £17,000 per annum
N. Print £15,000 per annum

Profit sharing ratio:

K. Mount 60%
N. Print 40%

No interest is to be charged on drawings or allowed on Current account balances.

You are required to prepare:

a A Trading, Profit and Loss and Appropriation account for the partnership for the year ended 30 November 19x9

b A clear calculation of balances on the partners' Current accounts as at 30 November 19x9.

(AAT)
► No answer given

10 Ganatri and Lucifer are in partnership sharing profits and losses in the ratio of 7 : 3 respectively.

The following information has been taken from the partnership records for the financial year ended 31 May 19x9.

Partners' Capital account Balances:

Ganatri £200,000
Lucifer £140,000

Partners' Current accounts balances as at 1 June 19x8

Ganatri £15,000 CR
Lucifer £13,000 CR

During the year ended 31 May 19x9 the partners made the following drawings from the partnership bank account.

Ganatri	£10,000 on 31 August 19x8
	£10,000 on 30 November 19x8
	£10,000 on 28 February 19x9
	£10,000 on 31 May 19x9
Lucifer	£7,000 on 31 August 19x8
	£7,000 on 30 November 19x8
	£7,000 on 28 February 19x9
	£7,000 on 31 May 19x9

Interest is to be charged on drawings at the rate of 12 per cent per annum. Interest is allowed on Capital accounts and credit balances on Current accounts at the rate of 12 per cent per annum.

Lucifer is to be allowed a salary of £15,000 per annum. The net profit of the partnership for the year ended 31 May 19x9 is £102,940.

You are required to prepare:

a A computation of the amount of interest chargeable on each partner's drawings for the year ended 31 May 19x9

b The Partnership Appropriation account for the year ended 31 May 19x9

c A computaion of the balance on each partner's Current account as at 31 May 19x9.

(AAT)

► Answer in appendix

11 A, B and C are in partnership, sharing profits and losses in the ratios 4 : 3 : 1. They are to alter their profit/loss ratios to 3 : 5 : 2.

The last Balance Sheet before the change was like this.

Balance Sheet as at 30 September 19x9

		£
Net assets (not including goodwill)		28,000
Capitals:	A	12,000
	B	9,600
	C	6,400
		28,000

The partners agree to bring in goodwill, being valued at £24,000 on the change.

You are required to prepare the Balance Sheets as at 1 October, 19x9 after goodwill has been taken into account if:

a The Goodwill account was opened

b The Goodwill account was not opened.

► No answer given

12 The partners are to change their profit/loss ratios as shown.

	Old ratio	New ratio
P	2	3
Q	3	4
R	4	3
S	1	2

They decide to bring in goodwill amounting to £36,000 on the change. The last Balance Sheet before any element of goodwill had been introduced was like this.

Balance Sheet as at 30 June 19x9

		£
Net assets (not including goodwill)		37,600
Capitals:	P	14,000
	Q	6,400
	R	10,000
	S	7,200
		37,600

You are required to prepare the Balance Sheets on 1 July, 19x9 after necessary adjustments have been made if:

a The Goodwill account was opened.

b The Goodwill account was not opened.

► Answer in appendix

13 The partnership agreement of X, Y and Z contains the following provision:
'Goodwill shall be valued at one and a half times the weighted average of net profits of the last three completed accounting periods. Weighting shall be one for the earliest year, two for the second year and three for the most recent year.'

Profits for the last three accounting years were: 19x6 – £22,000, 19x7 – £28,000 and 19x8 – £33,000.

Required: Valuation of goodwill at 1 January 19x9.

► No answer given

14 Right and Left are in partnership, sharing profits and losses equally. They decide to admit Centre. By agreement, goodwill valued at £12,000 is to be introduced into the business books. Centre is required to provide capital equal to that of Left after he has been credited with his share of goodwill.
The new profit-sharing ratio is to be 4 : 3 : 3 respectively for Right, Left and Centre.
The Balance Sheet before admission of Centre showed this situation.

	£
Fixed and current assets excluding cash	30,000
Cash	4,000
	34,000
Capitals: Right	16,000
Left	8,000
Current liabilities	10,000
	34,000

You are required to show:

a Journal entries for the admission of Centre

b Opening Balance Sheet of the new partnership

c Journal entries for writing off the goodwill which the new partners decided to do soon after the start of the new business.

► Answer in appendix

15 A, B and C who are in partnership sharing profits and losses in the ratio of 2 : 2 : 1, decide to dissolve the partnership on 30 September 19x9 at which date their Balance Sheet was like this.

A, B and C
Balance Sheet as at 30 September 19x9

	£	£
Fixed Assets (at WDV):		
Freehold property		60,000
Equipment		30,000
		90,000
Current Assets:		
Stock	16,000	
Debtors	9,000	
Bank	4,200	
	29,200	
Current Liabilities:		
Creditors	6,000	23,200
		113,200
Capital accounts:		
A	78,000	
B	26,000	
C	4,000	108,000
Current accounts:		
A	1,400	
B	(600)	
C	400	1,200
Loan – B		4,000
		113,200

The partners were unable to sell the business as a going concern and disposed of the assets separately for the following sums:

	£
Freehold property	62,000
Equipment	9,600
Stock	5,800

Debtors paid in full and creditors gave discounts

totalling £200. Dissolution expenses totalled £1,600.

You are required to prepare all the accounts of the partnership on dissolution.

► Answer in appendix

16 Anne, Bev and Chris, trading in partnership under the name 'Cosmetics' and sharing profits and losses in the ratio 2 : 1 : 1, received an offer from a chain store for the purchase of the entire business. The partnership Balance Sheet as at the date of offer was as follows.

Balance Sheet as at 30 September 19x9

	£	£
Fixtures and fittings		13,000
Motor vehicles		19,400
		32,400
Stock	34,400	
Bank	10,600	
	45,000	
Less: Creditors	13,600	31,400
		63,800
Capital accounts:		
Anne	26,000	
Bev	18,000	
Chris	14,000	58,000
Loan account – Anne		2,000
Current accounts:		
Anne	2,600	
Bev	800	
Chris	400	3,800
		63,800

The offer was for the purchase of the assets, excluding the balance at the bank for the sum of £80,000. The partners decided to accept the offer, and to dissolve their partnership on 30 September 19x9.

You are required to prepare all the accounts of the partnership on dissolution.

► No answer given

17 The Balance Sheet of A and B at 31 March, 19x9 was as follows.

	£	£
Fixed assets:		38,000
Current assets:		
Stock	23,600	
Debtors	9,500	
Cash	300	
		33,400
		71,400
Capital accounts:		
A	30,000	
B	28,000	
		58,000
Current accounts:		
A	3,800	
B	3,400	
		7,200
Current liabilities:		
Creditors		6,200
		71,400

The partnership was dissolved on 1 April, 19x9 on the following terms and conditions.

(i) The motor cars included in fixed assets were taken over by the partners at agreed values as A £4,000, B £6,000.
(ii) The remainder of the fixed assets were sold for £34,000.
(iii) The stock was valued at auction for £18,600.
(iv) The creditors were paid off less a 5 per cent discount.
(v) The debtors realised £9,200.
(vi) Expenses of realization were £500.
(vii) The profit sharing formula is:
10 per cent interest on capital, balance 3 : 2.

You are required to show the relevant accounts in the dissolution.

► Answerin appendix

19 Company accounts – an introduction

Chapter objectives

By the end of this chapter, you should be able to:

- explain how a company is formed
- distinguish between different types of company
- prepare final accounts for companies for internal use only
- understand the following terms: unlimited, limited, private, public, quoted and unquoted companies, memorandum of association, articles of association, Certificate of Incorporation, Trading Certificate, statutory books, owners' capital, debentures, share capital, preference shares, ordinary shares, deferred shares, risk capital, issues at par, issues at a premium, issues at a discount, share premium account, market issues of shares, bonus issues of shares/capitalization issues/scrip/stock dividend issue.

Introduction

We've so far discussed the accounting needs and methods relating to two types of business organization: sole traders and partnerships, which operate with a view to making a profit. In this chapter, we'll meet another type of business organization – the **company**. Although companies may be formed by Royal Charter, as in the case of the Hudson Bay Company, or by a special Act of Parliament, as was the East India Company, most companies are formed by incorporation or registration under the **Companies Acts**.

We shall begin with a brief account of how companies are formed by registration and the different types of company. Then, after outlining the accounting requirements of companies, there will be an explanation of the different items that would appear in the final accounts of companies. Finally, we'll look at how the final accounts of companies are prepared for internal use. The published accounts of companies are a specialized area and are outside the scope of this book.

Types of company

All companies have separate **legal entity** in the sense that they are treated as legal persons and they can therefore sue and be sued in a court of law. However, they are treated differently in some respects, depending on criteria such as the **limitation of liabilities**. Companies are normally classified into a number of types, as shown in Figure 19.1 below.

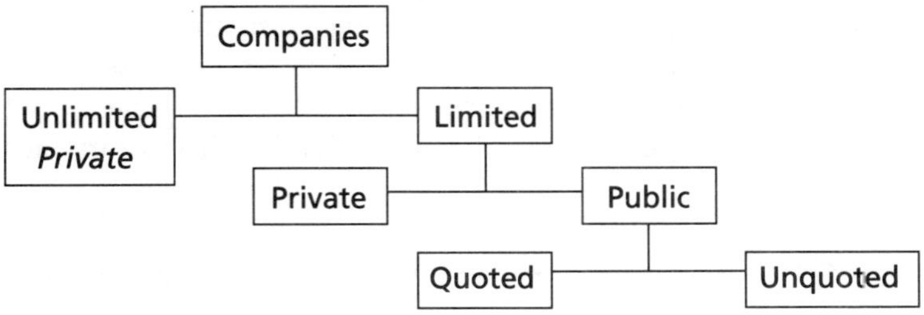

Figure 19.1
Classification of companies

► **Unlimited companies**: unlimited liabilities

Unlimited companies, like sole traders and partnerships, have unlimited liabilities for their debts and they are private companies. Such companies are very uncommon as they do not offer any real advantages over other forms of business organizations with unlimited liabilities, such as partnerships. **Limited companies**, on the other hand, are companies in which the members – that is, the **shareholders** – enjoy **limited liabilities**. This means that their liabilities are limited to the amount they have already contributed or have agreed to contribute to the company. There are two kinds of limited company: private and public.

> A company is a **private limited company** when it satisfies the following conditions:
> - it is registered as a private limited company
> - the right to transfer its shares is restricted
> - the number of members is limited to 50
> - any invitation to the public to subscribe to any **shares** or **debentures** (which will be explained later in the chapter) in the company is restricted
> - liabilities of the members are limited by shares or guarantee
> - the name ends with ' Limited ' or 'Ltd.'

► In a limited company liability is restricted to the amount contributed

Limited companies which are not private limited companies are called **public limited companies**. The name of a public limited company ends with 'Public Limited Company' or 'PLC'. A public limited company must have a minimum paid up share capital of £50,000. Both types of company must have at least two members. A public limited company must have at least two directors, whereas a private limited company may operate with one director. Although private limited companies are not permitted to offer shares or debentures to the general public, public limited companies may offer shares and debentures to the general public. They can increase the marketability of these securities by being quoted or listed on the **Stock Exchange**. Public limited companies whose securities are listed on the Stock Exchange are called **quoted** or **listed** companies; companies whose securities are not thus listed are known as **unquoted** or **unlisted** companies. For their securities to be listed or quoted on the Stock Exchange, companies must fulfil certain stringent conditions set out by the Stock Exchange. Normally, only large companies can afford to do so.

The formation of a registered company

Almost all companies are formed by registration. Anyone wishing to form a company must apply to the **Registrar of Companies,** sending a number of documents which include:

- the **Memorandum of Association**, signed by the first members of the company, which sets out the rules and regulations that will govern the company's dealings with the outside world. In particular, it contains the following details of the company:
  - name of the company
  - permanent address of the company
  - declaration of limited liability (for limited liability companies only)
  - capital of the company
- the **Articles of Association** which contain rules and regulations for

the internal management of the company. For example, it will define the duties and power of the directors and the rights of the shareholders. The **Companies Act** of 1985 contains a model set of articles, known as **Table A**, which can be adopted, in whole or in part, by companies seeking registration.

After completing some legal formalities, the Registrar of Companies will issue a **Certificate of Incorporation**, a document that is usually regarded as the company's birth certificate. A private company may start trading as soon as the Certificate is issued, but a public company has to raise its capital and to take some other legal steps before the Registrar will issue a **Trading Certificate** to enable it to commence business.

► Certificate of Incorporation

Accounting requirements of companies

Every company must keep books of accounts to record cash receipts and cash payments, purchases and sales of assets, liabilities incurred and purchases and sales of goods. These records should enable the company to prepare the final accounts which will show a true and fair view of the affairs of the company.

In addition to the books of accounts, a company is required to maintain another set of books, known as **statutory books**. Some examples of these books are:

► Statutory books

- a register of directors and secretaries
- an indexed register of members
- minutes books of meetings of members.

Every company should prepare, at the end of its financial year, a set of annual accounts, as listed below.

Annual accounts required by registered company

- a Profit and Loss account
- a Balance Sheet
- notes attached to the Profit and Loss account and the Balance Sheet
- a directors' report
- an auditors' report

The Companies Acts (of 1985 and 1989) state the formats and the specific requirements of the different accounts. These are advanced topics in company accounts which we shall not try to explore here.

The Balance Sheet

A Balance Sheet is a list of assets, liabilities and capital. In the Balance Sheet of a company, we find a number of new items under each of the three major headings: assets, liabilities and capital. Let's now explain some of these terms. We start with assets.

Assets

We can classify the assets that are listed in a company Balance Sheet into three main groups:

- intangible assets such as goodwill
- fixed (tangible) assets such as premises, and plant
- current assets such as stocks, debtors and cash.

► **Assets:**
- intangible
- fixed
- current

See also Chapter 3

▶ Assets are listed in order of convertibility

The assets are set out in ascending order of **liquidity**. Liquidity is the ease with which assets can be converted into cash. The listing of the assets in the Balance Sheet starts with the asset which is *most difficult* to convert into cash and ends by listing the asset which can be turned *most easily* into cash – or is cash itself.

Fixed assets are listed at cost less accumulated depreciation to date.

In company accounts, we often find an item called **investments** listed with other assets. These investments are shares and debentures of other companies, held for either a short period or a long period. **Long-term investments** are usually listed under fixed assets, whereas **short-term investments** are generally considered to be current assets. The purchase price or cost of such investments is shown in the Balance Sheet accompanied by a note of the current market price.

Liabilities

▶ **Liabilities**: owings but also sources of funds

Liabilities are what a company owes, but the liabilities shown in a Balance Sheet can also be thought of as sources of funds. The items listed under liabilities show where the money has come from to finance the assets of the company. The main liabilities or sources of funds of a company are as follows.

▶ **Liabilities:**
- owners' capital
- debentures
- loans
- current liabilities

See also Chapter 3

Owners' capital

A considerable part of the funds will be provided by shareholders, when they purchase shares when the company first started, or when it offers a new issue of shares. This is known as **share capital**. Owners' capital also includes both capital and revenue reserves. **Capital reserves** are similar to retained profits accumulated over the years from sources other than trading profit. Thus if shares are sold **at a premium**, i.e. at a price higher than the **nominal value**, the excess of the money received over and above the nominal value of the shares will be credited to a **capital reserve account**, called the **Share premium account**. These reserves are not distributable and cannot be given to shareholders as dividends. **Revenue reserves** and the balance on the Profit and Loss account, on the other hand, are **retained**, i.e. they are undistributed trading profits from previous years and are distributable. If the directors so desire, they can give these reserves to the shareholders in the form of increased dividends.

▶ Authorized share capital

In stating the capital of a company, we make a distinction between authorized share capital and issued share capital. **Authorized share capital** is the maximum amount of capital that a limited company is allowed to raise as share capital. This amount is stated in the Memorandum of Association and cannot be exceeded without altering the authorized share capital itself in the memorandum. Such a change requires strict adherence to the stipulated conditions. **Issued share capital** is the nominal value of the actual shares issued.

▶ Issued share capital

▶ Paid-up share capital

Not all of the issued share capital of a company may have been paid at a certain date. That part of the issued share capital that has been paid is known as the **paid up** or **called up share capital** and it is this amount which must be shown in the Balance Sheet.

An example will illustrate these different types of share capital.

Let's assume that AB PLC's Memorandum of Association states its share capital to be £1,000,000. On 1 January 19x0 AB PLC offered 500,000 shares of £1 each at par to the public on the following terms:

- 20p per share payable on application by 15 January 19x0
- 30p per share payable on allotment by 31 January 19x0
- 50p payable on 1 January 19x1.

Assuming that all the shares have been allotted and allotment money is received by the due date, then as at 31 January 19x0 AB PLC's authorized share capital will be £1,000,000, its issued share capital will equal £500,000 and its called up capital will be £250,000 (the actual amount of money called up by that date).

Debentures

Debentures appear quite frequently in company Balance Sheets. They are long-term loans – in the form of 'I owe yous' (IOUs). A company, say Alpha PLC, seeking a loan from another company, say Beta PLC, will write an IOU, called a **debenture certificate**, which will contain the following details:

► **Debentures**: long-term loans

- name and address of the borrower
- amount of the loan
- the fixed rate of interest (A 'five per cent debenture' has the rate of interest on the loan fixed at 5 per cent per annum.)
- date of maturity – not an exact date but a period, such as 2000–2001, during which the loan has to be repaid.

Alpha PLC will hand over this 'bond' to Beta PLC on receipt of the amount stated on the debenture certificate. Debentures, like stocks and shares, are **transferable** – that is, they can be bought and sold on the open market.

Debentures provide funds to companies, but, unlike shareholders, debenture holders are not regarded as owners of companies. Debenture holders do not get any dividends, but receive interest on the money loaned out at a fixed rate of interest.

Current liabilities

Besides the usual short-term liabilities such as trade creditors, accruals and bank overdrafts, we find two other common items under current liabilities of companies – **taxation** and **proposed dividends**. Companies do not pay income tax but they pay a tax on profits, known as **corporation tax**. When preparing the Profit and Loss account at the year end, corporation tax is estimated and shown as an appropriation. Since the tax has not been paid by the accounting date, but has to be paid (by most companies) within the next accounting year, it is shown as a current liability in the Balance Sheet. Similarly, dividend – once proposed – needs to be paid within a reasonable period; it is therefore included in current liabilities.

► **Current liabilities**: see also Chapter 3

► **Corporation tax**: paid on profits

► Current liabilities include tax and dividends

The Profit and Loss account for companies

Like a partnership, a company has an appropriation section in its Profit and Loss account, prepared for internal use. It shows the disbursements of profits which include corporation tax, paid and proposed dividends and transfer to one or more reserve accounts. Other than this, a company's Profit and Loss account is no different from that of any other business.

Classes of shares

A company's capital is called **share capital**. When we buy a share in a company we are, in effect, contributing to its capital and so we become a co-owner of the business, known as a **shareholder**. Again, we can buy and sell shares of a company freely and the price we pay for these shares depends on the **market forces** of **demand** and **supply**. Share prices fluctuate very frequently – they may change several times even in the course of an hour. If we have to value the share capital of a company at market price, we may get quite a large number of valuations during the year. This would require adjusting our share capital account many times over a given period. To overcome this problem of share valuation, companies in the UK always record share capital at **nominal value**, i.e. the value which is entered on the face of the **share certificate**. This is also a requirement of the Companies Acts. However, the market value of the share on the Balance Sheet date is normally given in the form of a note to the Balance Sheet.

► Types of shares

There are three main types of shares:

- preference shares
- ordinary shares
- deferred shares.

Preference shares

These shares earn a fixed rate of dividend. The fixed rate is printed on the share certificate – thus the holder of a 'five per cent preference share' will receive only a five per cent dividend *per annum* on the nominal value of the share. Another characteristic of preference shares is that they do not normally carry any voting rights because it is considered that these shares do not constitute the **risk capital** of the company. In other words, preference shareholders do not have much stake on their investment as they are more or less certain to get their fixed dividends. Preference shares could be either cumulative or non-cumulative. If a dividend cannot be paid to the holders of **cumulative** preference shares because of low or no profits made during the year, the amount owing is carried forward to the next or subsequent years. Holders of **non-cumulative** shares lose their dividends if profits are insufficient in any year to pay such dividends. Finally, preference shareholders have a preferential claim on the profits of the company *over* other shareholders and also take precedence over other shareholders (but not over debenture holders or creditors) in the event of liquidation.

Ordinary shares

All companies must have ordinary or **equity** shares. These carry voting rights but have no special dividend rights. In prosperous years, holders of ordinary shares receive a high dividend but in lean years they receive little or no dividend. Ordinary shares are risky because dividends are uncertain and their priority is low in the event of liquidation. Those who hold ordinary shares are the real risk-bearers of the company.

Deferred shares

These shares, also known as **founders' shares**, are now very rare but are sometimes issued to the original founders of the company. They receive dividends only after other types of shareholders – preference and ordinary – have been paid their dividends.

Issue of shares and debentures

Shares and debentures may be issued:
- at par
- at a premium
- at a discount.

Shares and debentures are issued **at par** when they are sold at their nominal or **face** value – a £1 share is sold for £1 only.

► Issued at par

Shares are issued **at a premium** when the issue price is more than their nominal value. When the issue price is lower than the nominal value, shares or securities are said to be issued **at a discount**.

► Issued at a premium

► Issued at a discount

Issue of shares at a discount is very rare and can be ignored. Shares issued at a premium are very common and company law requires that the amount of the **premium**, i.e. the excess of the issue price over the nominal value, should be put to a special reserve account called the **Share premium account**. The Share premium account is a capital reserve account and the amount to its credit cannot be distributed to the shareholders as dividends. To do so would amount to returning part of the capital to the providers of capital themselves!

Methods of share issue

There are three methods of issuing shares:
- market issue
- rights issue
- bonus issue.

Market issue

This is the normal method of raising initial or additional capital for a public limited company. **Market issue** involves an invitation to the general public – either through a **prospectus** or an **offer of sale** – to buy new shares in a company, at a price equal to the market price for a going concern *or* at an estimated price for a new company.

Rights issue

This is an invitation to existing shareholders to buy new shares in the company. Normally, the existing shareholders are offered new shares in proportion to the number of shares they already hold. The issue price will usually be below the current market price to make the offer attractive to them. Many companies prefer this method because it is less expensive than a market issue.

Bonus issue

A **bonus issue** is a free issue of new shares to the existing shareholders in proportion to the number of shares already held by them. The purpose of this type of share issue is to convert some of the reserves of the company into capital. Reserves are **capitalized** so this is also known as a **capitalization issue**. It may also be referred to as a **scrip** or a **stock dividend**.

► **Bonus issue**, or **capitalization issue** or **scrip** or **stock dividend**

FINAL ACCOUNTS OF A LIMITED COMPANY – AN ILLUSTRATION

Companies need to prepare a set of final accounts at the end of the financial year, in accordance with the provisions of the Companies Acts. These accounts are designed for publication and a copy should be forwarded to every shareholder. Most companies prepare a set of final accounts for internal use prior to the preparation of accounts for publication. Example 19.1 illustrates how accounts for internal use are prepared.

Example 19.1 The preparation of final company accounts for internal use

The following Trial Balance was extracted from the books of Popular Trading Company as at 30 September 19x2.

Popular Trading Company: Trial Balance

	DR £	CR £
500,000 ordinary shares of £1 each fully paid		500,000
300,000 10% preference shares of 50p ea.		150,000
Sales		3,050,000
Stocks – 1 September 19x1	100,000	
Share premium account		100,000
5% Debentures		100,000
Profit and Loss account		70,000
General reserve		50,000
Premises	800,000	
Furniture and fittings at cost	50,000	
Provision for depreciation on furniture and fittings		10,000
Motor vehicles at cost	100,000	
Provision for depreciation on motor vehicles		40,000
Debtors/Creditors	300,000	100,000
Wages and salaries	350,000	
Director's fees	100,000	
Other administrative expenses	240,000	
Selling and distribution	210,000	
Cash at bank	300,000	
Cash in hand	20,000	
Purchases	1,600,000	
	4,170,000	4,170,000

The following additional information is available.

(i) Closing stock was valued at £120,000.
(ii) Provision for debenture interest is to be made.
(iii) A provision for bad debts at 5 per cent of debtors is to be made.
(iv) Depreciate furniture and fittings at 10 per cent on cost, motor vehicle at 20 per cent, using the Reducing balance method.
(v) Provide for corporation tax of £175,000.
(vi) Preference dividend is to be paid in full.
(vii) An ordinary dividend of 10 per cent is proposed.
(viii) Transfer £20,000 to general reserve.

You are required to prepare for Popular Trading Company:

a A Trading and Profit and Loss account for the year ended 30 September 19x2.

b A Balance Sheet as at that date.

Solution

a

Popular Trading Company PLC

Trading and Profit and Loss account for the year ended 30 September 19x2

	£000	£000
Sales		3,050
Less cost of sales:		
Opening stock	100	
Add purchases	1,600	
	1,700	
Less closing stock	120	1,580
Gross profit		1,470
Less expenses :		
Wages and salaries	350	
Director's fees	100	
Administrative expenses	240	
Selling and distribution	210	
Debenture interest	5	
Provision for bad debts	15	
Depreciation on fixtures and fittings	5	
Depreciation on motor vehicles	12	937
Net profit		533
Less Appropriations:		
Tax	175	
Preference dividends	15	
Transfer to general reserve	20	
Ordinary dividend	50	
		260
Retained profit of the year		273
Add Profit and Loss a/c balance b/f		70
Profit and Loss a/c balance c/f		343

b

Popular Trading Company PLC
Balance Sheet as at 30 September 19x2

	Cost £000	Deprecn. £000	Net £000
Fixed Assets:			
Premises	800	–	800
Furniture and fittings	50	15	35
Motor vehicles	100	52	48
	950	67	883
Current Assets:			
Stocks		120	
Debtors	300		
Less provision	15	285	
Bank		300	
Cash		20	
		725	
Less Current Liabilities:			
Creditors	100		
Tax	175		
Preference dividend	15		
Ordinary dividend	50		
Debenture interest	5	345	
			380
			1,263
Less Debentures			100
			1,163
Ordinary shares			500
Preference shares			150
Share premium			100
General reserves			70
Profit and Loss account			343
			1,163

From these accounts prepared for internal use, it is relatively easy to prepare a Profit and Loss account and a Balance Sheet for publication. Published accounts should conform to the legal requirements as contained in the Companies Act and are outside the scope of this book. However, there is an example of published accounts in Chapter 1, in Figure 1.1. Go back to Chapter 1 and look at those accounts again – you'll probably be able to understand them now.

Chapter summary

- Most companies now are formed by registration with the Registrar of Companies.
- Most are limited liability companies where the liability of the members is limited to the amount of capital they provided.
- Public companies which raise capital through the stock exchange are called 'listed' or 'quoted' companies.
- The Trading and Profit and Loss account of a company includes an appropriation section which shows how the net profit of the year is appropriated in the form of corporation tax to the Inland Revenue and dividends to the shareholders.

ACT **19.1**

For each of questions 1 to 5, put a tick against the letter representing the best choice from among the four possible answers given.

1 The authorized share capital of a registered company is:
- **A** The minimum amount of share capital that the company may issue
- **B** The maximum amount of share capital that the company may issue
- **C** Another name for capital employed
- **D** Another name for equity capital.

2 When shares are issued at a premium, it means that:
- **A** The issue price is more than the nominal value
- **B** The issue price is exactly equal to the nominal value
- **C** The issue price is less than the nominal value
- **D** None of the above is true.

3 A person buys 1000 10 per cent preference shares of £0.50 each for £1,000. The current rate of interest is 15 per cent p.a. She will receive an annual dividend of:
- **A** £100
- **B** £150
- **C** £75
- **D** £50.

4 Which is the odd one out?
- **A** Goodwill
- **B** Plant and machinery
- **C** Debentures
- **D** Stocks.

5 The following items are taken from a company's Balance Sheet:

Ordinary shares	£100,000
Preference shares	£25,000
General reserve	£50,000
Debentures	£75,000

The equity capital of the company is:
- **A** £250,000
- **B** £200,000
- **C** £150,000
- **D** £100,000.

► Answers in appendix

6 Smith Brothers Ltd has an authorized capital of £500,000 divided into 300,000 ordinary shares of £1 each, and 200,000 8 per cent preference shares of £1 each. The following balances were extracted from the books of the company after it had prepared its Trading and Profit and Loss account for the year ended 31 March 19x9.

	DR £	CR £
Net profit of the year		65,000
Plant and machinery at cost	150,000	
Provision for depreciation on plant and machinery		30,000
Premises at cost	200,000	
Stocks	25,000	
Ordinary share capital, fully paid		200,000
8% Preference shares, fully paid		100,000
Debtors	40,000	
Creditors		25,000
Prepayments	15,000	
Accruals		5,000
Profit and Loss account balance – 31 March 19x8		15,000
General reserve		5,000
Bank	15,000	
	445,000	445,000

The company provides you with the following additional information.

(i) A provision of £15,125 for corporation tax is to be made.
(ii) The directors propose to pay a dividend of 10 per cent on ordinary shares.
(iii) £5,000 is to be transferred to the General Reserve.

You are required to :

a Prepare a Profit and Loss appropriation account for the year ended 31 March 19x9.
b Prepare a Balance Sheet as at 31 March 19x9.

► Answer in appendix

7 The following Trial Balance was extracted after the preparation of the Trading and Profit and Loss account at 31 December 19x0.

	DR £	CR £
150,000 ordinary shares of £1 each, fully paid		150,000
50,000 7.5% preference shares of £1 each, fully paid		50,000
Share premium		30,000
Profit and Loss account		55,000
Net profit of the year		100,000
Creditors		45,000
General reserve		50,000
Bank		15,000
Premises	209,000	
Plant and machinery at cost	175,000	
Provision for depreciation on plant and machinery		45,000
Fixtures and fittings at cost	20,000	
Provision for depreciation on fixtures and fittings		8,000
Motor vehicles at cost	80,000	
Provision for depreciation on motor vehicles		40,000
Stocks	43,000	
Debtors	60,000	
Accruals		12,000
Prepayments	10,000	
Cash	3,000	
	600,000	600,000

Additional information:

(i) A provision of £18,750 for Corporation tax is to be made.

(ii) An amount of £10,000 is to be transferred to the general reserve account.

(iii) A dividend of 15 per cent on ordinary shares is proposed.

You are required to prepare:

a A Profit and Loss Appropriation account for the year ended 31 December 19x0.

b A Balance Sheet as at that date.

► No answer given

8 The following list of balances was extracted from the books of Highbury Ltd at 31 December,19x9.

	£	£
Issued share capital:		
£1 ordinary shares		150,000
General reserve		16,000
Profit and Loss reserve at 31 December 19x8		12,276
5% Debentures		50,000
Premises at cost	40,000	
Machinery at cost	90,000	
Motor vehicles at cost	56,000	
Stock at 31 Dec 19x8	82,830	
Cash and bank	32,510	
Debtors	57,120	
Purchases	102,760	
Directors' remuneration	12,400	
Wages and salaries	22,744	
Sundry expenses	2,152	
Motor expenses	16,288	
Repairs to machinery	4,616	
Creditors		44,944
Provision for depreciation at 31 Dec. 19x8:		
Machinery		36,000
Motor vehicles		25,200
Sales		185,000
	519,420	519,420

Notes:

(i) Stock at 31 December 19x9: £108,600.
(ii) Motor expenses owing: £890.
(iii) Proposed ordinary dividend: 20 per cent.
(iv) Transfer £4,000 to general reserve.
(v) Make a provision for the debenture interest payable.
(vi) Provide for depreciation of all fixed assets at 20 per cent using the Reducing balance method.
(vii) The authorized share capital is £200,000.

You are required to prepare a Trading and Profit and Loss account for the year ended 31 December 19x9 and a Balance Sheet as at that date.

► Answer in appendix

9 The following Trial Balance was extracted from the books of ABC Limited on 31 March 19x9.

	DR £	CR £
Sales		604,000
Purchases	404,000	
Trade creditors		51,680
Trade debtors	60,000	
Premises at cost	200,000	
Plant and machinery at cost	80,000	
Motor vehicles at cost	30,000	
Stock at 1 April, 19x8	40,000	
Wages and salaries	93,820	
General expenses	45,800	
Carriage inwards	7,800	
Bad debts written off	1,480	
Cash in hand	2,320	
Bank balance		1,340
Authorized, issued and fully paid share capital: £1 ordinary shares		200,000
Provisions for depreciation at 1 April, 19x8:		
Plant and machinery		16,000
Motor vehicles		12,000
Discounts – net		5,200
Provision for doubtful debts		2,200
Profit and Loss reserve at 1 April, 19x8		11,800
General reserve		19,000
5% Debentures		42,000
	965,220	965,220

The following information is also provided.

(i) Stock at 31 March 19x9 was valued at £44,000.

(ii) The provision for doubtful debts is to be increased to £2,400.

(iii) At 31 March 19x9 wages due amounted to £980 and general expenses prepaid were £80.

(iv) Provision is to be made for debenture interest.

(v) Depreciation is to be provided as follows:
10 per cent per annum on cost for plant and machinery
20 per cent per annum on cost for motor vehicles.

(vi) £12,000 is to be transferred to the General Reserve.

(vii) The directors have proposed a dividend of 15 per cent on the ordinary shares.

You are required to prepare a Trading and Profit and Loss account for the year ended 31 March 19x9 and a Balance Sheet as at that date.

► No answer given

20 Source and application of funds

Chapter objectives

By the end of this chapter, you should be able to:

- explain the nature and significance of a funds flow statement
- list the various sources of funds that are available to a business
- list the different applications of these funds
- ascertain the net increase or decrease in working capital over a given period of time
- identify the net changes in the component parts of working capital over the same period
- prepare a Statement of Source and Application of Funds, as recommended in SSAP 10
- understand the following terms; funds, flow statement, statement of source and application of funds.

Introduction

In Chapter 12 we saw the need for the control of working capital and looked at the mechanics of three components of working capital: stock, debtors and creditors. This chapter extends that process to cover the whole area of working capital or **funds**. We shall see how the different sources of funds that are available are used or applied over a given period of time – or how funds move through the different activities of the business (not just trading activities) generating funds at some points and using them at some others. These movements of funds are normally presented in the form of a **Funds flow statement**, or – to use the title given by SSAP 10 – **the Statement of Source and Application of Funds.**

THE NATURE AND PURPOSE OF A FUNDS FLOW STATEMENT

► The function of a Funds flow statement is to trace the movements of assets, liabilities and capital

The two important financial statements that every business prepares at the end of its accounting year are the Trading and Profit and Loss account and the Balance Sheet. The Trading and Profit and Loss account shows how much profit or loss the company has earned over the year and the Balance Sheet shows how its assets, liabilities and capital have changed since the last Balance Sheet was prepared. Some of the changes in the Balance Sheet items are obviously related to, and dependent upon, the profits made during the year. The Profit and Loss account for the year, and the opening and closing Balance Sheets by themselves, though, do not explain fully how these changes have come about. What is needed is a statement linking the Profit and Loss account with the two Balance Sheets so that the changes in individual items can be properly understood. Such a link is provided by a Funds flow statement. Therefore, the purpose of a Funds flow statement is to trace the movements of assets, liabilities and capital which will eventually be reflected in an increase or a decrease in working capital and to indicate how the various activities of the business are financed. Moreover, the liquidity position of the business can be better understood by such a statement.

According to SSAP 10, every business with an annual turnover of more than £25,000 should prepare a Statement of Source and Application of Funds (Funds flow statement).

Sources of funds and their applications

It is not easy to give a precise definition of the term 'funds' – even SSAP 10 has not defined it. Many think that funds are the same thing as cash. However, we'll use this term in a wider sense and equate it with working capital with the proviso that working capital should not include taxation and dividends which, for purposes of the Funds flow statement, are (or should be) regarded as application of funds.

Sources of funds

The following are the major sources of funds:

- trading profit
- proceeds from the sale of fixed assets
- issue of shares for cash
- loans which will not require repayments within the next 12 months, e.g. debentures and bank loans.

In calculating the funds generated from the normal operations – e.g. trading – we very often have to make some adjustments to the net profit figure *before taxation* for items which do not involve the movement of funds. Good examples are depreciation and provisions for bad debts, and any profits or losses made on the disposal of fixed assets. Although a depreciation charge is treated as an expense, it does not involve an outflow of cash and is normally added back to net profit to give a more accurate figure for total generated from operations. We should make the same sort of adjustment for other provisions and for profit or loss on the sale of fixed assets. A profit on the disposal of an asset will be deducted from, and a loss added to, the net profit before taxation.

The other sources of funds, as listed above, are self-explanatory.

The applications of funds

The applications of funds indicate the way the various operations or activities are financed. They include:

- the purchase of fixed assets
- payment of tax
- payments of dividends, both preference and ordinary
- repayments of loans and debentures
- repayment of share capital.

Figure 20.1 shows the standard format of a Statement of Source and Application of Funds, as given in SSAP 10.

Example 20.1 demonstrates the actual preparation of a Statement of Source and Application of Funds.

Figure 20.1
Statement of Source and Application of Funds

Notice that the statement contains four distinct parts:

(i) sources of funds
(ii) applications of funds
(iii) change in working capital
(iv) changes in net liquid funds.

(i) and (ii) are self explanatory; (iii) is obtained by taking the difference between (i) and (ii); and (iv) refers to movements in bank and cash balances. (iii) and (iv) together show the net changes in the constituent parts of working capital over the year.

Statement of Source and Application of Funds for the year ended 31 December 19x9

	£	£
Sources of Funds:		
Net profit before taxation		X
Adjustments for items not involving the movements of funds:		
Depreciation		X
Total generated from operations:		X
Other sources:		
Issue of shares	X	
Loans raised	X	
Proceeds of fixed assets and investments sold	X	X
		X
Application of funds:		
Dividends paid	X	
Tax paid	X	
Fixed assets and investment purchases	X	
Loan repaid	X	(X)
Increase/(decrease) in working capital		X
Increase/(decrease) in stock	X	
Increase/(decrease) in debtors	X	
Decrease/(Increase) in creditors	X	
	X	
Movement in net liquid funds	X	(X)

Example 20.1 Preparation of a Statement of Source and Application of Funds

The following are the condensed Balance Sheets for Terrains Ltd for the years ended 31 March 19x1 and 19x2 and a summarized Profit and Loss account for the year ended 31 March 19x2.

Terrains Ltd
Balance Sheets as at 31 March

	19x1			19x2		
	£	£	£	£	£	£
Fixed assets at cost		60,000			72,000	
Less Depreciation		18,000	42,000		25,200	46,800
Current Assets:						
Stocks		20,750			30,000	
Debtors		20,200			20,000	
Bank		800			3,250	
		41,750			53,250	
Less Current Liabilities:						
Creditors	20,900			16,300		
Taxation	10,200			9,990		
Proposed Dividend	4,000	35,100		5,000	31,290	
			6,650			21,960
			48,650			68,760
Financed by						
Issued Share Capital			40,000			45,000
Profit and Loss a/c			8,650			23,760
			48,650			68,760

Trading and Profit and Loss account for the year ended 31 March 19x2

	£
Net Profits before Taxation	30,100
Tax on profits	9,990
	20,110
Retained Profits from last year	8,650
	28,760
Proposed dividend	5,000
Retained profits carried to next year	23,760

Note: There were no disposals of fixed assets during the year.

You are required to prepare a Statement of Source and Application of Funds for Terrains Ltd for the year to 31 March 19x2.

Solution

Terrains Ltd

Statement of Source and Application of Funds for the year ended 31 March 19x2

	£	£
Source of Funds		
Net profit before taxation		30,100
Adjustments for items not involving the movement of funds:		
Depreciation		7,200
Total generated from operations		37,300
Funds from other sources		
Issue of shares for cash		5,000
		42,300
Application of Funds		
Dividend paid	4,000	
Tax paid	10,200	
Purchase of fixed assets	12,000	26,200
Increase in working capital	16,100	
Increase in stocks	9,250	
Decrease in debtors	(200)	
Decrease in creditors	4,600	
Movement in net liquid funds:		
Increase in cash balances	2,450	16,100

Note:

1 Depreciation for the year is simply the difference between the accumulated depreciations of the two years, i.e. £25,200 – £18,000 = £7,200.

2 Notice the change in share capital as at 31 March 19x2. The increased amount of £5,000 must have been issued for cash during the year.

3 Dividend for 19x2 is £5,000 which appears on both the Profit and Loss account and the Balance Sheet of the year. Therefore dividend paid during the year must have been the amount due as at 31 March 19x1, i.e. £4,000.

4 Tax for the last year i.e. £10,200, must have been paid during the year as the tax liability appearing on the Balance Sheet on 31 March 19x2 is that of the current year as shown in the Profit and Loss account.

5 An increase in stock is an increase in working capital but a decrease in stock of £200 represents a decrease in working capital and is therefore shown as a negative figure, i.e. within brackets.

6 A decrease in creditors represents an increase in working capital and is therefore shown as a positive figure.

If however, the Profit and Loss account or the net profit of the year is not given, we have to calculate it by following the table given below.

Profit and Loss account balance at the end of year	X
Less Profit and loss account balance at start of year	X
Retained profit of the year	X
Add dividend for the year	X
Any transfer to reserve account	X
Net profit before taxation	X
Add tax on profit of the year	X
Net profit before taxation	X

The calculation of profits from Balance Sheet figures is demonstrated in Example 20.2.

Example 20.2 Calculation of profits from the Balance Sheet

Refer to Example 20.1. Consider the Balance Sheet, ignoring completely the Profit and Loss account given there. Calculate the net profit of the year.

Solution

Calculation of net profit before taxation for the year to 31 March 19x2

	£
Profit and Loss account balance at close of year at 31.3.x2	23,760
Less Profit and Loss account balance at 31.3.x1	8,650
Retained profit of the year	15,110
Add proposed dividend	5,000
Net profit after taxation	20,110
Add tax on profit of the year	9,990
Net profit before taxation	30,100

Note: The answer for the net profit before taxation is exactly the same as given in the Profit and Loss account.

Postscript: cash flow statements

► **FRS 1**: Financial Reporting Standard Cash flow statements

Since the completion of this chapter, a new development has occurred in relation to SSAP 10. The Accounting Standards Board has recently issued a new standard, called **FRS 1 (Financial Reporting Standard): Cash flow statements**, to replace SSAP 10. Large companies are now required to produce a cash flow statement (instead of Source and Application of Funds) as an integral part of their annual accounts. The standard came into force on 23 March, 1992.

As the new standard contains basically the same sort of information as SSAP 10, the principles that apply for the Source and Application of Funds Statement in its standard form still hold good, and as set out above, they provide a better understanding of the sources of funds and their application. However, an alternative presentation of the funds flow statement in the form of a cash flow statement will be equally useful. Example 20.1 is therefore represented below, using the standard format of the new Cash flow statement.

Example 20.3

Terrains Ltd

Cash flow statement for the year ended 31 March 19x2

	£	£
Net cash inflow from operating activities (Note 1)		23,650
Returns on investment and servicing of finance:		
Interest received	–	
Interest paid	–	
Dividends paid	(4,000)	

Net cash inflow/(outflow) from returns on investment and servicing of finance		(4,000)
Taxation:		
Corporation tax paid	(10,200)	
Tax paid		(10,200)
Investing activities:		
Payments to acquire intangible assets	–	
Payments to acquire fixed assets		(12,000)
Receipts from the sale of tangible fixed assets	–	
Net cash inflow/(outflow) from investing activities	(12,000)	
Net cash inflow/(outflow) before financing		(2,550)
Financing:		
Issue of ordinary share capital	5,000	
Purchases of debenture loans	–	
Net cash inflow from financing		5,000
Increase in cash or cash equivalents		2,450

Note:

1 Note that the increase in cash of £2,450, as given by the Cash flow statement is exactly the same as that given in the Source and Application of Funds.

2 The notes to the Cash flow statement are obligatory.

3 Both the Cash flow statement and the Source and Application of Funds statement give us similar information, but the figures in the Cash flow statement are presented in a manner which gives more information regarding the inflow and outflow of cash.

Notes to the cash flow statement

1 Reconciliation of operating profit to net cash inflow from operating activities

	£
Operating profit before taxation	30,100
Depreciation charges	7,200
Increase in stock	(9,250)
Decrease in debtors	200
Decrease in creditors	(4,600)
Net cash inflow from operating activities	23,650

2 **Analysis of changes in cash and cash equivalents during the year**

	£
Balance at 1 April, 19x1	800
Net cash inflow	2,450
Balance at 31 March, 19x2	3,250

3 **Analysis of the balances of cash and cash equivalents as shown in the Balance Sheet**

	19x2	19x1	Change in year
	£	£	£
Cash at bank and in hand	3,250	800	2,450
Short term investments	–	–	–
Bank overdraft	–	–	–
	3,250	800	2,450

4 **Analysis of changes in financing during the year**

	Share capital
	£
Balance at 1 April, 19x1	40,000
Cash inflow from financing	5,000
Balance at 31 March, 19x2	45,000

A similar analysis for debenture loan is to be given, if relevant.

Chapter summary

- A Funds flow statement (or a Statement of Source and Application of Funds) indicates the sources from which a business obtains funds or working capital and how it makes use of them.
- It starts by listing the sources of funds followed by a similar listing of applications of funds. The difference between these totals represents either an increase or decrease in working capital.
- It then shows how the change in working capital has come about by showing the movements or changes in each of the component items of working capital, with particular reference to the change in net liquid funds i.e. cash.
- Source and application of funds statement has now been superseded by ASB's first financial reporting standard (FRS1, Cash flow statements).

ACT **20.1**

1 The Balance Sheets of Piper Ltd, as at 31 December 19x0 and 31 December 19x1, are as follows.

	19x0	19x1
Fixed assets at cost less depreciation	80,000	120,000
Stocks	20,000	47,000
Debtors	20,000	36,000
Bank	10,000	
	130,000	203,000
Ordinary shares of £1 each	10,000	10,000
Profit and Loss account	58,000	138,000
Creditors	62,000	15,000
Overdraft		40,000
	130,000	203,000

Note: The net profit for 19x1 was £80,000 after charging depreciation of £10,000 on fixed assets.

You are required to prepare a Source and Application of Funds Statement for the year ended 31 December 19x1.

► No answer given

2 The Balance Sheets for Links Ltd for the years 19x5 and 19x6 were as follow.

	19x5 £	19x6 £
Fixed assets at cost	100,000	150,000
less provision for depreciation	30,000	40,000
	70,000	110,000
Current assets		
Stock	20,000	42,000
Debtors	8,700	31,000
Bank	21,300	–
	120,000	183,000
Ordinary shares of £1 each	50,000	100,000
Share premium	–	20,000
Profit and loss account	40,000	46,000
Creditors	30,000	6,400
Overdraft	–	10,600
	120,000	183,000

During the year ended 31 December 19x6, the company made a net profit of £20,000 out of which dividends of £14,000 had been paid.

You are required to prepare a Source and application of funds statement for the year ended 31 December 19x6.

► Answer in appendix

3 The Balance Sheets of Selkirk Ltd for the years ended 31 December 19x9 and 19x0 were as follow.

Selkirk Ltd
Balance Sheets as at 31 December

	19x9			19x0		
	£	£	£	£	£	£
Fixed Assets at cost		100,000			130,000	
Less Depreciation		30,000	70,000		43,000	87,000
Current Assets:						
Stocks		33,500			45,750	
Debtors		42,200			50,350	
Bank		1,000			5,500	
		76,700			101,600	
Less Current Liabilities:						
Creditors	35,450			34,250		
Taxation	10,000			12,500		
Proposed dividend	8,000	53,450		10,000	56,750	
Net Current Assets			23,250			44,850
			93,250			131,850
Financed by:						
Share capital			80,000			100,000
Profit and Loss a/c balance			13,250			31,850
			93,250			131,850

Summarized Profit and Loss account for the year ended 31 December 19x0

	£
Net profit before taxation	41,100
Taxation	12,500
	28,600
Retained profit from previous year	13,250
	41,850
Proposed dividend	10,000
Retained profit carried to next year	31,850

You are required to prepare a Statement of Source and Application of Funds for Selkirk Ltd for the year ended 31 December 19x0.

► No answer given

4 The following are the condensed Balance Sheets of AB Ltd for the years to 30 June 19x1 and 30 June 19x2.

AB Ltd
Balance Sheets as at 30 June

	19x1			19x2		
	£	£	£	£	£	£
Fixed assets at cost		232,000			306,000	
Less depreciation		82,000			112,600	
		150,000			193,400	
Current assets						
Stocks		50,000			61,600	
Debtors		40,750			51,000	
Bank		12,250			–	
		253,000			306,000	
Issued share capital		100,000			120,000	
Retained profits		50,000			60,500	
5% Debentures		50,000			50,000	
Taxation		12,000			15,000	
Dividends		10,000			12,000	
Overdraft		–			10,000	
Creditors		31,000			38,500	
		253,000			306,000	

AB Ltd's condensed Profit and Loss account for the year ended 30 June 19x2 is as follows.

AB Ltd
Profit and Loss account for the year ended 30 June 19x2

	£
Profit on ordinary activities before taxation*	37,500
Tax on profit on ordinary activities	15,000
	22,500
Retained profits brought forward	50,000
	72,500
Proposed dividend	12,000
Retained profits carried to next year	60,500

*Profit is calculated after charging depreciation of £30,600.

You are required to draw up a Flow of funds statement for the year ended 30 June 19x2.

► Answer in appendix

21 Analysis of financial information – an introduction to ratio analysis

Chapter objectives

By the end of this chapter, you should be able to:

- understand the meaning and significance of ratio analysis
- calculate a fair number of accounting ratios relating to the profitability, liquidity, assets usage, capital gearing and investment potential of a business and comment on their significance
- explain the limitations of ratio analysis
- understand the following terms: ratio analysis, capital structure (capital gearing/leverage), gross profit, net profit, rate of net profit, capital employed, return on capital employed, return on owner's equity, liquidity ratios, current (liquidity) ratio, quick (liquidity) ratio/acid test ratio, assets usage ratio, debtors ratio/average collection period, rate of stock turnover, ratio of sales to fixed assets, ratio of sales to assets value,capital structure ratios, gearing ratio, interest coverage, net worth ratio, investment ratio, earnings per share, dividend cover, dividend yield, price/earnings ratio/PE ratio, rate of payment to creditors.

Introduction

As explained in Chapter 1, the Balance Sheets and Profit and Loss accounts of a business provide different interested parties with information about its performance and financial standing. However, these accounts suffer from two limitations: firstly, the information is of historical nature and therefore does not reflect the current position, and secondly, the information is in condensed form so that many important details about assets, for example, such as their composition, are missed out. Nevertheless, financial statements are used by managers, shareholders, creditors and other interested parties to evaluate past performance, to monitor current position and to predict the future growth of the business.

This sort of analysis and interpretation of a set of accounts can be carried out in two ways. First, we can examine each key figure and compare it with the corresponding figure in previous accounts, in similar businesses or in the budget. Absolute figures by themselves are not particularly useful and it is only through comparisons that their significance can be properly understood. It is important to remember, though, that we have to be extremely careful in comparing absolute figures. Differences in accounting policies or in timing of transactions or in sizes of businesses make it difficult to compare absolute figures and draw relevant conclusions. This limitation brings us to the second method of analysing and appraising financial information, known as **ratio analysis**. This is the method that will be developed and used in the rest of this chapter.

The most useful way of comparing two sets of figures is through **ratios**, which show the relationship between two or more figures. Thus if there are four units of X and one unit of Y, the ratio of X to Y is four to one. We can also express Y as a **percentage** of X – 25 per cent in this example. However, accounting ratios should not be used in isolation – they should be compared with similar results obtained in previous accounting periods by the same business, or with results achieved by similar companies, or with predetermined standards or budgets for assessing the firm's profitability, liquidity, operating efficiency, stability and growth.

Comparative accounting ratios tend to show the strengths and weaknesses of a business and are therefore of great importance to their users.

The Profitability ratios

The following four ratios indicating the profitability of a business are most commonly used.

$$\text{Rate of gross profit} = \frac{\text{gross profit}}{\text{sales}} \times 100$$

The **gross profit percentage** or the **rate of gross profit** earned by a firm for a single year by itself does not tell us a great deal about its performance; but, as a general rule, the higher the rate, the better the performance of the business.

$$\text{Rate of net profit} = \frac{\text{net profit}}{\text{sales}} \times 100$$

The term 'net profit' may be defined, for purposes of ratio analysis, in more than one way. It may mean any of the following:

- profit before or after interest charges
- profit before or after taxation
- profit before interest and taxation
- profit after interest and taxation.

► **NPBIT**: net profit before interest and taxation

► **Consistency principle**: see Chapter 6

► **ROCE**: return on capital employed

However, the third definition seems to be the most popular so we'll define net profit as **net profit before interest and taxation** (NPBIT). Although the choice of definition of net profit is important, what is more important is to be consistent in using it. We must select a basis for calculating net profit, stick to it and go on using it consistently.

A low return on sales does not necessarily indicate inefficiency, as a low profit margin may be compatible with a very high turnover of stock, as is normally the case with many food supermarkets. It is therefore necessary to look at another measure of profitability – the **return on capital employed** (ROCE).

$$\text{ROCE} = \frac{\text{net profit before interest and taxation}}{\text{capital employed}} \times 100$$

Here again, there is a difference of opinion as to the precise meaning of the term 'capital employed', but the following definition is generally accepted:

Capital employed	= total net assets
	= fixed assets *less* depreciation ***plus*** current assets *minus* current liabilities

The return on capital employed is generally regarded as the best measure of profitability, indicating the efficiency with which the business is being run. This ratio can be broken down into two other ratios, as shown below.

► Return on capital employed is generally regarded as the best measure of profitability.

$$\frac{\text{NPBIT}}{\text{CE}} \times 100 = \frac{\text{NPBIT}}{\text{sales}} \times 100 \times \frac{\text{sales}}{\text{CE}}$$

Thus the ROCE represents the product of two ratios: the first one is the net profit ratio and the second one is the **asset turnover ratio**. It thus follows that a low ROCE, for example, indicates a low profit margin (NPBIT/sales ratio), or a low asset turnover, or both. Management should always try to earn the greatest possible ROCE.

$$\frac{\text{NPAIT} - \text{preference dividend}}{\text{ordinary share capital} + \text{reserves}}$$

► **ROOE**: return on owners' equity

► **NPAIT**: net profit after interest and taxation

The ROOE ratio measures the profitability of a company in terms of the capital provided by the owners of the company, i.e. the ordinary shareholders. Obviously, the ordinary shareholders (both existing and potential) would welcome a high ROOE.

Example 21.1 demonstrates how to calculate these profitability ratios.

Example 21.1 Calculating profitability ratios

Summarized Trading and Profit and Loss accounts of a company over a period of two years are as follows.

	Year 1 £	Year 2 £
Sales	200,000	300,000
Cost of sales	(120,000)	(190,000)
Gross profit	80,000	110,000
Expenses other than debenture interest	52,500	67,500
	27,500	42,500
Debenture interest	2,500	2,500
	25,000	40,000
Taxation	(6,000)	(9,000)
Net profit after taxation	19,000	31,000

The following additional information is also available:

Ordinary share capital	100,000	100,000
Retained profits	25,000	56,000
5% Debentures	50,000	50,000

You are required to:

a Calculate for each of the two years:

- **(i)** gross profit rate
- **(ii)** net profit rate
- **(iii)** return on capital employed
- **(iv)** return on equity capital.

b Comment on the performance of the company over the two years.

Solution

a	Year 1	Year 2
(i) Gross profit rate		
$= \frac{\text{gross profit}}{\text{sales}} \times 100$	$\frac{£80,000}{£200,000} \times 100$ = 40%	$\frac{£110,000}{£300,000} \times 100$ = 36.7%
(ii) Net profit rate		
$= \frac{\text{net profit}}{\text{sales}} \times 100$	$\frac{£27,500}{£200,000} \times 100$ = 13.75%	$\frac{£42,500}{£300,000} \times 100$ = 14.17%
(iii) ROCE		
$= \frac{\text{net profit}}{\text{capital employed}} \times 100$	$\frac{£27,500}{£175,000} \times 100$ = 15.7%	$\frac{£42,500}{£206,000} \times 100$ = 20.6%
(iv) Return on equity capital		
$= \frac{\text{NPIAT}}{\text{equity capital}}$	$\frac{£19,000}{£125,000} \times 100$ = 15.2%	$\frac{£31,000}{£156,000} \times 100$ = 19.9%

b **Comments:**

The gross profit percentage has decreased from 40% to 36.7% over the period. This may be due to an increased cost of purchases or a reduction in selling price. The net profit rate shows some improvement in spite of the drop in the gross profit rate. This indicates that in year 2 the company has managed to cut down its expenses in relation to the increase in sales value. Both the return on capital employed and the return on equity show considerable increase indicating good performance over the period.

ACT **21.1**

A Reeves owns a general purpose store. The following details are available about his business for the year ended 31 March 19x9.

Sales	£56,000
Cost of sales	£33,600
Expenses	£14,000
Capital employed	£52,500

Calculate the following ratios:

a gross profit percentage
b net profit percentage
c return on capital employed.

► Answer in appendix

Liquidity ratios

These ratios indicate the solvency of a business; they tell us whether a business has got sufficient funds to pay off the creditors. They are concerned with the working capital of a firm or the relationship between its current assets and its current liabilities. There are two main liquidity ratios:

► Liquidity – solvency

$$\text{Current ratio} = \frac{\text{current assets}}{\text{current liabilities}}$$

The **current ratio** is also known as the **working capital ratio**. Under normal circumstances, this ratio is expected to have a value of about 2 (2 : 1). A low value of this ratio indicates a tendency towards insolvency whereas a very high value indicates rather inefficient management of working capital.

► **Current ratio** or **working capital ratio**

$$\text{Quick ratio} = \frac{\text{current assets} - \text{stocks} - \text{investments}}{\text{current liabilities}}$$

This ratio is often called the **acid test ratio** because it is a very stringent test of liquidity in that it takes into account only the more liquid assets by the exclusion of stocks and short-term investments which are not easily convertible into cash. For a healthy position, a business should have a quick ratio in the region of 1. However, much will depend upon the type of the business concerned: some businesses could cope with a smaller ratio than others. A cash-and-carry business, for example, will require a much smaller ratio than a business whose sales consist mainly of credit sales. If the ratio exceeds 1 by too big a margin, it could be a sign of inefficiency, with too much money being tied up in current assets like stocks.

Let's now calculate these ratios in Example 21.2.

► **Quick ratio** or **acid test ratio**

► **Liquid assets**: easily convertible into cash

Example 21.2 Calculating the current ratio and the quick ratio

The Balance Sheets of a company as at 31 December 19x2 and 19x3 are as follow.

	19x2		19x3	
	£	£	£	£
Fixed assets		100,000		120,000
Current assets:				
Stock	40,000		55,000	
Debtors	50,000		50,000	
Cash	10,000		5,000	
	100,000		110,000	
Less Current liabilities				
Creditors	50,000		70,000	
		50,000		40,000
		150,000		160,000
Ordinary share capital		140,000		140,000
Reserves		10,000		20,000
		150,000		160,000

You are required to:

a Calculate the following for each year:
(i) current ratio **(ii)** quick ratio.

b Comment on your results.

Solution

a	19x2	19x3
Current ratio	$\frac{£100,000}{£50,000}$	$\frac{£110,000}{£70,000}$
	= 2	= 1.57
Quick ratio	$\frac{£100,000 - £40,000}{£50,000}$	$\frac{£110,000 - £55,000}{£70,000}$
	= 1.2	= 0.79

b **Comments**

It appears that the liquidity position of the company has worsened. Over the year, both the current ratio and the quick ratio have changed from a satisfactory level to a disturbingly low level.

ACT **21.2**

A sole trader's Balance Sheet as at 31 December, 19x0 was as follows.

	£	£
Fixed assets (net)		20,000
Current assets:		
Stocks	20,000	
Debtors	25,000	
Bank	5,000	
	50,000	
Less Current liabilities:		
Creditors	20,000	
		30,000
		50,000
Capital		50,000

► Answer in appendix

Calculate the following ratios:

a Current ratio

b Acid test ratio.

Assets usage ratios

► Assets usage ratios measure the efficiency with which assets are used.

These ratios indicate the efficiency with which the assets are employed in the business. Improved efficiency in the usage of assets will be reflected in greater profitability and more efficient use of such current assets as stocks and debtors. It will improve the liquidity position as well. Although it is possible to calculate many ratios relating to assets usage, the following are considered to be the most important.

$$\frac{\text{debtors}}{\text{credit sales}}$$

The debtors' ratio is also known as the **average collection period (of debt)**. The 'debtors' figure in the numerator may be taken as the average figure given by half the sum of opening and closing debtors. In the absence of the opening debtors figure, it is usual to take the year-end or closing debtors figure. Also, in the denominator we have used credit sales rather than total sales because these only give rise to debts outstanding. However, when credit sales are not given or known it is usual to take the total sales figure which will always be given in the Trading account.

In the absence of a discount incentive, debtors of approximately 45 days can be considered reasonable.

$$\text{Rate of stock turnover} = \frac{\text{cost of sales}}{\text{average stock}}$$

$$\text{where average stock} = \frac{1}{2}\,(\text{opening stock} + \text{closing stock})$$

► **Rate of stock turnover**: number of times a business turns over its stock in a time period

This ratio indicates the number of times a business turns over its stock in a year. However, it is possible to calculate the turnover ratio expressed in days:

$$\text{Rate of stock turnover (in days)} = \frac{\text{average stock}}{\text{cost of sales}} \times 365$$

It is impossible to give a precise value to this ratio that will indicate a satisfactory position in all cases. Much will depend upon the type of the business and the nature of the goods sold. A retailer will normally have a higher turnover than a manufacturer. Again, goods in daily use, e.g. food, will have a higher stock turn than semi-durable goods such as washing machines.

$$\text{Ratio of sales to fixed assets} = \frac{\text{sales}}{\text{fixed assets}}$$

► **Ratio of sales to fixed assets** shows how fixed assets generate sales.

This ratio indicates the efficiency with which fixed assets are being used to generate sales. It tells us by how much sales can be increased if investment in fixed assets is increased by £1. A low ratio implies that management is rather inefficient in the utilization of fixed assets. The size of the ratio depends largely on the type of business. A high capital investment results in a relatively low ratio. On the other hand, this ratio will be relatively high for a labour intensive business.

$$\text{Ratio of sales to assets value} = \frac{\text{sales}}{\text{FA + CA}} \text{ or } \frac{\text{sales}}{\text{NAV}}$$

where FA = fixed assets
CA = current assets
NAV = net assets value

We can express this ratio in two alternative forms, based on different interpretation of assets value. These are:

- total assets value (FA + CA)
- net assets value (NAV) = fixed assets + current assets – current liabilities.

Both ratios are used in assessing the rate at which assets' values are converted into sales revenue. Therefore, they indicate the ability of the assets to generate profits.

In Example 21.3, we'll now calculate these ratios.

Example 21.3 Calculating assets usage ratios

The final accounts of a sole trader for two successive years were as follows.

Trading and Profit and Loss account for the years ended 31 December

	19x3		19x4	
	£	£	£	£
Sales		450,000		500,000
Less Cost of Sales:				
Opening stock	50,000		60,000	
Add Purchases	280,000		320,000	
	330,000		380,000	
Less Closing stock	60,000	270,000	70,000	310,000
Gross profit		180,000		190,000
Less Expenses		110,000		120,000
Net profit		70,000		70,000

Balance Sheets as at 31 December

	19x3		19x4	
	£	£	£	£
Fixed assets		150,000		180,000
Current assets:				
Stock	60,000		70,000	
Debtors	55,000		50,000	
Bank	5,000		10,000	
	120,000		130,000	
Less Current liabilities				
Creditors	100,000		110,000	
		20,000		20,000
		170,000		200,000
Capital		130,000		170,000
Add Net profit		70,000		70,000
		200,000		240,000
Less Drawings		30,000		40,000
		170,000		200,000

You are required to:

a Calculate for each year:

(i) average collection period of debts
(ii) rate of stock turnover in number as well as in days
(iii) ratio of sales to fixed assets
(iv) ratio of sales to net asset value.

b Comment on the efficiency of the business in using its assets in the light of the ratios you have calculated in **a** above.

Solution

a (i) Average collection period $= \frac{\text{end-of-year debtors}}{\text{sales}} \times 365$

19x3 $\frac{£55,000}{£450,000} \times 365 = 44.6$ days

19x4 $\frac{£50,000}{£500,000} \times 365 = 36.5$ days

(ii) Rate of stock turnover $= \dfrac{\text{cost of sales}}{\frac{1}{2}(\text{cost opening stock + closing stock})}$

19x3 $\dfrac{£270{,}000}{\frac{1}{2}(£500{,}000 + £60{,}000)}$ = 4.9 times

19x4 $\dfrac{£3{,}170{,}000}{\frac{1}{2}(£60{,}000 + £70{,}000)}$ = 4.8 times

Rate of stock turnover in days $= \dfrac{\text{average stock}}{\text{cost of sales}} \times 365$

19x3 $\dfrac{£55{,}000}{£270{,}000} \times 365$ = 74 days

19x4 $\dfrac{£65{,}000}{£310{,}000} \times 365$ = 76.5 days

(iii) Ratio of sales to fixed assets

19x3 $\dfrac{£450{,}000}{£150{,}000}$ = 3 times

19x4 $\dfrac{£500{,}000}{£180{,}000}$ = 2.8 times

(iv) Ratio of sales to NAV

19x3 $\dfrac{£450{,}000}{£170{,}000}$ = 2.6 times

19x4 $\dfrac{£500{,}000}{£200{,}000}$ = 2.5 times

b **Comments:**

The assets ratios indicate that the efficiency with which the assets are being used has slightly deteriorated over the year. With the exception of the average collection period which shows marginal improvement, all other ratios show a slight downward trend.

ACT 21.3

The following figures were extracted from the books of a business at the end of a certain year.

	£
Opening stock	24,000
Closing stock	26,000
Purchases	42,000
Sales	60,000
Debtors	20,000
Fixed assets	30,000

Calculate:

a the rate of stock turnover
b the average collection period of debts in months
c the sales/fixed assets ratio.

► Answer in appendix

Capital structure ratios

These ratios indicate the effect of gearing on the dividend policy of a company, and also the risks the lenders take when advancing loans to the company. **Capital gearing**, also known as **leverage**, is a method of financing a business partly by ordinary shares and partly by fixed dividend shares (preference shares) and loan stock (debentures). The extent of the relationship between **equity** (or total) capital and fixed interest or dividend securities is measured by the gearing ratio.

► **Gearing** (or **leverage**): the extent to which a company is financed by loans and fixed interest stocks (debentures)

► High gearing means a high debt.

$$\text{Gearing ratio} = \frac{\text{fixed interest or dividend capital}}{\text{total capital (or equity capital)}}$$

where

equity capital = ordinary share capital + reserves

fixed interest or dividend capital = preference shares + long-term loans, i.e. debentures.

A company with a high proportion of debt capital, i.e. fixed interest securities, is known as a **high-geared company**. Likewise, a company that is **low-geared** has a low proportion of its capital in fixed interest or dividend securities. In years of good profits, where the rate of profits exceed the fixed interest or dividend payable, the ordinary shareholders will benefit from the surplus profits generated through high gearing. However, where profits are just a little above or below the high interest payable, the ordinary shareholders tend to subsidize the fixed interest stockholders and take a lower rate of dividend or sacrifice it altogether.

Besides the gearing ratio given above, it is possible to compute a number of other ratios which will indicate the extent of gearing of a business. One such ratio is:

$$\text{Interest coverage} = \frac{\text{net profit before interest and taxation}}{\text{interest payable}}$$

The **interest coverage ratio** tells us how many times the business is able to pay the annual interest on its debts out of the current year's profits. It therefore indicates the extent of the company's dependence on borrowed money. An interest cover of 5 or more is generally considered to be adequate.

► Net worth = paid up share capital + reserves

Another ratio relates the **net worth** of a business to its total assets:

$$\frac{\text{Net worth}}{\text{total assets}} = \frac{\text{paid up share capital + reserves}}{\text{fixed assets + current assets}}$$

As a general rule, a net worth ratio of 1 : 1 is considered to be satisfactory.

The calculation of these ratios is demonstrated in Example 21.4.

Example 21.4 Calculating capital structure ratios

The following are the Balance Sheets of two companies, High Ltd and Low Ltd, as at 31 March 19x4.

Balance Sheets as at 31 March 19x4

	High Ltd		Low Ltd	
	£	£	£	£
Fixed assets		200,000		180,000
Current assets	150,000		180,000	
Less Current liabilities	50,000		60,000	
		100,000		120,000
		300,000		300,000
Ordinary share capital		150,000		200,000
Retained profits		50,000		50,000
10% Debentures		100,000		50,000
		300,000		300,000

The following additional information is also available.

Net profit before interest and taxation, High Ltd, £100,000, Low Ltd £150,000

You are required to calculate three appropriate ratios which will help you to comment on the capital structure of the two companies.

Solution

	High Ltd	Low Ltd
Gearing ratio		
= debentures / total capital	£100,000 / £300,000	£50,000 / £300,000
	= 1 : 3	= 1 : 6
Interest coverage		
= NPBIT / interest payable	£100,000 / £10,000	£150,000 / £5,000
	= 10 times	= 30 times
Net worth / total assets	£200,000 / £350,000	£250,000 / £360,000
	= 0.57	= 0.69

Comments

Though both the companies have the same amount of capital employed, their capital structure is different. High Ltd has a much higher gearing than Low Ltd. Also, Low Ltd's interest coverage is three times greater than that of High Ltd, indicating High Ltd's great reliance on loan capital for financing its operations. Finally, Low Ltd finances 69 per cent of its total assets from its equity capital. The equivalent figure for High Ltd is much lower – only 57 per cent. High Ltd could be in trouble if the overall economic climate is poor but would do better in periods of increased economic activity.

ACT **21.4**

The following information relates to two companies, Ant Ltd and Bee Ltd.

	Ant Ltd £	*Bee Ltd* £
Ordinary shares	100,000	150,000
7.5% Preference shares	50,000	50,000
8% Debentures	50,000	–
	200,000	200,000

Calculate a gearing ratio for each company.

► Answer in appendix

Investment ratios

These ratios are important for existing and potential investors in quoted companies and also for top management, responsible for the overall Stock Exchange rating of their shares. There are four main ratios in this area:

$$\text{Earnings per share (EPS)} = \frac{\text{NPAIT} - \text{PD}}{\text{number of ordinary shares}}$$

where NPAIT = net profit after interest and taxation
PD = preference dividend

► SSAP requires every quoted company to publish its EPS.

The **earnings per share** (EPS) is always expressed in pence. Every quoted company is now required by SSAP 3 to state its EPS in the published accounts. A high EPS is usually reflected in the rising market price of the share.

$$\text{Dividend cover} = \frac{\text{NPAIT} - \text{PD}}{\text{total ordinary dividend payable}}$$

Dividend cover shows the company's ability to sustain dividend payments and a ratio of 2 or more will indicate adequate cover.

$$\text{Dividend yield} = \frac{\text{dividend per share}}{\text{market price of share}} \times 100$$

The **dividend yield** expresses the dividend as a return on the actual amount paid for the share and/or the current market price of the share. Investors, both existing and potential, will always welcome a high dividend yield.

$$\text{Price/earnings (P/E) ratio} = \frac{\text{market price of share}}{\text{EPS}}$$

The **price/earnings (P/E) ratio** is a good indicator of the market evaluation of the future prospects of a company. Generally speaking, a low P/E ratio suggests lack of confidence, whereas a high value indicates great confidence in the future prosperity of the company.

Example 21.5 illustrates the calculation of these ratios.

Example 21.5 Calculation of investment ratios

Craters Ltd has an issued share capital of £2 million as detailed below.

	£
Ordinary share capital of 50p each	1,500,000
500,000 10% Preference shares of £1 each	500,000
	2,000,000

The following extracts from its Profit and Loss accounts for the years ended 31 March 19x1 and 31 March 19x2 are provided.

	19x1 £000	*19x2* £000
Profit before taxation	1,300	1,700
Taxation	(325)	(420)
Profit after taxation	975	1,280
Dividends: Preference	(50)	(50)
Ordinary	(450)	(600)
Retained profit	475	630

The market price of the share was £2.50 at 31 March 19x1 and £3.00 at 31 March 19x2.

You are required to calculate the EPS, the dividend cover, the dividend yield and the P/E ratio for each of the two years and comment on them.

Solution

	19x1	19x2
EPS	$\frac{£975,000 - £50,000}{3,000,000}$	$\frac{£1,280,000 - £50,000}{3,000,000}$
	$= \frac{£925,000}{3,000,000}$	$= \frac{£1,230,000}{3,000,000}$
	= 30.8p	= 41p
Dividend cover	$\frac{£925,000}{£450,000}$	$\frac{£1,230,000}{£600,000}$
	= 2.1 times	= 2.1 times
Dividend yield	$\frac{£0.15}{£2.50} \times 100$	$\frac{£0.20}{£3.00} \times 100$
	= 6%	= 6.67%
Note: dividend per share	$\frac{£450,000}{3,000,000}$	$\frac{£600,000}{3,000,000}$
	= 15p	= 20p
P/E ratio	$\frac{250p}{30.8p}$	$\frac{300p}{41p}$
	= 8	= 7.31

Comments

The calculated ratios for the two years tend to show that the company's market standing has not significantly changed over the period under consideration. Only the EPS has increased from 30.8p to 41p reflecting an increase in retained profits per share. The dividend cover has remained constant and the dividend yield has increased marginally. The P/E ratio, on the other hand, shows a slight fall probably because of the increase in the price of the share from £2.50 to £3.00. On their own, the P/E ratios do not suggest a great deal of growth in the capital value of the share.

ACT **21.5**

The following information relates to AB Limited for the year ended 30 September 19x4.

Net profit after interest and taxation	£100,000
Ordinary dividend for the year	£40,000
Ordinary share capital of £1 each	£200,000
The current market share price	£3.00

Calculate:

a EPS
b Dividend cover
c Dividend yield
d P/E ratio.

► Answer in appendix

Other ratios

► Payment of creditors ratio

We've discussed the major ratios, subdivided into five main groups. However, it is possible to calculate many more ratios from a given set of final accounts of a company. Thus, for example, you can compute the **ratio of expense** (one for each item of expense) to sales. One ratio which may be of interest to analysts is the **rate of payment to creditors**. This ratio measures the average period of time taken by firms to pay their suppliers and is calculated as follows.

$$\text{Average payment period to creditors} = \frac{\text{average creditors}}{\text{credit purchase}} \times 365 \text{ (days)}$$

where

$$\text{average creditors} = \frac{1}{2}\text{ (opening creditors + closing creditors)}$$

If the opening creditors figure is not available, normal practice is to take the year-end or closing figure. Again, if the division between cash and credit purchases is not known, we use the total purchases figure in the computation.

Unlike the debtors' collection period, firms will welcome a longer payment period as it will allow them to use their working capital in a more efficient manner.

Limitations of ratio analysis

► The usefulness of ratios depends on skill in interpretation.

The calculation of ratios is easy, but their interpretation is difficult. The usefulness of ratio analysis depends on the skill of interpreting them usefully. However skillful interpreters – or analysts – may be, their analysis of the final accounts of a business in terms of ratios will be restricted by a number of limitations in ratio analysis itself. Some of these limitations relate to the underlying assumptions of ratio analysis and some relate to the inadequate financial information that is provided in the final accounts. We'll now look at some of these limitations.

Firstly, ratios taken in isolation are of very limited use. Ratios calculated from a company's accounts for a year must be compared with those of previous years to draw relevant conclusions. Also, they should be compared, wherever possible, with those of a similar company in the same trade, or with the average ratios for the industry or trade as a whole. With many trades or industries such figures for inter-firm comparisons are available through relevant trade associations. For many firms, however, such facilities are not available.

Secondly, we must remember that accounting ratios simply reflect the changes in performance indicators, but they do not necessarily explain those changes. For a proper explanation of these changes we need more information about the firm, which may not be easily available particularly to an external analyst.

Thirdly, accounting principles and policies tend to regulate the preparation of final accounts and differences in such policies may mar any attempt at comparing the ratios of two companies. Unless adjustments for such differences are made prior to the calculation of the relevant ratios, interpretations based on them will be of dubious value.

Fourthly, we must not give too much importance to any one single ratio. Interpretation based on one or two ratios may be misleading.

Thus, for example, a very high **return on capital employed** of a company may give the impression that all is well – but if we now calculate the **current ratio** of the same company, we might find that this ratio is very low, say 0.2, indicating that the very existence of the company is at stake.

Fifthly, the final accounts of a business are usually based on historic costing. The timing difference in acquiring similar assets, e.g. plant, will affect the depreciation charge and hence profit. In this situation, a comparison of the return on capital employed of two businesses will not truly reflect their relative performances.

Finally, major one-off transactions such as a special order of a significant amount may distort the true performance of a company.

Chapter summary

- Accounting ratios are used to interpret the final accounts of a business for evaluating its performance over a given period of time.
- They are usually subdivided into five groups corresponding to the major areas of performance: profitability, liquidity, assets usage, capital structure or gearing and investment.
- In using these ratios for the interpretation of accounts and the evaluation of performance of a business, you should remember the limitations of ratio analysis.

ACT **21.6**

For questions 1 to 6 put a tick against the letter that represents the best answer from among the four possible alternatives given.

1 The following details relating to a company were obtained on 31 December, 19x2:

Current ratio	2 : 1
Current liabilities	£30,000
Stocks	£25,000
Cash at bank and in hand	£5,000

Debtors on 31 December, 19x2 were:

A £30,000
B £15,000
C £12,000
D £10,000.

2 A company's total capital is made up as follows.

Ordinary share capital	£200,000
7.5% Preference shares	£50,000
10% Debentures	£50,000

Its gearing ratio is:

A 1
B 5
C $\frac{1}{5}$
D $\frac{1}{3}$.

► Answers in appendix

3 If a firm's rate of gross profit is 40 per cent, average stock is £10,000 and the rate of stock turnover is 9, its sales will be
A £150,000
B £144,000
C £126,000
D £90,000.

4 A company's return on capital employed and net profit percentage are 10 per cent and 12.5 per cent respectively. If its capital employed is £200,000, then its sales are:
A £20,000
B £25,000
C £160,000
D £1,600,000.

5 A company's share capital consists entirely of ordinary shares of 25 pence each and is £100,000. Its net profit after taxation for the year ended 31 December, 19x2 was £80,000. If the current market price of its share is £2, the P/E ratio will be:
A £40,000
B 10
C 0.8
D 20.

► Answers in appendix

6 State and explain the purpose of accounting ratios. Name three ratios and explain their usefulness.

► No answer given

4/5/95 - Homework

7 The following details relate to the business of J. Pym for the years ended 31 December 19x3 and 19x4.

	19x3 £	19x4 £
Stock – 1 January	18,500	25,250
Stock – 31 December	25,250	22,500
Sales :		
Cash	21,500	25,750
Credit	50,000	55,150
Purchases	56,750	53,750
Expenses	8,500	9,500
Cash in bank and at hand	3,000	4,000
Debtors	10,000	15,000
Creditors	18,750	20,340
Capital employed	50,000	55,000

You are required to:

a Prepare Trading and Profit and Loss accounts (in columnar form) for the years ended 31 December 19x3 and 19x4

b Calculate the following ratios for each of the two years 19x3 and 19x4:
(i) Gross profit percentage
(ii) Net profit percentage
(iii) Return on capital employed
(iv) Current ratio
(v) Acid test ratio

(vi) Rate of stock turnover
(vii) Average collection period of debt.

c Comment briefly on Pym's performance in running the business over the two year period, using the ratios you have calculated in **b** above.

► No answer given

8 The summarized accounts of J. Archibold, a retailer, for the years 19x1 and 19x2 are as follows.

Trading and Profit and Loss account for the year ended 31 December

	19x1		19x2	
	£	£	£	£
Sales		300,000		360,000
Less Cost of sales :				
Opening stock	30,000		31,000	
Purchases	200,000		274,000	
	230,000		305,000	
Closing stock	31,000	199,000	65,000	240,000
Gross profit		101,000		120,000
Less				
Other expenses		41,000		45,000
Net profit		60,000		75,000

Balance Sheets as at 31 December

	19x1			19x2		
	£	£	£	£	£	£
Fixed assets at cost less depreciation			80,000			107,000
Current Assets						
Stocks		31,000			65,000	
Debtors		30,000			40,000	
Bank balance		5,000			–	
		66,000			105,000	
Less Current Liabilities						
Creditors	25,500			38,000		
Bank overdraft	–	25,500		14,000	52,000	
			40,500			53,000
			120,500			160,000
Financed by:						
Capital			80,000			120,500
Add Net profit			60,000			75,000
			140,000			195,500
Less Drawings			19,500			35,500
			120,500			160,000

You are required to:

a Calculate the following ratios for each of the years 19x1 and 19x2:
(i) The rate of stock turnover
(ii) The rate of debtors turnover
(iii) The current ratio
(iv) The quick ratio
(v) The return on capital employed.

b Comment on the progress and position of J.Archibold's business in the light of the ratios you have calculated in answer to **a** above.

►**Answer in appendix**

22 Investment appraisal

Chapter objectives

By the end of this chapter, you should be able to:

- understand the meaning and significance of investment appraisal
- evaluate a number of similar projects and choose the best one by applying the payback method
- appraise and select the best project by using the return on investment method
- calculate the net present values of future streams of income and use them to choose the best project
- calculate and apply profitability index to the selection of the right project
- compare and contrast the relative merits and demerits of the different methods
- understand the following terms: investment appraisal, payback/capital recovery period, profitability index, return on investment method, discounted cash flow method, net present value method, internal rate of return, discounting factor, present value table.

INVESTMENT APPRAISAL

In Chapter 1 we saw that one of the major functions of management is decision-making, that is, choosing the most profitable course of action from amongst a number of available alternatives. The decision-making technique can be applied to the selection of capital or investment projects. A **capital project** normally involves an investment in fixed assets such as plant and machinery, either for the replacement of existing items or for expansion and growth. **Investment** in fixed assets requires a great deal of 'funds' or money. Even in the most prosperous of times, money is a scarce commodity – its supply is limited in relation to demand. Management's problem is therefore to decide how to make the best use of the limited resources available and for this purpose managers need to develop criteria for the acceptance or rejection of capital or investment proposals. This system of selecting and undertaking investment projects based on predetermined criteria is called **investment appraisal**. To appraise means to evaluate and our task in this chapter is to develop some methods for appraising investment projects or proposals.

► **Capital project:** investment in fixed assets

► **Investment appraisal**: evaluating and choosing between proposals for capital investment

All methods are usually based on a number of assumptions. These assumptions have a dual role. Firstly, they help us to develop the methods themselves in a simple manner by eliminating non-essential factors in the process, and, secondly, they remind us of the limitations of such methods when we try to apply them to practical problems. The

► Assumptions underlying investment appraisals

assumptions which underlie the process of investment appraisal include:

- Future costs and income can be estimated with reasonable accuracy.
- The cost of capital (to be defined later on) to the firm can be fairly estimated.
- Once adopted, the progress of the project will not be hindered by bottlenecks of, say, materials and labour.
- The effect of inflation and taxation will be ignored to restrict our analysis to simpler problems.

Methods of investment project appraisal

The principal methods of evaluating capital projects are:

- payback method
- return on investment (ROI) method
- discounted cash flow (DCF) method
- profitability index (PI) method.

Let's now explain each of these methods in turn.

The payback method of appraisal

► **Payback period or recovery period**: time needed to recover the amount invested

The **payback period method** begins with the calculation of the payback period of each project. The **payback period**, otherwise known as the **capital recovery period**, is the period over which the original outlay on the project can be recovered from the cash generated by the project. Once the payback periods of all the projects are worked out, a decision is taken as to which project(s) will be undertaken. This decision will depend upon the availability of funds or capital. If there is no shortage of capital, projects for which the payback periods are within a set amount of time will be selected. If, however, capital is scarce, that project with the shortest payback period, i.e. the project which recovers the initial investment most quickly, will be chosen. We see in Example 22.1 how this is done.

Example 22.1 Calculating the payback period

Three investment projects are open to a firm:

		Project L £	Project M £	Project N £
Cost		30,000	55,000	70,000
Net cash inflow: Year	1	15,000	30,000	–
	2	15,000	20,000	20,000
	3	6,000	20,000	25,000
	4	6,000	10,000	50,000
	5	4,000	10,000	50,000

The cash inflows are expected to arise uniformly throughout the year. You are required to:

a Calculate the payback period of each project

b State which project(s) will be chosen, assuming that the firm's policy is to undertake those projects which have a payback period of three years or less

c Indicate which projects should be undertaken, assuming further that only £50,000 is available for investment.

Solution

a Calculation of payback periods:

Project	L	M	N
Payback period (in years)	2 = 2	$2\frac{5,000}{20,000}$ = 2.25	$3\frac{25,000}{50,000}$ = 3.5

b Only Projects L and M will be selected as both of them have a payback period of less than three years.

c As the funds are restricted to £50,000, only one project can be chosen. Since Project L has a shorter payback period than either Project M or Project N, it will be chosen.

Note:

1 For Project L, the initial cost of £30,000 is expected to be recovered in two years (£15,000 + £15,000).

2 For Project M, only £50,000 is recovered in two years. This leaves a shortfall of £5,000 which will be obtained in the third year. £5,000 is a quarter of £20,000. Hence the payback period is 2.25 years.

3 Following the reasoning given for Project M, we see that the payback period for Project N is 3.5 years.

Advantages and disadvantages of the payback method

The advantages of the payback method include:

- The calculation of payback periods is very simple.
- During times of capital scarcity, it is sensible to choose projects based on payback periods.
- Calculations based on future events contain an element of uncertainty and the degree of uncertainty increases as we plan further into the future. Since the payback period usually takes in the early years of the project, there is greater certainty that the initial investment will be recovered within the estimated payback period.

Its main disadvantages are:

- It ignores the time value of money. In other words, it assumes that £1 receivable two years later is as good as £1 now.
- It takes no account of cash flows after the end of the payback period and therefore the overall profitability of the project.

ACT 22.1

Determine the payback period for each of the following projects and indicate which project will be chosen based on the payback method.

	Project A	*Project B*
Investment outlay	£10,000	£10,000
Estimated life	5 years	10 years
Annual net cash flow	£2,500	£2,000

► Answer in appendix

Return on investment (ROI) method

This method chooses an investment project based on its profitability. First of all, it measures the return on investment, which is similar to the return on capital employed, as explained earlier. It is usual to use average investment, rather than the total initial investment, and average annual profit to calculate the return on investment:

$$\text{ROI} = \frac{\text{average annual profit}}{\text{average investment}} \times 100$$

where $\text{average annual profit} = \frac{\text{total profit on the project}}{\text{working life of the project}}$

and

$\text{average investment} = \frac{1}{2}$ (initial investment – residual value).

The **residual value** is the estimated value of the project at the end of its working life. It is also known as the **scrap value.**

If a project has no residual or scrap value, average investment will be simply equal to half of the initial investment.

Once the **return on investment ratios** (ROIs) of the different projects are determined, they are then compared with a view to choosing the best project. At this stage, decisions are governed by one of the two criteria as listed below:

- If there is no shortage of capital, projects having a ROI in excess of a given minimum rate will be chosen.
- If funds are in short supply, projects having the higher ROIs will be selected.

The minimum rate usually corresponds to the firm's **cost of capital.** The calculation of the cost of capital to a firm is rather complex. For our purposes it is enough to say that the cost of capital simply refers to the cost of borrowing money to finance the project. We'll now show in Example 22.2 how the ROI method is used to select an investment project.

Example 22.2 Using the return on investment method of appraisal

Refer to the details of three projects L, M and N as given in Example 22.1 to answer the following questions.

a What is the ROI of each project?

b Which projects will be selected if the company's cost of capital is 23 per cent per annum?

c Which project will be chosen if only one project can be undertaken?

Solution

Project

	L	M	N
Total profit over the 5-year period	£46,000 – £30,000 = £16,000	£90,000 – £55,000 = £35,000	£145,000 – £70,000 = £75,000
Average annual profit	$\frac{£16,000}{5}$ = £3,200	$\frac{£35,000}{5}$ = £7,000	$\frac{£75,000}{5}$ = £15,000
Average investment	$\frac{£30,000}{2}$ = £15,000	$\frac{£55,000}{2}$ = £27,500	$\frac{£70,000}{2}$ = £35,000
a ROI	$\frac{£3,200}{£15,000} \times 100$ = 21.3%	$\frac{£7,000}{£27,500} \times 100$ = 25.5%	$\frac{£15,000}{£35,000} \times 100$ = 42.9%

b Projects M and N will be chosen as the ROIs of both of them are more than 23 per cent p.a.

c Project N will be selected as it has the highest ROI.

ACT **22.2**

Turnip Brothers & Company wishes to undertake a project for which the expected cash flows are as follows.

Investment expenditure	£20,000
Estimated life	5 years
Annual profit before depreciation	£6,500
Scrap value	nil

Calculate the return on investment.

► Answer in appendix

Advantages and disadvantages of the ROI method

The advantages of ROI are:

- It is easy to understand and easy to calculate.
- It is a measure of profitability and is therefore more meaningful in assessing the worth of a project.

Its disadvantages are:

- It does not consider the timing of the receipts and payments of cash which may be of considerable importance to a firm having an acute shortage of capital.
- It ignores the time value of money.

Discounted cash flow (DCF) methods

The **discounted cash flow** (DCF) method of investment appraisal takes into account both the profitability of projects and the timing of returns from them. It therefore combines the advantages of the two payback and ROI methods. It considers all cash flows over the expected life of the project, recognizing the importance of profitability in project evaluation. At the same time, it recognizes the timing of cash flows by working out the present values of all future flows of cash.

There are two approaches to project appraisal by the DCF technique. These are:

- The net present value (NPV) method
- The internal rate of return (IRR) method.

The first method is simpler and more popular than the second, so we shall look in detail at the NPV method and outline the IRR method.

The net present value (discounted cash flow) method

Under the net present value (NPV) method, the cash flows of the project are **discounted**, i.e. compounded in reverse, at a predetermined rate of interest (which usually corresponds to the cost of capital of the firm) to get the present values of all future cash flows and the sum of these present values will give the net present valu of the project – net because the initial outlay is deducted from the discounted net cash inflows resulting from the project.

After calculating the NPV of a project, three criteria are used for accepting or rejecting the project. These are:

- If the NPV is positive, the expected rate of return from the project will exceed the predetermined rate of discounting.
- If the NPV is equal to zero, the expected rate of return will exactly equal the predetermined rate.
- If the NPV is negative, the expected rate will be less than the predetermined rate.

It follows therefore that projects which satisfy either of the first two criteria will be accepted and projects with negative NPV will be rejected.

The NPV is calculated by discounting future cash inflows by a predetermined rate of interest, which for many firms is the current cost of capital. Discounting is compounding in reverse. The formula is the same as the compound interest formula from school mathematics.

> ***NVP formula***
>
> $A = P(1 + r)^t$,
> where
> A = the amount that is receivable at the end of t years
> P = the principal or the initial amount of investment
> r = the rate of interest expressed as a decimal. Thus 10% will be represented as 0.1 rather than 10/100.
> t = the time period – the number of years.

Example 22.3 below shows the calculation of compound interest.

Example 22.3 Calculation of compound interest

Calculate the compound interest on £1,000 at 10 per cent for 2 years.

Solution

Here $r = 0.1$
$t = 2$ years
$P = £1,000$

Putting these values in the compound interest formula, we get

$$A = £1{,}000\ (1 + 0.1)^2 = £1{,}000 \times 1.1^2 = £1{,}000 \times 1.21 = £1{,}210$$

Therefore, compound interest = $A - P$ = £1,210 – £1,000 = £210

So from the results in Example 22.3, £1,000 amounts to £1,210 in two years at 10 per cent per annum. We can put the same information in a different form: the present value of £1,210 receivable in two years' time at the discounting rate of 10 per cent is simply £1,000. As we value the present more than the future, an amount receivable in future is always worth less than its present value. Now, we can directly calculate the present value of a future sum by a transformation of the compound interest formula in the form:

► Present value formula

$$P = \frac{A}{(1 + r)^2} = A \times \frac{1}{(1 + r)^2}$$

If we use this formula to find the present value of £1,210 receivable in two years at 10 per cent, we get

$$P = £1{,}210 \times \frac{1}{(1.1)^2} = £1{,}210 \times \frac{1}{1.21}$$

$$= £1{,}210 \times 0.8264 = £999.94 = £1{,}000 \text{ (approximately)}$$

Now we see that the present value of £1,210 receivable in two years' time at 10 per cent p.a. is £1,000, the same result as we obtained from our compound interest calculations in Example 22.3 above.

In the transformed compound interest formula, the expression

► The discounting factor

$\frac{1}{(1 + r)^t}$ is known as the **discounting factor**. Once we know the discounting factor, weu can find the present value of any sum of money: we simply multiply the sum by the discounting factor. Thus, the present value of £560 receivable in two years' time at 10 per cent rate of interest is £560 × 0.8264 = £462.8. The discounting factor itself, in this example, is the present value of £1 receivable in two years' time.

As the number of years or the rate of interest changes, we need to find the new value of the discounting factor. This could be tedious or cumbersome to calculate by the formula. Fortunately, however, we don't need to do this. There is a ready reckoner available (see Appendix 1) which is called the **Present value table**. This table gives the present value of £1 receivable 1, 2, 3, etc years late at different rates of interest. Thus the present value of £1 in three years' time at 15 per cent rate of interest is, from the table, £0.6575. Therefore, the present value of £500 in three years' time at 15 per cent is £500 × 0.6575 = £328.75.

► **Present value table**: See Appendix 1, p. 368–9

ACT 22.3

Calculate the present values of the following sums.

a £10,000 receivable in 3 years at 8 per cent p.a.
b £12,345 receivable in 5 years at 12 per cent p.a.
c £897 receivable in 8 years at 14 per cent p.a.
d £20,000 receivable in 10 years at 20 per cent p.a.

► Answer in appendix

NPV and investment appraisal

We'll now apply this technique of present value in Example 22.4 to a problem involving investment appraisal.

Example 22.4 Using NVP in investment appraisal

Rainbow Ltd is contemplating acquiring a new machine and has two alternatives:

		Machine X	*Machine Y*
Cost		£10,000	£10,000
Estimated residual value		Nil	Nil
Estimated future profits,			
before depreciation: year	1	£5,000	£2,000
	2	£5,000	£3,000
	3	£3,000	£5,000
	4	£1,000	£5,000

The cost of capital to Rainbow Ltd is 16 per cent per annum.

You are required to:

a Calculate the NPV of each machine.
b Indicate which machine will be selected.

Solution

Year	*DF**	*Machine X*		*Machine Y*	
		Cash flows	*PV***	*Cash flows*	*PV***
0	1.000	(10,000)	(10,000)	(10,000)	(10,000)
1	0.862	5,000	4,310	2,000	1,724
2	0.743	5,000	3,715	3,000	2,229
3	0.641	3,000	1,923	5,000	3,205
4	0.552	1,000	552	5,000	2,760
NPV			500		(82)

* Discounting factor ** Present value

Note:

1 Investment is assumed to take place in year zero, i.e. the present period and that is why the discounting factor in year zero is 1. Investment implies an outflow of cash and is therefore represented by a negative figure, i.e. within a pair of brackets.

2 The DF values are obtained from the Present value table given on page 368–9.

3 The values in the PV columns are obtained by multiplying the values in the cashflow columns by their respective discounting factors.

4 The figures in each PV column are added to get the NPV of each project, remembering however that the first figure in each PV column is a negative figure.

b Machine X is to be preferred to Machine Y as its NPV is positive. The negative NPV for Machine Y implies that the expected return from it is below the current cost of capital of 16 per cent per annum.

The internal rate of return (IRR) method

► **Internal rate of return** (IRR) or **discounted yield** method

The internal rate of return method is also known as the **discounted yield** method. Using this method, a trial and error procedure is adopted to ascertain what interest rate must be employed in order to make the NPV of a project equal to zero. This involves choosing a rate arbitrarily in the first instance, discounting the future cash flows of the project at this rate and then examining the NPV to see if it is equal to zero. If not, a new rate must be chosen and the procedure repeated. Ultimately, the rate giving a NPV figure of zero is found and this rate is the **internal rate of return**. It is then compared with the predetermined rate and a decision is made on the basis of this comparison. The actual calculation of the IRR is beyond the scope of this book.

The profitability index

The NPVs of two projects having different costs may not tell us directly which is the better of the two projects. In this situation, we use another measure involving the NPV, known as the **profitability index** (PI), given by:

► Profitability index

$$PI = \frac{\text{sum of the present values of cash inflows}}{\text{cost of project or initial investment}}$$

If the PI is less than 1, the rate of return from the project seems to be lower than the cost of capital. If the PI = 1, the rate of expected return appears to be exactly equal to the cost of capital. A PI having a value greater than 1 shows that the expected rate of return is higher than the current cost of capital. If, however, there are several projects with profitability indices all greater than 1 then they will be arranged in descending order of profitability ratios and, based on this ranking, a decision will be taken as to how many of the projects can be undertaken.

Example 22.5 shows how the profitability index is used to appraise investment projects.

Example 22.5 Using the profitability index

A firm's current cost of capital is 15 per cent p.a. It is currently considering three projects whose cash flows are as follows:

Year	*Project 1* £	*Project 2* £	*Project 3* £
0	(12,000)	(17,000)	(22,000)
1	4,300	8,500	10,500
2	4,500	7,500	10,500
3	5,500	7,500	10,500
4	5,500	9,500	10,500

You are required to:

a Calculate the profitability index of each project.

b Rank the project in order of profitability.

Solution

Year	*DF* *	*Project 1*		*Project 2*		*Project 3*	
		*CI***	*PV****	*CI*	*PV*	*CI*	*PV*
1	0.870	4,300	3,741	8,500	7,395	10,500	9,135
2	0.756	4,500	3,402	7,500	5,670	10,500	7,938
3	0.658	5,500	3,619	7,500	4,935	10,500	6,909
4	0.572	5,500	3,146	9,500	5,434	10,500	6,006
Total			13,908		23,434		29,988

* Discounting factor **Cash inflow *** Present value

		Project 1	*Project 2*	*Project 3*
a	PI	$\frac{13{,}908}{12{,}000} = 1.159$	$\frac{23{,}434}{17{,}000} = 1.378$	$\frac{29{,}988}{22{,}000} = 1.363$
b	Ranking	3rd	1st	2nd

Note:

Each project in this example is profitable. However, if there is a shortage of capital or if the projects are mutually exclusive, we need to rank the projects in order of profitability to choose the best one(s). Two projects are **mutually exclusive** if the choice of one automatically precludes the selection of the other. Thus, the choice could be between two or more similar machines when the firm needs only one machine; the two machines are obviously mutually exclusive.

Chapter summary

- The system of selecting and undertaking investment (capital) projects based on predetermined criteria is called investment appraisal.
- The main methods or techniques of investment appraisal are: the payback method, the return on investment method, the discounted cash flow method with particular reference to the net present value of a project's future cash inflows and the profitability index method.

22.4

For questions 1 to 3 put a tick against the letter that represents the best answer from among the four possible alternative answers given.

1 The payback method selects capital projects on the basis of:
 A The total profitability of the projects
 B The net present value of projects
 C The recovery time of initial outlay of projects
 D The return on capital employed by the organization.

2 The discounting factor, as applied to the determination of present value of future cashflows is:
 A The same thing as the current rate of interest
 B Equal to $(1 + r)^t$ where r and t are rate of interest and time period respectively
 C Is equal to $1/(1+r)^t$ where r and t are rate of interest and time period respectively
 D The current cost of capital to the firm.

3 The profitability index of a capital project is:
 A The expected average profit of the project
 B The ratio between average profit and average investment
 C Another name for the internal rate of return
 D The ratio between the total present value of cash flows from the project and the initial outlay on the project.

► Answers in appendix

4 The following details relate to three capital projects which are being considered by the Board of Apex Ltd.

	Initial Cost £	Cash flows Year 1 £	Year 2 £	Year 3 £	Year 4 £
Project A	20,000	10,000	10,000	8,000	6,000
Project B	40,000	7,500	7,500	10,500	22,500
Project C	50,000	16,000	20,000	20,000	20,000

Assume that cash flows arise evenly throughout the year.

You are required to:

a Calculate the payback period of each project.

b State which projects will be chosen if the company's policy is to select those projects which have payback periods of less than three years.

c Indicate which projects will be selected if only £30,000 is available for investment.

► Answer in appendix

5 Refer to question 4 above and answer the following.

a Calculate the ROI of each project

b Indicate which project will be chosen if one and only one project can be undertaken.

► No answer given

6 Refer to question 4 again. Assuming that Apex Limited's cost of capital is 15 per cent:

a Calculate the NPV of each project

b Calculate the profitability index of each project

c Indicate which projects would be accepted if unlimited funds are available.

d Indicate which project will be selected if, because of capital rationing, only one project can be chosen.

► Answer in appendix

7 The following information relates to three possible capital expenditure projects. Because of capital rationing, only one project can be accepted.

Project	*A*	*B*	*C*
Initial cost	£ 200,000	£ 230,000	£ 180,000
Expected life	5 years	5 years	4 years
Scrap value expected	£10,000	£15,000	£8,000

Expected cash inflows year	£	£	£
1	80,000	100,000	55,000
2	70,000	70,000	65,000
3	65,000	50,000	95,000
4	60,000	50,000	100,000
5	55,000	50,000	–

The company estimates its cost of capital is 18 per cent and discount factors are:

Year	1	0.8475
	2	0.7182
	3	0.6086
	4	0.5158
	5	0.4371

Calculate:

a The payback period for each project
b The return on investment for each project
c The net present value of each project
d Which project should be accepted – give reasons
e Explain the factors management would need to consider, in addition to the financial factors, before making a final decision on a project.

(AAT)

► No answer given

8 A company is considering two capital expenditure proposals. Both proposals are for similar products and both are expected to operate for four years. Only one proposal can be accepted.
The following information is available.

	Proposal A £	*Proposal B* £
Initial investment	46,000	46,000
Profit year 1	6,500	4,500
Profit year 2	3,500	2,500
Profit year 3	13,500	4,500
year 4	Loss (1,500)	Profit 14,500
Estimated scrap value end year 4	4,000	4,000

Depreciation is charged on the straight line basis.
The company estimates its cost of capital at 20 per cent per annum.

Discount factors

Year	1	0.833
	2	0.694
	3	0.579
	4	0.482

Required:

a Calculate for both proposals:
 (i) the payback period to 1 decimal place
 (ii) the average rate of return on initial investment, to 1 decimal place
 (iii) net present value.

b Give two advantages for **each** of the methods of appraisal used in **a** above, and state with reasons which, if any, proposal you would recommend.

(AAT)

► Answer to **a** in appendix

23 Accounting and information technology

Chapter objectives

By the end of this chapter, you should be able to:

- explain the usefulness of computerised accounting
- outline the essentials of accounting data processing
- distinguish between computer hardware and software
- outline the main areas of accounting software.
- understand the meaning of the following terms: raw data, input data, output data, running balance method.

Introduction

Accounting is a financial data processing system. It is normally integrated into the kind of comprehensive management information system that is characteristic of most businesses today. Business data processing includes the systematic recording, classifying, filing, processing, storing and disseminating of information relating to various events, e.g. transactions occurring in the business. A very high proportion of data in a business originates in the Accounts section and this data can be processed either manually or electronically with computers. Until recently computers were primarily used by fairly big businesses and only a very restricted number of small businesses were computerized. Now the situation has fundamentally changed. Recent developments in computer technology, particularly in the area of silicon chips, have made it possible for even a very small business to own and use a computer today. Small computers – micros – are relatively cheap and have the capacity for dealing with the needs of most small businesses. Because of this ever increasing use of computers by smaller businesses, we shall look at the elements of a computer system, and some of the available accounting software.

COMPUTERIZED ACCOUNTING – ADVANTAGES

The use of computers in recording and processing accounting data does not affect the principles of book-keeping and accounting. Whatever the system, manual or electronic, the basic principles of double entry remain the same but computerized accounting has certain advantages over the manual system. Firstly, the computerized system is much faster than the manual system; it can update data very quickly. Secondly, the degree of accuracy is very high. Thirdly, computers can handle – quickly and easily – very complex mathematical and statistical calculations which are required, for example, in sales forecasting. Finally, they are very versatile – they can perform a wide variety of analyses of accounting data and produce different types of report very quickly, because of their ability to store and retrieve information at high speed. The layout and the presentation of accounts by a computerized system is different from that of the traditional horizontal ledger accounts. Computers produce accounts using the **running balance method**, and ledger accounts thus prepared do not have two sides – the traditional debit and credit sides. Instead they present one-sided accounts having three money columns to record debit entries, credit entries, and the up-to-date balance. Figure 23.1 below is a typical layout of a ledger account produced by a computer.

Date	Particulars	Debit	Credit	Balance

Figure 23.1
A typical layout of a computerized ledger a/c

The balance will be followed by DR or CR, to represent a debit or a credit balance respectively. Example 23.1 illustrates the running balance method of recording accounts.

Example 23.1 The running balance method

The following cash transactions relate to the business of John Timperley during the first week of March 19x2.

March 1	Balance b/f (cash in hand)	210 DR
2	Cash sales	200
4	Paid rent in cash	300
6	Cash sales	280
7	Cash drawings	100

Show how these transactions will be recorded in a computerized system.

Solution

Cash account

Date	Particulars	Debit	Credit	Balance
19x2 Mar				
1	Balance b/f			210 DR
2	Sales	200		410
4	Rent		300	110
6	Sales	280		390
7	Drawings		100	290 DR

Notice that cash receipts are still debited and cash payments are still credited. Also, see that debits are added to – or credits are deducted from – yesterday's balance to arrive at today's balance.

ELEMENTS OF A DATA PROCESSING SYSTEM

There are five elements in a data processing system: input, processing, output, storage and control, as shown in Figure 23.2.

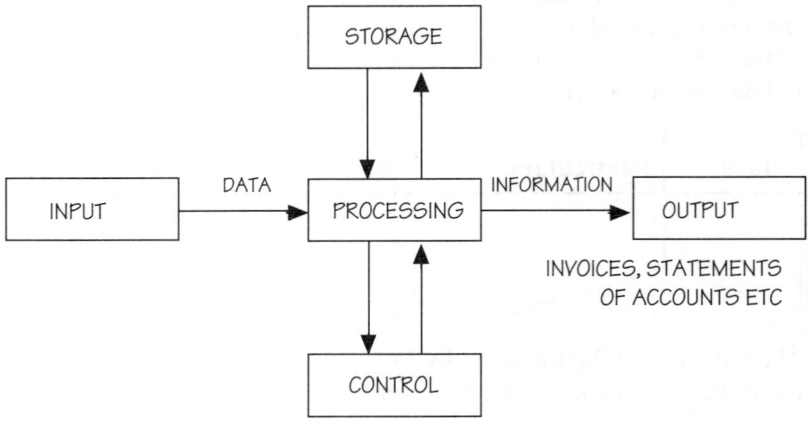

Figure 23.2
Elements of a data processing system

Input is raw data i.e. unprocessed data; they are **processed** to become useful information and **output**. Both input and output are **stored** and they can be retrieved whenever necessary. The **control** system is introduced to ensure that relevant and accurate output is obtained.

Elements of a computer system

Like the data processing system, the computer system has five elements: input, processing, output, storage and control. Depending on the type of the computer, terminal keyboards and bar code scanners are used for **input**. Processing is done by the **central processing unit** (CPU). The processed input becomes the **output** which is channelled through a printer, VDU (visual display unit) or to a **backing storage** – a magnetic tape or disc. Records are stored in master files through the media of tapes or discs. **Control** is performed by an internally stored program.

Hardware

The computer system is divided into two parts: the **hardware** and the **software**. The hardware is usually identified with the machine itself. If we consider a computer that will be used by a small business – a microcomputer – then the hardware will consist of:

- a microprocessor that is the central processing unit which contains the internal memory, the arithmetic/logic unit (popularly known as the ALU) and the control unit
- the keyboard which is the means of communicating with the processor, to input data and instructions to the computer
- the monitor (or the screen or the VDU) which is similar to a TV screen, and displays information present in the computer
- the printer which provides processed information i.e. output in printed form.

Mainframe computers are big and expensive machines with vast capacity, and they are used by big companies and public bodies such as the Ministry of Defence and local authorities. Big organizations will often have computer networks linking together a number of computers either locally (a **local area network** or LAN) or nationally or even internationally (known as a **wide area network** or WAN). A good example of a LAN is a network which connects the different departments of an organization. The advantages of a LAN lie in the sharing of expensive hardware devices such as a high-speed printer and high-capacity hard disc, data files and data discs. A WAN covers a much wider geographical area and has got the same advantages as those of a LAN.

Software

Computer **software** is made up of computer programs which give instructions to the computer to do specific jobs. **Computer users** can either write their own programs in a form understandable to the processors, or they can buy and use specific programs from specialist agencies. There is a great variety of such programs available for most types of computer, but since these programs are written for different types and makes of computer, it is difficult to discuss them in any detail without knowing what sort of computer a business is likely to use. Therefore our discussion of computer software will cover, in general terms, the types of program that will be suitable for the accounting system of a business, without going into specifics.

There are many **computer packages** – i.e. software – available for the accounting system of a business organization. The accounting system can be divided into a number of sub-systems for purposes of record-keeping, control and reporting. Some examples of such sub-systems are:

- wages and payroll
- purchases
- sales
- stock
- nominal ledger.

Separate packages for each of these sub-systems are available and can be used for specific tasks. Alternatively, integrated accounting systems are available which will cover all these sub-systems. These packages come with detailed operating instructions so – with a bit of practice and patience – the users can operate them. Moreover, most of these packages are menu-driven, that is, the functions in an individual package are listed in a main menu and then the main tasks within each main menu are listed and explained in a systematic manner. It is therefore possible for a user to master facilities offered by these packages within a reasonable period. Many companies selling software provide a free demonstration and advice service to their customers.

The software packages which will be particularly useful to small businesses are:

- spreadsheets
- databases
- integrated accounting systems.

We'll describe each of these in some detail.

Spreadsheets

A spreadsheet is a worksheet with a large number of rows and columns. Its use is varied, but some of its accounting applications are:

- cash-flow analysis
- sales forecasting
- budgeting
- stock control
- general ledger
- trading and profit and loss accounts
- balance sheets.

Spreadsheet packages are widely available; some are meant for a particular computer only, but others can be used on different computers. Thus, for example, Supercalc 3 is suitable for Amstrad and Apple machines, and Lotus 1-2-3 for IBM PC and IBM compatibles including Amstrad PC. All spreadsheets involve data processing with numerical data, repetitive and time-consuming calculations and a logical processing system.

A typical spreadsheet, when loaded into a computer, will show on the monitor (VDU) lines of empty rows and columns, as shown in Figure 23.3.

Figure 23.3
A typical spreadsheet

	A	B	C	D	E	F
1			C1			
2						
3						
4						
5						
6						
7						
8						

Notice that rows are numbered 1, 2, 3, ... and the columns are lettered A, B, C, ... Each box in the table is called a cell. Each cell is identified uniquely by column letter and row number. Thus C1 stands for the cell in Column C, Row 1. This reference is needed to manipulate the **cursor** – a 'blinking' oblong – which marks the current cell position.

The use of a spreadsheet can be demonstrated by constructing a Trading and Profit and Loss account for a business.

The first step is to insert the various descriptions or headings in your Trading and Profit and Loss account. Start with the title of the account: 'Trading and Profit and Loss account for the year ended ...' in the first row. Do this by varying the width of column A. In all spreadsheet programs, the width of a column can easily be varied by following a simple set of instructions that accompanies the spreadsheet being used. Leave Row 2 blank. You are now ready to start inserting the format of the account . You will need three columns, A, B and C, only. To start with, bring down the cursor to Column B, Row 3 and key in '£'– you may have to put a special sign like " before inserting any descriptive information. Consult your instruction manual.

Once you have typed in '£', you can see it at the top or bottom of the spreadsheet. This gives you the opportunity to correct any mistake you might have made. When you are satisfied that the right expression has been keyed in, press RETURN. You will see that the '£' now appears in the desired cell, i.e. B3. You must press RETURN after keying in any input so that the data or the command is registered in the relevant cell. In the same way, insert another '£' sign in C3. Continue inserting the following in the order given:

- "Sales" in A4
- "Cost of Sales:" in A5
- "Opening stock" in A6
- "Purchases" in A7
- "________" in B8
- "Closing stock" in A10
- "________" in B11
- "________" in C12
- "Gross Profit" in A13
- "Expenses:" in A14
- "Wages" in A15
- "Rent" in A16
- "Sundry expenses" in A17
- "________" in B18
- "________" in C19
- "Net profit" in A20
- "=========" in C21

A simple Trading and Profit and Loss account format is now ready for use. Save it by using the appropriate code for the machine.

We shall now examine how to use this format for preparing a Trading and Profit and Loss account from the data given below.

	£
Sales	50,000
Opening stock	8,000
Purchases	25,000
Closing stock	10,000
Wages	4,000
Rent	1,500
Sundry expenses	500

Move the cursor to C4, key in 50,000 and press RETURN. Immediately, 50,000 will appear in C4. Now insert 8,000 (opening stock) in B6 in the same way, followed by 25,000 (purchases) in B7. Key in the "_____" in B8. At this stage, you have to give a command to your computer to add up the opening stock and purchases. You give this command by inserting the formula, B6 + B7 or SUM(B6,B7), in cell B9. The manner in which the add formula is to be inserted may differ from spreadsheet to spreadsheet. Read your instruction manual to ensure the correct insertion of the formula. Now press RETURN. The sum of 8,000 and 25,000 which is 33,000 appears automatically in cell B9. Type in the closing stock of 10,000 in cell B10. It is time for giving another command to your computer. Insert the formula B10 – B9 in cell C11. Press RETURN. You will see that 23,000 which is the difference between 33,000 and 10,000, appears in C11. Again, you type in another formula, C4 – C11, in cell C13, to give you the gross profit of 27,000. Next, you insert the following figures:

- 4,000 (wages) in B15
- 1,500 (rent) in B16
- 500 (sundry expenses) in B17

Now, type in the formula B15 + B16 + B17 in cell C18. This will give you the total expenses of the business. Finally, you put in another formula, C13 – C18, in cell C20. The resulting figure of 21,000 is the net profit.

The completed spreadsheet is shown in Figure 23.4.

Figure 23.4
A completed spreadsheet

	A	B	C	D
1				
2				
3		£	£	
4	SALES		50,000	
5	COST OF SALES			
6	OPENING STOCK	8.000		
7	PURCHASES	25,000		
8		----------		
9		33,000		
10	CLOSING STOCK	10,000		
11		----------	23,000	
12			----------	
13	GROSS PROFIT		27,000	
14	EXPENSES			
15	WAGES	4,000		
16	RENT	1,500		
17	SUNDRY EXPENSES	500		
18		----------	6,000	
19			----------	
20	NET PROFIT		21,000	
22			==========	

The interesting thing about this account made by using the spreadsheet is that if you change any figure – say, closing stock figure – in it, all the arithmetical calculations will be automatically redone to give you revised gross profit and net profit. This is a quick and convenient way of computing future profit by taking different values of key items such as sales, purchases and expenses.

Before we leave this section, one word of caution. If you wish to introduce one or more additional items under the subheading 'expenses', you need to readjust your add formula to include the new items.

Spreadsheets are very versatile. They can print, edit and replicate. Some of them can even convert tabulated data into charts and graphs.

Databases

A database is a collection of data which is organized and integrated in a single set of files. This single file system can be comprehensive and contain all the information generated by an operation within an organization. The data that is collected and stored in a single databank can be extensive and may be independent of any application packages. Data from the same source can be used for a variety of purposes.

The user will set the format of each record and the details it will contain. The stored information can be easily ordered and sorted out according to specified criteria. Thus a database program can sort out sales by product, alphabetical order of customer names, geographical area or price range.

The availability of database software packages has increased considerably in recent years. Some of the main database software are:

- Delta 4
- dBase III and dBase IV
- DMS +

Integrated accounting systems

Nowadays, a variety of accounting packages are available. As we saw earlier, the accounting system can be subdivided into a number of sub-systems. We can buy a separate program for a specific area such as stock control. Such a specific program is known as a **module.** If an accounting package consists of one module, it is known as a **stand-alone module**. If a package consists of several modules, it is called a **suite**. If each individual module in a suite can be integrated with the others, it is known as an **integrated accounting system**.

In an integrated system, data entered in one module will be transferred automatically or by simple user request into any other module where the data has some relevance. Thus if there is an input in the invoicing module following the dispatch of an invoice to a customer, this can be easily passed to:

- the Sales Ledger to update the relevant customer's account
- the Stock module to update the stock file
- the Nominal Ledger to update the Sales account.

The main advantage of an integrated accounting system is that by making an entry in one account we can update several related accounts, and save time.

Many such integrated packages are available, the Sage accounting package being an example. Each package will contain all the necessary instructions to run the package. Many colleges run short courses on the use of such packages at a moderate cost.

Chapter summary

- The main advantages of a computerized accounting system are: speed, accuracy and versatility.
- The major elements in a data processing system are: input, processing, output, storage and control.
- The computer system is divided into hardware (the computer itself including the VDU and the printer) and software (programs/application packages).
- The accounting software packages which would be particularly useful to small businesses are: spreadsheets, databases and integrated accounting systems.

Appendix 1: Present value tables

PRESENT VALUE OF £1

Year	1%	2%	3%	4%	5%	6%	7%	8%	9%	10%
1	0.990	0.980	0.971	0.961	0.952	0.943	0.935	0.926	0.917	0.909
2	0.980	0.961	0.943	0.925	0.907	0.890	0.873	0.857	0.842	0.826
3	0.971	0.942	0.915	0.889	0.864	0.840	0.816	0.794	0.772	0.751
4	0.961	0.924	0.889	0.855	0.823	0.792	0.763	0.735	0.708	0.683
5	0.951	0.906	0.863	0.822	0.784	0.747	0.713	0.681	0.650	0.621
6	0.942	0.888	0.838	0.790	0.746	0.705	0.666	0.630	0.596	0.564
7	0.933	0.871	0.813	0.760	0.711	0.665	0.623	0.583	0.547	0.513
8	0.923	0.853	0.789	0.731	0.677	0.627	0.582	0.540	0.502	0.467
9	0.914	0.837	0.766	0.703	0.645	0.592	0.544	0.500	0.460	0.424
10	0.905	0.820	0.744	0.676	0.614	0.558	0.508	0.463	0.422	0.386
11	0.896	0.804	0.722	0.650	0.585	0.527	0.475	0.429	0.388	0.350
12	0.887	0.788	0.701	0.625	0.557	0.497	0.444	0.397	0.366	0.319
13	0.879	0.773	0.681	0.601	0.530	0.469	0.415	0.368	0.326	0.290
14	0.870	0.758	0.661	0.577	0.505	0.442	0.388	0.340	0.299	0.263
15	0.861	0.743	0.642	0.555	0.481	0.417	0.362	0.315	0.278	0.239
16	0.853	0.728	0.623	0.534	0.458	0.394	0.339	0.292	0.252	0.218
17	0.844	0.714	0.605	0.513	0.436	0.371	0.317	0.270	0.231	0.198
18	0.836	0.700	0.587	0.494	0.416	0.350	0.298	0.250	0.212	0.180
19	0.828	0.686	0.570	0.475	0.396	0.331	0.276	0.232	0.194	0.164
20	0.820	0.673	0.554	0.456	0.377	0.319	0.258	0.215	0.178	0.149
25	0.780	0.610	0.478	0.375	0.295	0.233	0.184	0.146	0.116	0.092

PRESENT VALUE OF £1

Year	12%	14%	15%	16%	18%	20%	24%	28%	32%	36%
1	0.893	0.877	0.870	0.862	0.847	0.833	0.806	0.781	0.758	0.735
2	0.797	0.769	0.756	0.743	0.718	0.694	0.650	0.610	0.574	0.541
3	0.712	0.676	0.658	0.641	0.609	0.579	0.524	0.477	0.435	0.398
4	0.636	0.592	0.572	0.552	0.516	0.482	0.423	0.373	0.329	0.292
5	0.567	0.519	0.497	0.476	0.437	0.402	0.341	0.291	0.250	0.215
6	0.507	0.456	0.432	0.410	0.370	0.335	0.275	0.227	0.189	0.158
7	0.452	0.400	0.376	0.354	0.314	0.279	0.222	0.178	0.143	0.116
8	0.404	0.351	0.327	0.305	0.266	0.233	0.179	0.139	0.108	0.085
9	0.361	0.308	0.284	0.263	0.226	0.194	0.144	0.108	0.082	0.063
10	0.322	0.270	0.247	0.227	0.191	0.162	0.116	0.085	0.062	0.046
11	0.287	0.237	0.215	0.195	0.162	0.135	0.094	0.066	0.047	0.034
12	0.257	0.208	0.187	0.168	0.137	0.112	0.076	0.052	0.036	0.025
13	0.229	0.182	0.163	0.145	0.116	0.093	0.061	0.040	0.027	0.018
14	0.205	0.160	0.141	0.125	0.099	0.078	0.049	0.032	0.021	0.014
15	0.183	0.140	0.123	0.108	0.084	0.065	0.040	0.025	0.016	0.010
16	0.163	0.123	0.107	0.093	0.071	0.054	0.032	0.019	0.012	0.007
17	0.146	0.108	0.093	0.080	0.060	0.045	0.026	0.015	0.009	0.005
18	0.130	0.095	0.081	0.069	0.051	0.038	0.021	0.012	0.007	0.004
19	0.116	0.083	0.070	0.060	0.043	0.031	0.017	0.009	0.005	0.003
20	0.104	0.073	0.061	0.051	0.037	0.026	0.014	0.007	0.004	0.002
25	0.059	0.038	0.030	0.024	0.016	0.010	0.005	0.002	0.001	0.000

Appendix 2: Assessment and examination

WRITTEN ASSIGNMENTS

Get briefed

The requirements for written assignments vary from subject to subject, course to course, examination board to examination board. If you are asked to complete a written assignment without being given detailed guidance on how it should be presented, you have every right to complain. This is not something you should be left to guess about.

Understanding the brief

Study the brief carefully. You can solve a lot of problems at this stage. It might be something as short as an essay title, or a long briefing for a marketing project. Right from the start try to imagine what the finished product will look like. This may well raise questions of interpretation. Make a list of these and ask for guidance from a tutor. If this is not forthcoming, discuss the problem with someone else. You will often find that simply putting your problem into words makes the problem disappear.

Organizing your time

For large pieces of work, especially those which require research, it is essential to make a plan showing what you are going to do and by when. All kinds of contingencies may cause problems for you: the book you require is on loan to someone else, the person you want to interview is on holiday, some data you require isn't published until after your deadline, etc. The better you plan, the easier you will find it to adjust to changing circumstances.

Organizing your mind

Many people find that the best way for them to organize their mind is to use a spider diagram like the one shown overleaf. Many of the spider's legs will turn out to be irrelevant, but at least you will know which ones are there to be cut off.

When you have thought around the assignments in this way and as you think further about it, you can start to assemble materials. Look at your lecture notes, activity responses and file cards. Check reading lists. Look at the contents pages and indexes of your textbooks. By the time you have done this you will probably have to draw another spider diagram.

Start drafting

Unless you are a very skilled writer, you simply won't be able to start writing an assignment at the beginning to reach a successful conclusion at the end. Before it reaches this point, your work will have to go through several drafts. Either keep your early drafts in note form or, if you write them more fully, be prepared to cut them and reassemble them in a different order. If you use a wordprocessor this is easy.

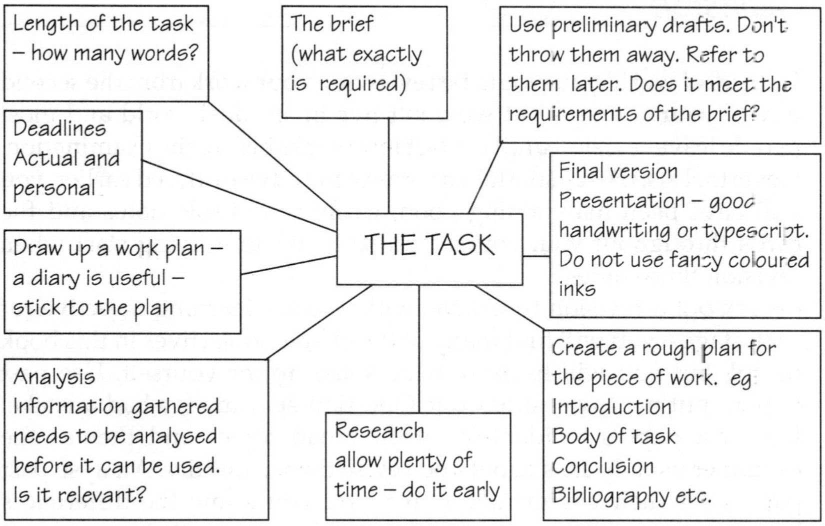

If you get stuck

If you get stuck, the first thing to do is to try to make a list of your difficulties. Say to yourself, 'I can't do this because . . . '. A lot of the confusion surrounding your difficulties will then disappear and the real problems should emerge. If you have any left, take the list of difficulties to a tutor or some other source of help. The worse things to do if you get stuck are to stay up night after night getting nowhere, or to give up without seeking advice.

Check before you finalize

When you have a draft, check it against the brief. Be tough with yourself. Will this draft, when written up, really meet the requirements? If it doesn't then make a list of the ways in which it fails. Use the list to redraft and rewrite.

Sleep on it

If you possibly can, leave the work alone for a few days. When you come back to it you will see its strengths and weaknesses more clearly.

The final version

This may be the second or third version. It should be clearly written and correctly spelled and punctuated. Leave wide margins on the page for tutor's comments. Make sure you follow any local requirements for length, line-spacing and structure. It may well require a bibliography. Failing any local advice, references quoted in the text should take one of the following forms:

Use either '(Kar, 1993)' or 'as Kar says (1993)'. Then at the end list the references in alphabetical order according to author name. For book references the references are: second name, initial or first name, publication date, publisher. For articles: second name, first name or initial, date, title, periodical title, volume, part or part number, page. Where your reference appears in a book edited by someone else: author's second name, initial or first name, date, title, editor's second name, initial or first name, title of book, publisher.

Check the final version and hand it in on time.

REVISION

► Make sure you know how you will be examined. How many exams? How long? What choice of questions? Will there be compulsory questions, essay questions, data-response questions, short answer questions? These all require different skills and different ways of revising.

► Establish how much of your syllabus you should revise.

► Check the assessment objectives which are printed in the syllabus document produced by your board.

► Read the Chief Examiner's reports for previous years. Note well what these reports say. Not only does the Chief Examiner have experience of the mistakes of thousands of students, he/she actually decides what is mistaken and what is correct.

In an ideal world you would be reviewing your work from the second day of your course – but we don't live in an ideal world and most people leave revision until the last few weeks before the examination. Nevertheless, if you have taken some of the advice offered earlier, you will have been maintaining good, easily retrievable notes and file cards throughout your course and so be off to a flying start when revision time comes.

Work out a revision timetable, with realistic learning objectives at each stage – you will find many of the chapter objectives in this book useful, but you will have to make some up for yourself. Use past papers, but **not** to question spot. Question-spotting is a bad mistake. Use past papers to identify which broad topics and themes the examiner usually asks about and revise them carefully. Analyse past papers for their commands. Make sure you know the differences between 'describe', 'account for', 'analyse', and so on. What you must not do is to revise actual questions and prepare model answers. Model questions rarely come up!

Ask yourself questions and answer them. Try to think like an examiner. As you approach different topics ask yourself, 'What questions could the examiner ask me about this?'

► Taking an active approach to revision is essential. Passive revision, i.e. sitting reading through notes and textbooks is both boring and ineffective.

► Revise with friends, discussing questions and trying to explain things to each other.

► Give yourself time off, especially on the day before the examinations start.

Revise actively

Make notes and summaries all the time. Make notes of notes, summaries of notes and notes of summaries. Annotate your notes with notes from a textbook and then produce a tidy version. Convert notes in continuous text into notes in diagram or table format, or vice versa.

As your revision proceeds, try to reduce the whole course to a series of trigger words and phrases – just enough to jog your memory. Practise writing your answers under the pressure of time. How much can you get down in the time available? Practise writing answers of that length.

Work in regular sessions with breaks every hour, but get used to working for three hours at a time before taking a longer break.

THE EXAMINATION

► Examiners want you to do well. They are instructed to mark your work by giving you credit for everything you do properly, not to penalize you for your mistakes. Your marks start at zero and go on up whenever you do something right. The examiner is looking for opportunities to reward positive achievements, so supply plenty of these and make it easy for the examiner to find them. Examination answers are vehicles for you to display your achievement.

Think of the examination as an opportunity for you to give a performance, with an audience of one – the examiner. You are displaying your knowledge, understanding and skills to someone who wants to applaud you.

Here are some key points to bear in mind:

- Make sure you know when and where the examination will be held. If it is an unfamiliar place, try to visit it beforehand and check your travel arrangements.
- The evening before the exam make sure you have all the pens, pencils and other equipment you will need.
- Arrive in good time, but don't stand around chatting. Go for a walk to loosen up and get the oxygen flowing to the brain.
- When the exam starts, read through the whole paper (or those parts which relate to your options).
- Do **not** start writing immediately, but settle down, get the feel of the paper, check the instructions and find the questions you feel

OK about. Take a few minutes to double check that you are following the rubric correctly.

- Choose your probable questions, but don't firm up your choice at this early stage.
- The marks allocated to each question, or parts of each question are a rough guide to how much you should write on each. If two marks are allocated, make two good points and stop. You won't get more than two marks however many brilliant points you make.
- Draw up a rough timetable for yourself – 'by 10.35 I should have finished the first question', etc.
- Start your first question. Now for the golden rule of exams:

ANSWER THE QUESTION SET: DO WHAT THE EXAMINER TELLS YOU TO DO.

- For all but very short answers, make a plan.
- Think all the time. Don't just try to remember things, but think about how to apply what you know to the question set.
- Don't overrun your time on a particular question. It takes much longer to get a few more marks at the end of an answer than at the beginning of another.
- Take rests during your exams. Loosen up physically; breathe, stretch, shut your eyes while you are thinking.
- Leave enough time for checking and polishing your answers. A single additional mark could mean a higher grade.

► If you suffer badly from nerves, learn to relax through the use of deep breathing techniques. Don't take pills, except under medical supervision. Don't drink alcohol before an exam. It relaxes the wrong part of your brain.

► The most common reason for candidates failing to get the marks they should is not lack of knowledge or skill, but failure to observe the golden rule. Make sure you do what the examiner asks you to do.

► Presentation and layout are important, because they should help the examiner to find your good points easily. Use short sentences and paragraphs to make your points clearly and concisely.

► GOOD LUCK!

Appendix 3

ANSWERS TO ACTIVITIES

Chapter 1

Activity 1.1 (page 5)

1 **a** F **b** F **c** F **d** F **e** T **f** T **g** F

2 **a** The primary objective of a manufacturing concern may be the maximization of profits consistent with stability and growth. A manufacturing firm may also have non-financial objectives such as the maintenance of high quality of the products it makes.

b The main difference between a private limited company and a public limited company is that a public company can make an issue of shares to the general public whereas a private company may only sell its shares privately, that is without advertising.

c A local sporting club will usually be a non-profit making organization. Consequently, its objective will be non-financial in nature – e.g. the promotion of different sporting activities.

d Planning and control are the two main elements of the management function. But both planning and control involve decision-making. To plan is to decide what is to be done. To control is to ensure that actual performance does not differ significantly from the plan or the standard set. Any deviation of the actual from the standard will call for management decisions. Decision-making thus embraces all aspects of the management process.

Chapter 2

Activity 2.1 (page 15)

Time taken = 40 hrs
Time allowed = 120 × 0.5 = 60 hrs
Therefore time saved = (60 – 40) hrs = 20 hrs
Total Wages = 40 × £3 + (20 × £3)
= £120 + £60
= £180

Activity 2.4 (page 23)

1 **a**

Eddie Banda	£	£
Gross pay		8,500
Less single person's allowance	3,000	
married couple's allowance	1,700	4,700
Taxable pay		3,800
Less income tax (25% × £3,800)		950
Net pay (annual)		2,850

$$\text{Net pay monthly} = \frac{£2,850}{12} = £237.50$$

b Joanne Kemp

	£	£
Gross salary		10,000
Less superannuation contribution		500
		9,500
Less personal allowance		3,000
Taxable income		6,500
Less income tax (25% × 6,500)		1,625
Net pay (annual)		4,875

$$\text{Net pay per month} = \frac{£4{,}875}{12} = £406.25$$

c Didar Singh

	£	£
Gross income		25,000.00
Less superannuation contribution (5% × £25,000)		1,250.00
		23,750.00
Less single person's allowance	3,000.00	
married couple's allowance	1,700.00	4,700.00
Taxable income		19,050.00
Less income tax (25% × £19,050)		4,762.50
Net income (annual)		14,287.50

$$\text{Net income per month} = \frac{£14{,}287.50}{12} = £1{,}190.63$$

2 a Julie Brown

	£
Gross interest payable = 14% × £15,000	2,100
Less tax relief (25% × £2,100)	525
Net interest payable	1,575

$$\text{Net interest payable per month} = \frac{£1{,}575}{12} = £131.25$$

b Steve Taylor

	£
Gross interest payable = 13.5% × £30,000	4,050.00
Less tax relief (25% × £4,050)	1,012.50
	3,037.50

$$\text{Net interest payable per month} = \frac{£3{,}037.50}{12} = £253.13$$

c Leslie Pitt

	£
Gross interest payable (14% × £60,000)	8,400
Less tax relief (restricted to mortgage of £30,000) 25% × £4,200	1,050
	7,350

Net interest payable per month = £612.50

Activity 2.5 (page 29)

2 Susan Drummond

	Normal hours	Overtime hours
Monday	8	–
Tuesday	8	1
Wednesday	8	0.5
Thursday	8	2.5
Friday	8	–
Saturday	–	8
Total	40	12

Gross wages $= £2.10 \times 40 + £2.10 \times 12 \times \frac{3}{2} = £84 + £\,37.80$

$= £121.80$

4 John Rees

a

	£
Basic gross wages = 40 × £2	80
Wages based on production	nil
Total weekly gross wages	80

b

	£
Basic gross wages	80
Wages based on production 1,250 × £0.10	125
Weekly gross wages	205

c

Basic gross wages	80
Wages based on production 1,700 × £0.12	204
Weekly gross wages	284

6 a

	£	£
Gross salary		14,750.00
Less superannuation contribution 5% × 14,750		737.50
		14,012.50
Less married person's allowance (3,000 + 1,720)		4,720.00
Taxable income		9,292.50

b Income tax liability = 25% × £9,292.50 = £2,323.13

c

	£	£
Gross salary		14,750.00
Less superannuation contribution	737.50	
NI contribution 6% × 14,750	885.00	
Income tax	2,323.13	3,945.63
Net pay		10,804.37

d

Interest on mortgage loan = 14% × £20,000	2,800
Less Tax rebate under MIRAS 25% × 2,800	700
Interest payable	2,100

8 **Eric and Paula**

Cash budget for the six months ending 30 Sept

	April £	May £	June £	July £	Aug £	Sept £
Opening balance	—	120	260	235	275	295
Receipts (A)	1,000	1,000	1,000	1,000	1,000	1,000
Total cash available (*x*)	1,000	1,120	1,260	1,235	1,275	1,295
Total payments (Sch B) – (*y*)	880	860	1,025	960	980	1,085
Closing balance	120	260	235	275	295	210

Schedule A

	April £	May £	June £	July £	Aug £	Sept £
Receipts						
Salary – Eric	600	600	600	600	600	600
– Paula	400	400	400	400	400	400
	1,000	1,000	1,000	1,000	1,000	1,000

Schedule B

	April £	May £	June £	July £	Aug £	Sept £
Payments						
Mortgage	300	300	300	300	300	300
Polltax	–	60	60	60	60	60
Household Insurance	100	–	–	–	–	–
Car tax	–	–	–	100	–	–
Car insurance	–	–	–	–	120	–
Gas and electricity	–	–	120	–	–	120
Petrol	60	60	60	60	60	60
Car servicing	–	–	–	–	–	60
Telephone	–	–	45	–	–	45
Life Assurance	–	20	20	20	20	20
Entertainment and General expenses	420	420	420	420	420	420
	880	860	1,025	960	980	1,085
Closing balances	120	260	235	275	295	210

Chapter 3

Activity 3.1 (page 37)

1 **a** Liabilities = £17,800 – £13,500 = £4,300
b Assets = £8,300 + £19,200 = £27,500
c *C* = £15,300 – £2,800 = £12,500
d *A* = £12,650 + £40,750 = £53,400
e *C* = £28,000 – £6,900 = £21,100
f *L* = £40,500 – £30,250 = £10,250

2

Assets	**Liabilities**
Office equipment	Bank overdraft
Cash in hand	Trade creditors
Motor vehicles	Loan from A. Lender
Stock of goods	
Plant and machinery	
Land and buildings	

3 Horizontal format

Albert King
Balance Sheet as at 31 December

	£	£		£
Premises		25,000		
Furniture		4,200	Capital	39,200
Stock		8,500		
Debtors		15,000		
Cash in hand		1,500		
		54,200		
Less Liabilities:				
Creditors	10,000			
Bank overdraft	5,000	15,000		
		39,200		39,200

Vertical format

Albert King
Balance Sheet as at 31 December

	£	£
Premises		25,000
Furniture		4,200
Stock		8,500
Debtors		15,000
Cash in hand		1,500
		54,200
Less Liabilities:		
Creditors	10,000	
Bank overdraft	5,000	15,000
		39,200
Financed by:		
Capital		39,200

Activity 3.2 (page 46)

For simplicity we shall show the ledger accounts in 'T' form.

Capital a/c Anne McDermot

	£		£
		Mar 1 Bank	12,000

Bank a/c

	£		£
Mar 1 Capital	12,000	Mar 2 Fixtures and fittings	1,200
Mar 9 R. Simons	100	Mar 3 Purchases	6,500
		Mar 10 Motor van	4,000

Fixtures and fittings a/c

	£		£
Mar 2 Bank	1,200		

Purchases a/c

		£			£
Mar 3	Bank	6,500			
Mar 8	Mod.W'salers Ltd	2,000			

Sales a/c

		£			£
			Mar 4	Cash	600
			Mar 6	R. Simons	100
			Mar 7	Cash	450

Cash a/c

		£			£
Mar 4	Sales	600	Mar 5	Wages	90
Mar 7	Sales	450			

Wages a/c

		£			£
Mar 5	Cash	90			

R. Simons a/c

		£			£
Mar 6	Sales	100	Mar 9	Bank	100

Modern Wholesalers Ltd a/c

		£			£
			Mar 8	Purchases	2,000

Motor van a/c

		£			£
Mar 10	Bank	4,000			

Activity 3.4 (page 51)

1 A **2** B **3** B **4** A **5** D

6
- Purchases account increases by £5,000 (+assets)
  Bank account decreases by £5,000 (–assets)
- Purchases account increases by £3,000 (+assets)
  AB Ltd's account decreases by £3,000 (+liabilities)
- Sales account increases by £600 (+revenue)
  Cash account increases by £600 (+assets)
- Cash and bank account increases by £2,000 (+assets)
  Loan account – (Sandra Jackson's) increases by £2,000 (+liabilities)

8

R. Jordan
Balance Sheet as at 31 December

	£	£	£
Fixed assets:			
Premises			30,000
Fixtures and fittings			2,150
Motor van			5,550
			37,700
Current assets:			
Stocks		10,500	
Debtors		10,350	
Cash in hand		100	
		20,950	
Less Current Liabilities:			
Creditors	8,250		
Bank overdraft	5,200	13,450	
Net current assets			7,500
			45,200
Less longterm liabilities			5,000
			40,200
Financed by:			
Capital			40,200

10

Capital a/c – Jim Coy

	£		£
		Mar 1 Bank	20,000

Fixtures and fittings a/c

	£		£
Mar 3 Bank	2,200		

Purchases a/c

	£		£
Mar 4 Bank	8,000		
Mar 5 A. Jackson	2,500		

Amanda Jackson a/c

	£		£
Mar 15 Bank	2,500	Mar 5 Purchases	2,500

Cash a/c

	£		£
Mar 8 Sales	750	Mar 10 Rent	250
Mar 20 Sales	500	Mar 25 Wages	150
		Mar 30 Drawings	200

Wages a/c

	£		£
Mar 25 Cash	150		

Drawings a/c

	£		£
Mar 30 Cash	200		

Bank a/c

	£		£
Mar 1 Capital	20,000	Mar 3 Fixtures and fittings	2,200
Mar 18 R. Banda	1,000	Mar 4 Purchases	8,000
		Mar 15 A. Jackson	2,500

Sales a/c

	£		£
		Mar 8 Cash	750
		Mar 9 R. Banda	1,500
		Mar 20 Cash	500
		Mar 27 R. Banda	500

R. Banda

	£		£
Mar 9 Sales	1,500	Mar 18 Bank	1,000
Ma 27 Sales	500		

Rent a/c

	£		£
Mar 10 Cash	250		

12

	Debit balance	Credit balance
Capital account		✓
Drawings account	✓	
Cash account	✓	
Wages account	✓	
Premises account	✓	
Sales account		✓
Purchases account	✓	
Rent account	✓	
Commission Received a/c		✓

14

Capital a/c – K. Harvey

		£			£
Mar 31	Balance c/d	15,000	Mar 1	Bank	15,000
			Apr 1	Balance b/d	15,000

Bank a/c

		£			£
Mar 1	Capital	15,000	Mar 2	Fixtures and fittings	2,150
Mar 20	R. Castle	250	Mar 3	Purchases	8,750
Mar 29	W. Roberts	500	Mar 18	Rent	250
Mar 29	J. Bain	200	Mar 30	D. Green	500
			Mar 31	Balance	4,300
		15,950			15,950
Apr 1	Balance b/d	4,300			

Fixtures and fittings a/c

		£			£
Mar 2	Bank	2,150	Mar 31	Balance c/d	2,270
Mar 12	Cash	120			
		2,270			2,270
Apr 1	Balance b/d	2,270			

Purchases a/c

		£			£
Mar 3	Bank	8,750	Mar 31	Balance c/d	11,850
Mar 4	D. Little	2,100			
Mar 22	D. Green	1,000			
		11,850			11,850
Apr 1	Balance b/d	11,850			

Sales a/c

		£			£
Mar 31	Balance c/d	2,575	Mar 4	Cash	375
			Mar 10	R. Castle	250
			Mar 10	W. Roberts	350
			Mar 10	J. Bain	180
			Mar 15	Cash	350
			Mar 25	W. Roberts	450
			Mar 25	J. Bain	220
			Mar 31	Cash	400
		2,575			2,575
Apr 1	Balance b/d	2,575			

Cash a/c

		£			£
Mar 4	Sales	375	Mar 8	Wages	150
Mar 15	Sales	350	Mar 12	Fixtures and fittings	120
Mar 31	Sales	400	Mar 28	Wages	180
			Mar 31	Balance b/d	675
		1,125			1,125
Apr 1	Balance b/d	675			

D. Little a/c

		£			£
Mar 31	Balance c/d	2,100	Mar 6	Purchases	2,100
			Apr 1	Balance b/d	2,100

Wages a/c

		£			£
Mar 8	Cash	150	Mar 31	Balance c/d	330
Mar 28	Cash	180			
		330			330
Apr 1	Balance b/d	330			

R. Castle a/c

		£			£
Mar 10	Sales	250	Mar 20	Bank	250

W. Roberts a/c

		£			£
Mar 10	Sales	350	Mar 29	Bank	500
Mar 25	Sales	450	Mar 31	Balance c/d	300
		800			800
Apr 1	Balance b/d	300			

J. Bain a/c

		£			£
Mar 10	Sales	180	Mar 29	Bank	200
Mar 25	Sales	220	Mar 31	Balance c/d	200
		400			400
Apr 1	Balance b/d	200			

Rent a/c

		£			£
Mar 18	Bank	250	Mar 31	Balance c/d	250
Apr 1	Balance b/d	250			

D. Green a/c

		£			£
Mar 29	Bank	500	Mar 22	Purchases	1,000
Mar 31	Balance c/d	500			
		1,000			1,000
			Apr 1	Balance b/d	500

K. Harvey
Trial Balance as at 31 March

	DR £	CR £
Capital		15,000
Bank	4,300	
Fixtures and fittings	2,270	
Purchases	11,850	
Sales		2,575
Cash	675	
D. Little		2,100
Wages	330	
W. Roberts	300	
J. Bain	200	
Rent	250	
D. Green		500
	20,175	20,175

16

Stock a/c

		£			£
Mar 1	Balance b/d	5,500			

Little a/c

		£			£
Mar 1	Balance b/d	560	Mar 31	Balance c/d	810
Mar 4	Sales	250			
		810			810
Apr 1	Balance b/d	810			

Smith a/c

		£			£
Mar 1	Balance b/d	500	Mar 10	Bank	500
Mar 4	Sales	175	Mar 31	Balance c/d	175
		675			675
Apr 1	Balance b/d	175			

Johnson a/c

		£			£
Mar 1	Balance b/d	100	Mar 28	Bank	220
Mar 4	Sales	120			
		220			220

Cash a/c

		£			£
Mar 1	Balance b/d	100	Mar 13	Wages	150
Mar 2	Sales	200	Mar 31	Wages	150
Mar 16	Sales	300	Mar 31	Balance c/d	300
		600			600
Apr 1	Balance b/d	300			

Bank a/c

		£			£
Mar 1	Balance b/d	2,140	Mar 6	Day	150
Mar 10	Smith	500	Mar 24	Choudhury	300
Mar 28	Johnson	220	Mar 31	Balance c/d	2,410
		2,860			2,860
Apr 1	Balance b/d	2,410			

Fixtures and fittings a/c

		£			£
Mar 1	Balance b/d	2,000			

Day a/c

		£			£
			Mar 6	Bank	150
Mar 1	Balance b/d	150			
Mar 31	Balance c/d	500	Mar 20	Purchases	500
		650			650
Apr 1	Balance b/d	500			

Choudhury a/c

		£			£
Mar 24	Bank	300	Mar 1	Balance b/d	300

Capital a/c – Teresa London

		£			£
			Mar 1	Balance b/d	10,450

Sales a/c

		£			£
Mar 31	Balance c/d	1,045	Mar 2	Cash	200
			Mar 4	Little	250
			Mar 4	Smith	175
			Mar 4	Johnson	120
			Mar 16	Cash	300
		1,045			1,045
			Apr 1	Balance b/d	1,045

Wages a/c

		£			£
Mar 13	Cash	150	Mar 31	Balance c/d	300
Mar 31	Cash	150			
		300			300
Apr 1	Balance b/d	300			

Purchases a/c

		£			£
Mar 20	Day	500	Mar 31	Balance c/d	500
Apr 1	Balance b/d	500			

Teresa London
Balance Sheet as at 31 March

	DR £	CR £
Stock	5,500	
Little	810	
Smith	75	
Cash	300	
Bank	2,410	
Fixtures and fittings	2,000	
Day		500
Capital		10,450
Sales		1,045
Wages	300	
Purchases	500	
	11,995	11,995

18

	DR			CR		
	Personal	Nominal	Real	Personal	Nominal	Real
Good bought on credit from I Green – £500		✓		✓		
Sold goods on credit to Hutchinson £250	✓				✓	
Withdrew cash for personal use	✓					✓
Bought office furniture for cash			✓			✓
Paid rent by cheque		✓				✓

Chapter 4

Activity 4.1 (page 72)

1 D **2** B **3** C **4** A **5** D

6

Cash Book

		C £	B £			C £	B £
Apr 1	Capital		10,000	Apr 2	Rent and Rates		500
Apr 6	Sales	450		Apr 4	Purchases		5,000
Apr 8	B.Wilson		150	Apr 7	R. Thornton		550
Apr 15	Sales	600	150	Apr 10	Wages	150	
Apr 25	Sales			Apr 20	T. Burton		120
				Apr 30	Wages	150	
				Apr 30	Balance c/d	750	4,130
		1,050	10,300			1,050	10,300
May 1	Balance b/d	750	4,130				

8

Cash Book

		C £	B £			C £	B £
Dec 1	Balance b/d	250		Dec 1	Balance b/d		500
Dec 2	Sales	400		Dec 11	Bank	800	
Dec 5	A. Rogers		210	Dec 15	S. Kapoor		200
Dec 10	Sales	420		Dec 20	Drawings		600
Dec 11	Cash		800	Dec 25	Insurance		225
Dec 18	Sales		400	Dec 28	Wages	400	
Dec 26	Sales	375		Dec 30	S. Hart		115
Dec 31	R. Coping		90	Dec 31	Balance b/d	245	
Dec 31	Balance c/d		140				
		1,445	1,640			1,445	1,640
Jan 1	Balance b/d		245	Jan 1	Balance b/d		140

10 a

Cash Book

19x8		D £	C £	B £	19x8		D £	C £	B £
April 1	Balance b/d		150		April 1	Balance b/d			300
April 6	Sales		50	200	April 6	Wages		60	
April 12	R. Logan	15		285	April 7	Electricity		90	
April 13	Sales		100	200	April 10	E. Hague	4		76
April 20	Sales		50	275	April 13	Wages		60	
April 20	J. Coy	10		165	April 15	Sundry expenses		50	
April 27	Sales		100	150	April 15	Rent			200
April 27	B. Dillons	11		199	April 20	Wages		60	
					April 20	D. Crowther	10		185
					April 25	Telephone		90	
					April 25	S. Singh	20		260
			20		April 27	Wages		60	
					April 30	Balance c/d			453
		36	550	1,474			34	470	1,474
May 1	Balance b/d		470	453				20	20

b Personal accounts

R. Logan a/c

			£				£
19x8				19x8			
Apr	1	Balance b/d	300	Apr	12	Bank	285
				Apr	12	Discount allowed	15
			300				300

J. Coy a/c

			£				£
19x8				19x8			
Apr	1	Balance b/d	175	Apr	20	Bank	165
				Apr	20	Discount allowed	10
			175				175

B. Dillons a/c

			£				£
19x8				19x8			
Apr	1	Balance b/d	210	Apr	27	Bank	199
				Apr	27	Discount allowed	11
			210				210

E. Hague a/c

			£				£
19x8				19x8			
Apr	10	Bank	76	Apr	1	Balance b/d	80
Apr	10	Discount received	4				
			80				80

D. Crowther a/c

			£				£
19x8				19x8			
Apr	20	Bank	185	Apr	1	Balance b/d	195
Apr	20	Discount rec'd.	10				
			195				195

S. Singh a/c

			£				£
19x8				19x8			
Apr	25	Bank	260	Apr	1	Balance b/d	280
Apr	25	Discount rec'd.	20				
			280				280

c In the General Ledger

Discount allowed a/c

		£				£
19x8						
Apr 30	Total for the month	36				

Discount received a/c

		£			£
19x8			19x8		
			Apr 30	Total for the month	34

12

Cash Book (Bank columns only)

		£			£
19x9			19x9		
Dec 31	Balance b/d	1,034			
Dec 31	Dividends	620	Dec 31	Bank charges	34
			Dec 31	Insurance (DD)	260
			Dec 31	Balance c/d	1,360
		1,654			1,654

J. Samuelson
Bank Reconciliation Statement as at 31 Dec 19x9

	£	£
Bank statement balance		1,658
Add cheques paid into bank but not yet entered in the bank statement		392
		2,050
Less cheques drawn but not yet presented for payment		690
Balance as per the (adjusted) cash book		1,360

14

Petty Cash Book

£	Date	Details	Voucher number	Total £	Postage £	Stationery £	Carriage £	Sundry expenses £
25.00	Mar 1	Balance b/d						
55.00	Mar 1	Cash						
	Mar 1	Postage		5.90	5.90			
	Mar 2	Stationery		10.60		10.60		
	Mar 4	Sundry expenses		3.75				3.75
	Mar 9	Carriage		6.30			6.30	
	Mar 12	Postage		5.95	5.95			
	Mar 19	Postage		4.90	4.90			
	Mar 21	Sundry expenses		5.25				5.25
	Mar 23	Carriage		3.80			3.80	
	Mar 25	Postage		8.05	8.05			
	Mar 26	Stationery		4.50		4.50		
	Mar 31	Carriage		5.30			5.30	
				64.30	24.80	15.10	15.40	9.00
	Mar 31	Balance b/d		15.70				
80.00				80.00				

Chapter 5

Activity 5.1 (page 92)

1 a Recording unusual transactions of infrequent occurrence such as the disposal of fixed assets

b Correction of errors

2
- Errors of original entry
- Errors of omission
- Errors of commission
- Errors of principle
- Compensating errors
- Errors of reversal

3 a An error of principle occurs when a transaction is posted to an account in the wrong group. An example of this type of error is if a piece of furniture purchased on credit from Northwest Furniture Ltd for £500 is posted as:
- debit the Purchases account with £500
- credit the Northwest Furniture Ltd with £500

These entries are obviously wrong as furniture – a fixed asset – is entered into the Purchases account which records buying of goods for resale. To rectify this error we need the following entries:
- debit the Furniture account with £500
- credit the Purchases account with £500

b In an error of reversal, two entries in the ledger are made the wrong way round. Thus cash sales of £600, recorded as
- debit the Sales account with £600 and,
- credit the Cash account with £600

represent such an error. To rectify this, we need to:
- debit the Cash account with £1,200
- credit the Sales account with £1,200

The amount is doubled in each case to cancel the original wrong entry of £600 and enter the correct value of £600 thus giving a total of £1,200.

Activity 5.2 (page 94)

1 D **2** A **3** B **4** C **5** D

6

Sales Day Book Page 1

Date	Customer's account	Invoice no.	Folio	Amount £
19x9				
June 1	R. Islam	00121		500
June 8	Brown and Brown Co	00122		1,000
June 20	R. Islam	00123		800
June 25	Brown and Brown Co	00124		1,200
June 30	Joan Cummings	00125		600
	Transferred to Sales account			4,100

Ledger accounts

R Islam a/c

		£			£
19x9			19x9		
June 1	Sales	500			
June 20	Sales	800			

Brown and Brown Co a/c

		£			£
19x9			19x9		
June 8	Sales	1,000			
June 25	Sales	1,200			

Joan Cummings a/c

		£			£
19x9			19x9		
June 30	Sales	600			

Sales a/c

		£			£
19x9			19x9		
			June 30	Sundry debtors	4,100

8

Purchases Day Book

Date	Suppliers' a/c	Invoice no.	Folio	Amount £
19x3				
Sept 1	A. Chang			800
6	Rani Patel			700
12	A. Chang			900
15	Rani Patel			500
25	R. King			400
30	R. King			550
	Total transferred to Returns Outwards a/c			3,850

Returns Outwards Book

Date	Suppliers' a/cs	Invoice no.	Folio	Amount £
19x3				
Sept 20	A. Chang			200
Sept 28	Rani Patel			150
	Total transferred to Returns Outwards a/c			350

Ledger accounts

A. Chang a/c

		£			£
19x3			19x3		
Sept 20	Retns Outwards	200	Sept 1	Purchases	800
			Sept 12	Purchases	900

Rani Patel a/c

		£			£
19x3			19x3		
Sept 28	Retns Outwards	150	Sept 6	Purchases	700
			Sept 15	Purchases	500

R. King a/c

		£			£
19x3			19x3		
			Sept 25	Purchases	400
			Sept 30	Purchases	550

Purchases a/c

		£			£
19x3			19x3		
Sept 30	Sundry creditors	3,850			

Returns Outwards a/c

		£			£
19x3			19x3		
			Sept 30	Sundry creditors	350

10

Purchases Day Book

Date	Suppliers' a/c	Invoice no.	Folio	Amount £
19x3				
Nov 2	C. Singh	0701		500
Nov 3	A. Mahendra	0810		800
Nov 10	B. Jacobs	1122		920
Nov 18	A. Mahendra	0999		750
Nov 25	AB Ltd	1987		990
Nov 30	B. Jacobs	0678		620
	Total transferred to Purchases a/c			4,580

Returns Outwards Book

Date		Suppliers' a/c	Credit note no.	Folio	Amount £
19x3					
Nov	7	B Jacobs	0089		150
Nov	12	A. Mahendra	0910		200
Nov	20	C. Singh	0825		175
Nov	29	AB Ltd	0930		100
		Total transferred to Returns Outwards a/c			625

c Purchases Ledger accounts

A. Mahendra a/c

			£				£
19x3				19x3			
Nov	12	Returns Outwards	200	Nov	1	Balance b/d	850
				Nov	3	Purchases	800
				Nov	18	Purchases	750

B. Jacobs a/c

			£				£
19x3				19x3			
Nov	7	Returns Outwards	150	Nov	1	Balance b/d	500
				Nov	10	Purchases	920
				Nov	30	Purchases	620

C. Singh a/c

			£				£
19x3				19x3			
Nov	20	Returns Outwards	175	Nov	1	Balance b/d	450
				Nov	2	Purchases	500

AB Ltd a/c

			£				£
19x3				19x3			
Nov	29	Returns Outwards	100	Nov	25	Purchases	990

d Nominal Ledger accounts

Purchases a/c

			£				£
19x3				19x3			
Nov	1	Balance b/d	2,000				
Nov	30	Sundry creditors	4,580				

Returns Outwards a/c

			£				£
19x3				19x3			
				Nov	1	Balance b/d	200
				Nov	30	Sundry creditors	625

12

The Journal

Date			DR	CR
19x1				
Aug 1	B. Singher		200	
	B. Singh			200
	Correction of entry made in the wrong debtor's account.			
Aug 10	Cash		250	
	Sales			250
	An error of omission is now corrected.			
Aug 15	Office machine		150	
	Purchases account			150
	Correction of overstated purchases and understated office machine.			
Aug 20	Rita Hughes		9	
	Sales			9
	Correction of original entries as sale of £256 which should have been £265.			
Aug 25	Discount allowed		150	
	Discount received			150
	Correction of entry made in the wrong discount account.			
Aug 30	Sales account		50	
	Disposal of Assets account			50
	Correction of overstated sales and understated disposal of assets account.			

Chapter 7

Activity 7.1 (page 106)

1 Two examples of zero–rated supplies are:
- books and newspapers
- children's clothes

2 Any trader or organization whose turnover is in excess of a certain minimum prescribed by the government from time to time must register for VAT.

3 Three examples of exempt supplies are:
- Postal services
- Medical services
- Insurance premiums

Activity 7.2 (page 111)

	Gross sales		a VAT	b Net sales*
	£		£	£
(i)	780	780 × 17.5/117.5 =	116.17	663.83
(ii)	1,000	1000 × 17.5/117.5 =	148.94	851.06
(iii)	540	540 × 17.5/117.5 =	80.43	459.57

* (Gross sales – VAT)

Activity 7.3 (page 112)

4

Sales Day Book

Date	Account	Invoice no	Folio	Net £ p	VAT £ p	Gross £ p
19x4						
April 1	K. Roberts			160	28	188
April 7	M. Mohendra			200	35	235
April 8	Sen and Co.			250	43.75	293.75
April 15	K. Roberts			125	21.88	146.88
April 20	M. Mohendra			150	26.25	176.25
April 25	R. London			80	14	94
April 30	Sen and Co.			150	26.25	176.25
				1,115	195.13	1,310.13

Sales Ledger accounts

K. Roberts a/c

	£		£
19x4		19x4	
Apr 1 Sales	188.00		
Apr 15 Sales	146.88		

M. Mohendra a/c

	£		£
19x4		19x4	
Apr 7 Sales	235.00		
Apr 20 Sales	176.25		

Sen and Co. a/c

	£		£
19x4		19x4	
Apr 8 Sales	293.75		
Apr 30 Sales	176.26		

R. London a/c

	£		£
19x4		19x4	
Apr 25 Sales	94		

General Ledger accounts

Sales a/c

	£		£
19x4		19x4	
		Apr 30 Total for month	1,115

VAT a/c

	£		£
19x4		19x4	
		Apr 30 Total for month	195.13

Chapter 8

Activity 8.1 (page 117)

1 a

	£
Opening stock	3,000
Add Purchases	50,000
	53,000
Less Closing stock	5,000
Cost of sales	48,000

b

	£
Opening stock	4,900
Add Purchases	27,950
	32,850
Less Closing stock	2,100
Cost of sales	30,750

c

	£	£
Opening stock		9,275
Add Purchases	65,550	
Less Returns out	2,750	62,800
		72,075
Less Closing stock		10,000
Cost of sales		62,075

d

	£	£
Opening stock		9,575
Add Purchases	45,780	
Less Returns out	5,150	40,630
Add Carriage in		1,250
		51,455
Less Closing stock		4,780
Cost of sales		46,675

2 a

	£
Sales	55,000
Less cost of sales	32,000
Gross profit	23,000
Less expense	12,800
Net profit	10,200

b

	£
Sales	75,000
Less returns in	5,000
	70,000
Less cost of sales	60,250
Gross profit	9,750
Less expenses	10,250
(Net) Loss	(500)

c

	£
Sales	64,750
Less Returns in	3,750
	61,000
Less Cost of sales	69,250
(Gross) Loss	(8,250)
Less Expenses	12,800
(Net) Loss	(21,050)

3 a

	£	£	£
Sales			80,000
Less Returns in			3,700
			76,300
Less Cost of sales:			
Opening stock		5,000	
Add Purchases	50,000		
Less Returns out	5,000		
		45,000	
Carriage in		2,150	
		52,150	
Less Closing stock		6,000	
			46,150
Gross profit			30,150
Less Expenses			29,000
Net profit			1,150

b

	£	£	£
Sales			75,500
Less Returns in			4,250
			71,250
Less Cost of sales:			
Opening stock		7,500	
Add Purchases	55,555		
Less Returns out	2,900		
		52,655	
Carriage in		2,500	
		62,655	
Less Closing stock		6,000	
			56,655
Gross profit			14,595
Less Expenses			17,865
(Net) Loss			(3,270)

c

	£	£	£
Sales			99,990
Less Returns in			5,450
			94,540
Less Cost of sales:			
Opening stock		9,999	
Add Purchases	94,880		
Less Returns out	3,333		
		91,547	
Carriage in		2,215	
		103,761	
Less closing stock		1,880	101,881
(Gross) Loss			(7,341)
Less expenses			19,465
(Net) Loss			(26,806)

Activity 8.2 (page 125)

1 B **2** B **3** A **4** C **5** A

6 **(i)** Horizontal format

D. Spencer
Trading and Profit and Loss account for the year ended 31 December 19x0

	£		£
Opening stock	5,000	Sales	50,000
Add purchases	35,500		
	40,500		
Less closing stock	6,000		
Cost of sales	34,500		
Gross profit c/d	15,500		
	50,000		50,000
Administrative expenses	2,500	Gross profit b/d	15,500
Advertising expenses	1,500		
Transport expenses	1,000		
Occupancy expenses	1,500		
	6,500		
Net profit	9,000		
	15,500		15,500

(ii) Vertical format

D. Spencer
Trading and Profit and Loss account for the year ended 31 December 19x0

	£	£
Sales		50,000
Less cost of sales:		
Opening stock	5,000	
Add purchases	35,500	
	40,500	
Less closing stock	6,000	34,500
Gross Profit		15,500
Less expenses:		
Administrative expenses	2,500	
Advertising expenses	1,500	
Transport expenses	1,000	
Occupancy expenses	1,500	6,500
Net Profit		9,000

8 a

Julie Hampshire
Trading and Profit and Loss account for the year ended 31 March 19x0

	£	£	£
Sales			35,150
Less returns in			210
			34,940
Less cost of sales:			
Opening stock		5,000	
Add purchases	21,500		
Less returns out	325	21,175	
		26,175	
Less closing stock		5,780	20,395
Gross profit			14,545
Less expenses:			
Rates		905	
Heating and lighting		1,720	
Wages		11,000	
Insurance		500	
Sundry expenses		825	
Motor expenses		3,110	18,060
Net Loss			(3,515)

b

Julie Hampshire
Balance Sheet as at 31 March 19x0

	£	£	£
Fixed Assets:			
Premises			38,000
Fixtures and fittings			1,500
Motor van			6,000
			45,500
Current Assets:			
Stock		5,780	
Debtors		4,160	
Cash at bank		4,000	
Cash in hand		120	
		14,060	
Less Current Liabilities:			
Creditors		3,250	
Net Current Assets:			10,810
			56,310
Financed by:			
Capital			65,425
Less Loss			3,515
Less Drawings		5,600	9,115
			56,310

10 a

Billy Cooper
Trading and Profit and Loss account for the year ended 31 December 19x0

	£	£	£
Sales			101,890
Less cost of sales:			
Opening stock		21,980	
Add purchases		74,294	
Add carriage on purchases		260	
		96,534	
Less closing stock		25,750	70,784
Gross profit			31,106
Add commission received			1,250
			32,356
Less expenses:			
Carriage outwards		615	
Wages and salaries		14,785	
Interest on loan		1,000	
Rates		1,250	
Advertising		620	
Heating and lighting		1,640	
Sundry expenses		790	
Repairs to building		1,125	21,825
Net profit			10,531

b

Billy Cooper
Balance Sheet as at 31 December 19x0

	£	£	£
Fixed Assets:			
Land and buildings			25,000
Fixtures			4,500
			29,500
Current Assets:			
Stock		25,750	
Debtors		12,350	
Cash at bank		2,380	
Cash in hand		175	
		40,655	
Less Current Liabilities:			
Creditors		9,780	
Net Current Assets:			30,875
			60,375
Less Longterm Liabilities:			
Loan from R. McKay			10,000
			50,375
Financed by:			
Capital			50,344
Add net profit			10,531
			60,875
Less drawings			10,500
			50,375

12 a

C. Dickens
Trading and Profit and Loss account for the year ended 31 December 19x2

	£	£	£
Sales			110,250
Less Returns inwards			750
			109,500
Less cost of sales:			
Opening stock		12,000	
Add purchases	85,900		
Less returns out	875	85,025	
Carriage in		705	
		92,730	
Less closing stock		20,190	65,540
Gross profit			43,960
Add discount received			910
			44,870
Less expenses:			
Discount allowed		320	
Rates		1,480	
Interior decorations		1,200	
Interest		750	
Salaries and wages		18,750	
Heating and lighting		1,830	
Motor expenses		2,310	
Insurance		950	
General expenses		880	28,470
Net profit			16,400

b

C. Dickens
Balance Sheet as at 31 December 19x2

	£	£	£
Fixed Assets:			
Premises			30,000
Fixtures			3,500
Motor vehicles			7,000
			40,500
Current Assets:			
Stock		20,190	
Debtors		15,900	
Cash at bank		2,225	
Cash in hand		250	
		38,565	
Less Current Liabilities:			
Creditors		16,800	
Net Current Assets:			21,765
			62,265
Less Longterm Liabilities:			
Loan from J. Austin			7,500
			54,765
Financed by:			
Capital			48,565
Add net profit			16,400
			64,965
Less drawings			10,200
			54,765

Chapter 9

Activity 9.1 (page 136)

1 a Accrued expense
  b Yes, you show it as an addition to the heating and lighting expense figure given in the Trial Balance.
  c Yes, you show this item as an accrual under Current Liabilities.

2

Insurance a/c

			£				£
May	5	Bank	800	Dec	31	Profit & Loss a/c	1,200
Oct	8	Bank	800	Dec	31	Balance b/d	400
			1,600				1,600
Jan	1	Balance b/d	400				

3 Any non–trading income due for the year but not yet received will be shown as income and added to gross profit.

4

Rent receivable a/c

			£				£
Dec	31	Profit & Loss a/c	3,600	Jan	2	Bank	900
				Apr	3	Bank	900
				July	2	Bank	900
				Dec	31	Balance c/d	900
			3,600				3,600
Jan	1	Balance b/d	900				

This balance will be shown as a current asset in the Balance Sheet.

Activity 9.2 (page 137)

1 B 2 A

4 a

Arthur King
Trading and Profit and Loss account for the year ended 31 December 19x2

	£	£	£
Sales			120,250
Less returns inwards			600
			119,650
Less cost of sales:			
Opening stock		22,400	
Add purchases	99,900		
Less returns out	650	99,250	
		121,650	
Less closing stock		25,880	95,770
Gross profit			23,880
Add discount received			800
			24,680

	£	£	£
Less expenses:			
Business rates		3,500	
Wages	6,800		
Add amount due	250	7,050	
Heating and lighting		2,600	
Motor van expenses		5,750	
Discount allowed		560	
Sundry expenses		2,880	
Insurance	2,860		
Less amount prepaid	715	2,145	24,485
Net profit			195

b

Arthur King
Balance Sheet as at 31 December 19x2

	£	£	£
Fixed Assets:			
Premises			45,500
Fixtures			4,500
Motor van			12,600
			62,600
Current Assets:			
Stocks		25,880	
Trade debtors		10,300	
Prepayments		715	
Cash in hand		800	
		37,695	
Less Current Liabilities:			
Trade creditors	20,950		
Accruals	250		
Bank overdraft	7,000	28,200	
Net Current Assets:			9,495
			72,095
Financed by:			
Capital			80,300
Add net profit			195
			80,495
Less drawings			8,400
			72,095

Chapter 10

Activity 10.1 (page 144)

1 Every businessman knows from experience that a certain proportion of the total debtors fail to settle their debts each year. If nothing is done about it, the profits of the business will be overstated. It is therefore common practice to make a provision for bad debts so that a more realistic net profit figure is obtained at the end of any given year.

2 • debit the Bad Debts account
• credit the Debtors account

3 The effect of bad debts is to reduce the net profit of a business.

4 Only the increase in provision for bad and doubtful debts – that is £100 in this case – will be shown as an expense in the Profit and

Loss account and the new provision – i.e. £250 – will be shown as a deduction from the debtors' figure in the Balance Sheet.

5 Add the decrease in provision for bad debts – i.e. £100 – to the gross profit in the Profit and Loss account, because a decrease in provision is similar to an unexpected gain.
In the Balance Sheet, the new provision – £100 – will be deducted from the debtors' figure.

Activity 10.2 (page 145)

1 C 2 D

4 a

Tip Top Dealers Ltd
Provision for Doubtful Debts account

		£			£
19x9			19x9		
31 May	Profit and Loss	168	June 1	Balance b/d	410
31 May	Balance c/d (see Note 1)	242			
		410			410
19x9			19x9		
			June 1	Balance b/d	242

Note 1

	£	£
Sales ledger debit at 31 May 19x9 balance		12,360.00
Less bad debts written off:		
L. Pink	210.00	
G. Slack	50.00	260.00
		12,100.00

Provision for doubtful debts at 31 May 19x9
= 2% of £12,100 = £242.00

b **Balance Sheet as at 31 May 19x9**

	£
Debtors (see Note 2)	12,512
Creditors (see Note 3)	8,064

Note 2

	£
Debtors	
Sales Ledger Control account (DR balance)	12,360
Less bad debts written off (see Note 1)	260
	12,100
Less provision for doubtful debts	242
	11,858
Purchases Ledger Control account (DR balance)	654
	12,512

Note 3

	£
Creditors	
Purchases Ledger Control account (CR balance)	7,348
Sales Ledger Control account (CR balance)	716
	8,064

Chapter 11

Activity 11.1 (page 152)

1 Annual depreciation = $\frac{£35{,}000 - £5{,}000}{10} = \frac{£30{,}000}{10} = £3{,}000$

2 $r = 1 - \sqrt[n]{\frac{R}{C}} = 1 - \sqrt[5]{\frac{2{,}000}{15{,}000}} = 1 - \sqrt[5]{0.133}$

$= 1 - 0.67 = 0.33$

$= 33\%$

3

Year	No. of unexpired years of asset life	Cost – residual value	Depreciation
1	5	35,000 – 5,000 30,000	$30{,}000 \times \frac{5}{15}$ = £10,000
2	4		$30{,}000 \times \frac{4}{15}$ = £8,000

4 Depreciation = £16,000 – £15,500 = £500

Activity 11.2 (page 156)

1

	£
Cost	2,500
Less depreciation	2,000
WDV	500
Proceeds of sale	600
Profit	100

2

	£
WDV	1,500
Less sale proceeds	1,200
Loss	300

3
- debit the Profit and Loss account
- credit the Provision for Depreciation account

4 **Asset disposal a/c**

Cost of the asset	*X*	Provision for depreciation	*X*
Cash	*X*		

The balancing figure will represent either a profit or a loss on disposal.

Activity 11.3 (page 162)

1 C 2 B

4 a

Equipment a/c

			£				£
19x5				19x5			
Jan	1	Balance b/d	10,000	Jan	1	Disposal – Equipment	10,000
Jan	1	Johnson & Johnson	13,000	Dec	31	Balance c/d	13,000
			23,000				23,000
19x6							
Jan	1	Balance b/d	13,000				

b

Provision for depreciation – Equipment a/c

			£				£
19x1				19x1			
Dec	31	Balance c/d	2,000	Dec	31	Profit & Loss a/c	2,000
19x2				19x2			
Dec	31	Balance c/d	4,000	Jan	1	Balance b/d	2,000
				Dec	31	Profit & Loss a/c	2,000
			4,000				4,000
19x3				19x3			
Dec	31	Balance c/d	6,000	Jan	1	Balance b/d	4,000
				Dec	31	Profit & Loss a/c	2,000
			6,000				6,000
19x4				19x4			
Dec	31	Balance c/d	8,000	Jan	1	Balance b/d	6,000
				Dec	31	Profit & Loss a/c	2,000
			8,000				8,000
19x5				19x5			
Dec	31	Disposal – Equipment	8,000	Jan	1	Balance b/d	8,000
Dec	31	Balance c/d	2,600	Dec	31	Profit & Loss a/c	2,600
			10,600				10,600
				19x6			
				Jan	1	Balance b/d	2,600

c

Disposal of equipment a/c

			£				£
19x5				19x5			
Jan	1	Equipment	10,000	Jan	1	Bank	2,500
Dec	31	Profit & Loss a/c	500	Dec	31	Provision for dep'n – Equipment	8,000
			10,500				10,500

d

Profit and Loss account for the year ended 31 December 19x5 (extract only)

Gross profit	*x*
Add profit on disposal of equipment	500

Balance Sheet as at 31 December 19x5

Fixed Assets:	£
Equipment at cost	13,000
Less depreciation	2,600
	10,400

6 a

Motor vehicles at cost a/c

			£				£
19x7				19x8			
Oct	1	Bank (van E676 TVX)	28,000	Dec	31	Lorry disposal (E438 CBA)	36,000
19x9				19x9			
		Bank Lorry E438 CBA	36,000	Sept	30	Balance c/d	75,720
			64,000				
Feb	1	Bank Van E779 GMS	16,000				
April	1	Direct labour Van E779 GMS	1,880				
		Direct material	3,200				
		Variable o'heads.	1370				
		Fixed overheads (0.25 · £5,080)	1,270				
July	1	Bank Van F934 KTA	24,000				
			111,720				111,720
19x9							
Oct	1	Balance b/d	75,720				

b

Provision for depreciation – Motor vehicles a/c

			£				£
19x8				19x8			
Dec	31	Lorry disposal E438 CBA	7,200	Sept	30	Profit & Loss a/c (Note 1)	11,000
19x9				19x9			
				Sept	30	Profit & Loss a/c (Note 2)	10,972
Sept	30	Balance c/d	14,772				
			21,972				21,972
				19x9			
				Oct	1	Balance b/d	14,772

c

Lorry (E438 CBA) disposal a/c

			£				£
19x8				19x8			
Dec	31	Motor vehicles at cost	36,000	Dec	31	Provision for depreciation – Motor vehicles	7,200
				Dec	31	John Kerry	21,680
				19x9			
				Sept	30	Profit & Loss a/c	7,120
			36,000				36,000

d **Motor vehicles – Insurance a/c**

			£			£
19x7				19x8		
Oct	1	Fairdeal Insurance (E676 TVX)	5,000	Sept 30	Profit & Loss a/c (Note 3)	8,750
				Sept 30	Balance c/d	1,250
19x8						
Jan	1	Fairdeal Insurance (E438 CBA)	5,000			
			10,000			10,000
19x8				19x9		
Oct	1	Balance b/d	1,250	Sept 30	Profit & Loss a/c (Note 4)	10,833
Oct	1	Fairdeal Insurance	5,000	Sept 30	Balance c/d	5,417
19x9						
Feb	1	Fairdeal Insurance	5,000			
July	1	Fairdeal Insurance	5,000			
			16,250			16,250
19x9						
Oct	1	Balance b/d	5,417			

Note 1

Calculation of provision for depreciation for the year ended 30 September 19x8:

E676 TVX 20% × £28,000 = £5,600

E438 CBA 20% × 0.75 $\left(=\frac{9}{12}\right)$ × £36,000 = £5,400

£11,000

Note 2

Calculation of provision for depreciation for the year ended 30 September 19x9:

E676 TVX 20% × £28,000 = £5,600

E438 CBA 20% × 0.25 $\left(=\frac{3}{12}\right)$ × £36,000 = £1,800

E779 GMS 20% × 0.5 $\left(=\frac{6}{12}\right)$ × £23,720 = £2,372

F493 KTA 20% × 0.25 $\left(=\frac{3}{12}\right)$ × £24,000 = £1,200

£10,972

Note 3

Calculation of insurance cost for the year ended 30 September 19x8:

E676 TVX 1 × £5,000 = £5,000

E438 CBA 0.75 $\left(=\frac{9}{12}\right)$ × £5,000 = £3,750

£8,750

Note 4

Calculation of insurance cost for the year ended 30 September 19x9:

E676 TVX 1 × £5,000 = £5,000

E438 CBA 0.25 $\left(=\frac{3}{12}\right)$ × £5,000 = £1,250

E779 GMS 0.67 $\left(=\frac{8}{12}\right)$ × £5,000 = £3,333

F493 KTA 0.25 $\left(=\frac{3}{12}\right)$ × £5,000 = £1,250

£10,833

10

Mr Chai
Trading and Profit and Loss account for the year ended 30 April 19x7

	£	£	£
Sales			259,870
Less returns in			5,624
			254,246
Less Cost of sales:			
Opening stock		15,654	
Add purchases	135,680		
Less returns out	13,407	122,273	
Carriage in		11,830	
		149,757	
Less closing stock		17,750	132,007
Gross profit			122,239
Add discount received			1,750
			123,989
Less expenses:			
Increase in provision for bad debts		223	
Discount allowed		2,306	
Carriage outwards		4,562	
Rent, rates and insurance	25,973		
Less insurance prepaid	1,120		
	24,853		
Rates prepaid	5,435	19,418	
Heating and lighting	11,010		
Add amount due	1,360	12,370	
Postage, stationery and telephone		2,410	
Advertising		5,980	
Salaries and wages		38,521	
Bad debts		2,008	
Depreciation		12,074	99,872
Net profit			21,117

Mr Chai
Balance Sheet as at 30 April 19x7

	£	£	£
Fixed Assets:			
Fixtures and fittings at cost			120,740
Less depreciation			63,020
			57,720
Current Assets:			
Stocks		17,750	
Trade debtors	24,500		
Less provision for bad debts	735	23,765	
Prepayments (1120+5435)		6,555	
Cash at bank		4,440	
Cash on hand		534	
		53,044	
Less Current Liabilities:			
Trade creditors	19,840		
Accruals	1,360	21,200	
Net Current Assets:			31,840
			89,564

Financed by:	
Capital	83,887
Add net profit	24,117
	108,004
Less drawings	18,440
	89,564

Chapter 12

Activity 12.1 (page 183)

a FIFO

b

Date	RECEIPTS			ISSUES			BALANCE		
	Quantity	Rate £	Value £	Quantity	Rate £	Value £	Quantity	Rate £	Value £
1983 Jan 2	100	5	500				100	5	500
Jan 6	200	5.20	1,040				100 + 200 300	5 5.20	500 + 1,040 1,540
Jan 8				100 + 50 150	5 5.20	500 + 260 760	150	5.20	780
Jan 12	250	5.30	1,325				150 + 250 400	5.20 5.30	780 + 1,325 2,105
Jan 15				150 + 70 220	5.20 5.30	780 + 371 1,151	180	5.30	954

c

Date	RECEIPTS			ISSUES			BALANCE		
	Quantity	Rate £	Value £	Quantity	Rate £	Value £	Quantity	Rate £	Value £
1983 Jan 2	100	5	500				100	5	500
Jan 6	200	5.20	1,040				100 + 200 300	5 5.20	500 + 1,040 1,540
Jan 8				150	5.20	780	100 + 50 150	5 5.20	500 + 260 760
Jan 12	250	5.30	1,325				100 50 + 250 400	5 5.20 5.30	500 260 + 1,325 2,085
Jan 15				220	5.30	1,166	100 50 + 30 180	5 5.20 5.30	500 260 + 159 919

Activity 12.2 (page 185)

1 B **2** B **3** A **4** D

6

Purchases Ledger control a/c

	£		£
19x2		19x2	
Apr 30 Returns outwards	3,540	Apr 1 Balance b/d	25,690
Apr 30 Cash/Bank	75,350	Apr 30 Purchases Day Book	83,938
Apr 30 Discount rec'd	2,129		
Apr 30 Balance c/d	28,609		
	109,628		109,628
		May 1 Balance b/d	28,609

8 a

Creditors control a/c

	£		£
Returns outwards	21,555	Balance b/f	96,504
Set off to sales ledger	5,454	Purchases	874,210
Discount received	16,350		
Cash	820,311		
Balance b/f	107,044		–
	970,714		970,714

b Journal entries

	DR £	CR £
Purchases a/c	180	
Creditors Control a/c		180
Creditors Control a/c	211	
Returns Outwards a/c		211
Creditors Control a/c	60	
Purchases a/c		60

c Corrected Control a/c

Creditors Control a/c

	£		£
Returns Outwards	211	Uncorrected balance b/f	107,044
Purchases	60	Purchases	180
Corrected balance c/f	106,953		
	107,224		107,224

d

	£
Total of balances on individual creditors a/cs	106,984
Add increase in invoice value	180
	107,164
Less debit note not entered	211
Corrected total of individual creditor balances	106,953

e If the totals in **c** and **d** agree, there is evidence that all entries in the a/cs are correct and that the correct total for creditors as at 30 November 19x9 is £106,953. However there still could be some errors which would not affect the equality of the two totals e.g. an invoice missed out altogether.

10 a (i) Stores Ledger a/c: FIFO method

Date	RECEIPTS			ISSUES			BALANCE		
	Quantity	Rate £	Value £	Quantity	Rate £	Value £	Quantity	Rate £	Value £
19x1 Jan	100	50	5,000				100	50	5,000
Feb	50	55	2,750				100 + 50 150	50 55	5,000 + 2,750 7,750
March				30	50	1,500	70 + 50 120	50 55	3,500 + 2,750 6,250
April	80	61	4,880				70 50 + 80 200	50 55 61	3,500 2,750 + 4,880 11,130
May				70 + 40 110	50 55	3,500 + 2,200 5,700	10 + 80 90	55 61	550 + 4,800 5,430
June				10 + 40 50	55 61	550 + 2,440 2,990	40	61	2,440

The value of Closing stock using FIFO is £2,440.

(ii) Stores Ledger a/c: LIFO method

Date	RECEIPTS			ISSUES			BALANCE		
	Quantity	Rate £	Value £	Quantity	Rate £	Value £	Quantity	Rate £	Value £
19x1 Jan	100	50	5,000				100	50	5,000
Feb	50	55	2,750				100 + 50 150	50 55	5,000 + 2,750 7,750
March				30	55	1,650	100 + 20 120	50 55	5,000 + 1,100 6,100
April	80	61	4,880				100 20 + 80 200	50 55 61	5,000 1,100 + 4,880 10,980
May				80 20 + 10 110	61 55 61	4,880 1,100 + 610 6,590	90	50	4,500
June				50	50	2,500	40	50	2,000

The value of Closing stock using LIFO is £2,000.

(iii) Stores Ledger a/c: AVCO method

Date	RECEIPTS			ISSUES			BALANCE		
	Quantity	Rate £	Value £	Quantity	Rate £	Value £	Quantity	Rate £	Value £
19x1 Jan	100	50	5,000				100	50	5,000
Feb	50	55	2,750				100 + 50 150	50 55 51.67	5,000 2,750 7,750
March				30	51.67	1,550	120	51.67	6,200
April	80	61	4,880				120 + 80 200	51.67 61 55.4	6,200 4,880 11,080
May				110	55.4	6,094	90	55.4	4,986
June				50	55.4	2,770	40	55.4	2,216

The value of Closing stock using AVCO is £2,216.

b Trading account for the six months ending 30 June 19x1

	FIFO		LIFO		AVCO	
	£	£	£	£	£	£
Sales (note 1)		14,720		14,720		14,720
Less cost of sales: Purchases	12,630		12,630		12,630	
Less closing stock	2,440	10,190	2,000	10,630	2,216	10,414
Gross profit		4,530		4,090		4,306

Note 1

Sales for the six months:		£
March	30 @ £75	2,250
May	110 @ £77	8,470
June	50 @ £80	4,000
		14,720

Note 2

Purchases		£
January	100 @ £50	5,000
February	50 @ £55	2,750
April	80 @ £61	4,880
		12,630

12 a Perpetual Inventory Method: FIFO

Date	RECEIPTS			ISSUES			BALANCE		
	Quantity	Rate £	Value £	Quantity	Rate £	Value £	Quantity	Rate £	Value £
19x1 July	260	20	5,200				260	20	5,200
August				120	20	2,400	140	20	2,800
Sept	140	21	2,940				140 +140 280	20 21	2,800 + 2,940 5,740
Oct				140 + 20 160	20 21	2,800 420 3,220	120	21	2,520
Nov	180	22	3,960				120 +180 300	21 22	2,500 + 3,960 6,480
Dec				120	21	2,520	180	22	3,960

Perpetual Inventory Method: LIFO

Date	RECEIPTS			ISSUES			BALANCE		
	Quantity	Rate £	Value £	Quantity	Rate £	Value £	Quantity	Rate £	Value £
19x1 July	260	20	5,200				260	20	5,200
Aug				120	20	2,400	140	20	2,800
Sept	140	21	2,940				140 + 140 280	20 21	2,400 + 2,940 5,740
Oct				20 + 140 160	20 21	400 + 2,900 3,340	120	20	2,400
Nov	180	22	3,960				120 + 180 300	20 22	2,400 + 3,960 6,360
Dec				120	22	2,640	120 + 60 180	20 22	2,400 + 1,320 3,720

b Valuation of closing stock based on periodic inventory valuation method:

FIFO Method:	180	@ £22 =	£3,960
LIFO Method:	60	@ £22 =	£1,320
	120	@ £20 =	£2,400
	180		£3,720

c

Trading and Profit and Loss account for the six months ended 31 December 19x1

	FIFO		LIFO	
	£	£	£	£
Sales (Note 1)		10,460		10,460
Less cost of sales				
Purchases (Note 2)	11,960		11,960	
Less closing stock	3,960	8,000	3,660	8,240
		2,460		2,220
Less expenses		600		600
Net profit		1,860		1,620

			£
Note 1	Sales		£
Aug	120 @ £26	=	3,120
Oct	160 @ £26	=	4,160
Dec	120 @ £26.50	=	3,180
			10,460
Note 2	Purchases		
July	260 @ £20	=	5,200
Sept	140 @ £20	=	2,800
Nov	180 @ £22	=	3,960
			11,960

d

Balance Sheet as at 31 December 19x1

	FIFO		LIFO	
	£	£	£	£
Fixed Assets:		10,000		10,000
Current Assets				
Stock	3,960		3,720	
Bank (Note 1)	2,900	6,860	2,900	6,620
		16,860		16,720
Opening capital (£10,000 + £5,000)		15,000		15,000
Add net profit		1,860		1,620
		16,860		16,620

Note 1 It is assumed that all purchases and sales are for cash only.

	£
Opening balance	5,000
Add sales receipts	10,460
	15,460
Less purchases	11,960
	3,500
Less expenses	600
Closing cash balance	2,900

Chapter 14

Activity 14.1 (page 214)

1 Capital = £33,500 – £20,150 = £13,350

2 a Profit = £20,000 – £15,000 = £ 5,000
b Profit = £20,000 – £15,000 + £2,000 = £7,000

3 Profit = £21,000 – £18,500 + £3,000 – £2,000 = £ 3,500

Activity 14.2 (page 217)

1 a Cost of sales = £6,500 + £15,000 – £7,500 = £14,000

$$40\% = \frac{GP}{14{,}000 + GP}$$

0.4(14,000 + GP) = GP

or 5,600 + 0.4 × GP = GP

or 5,600 = GP – 0.4 × GP = 0.6 × GP

$$\text{Therefore GP} = \frac{5{,}600}{0.6} = £9{,}333$$

Therefore S = £14,000 + £9,333 = £23,333

b $$\frac{1}{3} = \frac{GP}{14{,}000}$$

$$\text{Therefore GP} = \frac{1}{3} \times 14{,}000 = £4{,}667$$

Sales = £14,000 + £4,667 = £18,667

c $$0.3 = \frac{GP}{30{,}000}$$

Therefore GP = 30,000 × 0.3 = £9,000

d $$0.25 = \frac{GP}{COS} = \frac{GP}{50{,}000 - GP}$$

Therefore 0.25(50,000 – GP) = GP

or 12,500 – 0.25 × GP = GP

or 12,500 = GP + 0.25 × GP

or 12,500 = 1.25 × GP

$$\text{Therefore GP} = \frac{12{,}500}{1.25} = £10{,}000$$

2 a Cost of sales = £8,000 + £20,000 – £7,150 = £20,850

$$\text{Now } 0.2 = \frac{GP}{28{,}850}$$

Therefore GP = 0.2 × 20,850 = £4,170

b Sales = £20,850 + £4,170 = £25,020

3 a $$0.3 = \frac{GP}{40{,}000}$$

Therefore GP = 0.3 × 40,000 = £12,000

Therefore cost of sales = £40,000 – £12,000 = £28,000

Therefore purchases = £28,000 + £5,900 – £6,250 = £27,650

Activity 14.3 (page 224)

1 A 2 C 3 D 4 D 5 C

6 a

Jim Hodges

Statement of affairs as at 1 January 19x1

	£	£	£
Fixed Assets:			
Premises at cost			20,000
Fixtures at WDV			1,600
			21,600
Current Assets:			
Stocks		6,350	
Debtors		4,800	
Prepayments		500	
Cash at bank		1,000	
Cash in hand		200	
		12,850	
Less Current Liabilities:			
Creditors	7,000		
Accruals	200	7,200	
Net Current Assets			5,650
			27,250
Financed by:			
Capital			27,250

b

Jim Hodges

Statement of affairs as at 31 December 19x1

	£	£	£
Fixed Assets:			
Premises at cost			20,000
Fixtures at WDV			1,400
			21,400
Current Assets:			
Stocks		5,980	
Debtors		5,500	
Prepayments		350	
Cash at bank		250	
Cash in hand		300	
		12,380	
Less Current Liabilities:			
Creditors	6,200		
Accruals	400	6,600	
Net Current Assets:			5,780
			27,180
Financed by:			
Capital			27,180

c

	£
Capital at close of year	27,180
Less capital at start of year	27,250
	(70)
Add drawings	4,800
Net profit	4,730

8 a

Mary Grimes

Trading and Profit and Loss account for the year ended 31 August 19x8

	£	£
Sales (W1)		98,180
Less cost of sales:		
Opening stock	4,900	
Purchases (W2)	70,990	
	75,890	
Less closing stock	5,900	69,990
Gross profit		28,190
Add discount received		1,100
Add profit on sale of motor vehicle (W3)		100
		29,390
Less expenses:		
Rent and rates (W4)	2,660	
Repairs and renewals	650	
Insurances (W5)	760	
Wages	15,100	
Postages and stationery	1,360	
Motor vehicle expenses	3,350	
Motor vehicle depreciation	2,600	
Bad debts written off	300	26,780
Net Profit		2,610

b

Mary Grimes

Balance Sheet as at 31 August 19x8

	£	£	£
Fixed Assets:			
Motor vehicles, at cost		13,000	
Less provision for depreciation		2,600	10,400
Current Assets:			
Stock in trade		5,900	
Trade debtors (W6)		9,200	
Prepayments		200	
Balance at bank		2,010	
		17,310	
Less Current Liabilities:			
Trade Creditors	2,590		
Accruals	260	2,850	
Net Current Assets:			14,460
			24,860
Represented by:			
Capital – 1 Sept 19x7 (W7)			11,450
Add sale of private yacht			20,000
Net profit of the year			2,610
			34,060
Less drawings			9,200
			24,860

for workings see page 420

Workings

W1: Sales	£
Trade debtors at 31 August 19x8	9,500
Receipts from debtors	96,000
	105,500
Less trade debtors at 1 Sept 19x7	7,320
	98,180

W2: Purchases	
Creditors at 31 August 19x8	2,590
Prepayments to suppliers	72,000
Discounts received	1,100
	75,690
Less creditors at 1 Sept 19x7	4,700
	70,990

W3: Sale of motor vehicle (A123 BWA)	
At Cost	10,000
Less provision for depreciation at 1 Sept 19x7	8,000
	2,000
Sale proceeds	2,100
Profit on sale	100

W4: Rent and rates	
Accruals at 31 August 19x8	260
Payments	2,600
	2,860
Less accruals at 1 Sept 19x7	200
	2,660

W5: Insurances	
Prepaid at 1 Sept 19x7	160
Payments	800
	960
Less prepaid at 31 August 19x8	200
	760

W6: Trade debtors	
At 31 August 19x8	9,500
Less bad debts written off	300
	9,200

W7: Capital at 1 Sept 19x7	£	£	£
Motor Vehicle at cost		10,000	
Less provision for depreciation		8,000	2,000
Stock in trade		4,900	
Trade debtors		7,320	
Prepayments		160	
Bank		1,970	
		14,350	
Less : Trade Creditors	4,700		
Accruals	200	4,900	9,450
			11,450

Chapter 15

Activity 15.1 (page 235)

1

Subscription a/c

	£		£
Balance b/d (in arrears)	475	Balance b/d (in advance)	225
Ide Account	12,465	Cash	12,580
Balance c/d	180	Balance c/d	315
	13,120		13,120

Alternatively:

	£
Cash received during 19x1	12,580
Add amount received in the previous year for 19x1	225
	12,805
Less amount received this year for the last year	475
	12,330
Add amount due for this year	315
	12,645
Less amount received in the current year for the next year	180
Amount transferred to Income and Expenditure a/c	12,465

2

Creditors Control a/c

	£		£
Cash	25,800	Balance b/d	10,100
Balance c/d	9,950	Purchases	25,650
	35,750		35,750

Bar Trading account for the year ended 31 March 19x2

	£	£
Sales		40,500
Less Cost of sales:		
Opening stock	12,900	
Add Purchases	25,650	
	38,550	
Less Closing stock	11,850	26,700
Gross profit		13,800

Activity 15.2 (page 240)

1 C **2** D **3** A **4** B **5** D

6 b

Allage Sporting Club
Income and Expenditure account
for the year ended 31 December 19x2

	£	£	£
Income:			
Donations			5,750
Subscriptions (W1)			2,675
Profit from the sale of refreshments (W2)			1,500
Sale of lottery		2,000	
Less lottery ticket prizes		560	1,440
			11,365
Less expenses:			
Insurance, water and community charges	1,050		
Less amount prepaid	250		
		800	
Lighting and heating	800		
Add electricity bill due	250	1,050	
General expenses		972	
Depreciation of equipment (£13,000 + £9,750)		3,250	6,072
Surplus of income over expenditure			5,293

Workings

W1: Subscriptions	£
Cash collected for 19x2	2,500
Subscriptions owing	175
	2,675

W2: Income from the sale of refreshments

	£	£
Sales of refreshments		4,500
Less cost of sales:		
Opening stock	5,000	
Add purchases	2,800	
	7,800	
Less closing stock	4,800	3,000
Profit		1,500

Allage Sporting Club
Balance Sheet as at 31 December 19x2

	£	£	£
Fixed Assets:			
Land and Buildings	150,000	–	150,000
Equipment	13,000	3,250	9,750
	163,000	3,250	159,750
Current Assets:			
Bar stocks		4,800	
Sales in advance and subscriptions in arrears		175	
Prepayments		250	
Bank		16,068	
		21,293	
Less Current Liabilities:			
Subscriptions paid in advance	500		
Accruals	250	750	
Net Current Assets:			20,543
			180,293
Represented by:			
Accumulated fund – 1.1.x2			175,000
Add surplus of income over expenditure			5,293
			180,293

8 a

Subscription account for the year ended 31 May 19x9

	£		£
Subscriptions in arrears b/d	278	Subscriptions in advance b/d	90
Income and expenditure a/c	6,024	Cash and Bank	6,127
Subscriptions in advance c/d	135	Subscriptions in arrears c/d	220
	6,437		6,437

b

Regalia Trading account for the year ended 31 May 19x9

	£	£
Sales		1,880
Less cost of sales:		
Opening stock	255	
Purchases (W1)	1,288	
	1,543	
Less closing stock	298	1,245
Profit		635

Workings

W1: Calculation of purchases of Regalia	£
Cash paid	1,145
Less amount owing to suppliers at start of year	228
	917
Add amount owing to suppliers at close of year	371
Purchases	1,288

c

The Monarchs MCC
Income and Expenditure account for the year ended 31 May 19x9

	£	£	£
Income:			
Subscriptions			6,024
Donations			350
Profit on sale of regalia			635
Less expenses:			
Secretarial expenses		440	
Rent		2,750	
Meeting expenses		2,200	
Subscription to National Body		500	
Stationery and printing		345	
Depreciation		683	6,918
Surplus of income over expenditure			91

10 a

Calculation of Accumulated Funds as at 1 August 19x5

	£	£
Assets:		
Equipment		975
Subscriptions in arrears		65
Stocks of competition prizes		38
Cash and bank balances		210
		1,288
Less Liabilities:		
Subscriptions in advance	10	
Suppliers of competition prizes	58	68
Accumulated Funds		1,220

b (i)

Subscription a/c

		£			£
19x5			19x5		
Aug 1	Balance b/f (Subs in arrears)	65	Aug 1	Balance b/f (subs in advance)	10
19x6			19x6		
July 31	Income & expenditure	1,980	July 31	Receipts & payments	1,987
July 31	Balance c/f (subs in advance)	37	July 31	Balance c/f (subs in arrears)	85
		2,082			2,082

(ii)

Competition prizes a/c

			£				£
19x5				19x5			
Aug	1	Balance b/f (stocks)	38	Aug	1	Balance b/f (creditors)	58
19x6				19x6			
July	31	Receipts & payments	270	July	31	Stocks c/f	46
July	31	Creditors c/f	68	July	31	Cost of prizes used	272
			376				376

c

Miniville Rotary Club
Income and Expenditure account for the year ended 31 July 19x6

	£	£
Income:		
Subscriptions		1,980
Competition ticket sales	437	
Less cost of sales	272	165
Rent refund		500
Donations		177
		2,822
Less expenses:		
Secretarial expenses	163	
Rent	1,402	
Visiting speakers' expenses	1,275	
Stationery and printing	179	
Donations to charity	35	
Depreciation	195	3,249
Deficit for the year		(427)

Miniville Rotary Club
Balance Sheet as at 31 July 19x6

	£	£	£
Fixed Assets:			
Equipment, at cost		1,420	
Less accumulated depreciation (W1)		640	780
Current Assets:			
Stocks of competition prizes		46	
Subscriptions in arrears		85	
		131	
Less Current Liabilities:			
Suppliers of competition prizes	68		
Subs in advance	37		
Bank and cash	13	118	
			13
			793
Accumulated fund			
As at 1 August 19x5			1,220
Less deficit for the year			427
			793

Workings

W1 **Equipment a/c**

		£			£
19x5			19x6		
Aug 1	Balance b/d	975	July 31	Depreciation	195
			July 31	Balance c/d	780
		975			975

Chapter 16

Activity 16.1 (page 247)

Statement of cost of raw materials used

	£	£
Opening stock of materials		7,500
Add Purchases	49,500	
Less Returns out	2,250	47,250
Add carriage on purchases		750
		55,500
Less closing stock		8,250
Cost of materials used		47,250

Activity 16.2 (page 248)

Statement of prime cost

	£	£
Opening stock of materials		10,000
Add Purchases	60,500	
Less Returns out	2,500	58,000
Add Carriage on purchases		1,500
		69,500
Less Closing stock		8,900
Cost of material used		60,600
Add Direct wages		27,500
Add Royalties		5,000
		93,100

Activity 16.3 (page 250)

Anne Hart Manufacturing account for the year ended 31 March 19x0

	£	£
Opening stock of materials		8,000
Add Purchases	65,000	
Less Returns out	1,500	63,500
Add Carriage in		900
		72,400
Less Closing stock of materials		11,500
Cost of materials used		60,900
Add Manufacturing wages		29,750
Royalties		1,200
Prime Cost		91,850
Add Production overheads:		
Indirect factory wages	12,250	
Factory rent and rates	5,800	

	£	£
Factory power	5,500	
Factory heating and lighting	3,750	
Factory general expenses	4,750	
Depreciation plant & machinery	2,750	34,800
Production cost of goods completed		126,650

Activity 16.4 (page 251)

Anne Hart
Adjusted Manufacturing account for the year ended 31 March 19x0

	£	£
Opening stock of materials		8,000
Add Purchases	65,000	
Less Returns out	1,500	63,500
Add Carriage in		900
		72,400
Less Closing stock of materials		11,500
Cost of material used		60,900
Add Manufacturing wages		29,750
Royalties		1,200
Prime Cost		91,850
Add Production overheads:		
Indirect factory wages	12,250	
Factory rent and rates	5,800	
Factory power	5,500	
Factory heating and lighting	3,750	
Factory general expenses	4,750	
Depreciation plant & machinery	2,750	34,800
Production cost of the year		126,650
Add Opening WIP		5,150
		131,800
Less Closing WIP		7,200
(Adjusted) Cost of goods completed		124,600

Activity 16.5 (page 253)

Didar Singh
Trading account for the year ended 31 March 19x0

	£	£
Sales		100,000
Less Cost of goods sold:		
Opening stock of finished goods	8,800	
Add Cost of goods manufactured	57,500	
Add Purchases of finished goods	10,000	
	76,300	
Less Closing stock of finished goods.	9,250	67,050
Gross profit		32,950

Activity 16.6 (page 257)

1 D **2** A **3** C **4** B **5** C

6

Dot Ashworth
Manufacturing account for the year
ended 31 March 19x3

	£	£	£
Opening stock of raw materials			20,250
Add purchases of raw materials			160,900
Add carriage on purchases			1,100
			182,250
Less closing stock of raw materials			25,950
Cost of raw materials used			156,300
Add maunfacturing wages		65,750	
Add manufacturing wages due		530	66,280
Prime Cost			222,580
Manufacturing overheads			
Power		20,320	
Manfacturing expenses		7,830	28,150
			250,730
Add opening work in progress			15,750
			266,480
Less closing work in progress			20,370
			246,110

Chapter 17

Activity 17.1 (page 266)

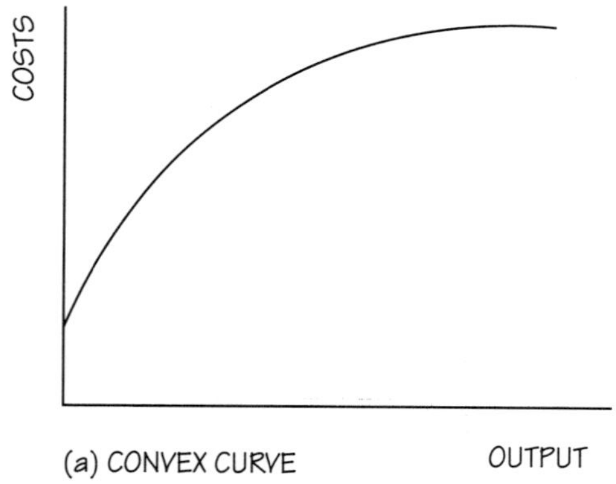

(a) CONVEX CURVE

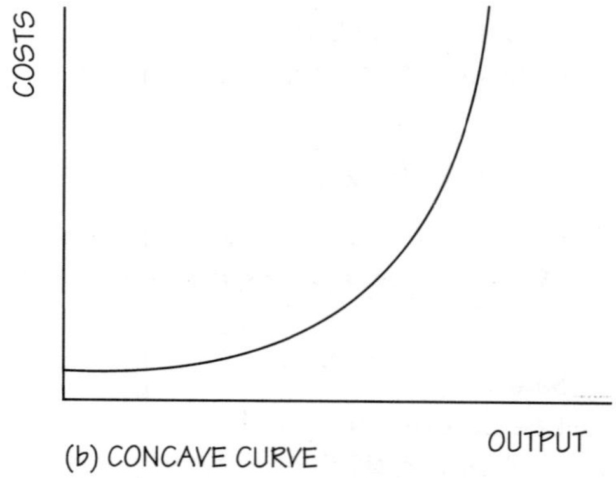

(b) CONCAVE CURVE

Non-linear semi-variable cost curves

Activity 17.2 (page 269)

1 **a** Contribution per unit = £25 – (£7 + £4 + £4)
= £25 – £15 = £10

b P/V ratio = $\frac{10}{25}$ = 0.4 or 40%

c BEP (in units) = $\frac{£40,000}{£10}$ = 4,000 units

d BEP (£) = $\frac{\text{£40.000}}{0.4}$ = £100,000

e $\frac{C}{\text{£130,000}} = 0.4$

Therefore C = £130,000 × 0.4 = £52,000

Therefore NP = £52,000 – £40,000 = £12,000

f C = £50,000 + £40,000 = £90,000

CPU = £10

Therefore sales in units required to earn a profit of £50,000

= $\frac{\text{£90,000}}{\text{£10}}$ = 9,000 units

g C = £60,000 + £40,000 = £100,000

$\frac{\text{£100,000}}{S} = 0.4$

Therefore S = $\frac{\text{£100,000}}{0.4}$ = £250,000

2 Change in sales = £20,000

Change in profit= £5,000

The change in profit is simply the change in contribution as fixed costs are – by definition – fixed. Therefore, the contribution from £20,000 is simply £5,000.

a P/V ratio $\frac{\text{£5,000}}{\text{£20,000}} = \frac{1}{4}$ = 0.25 or 25%

b To determine the BEP we need to calculate the fixed costs as follows.

	1st Year	2nd Year	Change
	£	£	£
Sales	100,000	120,000	20,000
Profit	20,000	25,000	5,000
TC	80,000	95,000	15,000

The change of £15,000 in total cost is due to the change in VC. Therefore the variable cost corresponding to sales of £20,000 is £15,000.

VC = $\frac{15,000}{20,000}$ × 100 = 75% of sales

Therefore VC in year 1 = £100,000 × 75% = £75,000

Therefore FC = TC – VC = £80,000 – £75,000 = £5,000

Therefore BEP (£) = $\frac{\text{£5,000}}{0.4}$ = £20,000

3 **a** P/V ratio = $\frac{\text{£200,000} - \text{£120,000}}{200,000} = \frac{80,000}{200,000} = \frac{2}{5}$ = 40%

b BEP (£) = $\frac{\text{£60,000}}{0.4}$ = £150,000

c C = £60,000 + £50,000 = £110,000

$\frac{\text{£100,000}}{S} = 0.4$

Therefore S = $\frac{\text{£100,000}}{0.4}$ = £275,000

Activity 17.3 (page 271)

1

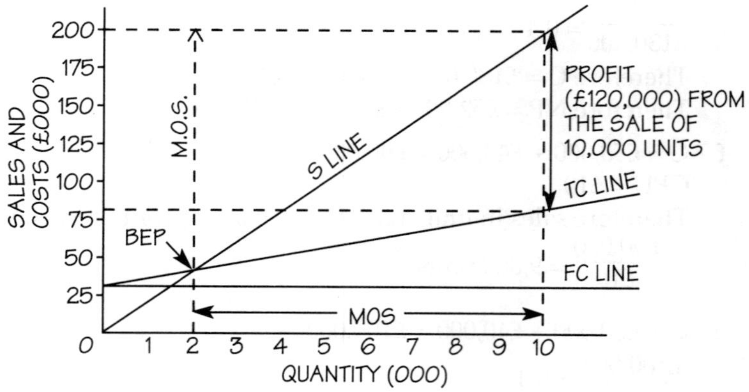

a BEP = 2,000 units or £40,000 of sales
b Expected profit = £120,000 from the sales of 100,000 units
c Margin of safety = 8,000 units or £160,000

2

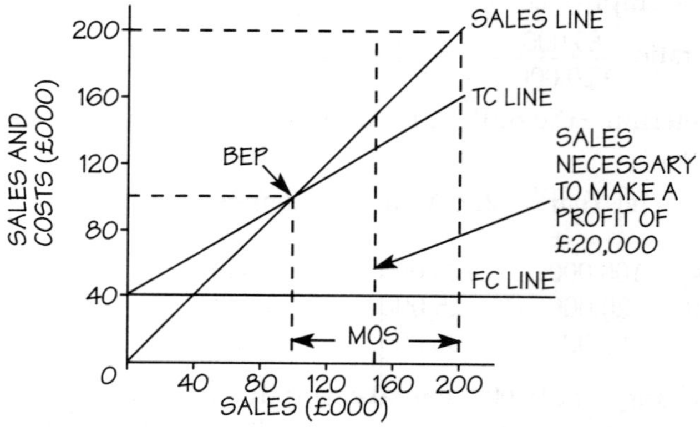

a BEP = £100,000
b Margin of safety = £200,000 – £100,000 = £100,000
c Sales necessary to make a profit of £20,000 = £150,000

Activity 17.4 (page 273)

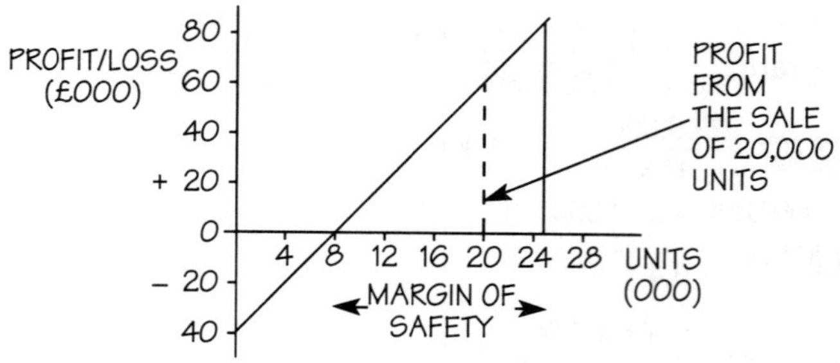

a BEP = £8,000
b Margin of safety = 25,000 – 8,000 = 17,000 units
c Profitfrom the sale of 20,000 units = £60,000

Activity 17.5 (page 275)

1 B **2** D **3** B **4** C **5** D

6 **a** Contribution per unit (CPU) = £20 – £12 = £8

b Total contribution = 50,000 × £8 = £400,000

c P/V ratio = $\frac{£8}{£20}$ = 0.4 = 40%

d BEP in units = $\frac{£50,000}{£8}$ = £6,250

e BEP (£) = $\frac{£50,000}{0.4}$ = £125,000

f Margin of safety = 50,000 – 6,250 = 43,750 units.

g

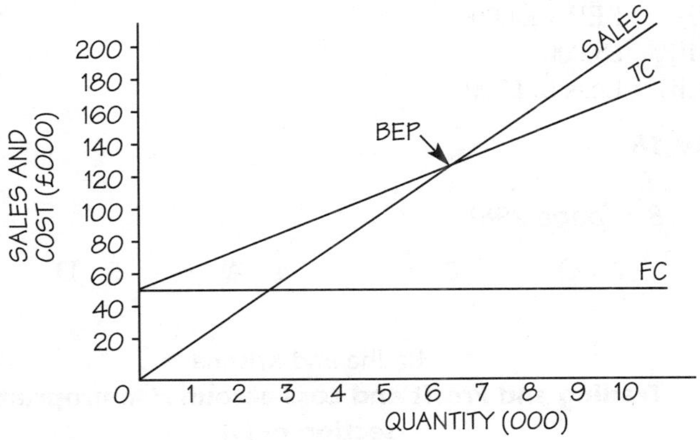

h, j, k

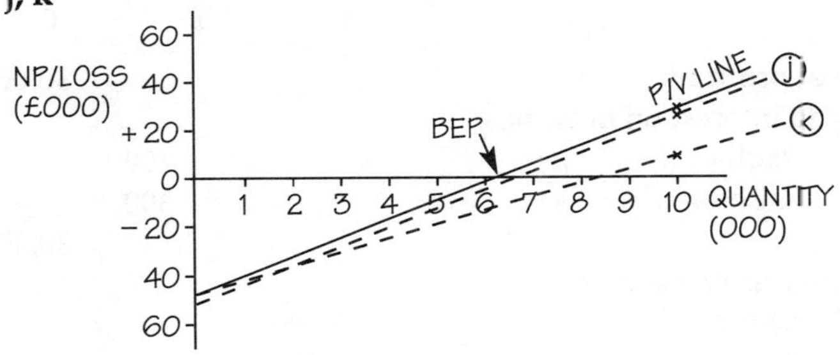

i C = NP + FC = £30,000 + £50,000 = £80,000

Now C = $\frac{0.4}{S}$

or £80,000 = 0.4 × 5

Therefore *S* = $\frac{£80,000}{0.4}$ = £200,000

Therefore sales in units to attain a net profit of £30,000

= $\frac{£80,000}{0.4}$ = 10,000 units

9 **a** BE sales in units = $\frac{£35,000}{£10}$ = 3,500 units

b BE sales (£) = $\frac{£35,000}{0.4}$ = £87,500

11 a

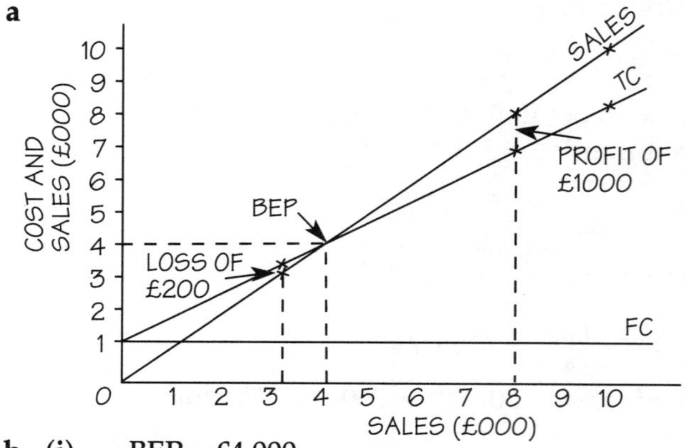

b **(i)** BEP = £4,000
(ii) £8,000
(iii) Loss of £200

Chapter 18

Activity 18.1 (page 298)

1 B **2** C **3** C **4** A **5** D

6 a

Radha and Krishna
Trading and Profit and Loss account (Appropriation section only)
for the year ended 30 June 19x2

	£	£	£
Net profit b/f			30,000
Add interest on drawings:			
Radha		150	
Krishna		300	450
			30,450
Interest on capitals:			
Radha	2,000		
Krishna	2,500	4,500	
Salary – Krishna		6,000	10,500
			19,950
Share of profits:			
Radha		9,975	
Krishna		9,975	19,950

b

Current accounts

	£	£		£	£
19x2			19x2		
	Radha	Krishna		Radha	Krishna
Jun 30 Interest on drawings	150	350	Jun 30 Interest on capital	2,000	2,500
Jun 30 Drawings	2,500	5,000	Jun 30 Salary		6,000
Jun 30 Balance c/d	9,325	13,125	Jun 30 Share of profits	9,975	9,975
	11,975	18,475		11,975	18,475
			July 1 Balance b/d	9,325	13,125

10 a Calculation of Interest on drawings

Ganatri

Date	Drawings	Rate	Proportion of year	Interest charged
31 Aug x8	10,000	12%	0.75	900
30 Nov x8	10,000	12%	0.50	600
28 Feb x9	10,000	12%	0.25	300
31 May x9	10,000	12%	0	0
	40,000			1,800

Lucifer

Date	Drawings	Rate	Proportion of year	Interest charged
31 Aug x8	7,000	12%	0.75	630
30 Nov x8	7,000	12%	0.50	420
28 Feb x9	7,000	12%	0.25	210
31 May x9	7,000	12%	0	0
	28,000			1,260

b

Ganatri and Lucifer
Appropriation account for the year ended 31 May 19x9

	£	£	£
Net profit for the year			102,940
Add interest on drawings			
Ganatri		1,800	
Lucifer		1,260	3,060
			106,000
Interest on capital			
Ganatri	25,800		
Lucifer	18,360	44,160	
Salaries – Lucifer		15,000	59,160
Balance divisible			
Ganatri		32,788	
Lucifer		14,052	46,840

c Current accounts

	£ Ganatri	£ Lucifer		£ Ganatri	£ Lucifer
Drawings	40,000	28,000	Balance b/f	15,000	13,000
Interest on drawings	1,800	1,260	Interest on capital and current a/cs	25,800	18,360
Balance c/d	31,788	31,152	Salaries		15,000
			Share of profits	32,788	14,052
	73,588	60,412		73,588	60,412
			Balance b/d	31,788	31,152

12 a When Goodwill account is maintained:

Capital accounts

P	$\frac{2}{10}$	7,200
Q	$\frac{3}{10}$	10,800
R	$\frac{4}{10}$	14,400
S	$\frac{1}{10}$	3,600
		36,000

The Capital accounts will be credited with the relevant amounts. Thus the partners' new capitals will be as follows:

	Opening capital	Goodwill	New capital
	£	£	£
P	14,000	7,200	21,200
Q	6,400	10,800	17,200
R	10,000	14,400	24,400
S	7,200	3,600	10,800
			73,600

P, Q, R and S
Balance Sheet as at 1 July 19x9

	£
Goodwill	36,000
Net assets (excluding goodwill)	37,600
	73,600
Capitals:	
P	21,200
Q	17,200
R	24,400
S	10,800
	73,600

b When Goodwill account is not maintained:
In this case Goodwill will be written off in the new profit-sharing ratios. Starting with the capital balances as in **a** above, we show the effect of deletion of Goodwill on the Capital balances.

		Capital balances as above	Goodwill written	Adjusted capital balance
		£	£	£
P	$\frac{3}{12}$	21,200	9,000	12,200
Q	$\frac{4}{12}$	17,200	12,000	5,200
R	$\frac{3}{12}$	24,400	9,000	15,400
S	$\frac{2}{12}$	10,800	6,000	4,800
			36,000	37,600

P, Q, R and S
Balance Sheet as at 1 July 19x9

	£
Net assets (excluding goodwill)	37,600
Capitals:	
P	12,200
Q	5,200
R	15,400
S	4,800
	37,600

14 a The Journal

	DR	CR
	£	£
Goodwill	12,000	
Capital account – Right		6,000
Capital account – Left		6,000
Being the division of goodwill between the existing partners		
Bank	14,000	
Capital account – Centre		14,000
Introduction of capital by Centre		

b

Right, Left and Centre
Balance Sheet after admission of Centre

			£
Fixed and current assets excluding cash and goodwill			30,000
Goodwill			12,000
Cash		(£4,000 + £14,000)	18,000
			60,000
Capitals:	Right	(£16,000 + £6,000)	22,000
	Left	(£8,000 + £6,000)	14,000
	Centre		14,000
			50,000
Current liabilities			10,000
			60,000

c The Journal

		DR	CR
		£	£
Capital:			
Right – $\frac{4}{10}$	4,800		
Left – $\frac{3}{10}$	3,600		
Centre – $\frac{3}{10}$	3,600		
		12,000	
Goodwill written off			12,000

15

Freehold property a/c

		£			£
19x9			19x9		
Oct 1	Balance b/d	60,000	Sept 30	Realization	60,000

Equipment a/c

		£			£
19x9			19x9		
Oct 30	Balance b/d	30,000	Sept 30	Realization	30,000

Stocks a/c

		£			£
19x9			19x9		
Oct 1	Balance b/d	16,000	Sept 30	Realization	16,000

Debtors a/c

		£			£
19x8			19x9		
Oct 1	Balance b/d	9,000	Sept 30	Realization	9,000

Bank a/c

		£			£
19x9			19x9		
Oct 1	Bank b/d	4,200	Sept 30	Loan a/c – B	4,000
Sept 30	Realization (freehold premises)	62,000	Sept 30	Creditors	5,800
Sept 30	Equipment	9,600	Sept 30	Realization	1,600
Sept 30	Stocks	5,800	Sept 30	Capital a/c – A	67,400
Sept 30	Debtors	9,000	Sept 30	Capital a/c – B	13,400
Sept 30	Capital a/c – C	1,600			
		92,200			92,200

Creditors a/c

		£			£
19x9			19x9		
Sept 30	Realization discount	200	Sept 30	Balance b/d	6,000
Sept 30	Bank	5,800			
		6,000			6,000

Capital accounts

19x9		£ A	£ B	£ C	19x9		£ A	£ B	£ C
Sept 30	Current account		600		Sept 30	Balance b/d	78,000	26,000	4,000
Sept 30	Bank	79,400	25,400		Sept 30	Current account	1,400		400
		79,400					79,400		

Current accounts

19x9	£ A	£ B	£ C	19x9	£ A	£ B	£ C
Sept 30 Balance b/d		600		Sept 30 Balance b/d	1,400		400
Sept 30 Capital account	1,400		400	Sept 30 Capital		600	
	1,400	600	400		1,400	600	400

Loan account – B

	£		£
19x9		19x8	
Sept 30 Bank	4,000	Oct 1 Balance b/d	4,000

Realization a/c

	£		£
19x9		19x9	
Sept 30 Freehold property	60,000	Sept 30 Bank (freehold premises)	62,000
Equipment	30,000	Bank (equipment)	9,600
Stock	16,000	Bank (stock)	5,800
Debtors	9,000	Bank (debtors)	9,000
Dissolution expenses	1,600	Discount rec'd.	200
		Capital accounts :	
		A – 12,000	
		B – 12,000	
		C – 6,000	30,000
	116,600		116,600

Capital accounts

19x9	£ A	£ B	£ C	19x9	£ A	£ B	£ C
Sept 30 Current account		600		Oct 1 Balance b/d	78,000	26,000	4,000
Sept 30 Realisation	12,000	12,000	6,000	19x9			
Sept 30 Bank	67,400	13,400		Sept 30 Current account	1,400		400
				Sept 30 Bank			1,600
	79,400	26,000	6,000		79,400	26,000	6,000

17

Realization a/c

	£		£
19x9		19x9	
Fixed Assets	38,000	Bank (fixed assets)	34,000
Stock	23,600	Bank (stock)	18,600
Debtors	9,500	Car taken over by A	4,000
Expenses (bank)	500	Car taken over by B	6,000
Capital accounts		Debtors	9,200
A – 306		Creditors: discount received	310
B – 204	510		
	72,110		72,110

Cash/Bank a/c

		£			£
19x9			19x9		
Mar 31	Balance b/d	300	April 1	Realization expenses	500
April 1	Fixed assets realization	34,000	April 1	Creditors	5,890
April 1	Stock (realization)	18,600	April 1	Capital accounts	
April 1	Debtors (realization)	9,200		A – 30,106	
				B – 25,604	55,710
		62,100			62,100

Capital accounts

		£	£			£	£
19x9		A	B	19x9		A	B
April 1	Realization (cars taken over)	4,000	6,000	Mar 31	Balance b/d	30,000	28,000
				Apr 1	Current account	3,800	3,400
April 1	Bank	30,106	25,604	Apr 1	Realisation	306	204
		34,106	31,604			34,106	31,604

Chapter 19

Activity 19.1 (page 317)

1 B 2 A 3 D 4 C 5 C

6 a

Smith Brothers Ltd
Appropriation account for the year ended 31 March 19x9

	£	£	£
Net profit b/f			65,000
Profit and loss account balance b/f			15,000
			80,000
Less appropriations:			
Corporation tax		15,125	
Preference dividend		8,000	
Ordinary dividend		20,000	
Transfer to General Reserve		5,000	48,125
Profit and Loss account c/f			31,875

b

Smith Brothers Ltd
Balance Sheet as at 31 March 19x9

	£	£	£
Fixed Assets:			
Premises	200,000	–	200,000
Plant and machinery	150,000	30,000	120,000
	350,000	30,000	320,000

Current Assets:			
Stocks		25,000	
Debtors		40,000	
Prepayments		15,000	
Bank		15,000	
		95,000	
Less Current Liabilities:			
Creditors	25,000		
Accruals	5,000		
Corporation tax	15,125		
Dividends: Preference.	8,000		
Ordinary	20,000	73,125	
Net Current Assets:			21,875
			341,875
Financed by:			
Share capital and reserves			
Ordinary shares			200,000
8% preference shares			100,000
General reserves			
(£5,000 + £5,000)			10,000
Profit and Loss account balance			31,875
			341,875

8 a

Highbury Ltd
Trading and Profit and Loss account for the year ended 31 December 19x9

	£	£	£
Sales			185,000
Less cost of sales:			
Opening stock		82,830	
Add purchases		102,760	
		185,590	
Less closing stock		108,600	76,990
Gross profit			108,010
Less expenses:			
Directors' remuneration		12,400	
Wages and salaries		22,744	
Sundry expenses		2,152	
Motor expenses	16,288		
Add amount owing	890	17,178	
Repairs to machinery		4,616	
Debenture interest		2,500	
Depreciation on machinery		10,800	
Depreciation on motor vehicles		6,160	78,550
Net profit			29,460
Add Profit and Loss reserve b/f			12,276
			41,736
Less appropriations			
Transfer to general reserve		4,000	
Ordinary dividends		30,000	34,000
Profit and Loss account reserve c/f			7,736

b

Highbury Ltd
Balance Sheet as at 31 December 19x9

	£	£	£
Fixed Assets:			
Premises	40,000		40,000
Machinery	90,000	46,800	43,200
Motor vehicles	56,000	31,360	24,640
	186,000	78,160	107,840
Current Assets:			
Stocks		108,600	
Debtors		57,120	
Cash and bank		32,510	
		198,230	
Less Current Liabilities:			
Creditors	44,944		
Motor expenses owing	890		
Debenture interest	2,500		
Ordinary dividend	30,000	78,334	
Net Current Assets:			119,896
			227,736
Less Longterm Liabilities:			
5% of Debentures			50,000
			177,736
Issued share capital			150,000
General reserve			20,000
Profit and Loss reserve			7,736
			177,736

Chapter 20

Activity 20.1 (page 328)

2

Links Ltd
Statement of Source and Application of Funds
for the year ended 31 December 19x6

	£	£
Source of funds		
Net profit		20,000
Adjustment for items not involving the movement of funds:		
Depreciation (£40,000 – £30,000)		10,000
Total generated from operations		30,000
Funds from other sources		
Issue of shares for cash		70,000
		100,000
Application of funds		
Dividends paid	14,000	
Purchase of fixed assets (W1)	50,000	64,000
Increase in working capital		36,000
Increase in stocks	22,000	
Increase in debtors	22,300	

Decrease in creditors	23,600	
Movement in net liquid funds		
Decrease in cash balances	(31,900)	36,000

4

AB Ltd
Flow of funds statement for the year ended 30 June 19x2

	£	£
Source of funds		
Net profit before taxation		37,500
Adjustments for items not involving the movement of funds:		
Depreciation		30,600
Total generated from operations		68,100
Funds from other sources		
Issue of shares for cash		20,000
		88,100
Application of Funds		
Dividends paid	10,000	
Tax paid	12,000	
Purchase of fixed assets	74,000	(96,000)
Decrease in working capital		(7,900)
Increase in stocks	11,600	
Increase in debtors	10,250	
Increase in creditors	(7,500)	
Movement in net liquid assets		
Decrease in cash balances	(22,250)	(7,900)

Chapter 21

Activity 21.1 (page 334)

Workings	£
Sales	56,000
Less Cost of sales	33,600
Gross profit	22,400
Less Expenses	14,000
Net profit	8,400

a $\text{GP\%} = \dfrac{£22{,}400}{£56{,}000} \times 100 = 40\%$

b $\text{NP\%} = \dfrac{£8{,}400}{£56{,}000} \times 100 = 15\%$

c $\text{ROCE} = \dfrac{£8{,}400}{£52{,}500} \times 100 = 16\%$

Activity 21.2 (page 336)

a $\text{Current ratio} = \dfrac{£50{,}000}{£20{,}000} = 2.5 \text{ or } 5:2$

b $\text{Acid test ratio} = \dfrac{£50{,}000 - £20{,}000}{£20{,}000} = \dfrac{£30{,}000}{£20{,}000} = 1.5 \text{ or } 3:2$

Activity 21.3 (page 339)

a Rate of stock turnover

$$= \frac{£24{,}000 + £42{,}000 - £26{,}000}{\frac{1}{2}(£24{,}000 + £26{,}000)}$$

$$= \frac{£40{,}000}{£25{,}000} = 1.6 \text{ times}$$

b Average collection period of debt = $\frac{£20{,}000}{£60{,}000} \times 365 = 122$ days

c Sales/FA = $\frac{£60{,}000}{£30{,}000} = 2$ (or 2 : 1)

Activity 21.4 (page 341)

	A Ltd	B Ltd
Gearing ratio = $\frac{\text{debenture + PS}}{\text{total capital}}$	$\frac{£100{,}000}{£200{,}000}$	$\frac{£50{,}000}{£200{,}000}$
	$= \frac{1}{2}$ or 1 : 2	$= \frac{1}{2}$ or 1 : 4

Activity 21.5 (page 343)

a EPS = $\frac{£100{,}000}{20{,}000} = 50p$

b Dividend cover = $\frac{£100{,}000}{£40{,}000} = 2.5$ times

c Dividend yield = $\frac{20}{300} \times 100 = 6.67\%$

Dividend per share = $\frac{£40{,}000}{200{,}000} = 20p$

d P/E ratio = $\frac{300}{50} = 6$

Activity 21.6 (page 345)

1 A **2** D **3** A **4** C **5** B

8 a

	19x1	19x2
(i) Rate of stock turnover		
$\frac{\text{COS}}{\text{AS}}$	$\frac{£199{,}000}{(£30{,}000 + £31{,}000)}$	$\frac{£240{,}000}{(£31{,}000 + £65{,}000)}$
	= 6.5 times	= 5 times
(ii) Rate of debtors' turnover		
$\frac{\text{Debtors}}{\text{Sales}} \times 365$	$\frac{£30{,}000}{£300{,}000} \times 365$	$\frac{£40{,}000}{£360{,}000} \times 365$
	= 36.5 days	= 40.6 days
(iii) Current ratio		
$\frac{\text{CA}}{\text{CL}}$	$\frac{66{,}000}{25{,}000}$	$\frac{105{,}000}{52{,}000}$
	= 2.59	= 2.02

(iv) Quick ratio

$\frac{\text{CA} - \text{stocks}}{\text{CL}}$	$\frac{35{,}000}{25{,}000}$	$\frac{40{,}000}{52{,}000}$
	= 1.37	= 0.77

(v) Return on capital employed

$\frac{\text{NP}}{\text{CE}} \times 100$	$\frac{£60{,}000}{120{,}000} \times 100$	$\frac{£75{,}000}{160{,}000} \times 100$
	= 49.8%	= 46.8%

Chapter 22

Activity 22.1 (page 351)

	Project A	**Project B**
Payback period	$\frac{£10{,}000}{£2{,}500} = 4$ years	$\frac{£10{,}000}{£2{,}000} = 5$ years

Project A will be chosen.

Activity 22.2 (page 353)

Annual depreciation = $\frac{£20{,}000}{5}$ = £ 4,000

Therefore annual profit = £ 6,500 – £4,000 = £2,500

Average investment = $\frac{1}{2}$ × £20,000 = £10,000

Therefore ROI = $\frac{£2{,}500}{£10{,}000}$ × 100 = 25%

Activity 22.3 (page 355)

a Present value = £10,000 × 0.794 = £7,940
b Present value = £12,345 × 0.567 = £7,000
c Present value = £897 × 0.351 = £315
d Present value = £20,000 × 0.162 = £3,240

Activity 22.4 (page 357)

1 C   **2** C   **3** D

4

Year	Project A Net cash in-flow £	Project A Cum.* cash in-flow £	Project B Net cash in-flow £	Project B Cum.* cash in-flow £	Project C Net cash in-flow £	Project C Cum.* cash in-flow £
1	10,000	10,000	7,500	7,500	16,000	16,000
2	10,000	20,000	7,500	15,000	20,000	36,000
3	8,000	28,000	10,500	25,500	20,000	56,000
4	6,000	34,000	22,500	48,000	20,000	76,000

* Cumulative

a Payback period

Project A	Project B	Project C
2 years	$3\frac{14,500}{22,500}$ = 3.64 years	$2\frac{14,500}{20,000}$ = 2.7 years

b Projects A and C
c Project A

6 a

Year	DF	Project A CI	Project A PV	Project B CI	Project B PV	Project C CI	Project C PV
0	1.000	(20,000)	(20,000)	(40,000)	(40,000)	(50,000)	(50,000)
1	0.870	10,000	8,700	7,500	6,525	16,000	13,920
2	0.756	10,000	7,560	7,500	5,670	20,000	15,120
3	0.658	8,000	5,264	10,500	6,909	20,000	13,160
4	0.572	6,000	3,432	22,500	12,870	20,000	11,440
NPV			4,956		(8,026)		3,640

b Profitability index

Project A	Project B	Project C
$\frac{24,956}{20,000}$ = 1.25	$\frac{31,974}{40,000}$ = 0.8	$\frac{53,640}{50,000}$ = 1.07

c If unlimited funds are available, it is advisable that projects A and C are accepted, because in both cases the extracted rate of return will be higher than the cost of capital to the firm. Project B's expected return will be lower than the cost of capital as indicated by the negative NPV of the project.

d Of the two projects A and C, project A has a higher NPV indicating that its rate of return is higher than that of project C. We therefore suggest that project A be accepted under conditions of capital rationing.

8 a **Proposal A**

Year	Profit	Depreciation	Cash flow	Cumulative cash flow
	£	£	£	£
1	6,500	10,500	17,000	17,000
2	3,500	10,500	14,000	31,000
3	13,500	10,500	24,000	55,000
4	(1,500)	10,500	9,000	64,000
4			4,000	68,000
	22,000	42,000	68,000	

Proposal B

Year	Profit	Depreciation	Cash flow	Cumulative cash flow
	£	£	£	£
1	4,500	10,500	15,000	15,000
2	2,500	10,500	13,000	28,000
3	4,500	10,500	15,000	43,000
4	14,500	10,500	25,000	68,000
4			4,000	72,000
	26,000	42,000	72,000	

Note:

1 Annual depreciation is calculated as follows:

$$\text{Depreciation} = \frac{£45{,}000 - £4{,}000}{4} = £10{,}500$$

2 Cash in-flows in column 4 are obtained by adding the profit figure (column 2) to the depreciation figure (column 3).

3 Year 4 appears twice in the table. The second 4 is included to show the scrap value of the proposals.

(i) Payback period is calculated as follows:

Proposal A

$$2 + \frac{£15{,}000}{£24{,}000} \text{ years}$$

= 2.6 years

Proposal B

$$3 + \frac{£3{,}000}{£25{,}000} \text{ years}$$

= 3.1 years

(ii) Average rate of return:

Proposal A

$$\text{Average profit} = \frac{£22{,}000}{4}$$

= £5,500

Proposal B

$$\text{Average profit} = \frac{£26{,}000}{4}$$

= £6,500

Therefore average rate of return =

$$\frac{\text{average profit}}{0.5(\text{total invested} - \text{scrap value})} \times 100\%$$

$$= \frac{\text{average profit}}{0.5(£46{,}000 - £4{,}000)} = \frac{\text{average profit}}{£21{,}000}$$

Proposal A

$$\frac{£5{,}500}{£21{,}000} \times 100$$

= 26%

Proposal B

$$\frac{£6{,}500}{£21{,}000} \times 100$$

= 31%

(iii) NPV

Year	**DF**	**Proposal A Cash flow**	**PV**	**Proposal B Cash flow**	**PV**
0	1.000	(46,000)	(46,000)	(46,000)	(46,000)
1	0.833	17,000	14,161	15,000	12,495
2	0.694	14,000	9,716	13,000	9,022
3	0.579	24,000	13,896	15,000	8,685
4	0.482	9,000	4,338	25,000	12,050
4	0.482	4,000	1,928	4,000	1,928
NPV			(1,961)		(1,820)

Appendix 4

GLOSSARY OF ACCOUNTING AND FINANCIAL TERMS

Account A chronological record of business transactions in the Ledger
Accountant A person who practises accountancy
Accounting The collection, classification, recording and interpretation of business transactions
Accounting equation States, in its basic form, that
assets – liabilities = capital
Accounting policies The accounting methods followed by a business, in a consistent manner, in preparing the final accounts to give a true and fair view of the business
Accounting principles The concepts and conventions which are used in preparing financial statements
Accounting ratio A relationship between two financial figures
Accounting standards A set of standards (i.e. rules) which are expected to be followed by the accountancy profession
Acid test ratio A ratio between liquid assets (current assets – stocks) and current liabilities
Accruals Expenses which have been incurred but not yet paid
Accumulated fund The same thing as capital for a non-trading organization
Appropriation account That part of the Profit and Loss account of a partnership or a company which shows the division of the net profit
Articles of Association A set of internal rules for the operation of an incorporated company
Assets Any resources, tangible or intangible, that are owned by a business
Auditing An examination of the accounts of a business by an independent person, called the auditor
Authorized capital The maximum amount of share capital that a company may raise; the amount is stated in the Memorandum of Association
Average cost (avco) A method of valuing stock at cost, usually calculated by dividing the value of stocks at cost by the number of units in stock

Bad debt A debt that is considered to be irrecoverable
Balance Sheet A financial statement of a business at a given point in time in terms of its assets, liabilities and capital
Bank reconciliation statement A statement explaining the difference between the cash book balance and the bank statement balance
Bonus issue An issue of new shares to the existing shareholders by capitalizing reserves; also known as a scrip issue or a capitalization issue
Book-keeping (double-entry) The system of recording transactions in the books of accounts according to the principles of double entry
Books of prime (or original) entry Books of accounts into which transactions are first recorded before posting to the Ledger
Book value The value of an asset at cost minus accumulated depreciation

Called–up share capital Share capital which has been paid up or requested for payment
Capital Money or money's worth contributed by the owner(s) into the business; alternatively,
capital = assets – liabilities
Capital expenditure Expenditure on fixed assets such as plant and machinery
Cash budget A statement of expected receipts and payments of cash over a given future period of time
Capital reserve A reserve which cannot be paid as dividends to the shareholders; when shares are issued at a price higher than the nominal value, the amount of the excess, called the *premium*, is credited to a *capital reserve account*, known as the *share premium account*
Control account A memorandum account of which the balance is equal to the total balances of similar accounts, such as individual debtors
Cost of sales The cost of goods sold in a period; equal to the sum of opening stock and purchases, less closing stock
Credit The right hand side of a ledger account/cash book
Credit note A document sent by a supplier to a debtor for goods returned
Creditors Individuals or companies to whom a business owes money
Current accounts Accounts maintained in the names of partners in a partnership business to record transactions between the partners and the partnership
Current assets Assets held for less than a year with the intention of converting them into cash
Current liabilities Liabilities (i.e. debts) that need to be repaid within a year
Current ratio A ratio between current assets and current liabilities

Data Quantitative information
Database A collection of data, in a single file, independent of the application programs which use them
Debenture A document of indebtedness; many companies borrow money by the issue of debentures
Debit The left hand side of a ledger account/cash book
Debit note A document sent to the supplier whose account is intended to be debited for goods returned
Debtors Individuals or organizations who owe money to a business
Debtors' payment period Average collection period of debts given by: $\frac{\text{debtors}}{\text{sales}} \times 100$
Depreciation A measure of the decrease in the value of a fixed asset because of normal wear and tear, obsolescence or simply the passage of time
Diminishing balance A method of depreciation whereby a fixed percentage of the written down value (i.e. book value) of an asset is written off each year
Discount allowed An allowance given to the credit customers of a business for prompt payment; treated as a business expense
Discount received An allowance received by a business from its creditors for prompt payment; treated as a non-trading income
Dissolution of partnerships The closing of a partnership
Dividend A payment to the shareholders out of the profits of the company

Dividend cover The number of times the proposed dividend can be paid to the shareholders out of the current year's profits after taxation
Dividend yield A measure of the true return on the money invested in the ordinary shares of a company; given by:

$$\frac{\text{dividend per share}}{\text{market price of share}} \times 100$$

Drawings Money or goods taken out by a sole trader or a partner from the business for her/his personal use

Earnings per share An investment ratio which is obtained by dividing the number of ordinary shares into the profit of the year that belongs to the ordinary shareholders

FIFO 'First in, first out'; method of stock valuation
Fixed assets Assets which have a working life of more than a year

Gearing A measure of the reliance of a business on borrowed money; calculated as a ratio between fixed interest/dividend bearing capital and total capital
Goodwill A money value given to the reputation of a business, estimated as the excess of cost of purchase over the net value of tangible assets
Gross profit The difference between sales revenue and cost of sales

Hardware The physical components of a computer system such the processor, the monitor, the keyboard or the printer

Imprest A fixed amount of cash that is used to meet petty (small) expenses over a given period, usually a month
Income and expenditure account Income statements (such as the Trading and Profit and Loss accounts) of non-profit making organizations
Incomplete records Accounting records which are not maintained in accordance with the principles of double-entry book-keeping
Investments Assets consisting of shares and loan stocks of other companies
Issued capital That part of the authorized share capital of a company which has actually been issued to the shareholders

Ledger The main book of accounts which is kept according to the principles of double-entry book-keeping
Longterm liabilities Liabilities which need to be paid after the expiry of at least one year
LIFO 'Last in, first out', a method of stock valuation
Liquidity The ease with which assets can be converted into cash
Liquidity ratio A ratio between current assets and current liabilities

Memorandum of Association Similar to a company's constitution; this document together with the Articles of Association must be submitted to the Registrar of Companies by an organization seeking registration
Mortgage A transaction in which an asset is given as security for a loan

Net present value The present value of net income receivable in a future period
Net profit Gross profit minus expenses

Ordinary shares The equity capital of a business

Partnership A business owned by two or more individuals
Periodic inventory A method of recording movements of stocks on a periodic basis
Perpetual inventory A method of recording movements of stocks on a continuous basis
Preference shares Those shares on which shareholders receive a fixed rate of dividend
Prepayments Amounts paid in advance for the next accounting period
Price earnings ratio An investment ratio which is calculated by dividing EPS (earnings per share) into market price of a share
Prime cost The sum of all direct costs

Quick ratio An accounting ratio to measure the liquidity position of a business; calculated by dividing current liabilities into liquid assets (current assets – stocks)

Revenue reserves Reserves created out of retained profits of a company
Return on capital employed A profitability ratio which expresses net profit as a percentage of capital employed
Rights issue An issue of new shares to the existing shareholders of a company

Software A computer program
Spreadsheet A computer program which enables us to arrange and manipulate data in rows and columns; suitable for cash budgets and financial statements
SSAP Statement of Standard Accounting Practice; statements which provide standards for the accountancy profession
Straight-line method A method of depreciation whereby the cost of an asset minus any scrap value is depreciated over its working life in equal instalments
Suspense account A ledger account where any discrepancy between the debit total and the credit total in a trial balance is first posted

Trial Balance A list of balances, classified into debit and credit balances, extracted from the Ledger at any given point in time
Turnover Total net sales in a period

VAT Value Added Tax; a tax levied by HM Customs and Excise on the supply of some goods and services
Variable cost A cost that varies with the quantity produced; also known as marginal cost

Working capital The difference between current assets and current liabilities; also known as *net current assets*
Work in progress Partly finished goods
Written down value The net book value of an asset which is obtained

Index